Potomac Squire

Books by ELSWYTH THANE

FICTION

Riders of the Wind
Echo Answers
Cloth of Gold
His Elizabeth
Bound to Happen
Queen's Folly
Tryst
Remember Today
From This Day Forward
Melody
The Lost General
Letter to a Stranger

THE WILLIAMSBURG NOVELS

Dawn's Early Light
Yankee Stranger
Ever After
The Light Heart
Kissing Kin
This Was Tomorrow
Homing

NONFICTION

The Tudor Wench
Young Mr. Disraeli
England Was an Island Once
The Bird Who Made Good
Reluctant Farmer
The Family Quarrel
Washington's Lady
Potomac Squire

PLAYS

The Tudor Wench
Young Mr. Disraeli

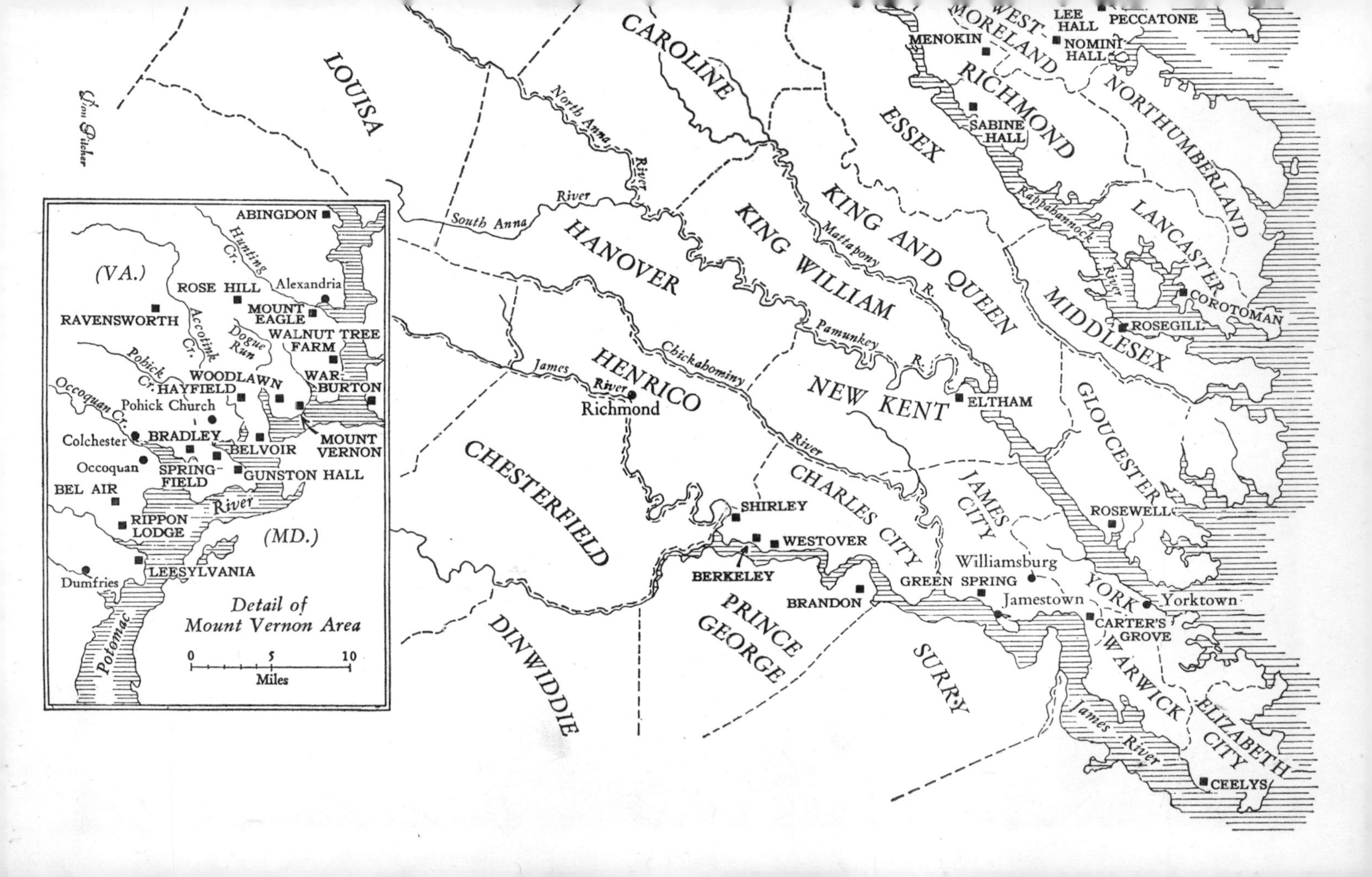
LOUISA
CAROLINE
WEST-
MORELAND
LEE
HALL
PECCATONE
MENOKIN
NOMINI
HALL
RICHMOND
SABINE
HALL
NORTHUMBERLAND
ESSEX
KING AND QUEEN
KING WILLIAM
HANOVER
LANCASTER
COROTOMAN
ROSEGILL
MIDDLESEX
Rappahannock River
Mattapony R.
Pamunkey R.
North Anna River
South Anna River
Chickahominy River
HENRICO
James River
Richmond
NEW KENT
ELTHAM
GLOUCESTER
ROSEWELL
JAMES
CITY
CHESTERFIELD
CHARLES CITY
SHIRLEY
WESTOVER
BERKELEY
BRANDON
GREEN SPRING
Williamsburg
Jamestown
YORK
Yorktown
CARTER'S
GROVE
WARWICK
ELIZABETH
CITY
CEELYS
DINWIDDIE
PRINCE
GEORGE
SURRY
James River
Dion Pitcher
ABINGDON
Hunting Cr.
(VA.)
ROSE HILL
Alexandria
MOUNT
EAGLE
RAVENSWORTH
Accotink Cr.
Dogue Run
WALNUT TREE
FARM
Pohick Cr.
WOODLAWN
WAR-
BURTON
Occoquan Cr.
HAYFIELD
Pohick Church
Colchester
BRADLEY
MOUNT
VERNON
BELVOIR
Occoquan
SPRING-
FIELD
GUNSTON HALL
BEL AIR
River
RIPPON
LODGE
(MD.)
Dumfries
LEESYLVANIA
Potomac
Detail of
Mount Vernon Area
0
5
10
Miles

Potomac Squire

by

ELSWYTH THANE

DUELL, SLOAN AND PEARCE

New York

First Edition

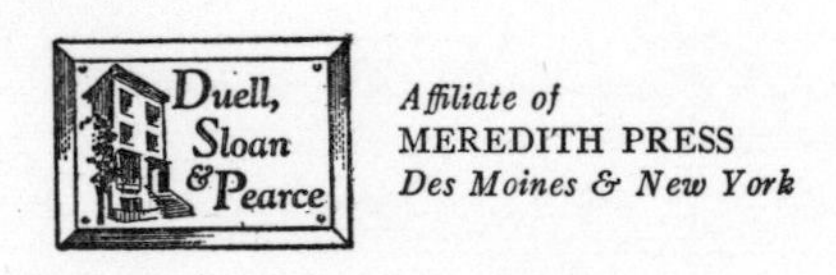

Affiliate of
MEREDITH PRESS
Des Moines & New York

Library of Congress Catalogue Card Number: 63-10346

MANUFACTURED IN THE UNITED STATES OF AMERICA FOR MEREDITH PRESS

VAN REES PRESS • NEW YORK

To

The Present Staff at Mount Vernon
Who made welcome a Stranger
(herself a Yankee)
With true Washingtonian Courtesy,
Kindness, and Hospitality

Illustrations

following page 48

Mount Vernon from the South, from a Sketch by Latrobe

Mount Vernon from the West, from an Aquatint by Parkyns

Perspective Through the Portico at Mount Vernon, from a Water-Color Sketch by Alexander Jackson Davis

"Classical Group at Mount Vernon," by Latrobe

Washington's Own Map of the Five Farms of the Mount Vernon Estate

The Dining-room at Mount Vernon

The Ceiling of the Great Room at Kenmore

Tobias Lear

Fanny Bassett, by Robert Edge Pine

Colonel David Humphreys, by Gilbert Stuart

John Parke Custis ("Jacky")

Eliza Parke Custis, by Gilbert Stuart

Martha Parke Custis ("Patty"), by Robert Edge Pine

Nelly Custis, supposed by Gilbert Stuart

Page from Washington's Diary in August, 1785

George Washington's Book Plate

The plan of the cherry walk at Gunston Hall on page 70 appeared in *Virginia Cavalcade*, Richmond, Virginia, 1951.

The plans of the first and second floors of Mount Vernon, on page 253 are from the Mount Vernon Handbook, and are reproduced by permission of the Mount Vernon Ladies' Association.

Foreword

It will be noted that I have used many quotes from contemporary letters and memoirs. The reason for this, if anyone requires a reason, is that to pre-digest, cut, or break up such material so as to embed it in my text would be to rob it of life and color. Washington speaks for himself to the extent of thirty-nine large volumes in the Fitzpatrick edition of the *Collected Writings*, and four volumes of the published *Diary*.

No one—except a fanatic like me—is going to lift a single one of those heavy, unaccommodating books off the far shelves of the few libraries which possess the set, and if anyone did, the chances are that it would fall open at the wrong place to pages of doubtful interest. But if someone (like me) will take the trouble to mine the mass of material available, almost with a pick and shovel, as I have done, into more than two dozen closely written indexed notebooks of personalities and domestic highlights, these act as guide lines, like Ariadne's thread, for specialized tours through the thicket of words. This way Washington's more private hours, his family life, his daily exasperations and satisfactions, his friends and visitors, are brought to light, and the mountain comes to Mohammed. This way I bring you Washington himself—not a man on a monument, not the father of his country, but a very human *pater familias*, often harassed by his responsibilities for other men's children, often rather hard up, often somewhat testy, often benign and humorous, often wise and tolerant.

What he ordered from his agents abroad and later in Baltimore and Philadelphia; what he provided for his household to eat and wear; what he put on the shelves of his always increasing library, and read aloud to the family in the evenings around the fire; what he wrote down in the conscientious effort to guide and advise his young people; what he permitted his friends to know of his emotions while the Presidential doom gathered on his horizon; what he asked of his managers at home while his public duties pinned him down elsewhere—these are best discovered in his own resounding sentences (which were likely to become more involved in proportion to his earnestness) instead of in any pale paraphrase more expedient to the modern eye.

As the dedicated go-between, I adjure you not to skip; but to slow down to the stately eighteenth-century style of life, and learn to know a man who was always courteous, always dignified, even in anger—and he could be angry!—and whose carefully trimmed quill was never driven into a scrawl. Douglas Southall Freeman, in the sixth volume of what should be considered the best Life of Washington so far, put it all into a sentence: "His continuing commission, never outdated, never expiring, was that of self-command."

The memoirs and diaries like Elkanah Watson's, Niemcewicz's, Latrobe's, and Hunter's, and family letters like Winsor's and Mrs. Carrington's, are not easily available, are not generally known to exist; and yet words set down within hours after the writers had been in Washington's actual presence are surely worth more than some warmed-over twentieth-century hindsight. These people "saw Shelley plain." Read, then, as they wrote it.

In establishing the story of a large family—and most Virginian families in the eighteenth century were large—there is always at first what may seem to the hasty (one must not say *lazy*) reader an overabundance of names. It is like entering the drawing-room belated, after the party has begun, when the introductions come thick and fast, in a blur of faces. But as the evening progresses and one moves from group to group and the conversation of each embraces the newcomer, the strangeness wears off, and what appeared to be confusion clarifies itself into personalities, friends and neighbors, among whom one begins to feel at ease.

Because of the terror which descends on some otherwise quite intelligent people when confronted by an assemblage of strangers—in the days when one went to parties by horse and carriage this form of stage-fright began at the entrance to the driveway and was known as *gravel panic*—your kindhearted author has prepared a list, a cast of characters, to which the timid reader may refer if he begins to reel, with the assurance that before long he will be able to recognize his fellow guests without prompting. Because if he turns back at the first chapter, if he doesn't persevere a little, he will go poorer all his life for not having known his forefathers at home.

Now, watch how easy it is.

George Washington's father, Augustine Washington (1694–1743) married as his first wife Jane Butler, by whom he had two surviving children:

(1) Lawrence (1718–1752)
(2) Augustine ("Austin") (1720–1762)

By his second wife, Mary Ball, he had five surviving children:

(3) GEORGE (1732–1799)
(4) Betty (1733–1797)
(5) Samuel (1734–1781)
(6) John Augustine (1736–1787)
(7) Charles (1738–1799)

Lawrence Washington (1) (Mount Vernon) married Anne Fairfax, and their several children all died in infancy.
"Austin" Washington (2) (Wakefield, at Pope's Creek) married Anne Aylett, by whom he had several daughters and a son:

(a) William Augustine (1757–1810)

GEORGE WASHINGTON (3) married Martha (Dandridge) Custis (1731–1802), a widow with two little children, Jack and Patsy Custis. There were no children of this marriage.
Betty Washington (4) married Fielding Lewis (1725–1781) of Fredericksburg, who built for her the house called Millbank (now known as Kenmore) and by whom she had six surviving children:

(a) Fielding, Jr. (1755–1800)
(b) Betty (1758–18–)
(c) George Fielding (1760–1821)
(d) Lawrence (1767–1839)
(e) Robert (1769–1829)
(f) Howell (1771–1822)

Samuel Washington (5) (Harewood) married five times and had six children:

(a) Thornton (1760–1799)
(b) Tristram (1763–1768)
(c) Ferdinand (1767–1788)
(d) George Steptoe (1773–1808)
(e) Lawrence Augustine (1775–1825)
(f) Harriot (1776–1822)

John Augustine (6) (Bushfield) married Hannah Bushrod, by whom he had four surviving children:

(a) Jane (1758–1791)
(b) Mildred (1760–18–)
(c) Bushrod (1762–1829)
(d) Corbin (1765–1799)

Charles Washington (7) (Happy Retreat) married Mildred Thornton, by whom he had several children, one of whom was:

(a) George Augustine (1763–1793)

In the next generation a few personalities stand out among Washington's numerous nieces and nephews.

William Augustine (2a) of Wakefield married as the first of three wives his cousin Jane Washington (6a) of Bushfield.

George Fielding Lewis of Fredericksburg and his brothers Robert and Howell were at different times aides and secretaries to George Washington, and their brother Lawrence lived at Mount Vernon after the Presidency and married Martha Washington's granddaughter, Eleanor Parke Custis (see below).

George Steptoe Washington (5d) and his brother Lawrence Augustine and their sister Harriot composed the troublesome younger generation at Harewood.

Bushrod Washington (6c) of Bushfield married Julia Anne Blackburn of Rippon Lodge. He was named Washington's heir after Martha in the General's will. Bushrod's marriage was childless, his wife a chronic invalid, so that at his death Mount Vernon passed again to a nephew, John Augustine II, son of Bushrod's younger brother Corbin and another Blackburn girl.

George Augustine Washington (7a) of Happy Retreat served as

aide to Washington during the war, and as manager of Mount Vernon during the early years of the Presidency. He married Martha's niece, Fanny Bassett, by whom he had three surviving children: Maria, Fayette, and Charles Augustine Washington. He died at the age of thirty, and his widow married Tobias Lear, who lived for many years in the Washington household as secretary and tutor.

Lund Washington, born in 1737 in the Chotank district to the south of Mount Vernon, was related to George by a distant cousinship, being descended from a younger brother of the early Washington line in America. He married in 1779 Elizabeth Foote, who was in an obscure way his cousin, and none of their children survived infancy. He died in 1796 at his own house, Hayfield, which he had built in 1784–5 on land adjacent to Mount Vernon, to which he had retired at the end of the war years.

On the Custis side, Martha was one of eight children, and after her marriage to Washington remained in close touch with her family in New Kent County on the Pamunkey, especially with:

(1) Bartholomew Dandridge (1737–1784) who had a son Bartholomew II, who was for a time secretary to Washington during the Presidency.
(2) Anne Dandridge ("Nancy") (1739–1777) who married Burwell Bassett of Eltham in New Kent County, by whom she had several children, in particular:
    (a) Fanny Bassett (1767–1796) who married Washington's nephew, George Augustine Washington (7a above), and after his death married Tobias Lear.

Martha's son, John Parke Custis ("Jacky") married Eleanor Calvert of Mount Airy in Maryland, by whom he had four children:

(a) Eliza Parke Custis (1776–1832) who married Thomas Law.
(b) Martha Parke Custis ("Patty") (1777–18–) who married Thomas Peter.
(c) Eleanor Parke Custis ("Nelly") (1779–1852) who married Lawrence Lewis (4d above).
(d) George Washington Parke Custis (1781–1857) who married Mary Lee Fitzhugh of Chatham and Ravensworth.

After Jacky's early death in 1781 his widow married Dr. David Stuart of Hope Park, by whom she had numerous children.

In the immediate Mount Vernon neighborhood, the Carters, the Lees, and the Fitzhughs in their legions baffle even the professional genealogist. It is enough to record that when old "King" Carter of Corotoman on the Rappahannock died in 1732, the year George Washington was born, he was possessed of some 200,000 acres and he left some dozen children, most of whom married into other large, well-to-do families and established famous houses of their own. His eldest son John Carter married the heiress of Shirley on the James, who was Elizabeth Hill, and his offspring became identified with that mansion. Robert Carter, Jr., lived at Nomini Hall in Westmoreland County, and hired as a tutor for his children a Princeton man named Philip Fithian, who set down in his diary an invaluable picture of life on a pre-Revolution Potomac plantation. Charles, the third Carter son, had a house on the Rappahannock called Cleve; his brother Landon had nearby Sabine Hall; their sister Elizabeth married a Burwell and lived at Carter's Grove on the James; Judith married Mann Page of Rosewell on the York; Anne married Benjamin Harrison IV of Berkeley; Lucy married first the Eagle's Nest Fitzhugh, and second the Brandon Harrison.

Thomas Lee of Stratford died in 1750, leaving six sons and two daughters; Philip Ludwell Lee inherited Stratford; Thomas Ludwell Lee built Belleview; Richard Henry Lee called his house Chantilly; Francis Lightfoot Lee had Menokin; William and Arthur's associations turned towards England; Hannah Lee married a Corbin of Peccatone—and when at his death in 1778 she inherited the property, she protested long and loud against the taxation of women when they were not allowed to vote. This same Hannah Lee Corbin took one Dr. Hall as her second husband, lived with him at Peccatone, and insisted that her children by him should still bear the surname of Corbin. Her sister Alice married a Philadelphia Shippen. First cousin to this line of Lees was the spectacular Lighthorse Harry of Leesylvania, near Dumfries, who by his second wife fathered Robert E. Lee; who tied a bowknot on the strands of lineage by marrying the daughter of George Washington Parke Custis.

You see how simple it is.

As for the Fitzhughs, there was Henry of the Potomac Eagle's Nest, whose widow Lucy Carter Fitzhugh the Washingtons visited; and there were Henry's son William of Chatham, near Fredericksburg, and later of Ravensworth; and another William of Marmion on the Potomac, cousins, both Washington's lifelong friends; and the latter's son John Fitzhugh of Marmion.

The Digges family included William of Warburton Hall, opposite Mount Vernon on the Maryland shore; his daughters Teresa ("Tracy"), Elizabeth, Nancy, and Jenny; his son George; and his brother Ignatius.

There were two Galloways: Samuel of Tulip Hill near Annapolis, whose daughter aspired briefly to Jacky Custis during his schooldays; and Benjamin Franklin's friend Joseph of Philadelphia. Both brothers proved to be obstinate Tories.

The Fairfaxes of Belvoir were the sixth lord, Thomas, who lived most of the time at his wilderness mansion called Greenway Court in the Shenandoah Valley; his cousin William, on the Potomac; William's sons, George William Fairfax and Bryan, both boyhood companions of Washington, and their sisters Anne, Sarah, and Hannah Fairfax.

George Mason's Gunston Hall lay on the riverbank just below Belvoir, and these were the two nearest neighbors to Mount Vernon on the south.

Mason's neighbors were the Cockburns of Springfield, the Tripletts of Round Hill, the Blackburns of Rippon Lodge, and the Masseys of Bradley.

John Carlyle, who married Sarah, the second Fairfax daughter; William Ramsay, Dr. Laurie, Dr. Rumney, Dr. Craik, the clergyman Mr. Green, and the lawyer Robert Hanson Harrison were all Alexandria residents.

At Fredericksburg on the Rappahannock were Fielding Lewis, who had married Washington's only sister Betty; George Weedon, who with Washington's brother Charles established a prosperous tavern in Caroline Street—the building still stands intact; and Hugh Mercer, the apothecary-doctor, whose shop can still be seen. Both Weedon and Mercer became generals in the American Army during the war. And across the river, on the old family place called the Ferry Farm, lived Washington's mother.

Two of his brothers, Charles and Samuel Washington, lived in the vicinity of Fredericksburg until they built handsome houses near Winchester in the Shenandoah Valley during the late '60's. Also in the west, at Fairfield, was Warner Washington, son of Augustine's elder brother John, first cousin to George and fifteen years his senior—who married as his second wife the youngest Fairfax daughter, Hannah.

George's half-brother Austin was at the house he called Wakefield, in Westmoreland County. And still further southward where Nomini Creek joined the Potomac, John Augustine Washington lived at Bushfield, inherited from his wife's father.

Down the River, along with the Lee houses, lay Hickory Hill and Peccatone, of the turbulent Turbervilles and Corbins. Fithean recorded that George Turberville, to cure his coachman of running away, chained him to the seat of the chariot when the family went visiting, where the poor fellow remained even when the horses were released from the harness. Still further south lay the Wormeleys' magnificent Rosegill, Mann Page's splendid Rosewell, and the other great mansions of the James and York Rivers. Williamsburg was there, near the mouths of the James and York, and at the falls of the James was Richmond, which until the government was moved there during the war remained a country town. That was Washington's Virginia—from Alexandria to Williamsburg. And but for the determination of a German king in England to rule America Germanically, that would have been Washington's life, into a peaceful old age.

Potomac Squire

I

GEORGE WASHINGTON'S lifetime of public service consisted of some six years of Indian fighting on the western frontier, beginning when he was twenty-one, eight years of the Revolutionary War, and eight years of the Presidency—which adds up to roughly twenty-two years during which his duties kept him away from home, or permitted only brief stop-overs there on the way to or from his public obligations. If the years of continuous residence at Mount Vernon are counted up they come to sixteen between his marriage and the first Continental Congress (interrupted even then by his faithful attendance as a Burgess in the Assembly at Williamsburg), five years between the war and the first inauguration, and something over two years after the second term was finished—which amounts to about twenty-three. His early youth had been divided among the households of his widowed mother at the Rappahannock farm near Fredericksburg, and his married half-brothers at Mount Vernon and Wakefield.

Half his mature life, then, was actually spent in the enjoyment of the plantation to which he was devoted, and without those tranquil intervals he might have found it impossible to support the burden of the other half.

Not until the death of his half-brother Lawrence's widow in 1761, some two years after George had resigned from the colonial militia and brought Martha to the house as a bride, did Mount Vernon come into his actual possession by the terms of Lawrence's will. But for nearly ten years before then he had leased the estate from Anne and her second husband, and he made extensive alterations to the house just previous to his marriage, such as raising the roof to a full two stories and a half, to provide third-floor rooms.

From that time until the year of his death, he never ceased to dream about, design, and increase the property which was his pride and his perpetual preoccupation. Even during the worst days of the Revolution, he carried always in his mind's eye the map of his land and the plan of his house, and he often sat late at his writing-table when the military correspondence was done, to devise long, detailed letters to his cousin Lund Washington, who managed the place for him during his absence at the war. He wrote instructions for planting trees, sowing crops, directing slave and tenant labor, and rebuilding the mansion house and its dependencies. Later, while he was President, and Lund had retired to his own acres nearby, Washington wrote in the same way to a succession of unsatisfactory hireling managers and incompetent relatives to whom he was forced to entrust the estate business and improvements which he was unable to supervise personally.

As so much of the work was done while he was away, it is possible to follow most of its progress by his correspondence. When he was at home he kept a diary of his undertakings and experiments, as well as the Mount Vernon weather, the planting and the harvesting, his yearly inventories and accounts, and the countless visitors. His almost daily entries are sparse and colorless at first glance, but when studied against the background of the variety of persons mentioned, and the homely round of his busy days, they contain many fascinating clues to his private life. Whole volumes of the Diary between 1760 and 1775 are missing or were not kept up, and he allowed it to lapse again during the war and the Presidency. Provided with an index and footnotes by Dr. John C. Fitzpatrick, the entire available text was published in four volumes in 1925 by the Mount Vernon Ladies' Association, and there the patient biographer can find a key to a very different man from the general on horseback.

So it is largely in his own words, and those of his workmen and representatives, that we can now become as it were a member of his inner circle and join him on his own hearth, where we will never catch him at a disadvantage—for he never appeared at the dinner table in his riding clothes, or without powder in his hair. Except for an occasional addition for clarity's sake, mainly in his habitual abbreviations, the text of Washington's letters, diaries, and invoices is reproduced here as it appears in the original. Ignorant amusement at his variable spelling, like credence of the stale Sally Fairfax legend, has been firmly dealt with by Dr. Fitzpatrick who, after the publication of the Diary, prepared for the printer the thirty-nine volumes of the Bicentennial Edition of Washington's Writings, from which the excerpts quoted here have been taken. It must be remembered that before Dr. Johnson's Dictionary was published in England in 1757 (when Washington was twenty-five) there had been no single authority for uniform spelling. Children learned from tutors or schoolmasters who used the few small exercise books then in existence, which differed somewhat from each other, or made rules of their own. There was a general eighteenth-century tendency towards uniformity, which recognized out and out phonetic illiteracy with its own amusement—witness the novelist Richardson's character who was said to spell "pretty well, for a lord"—but inconsistency in spelling still was such that even in printed books the same word could appear on the same page in two different forms. The random capitalization was even more inconsistent, and bore no apparent relation to emphasis or meaning. Washington's later letters adhere more closely to standard modern usage—he spelled *opportunity* with an *e* to the end of his life, and why not?—but Hamilton, Jefferson, Monroe, and even Johnson himself were often at permanent variance with twentieth-century rules. Washington's favorite secretary, Tobias Lear, Harvard, '83, always wrote "*umbrilla,*" and doubtless pronounced it the same.

In Dr. Fitzpatrick's Foreword to his own Life of Washington (*George Washington Himself*, 1933) he says: "It is a matter of amazement that biographers could think that the story of George Washington has been told, merely because so many enthusiastic writers have cheerily rushed into print with so-called complete lives of the First American while less than half the facts were at their command. A George Washington has thus been created in the public mind who is, unfortunately, utterly unlike the real man, yet who is, again unfortunately, cherished by that public to such an extent that it refuses to accept anything which contradicts or omits the false proportions or misplaced highlights of the accustomed portrait. If the cherished but palpably untrue is omitted the biographer is set down as knowing very little about Washington; if the untruths are alluded to and strange new facts substituted therefor the biographer is almost forced into argumentative discourse, which is well nigh fatal to good biography."

Granting that such stirring events as took place at Trenton, Valley Forge, and Yorktown, along with the less spectacular political crises and perplexities which confronted the first President of the United States, are familiar to many readers today—a story so inspiring and so touchingly simple in this atomic age can always bear repeating. But within its limits Washington stands alone, the harassed, poker-faced man at the helm, who except in rare instances bore his many disasters without flinching and his few triumphs without visible exultation. At Mount Vernon, however, he permitted himself to relax into the family life of the Virginia planter—the sort of every-day routine which his brothers and neighbors maintained, and which he himself preferred. He watched from the parlor doorway while Martha's children and their little friends twirled and curtseyed under the direction of the itinerant dancing-master. He wrote out explicit orders to his London agents for the children's clothing and school-books and toys, as well as for the plantation necessities, and his and Martha's own requirements. He rode the rounds of his farms daily, superintending the work and health of his people and his livestock. He laid out walks and groves, gardens and orchards, and personally saw to the grafting of his fruit trees. He invented a plough.

It is this second life of his, behind the scenes and between the acts, that this book is designed to reveal. He was never, in his own mind nor in the eyes of his devoted family, a man on a pedestal. He was a loving and lovable human being, a good neighbor, a generous host, a considerate husband, and a dedicated farmer. In spite of his reputation as one of the wealthiest men in Virginia, his financial affairs were often critical. His assets were mainly in land, crops, and stock, and his many improvident relatives and friends made frequent demands on him, so that he was always short of ready cash.

Contemplated beside the elegant interiors of his sister Betty's house at Fredericksburg, or of his friend George Mason's Gunston Hall and the lavish Carter, Lee, and Burwell houses, or the James River mansions where he was a welcome guest, Mount Vernon's rooms were of an austere simplicity, so that one wonders if he ever regretted the comparative lack of adornment of his own house in the form of carved woodwork and ornate plaster ceilings and mantelpieces. It is probable that if he had been spared even the demands of the Presidency, and had been able to put those eight valuable years of his prime to good account at home, nursing and improving his property as he knew so well how to do, he would have shown a far greater yearly profit and built up a larger fortune, some of which might have gone to embellish his stately rooms.

The Hunting Creek land, which was to be known as Mount Vernon, was left by his father's will to George's elder half-brother Lawrence. Augustine Washington had dwelt there briefly with his second wife Mary and her small children before establishing his household permanently on the Rappahannock farm across the River from Fredericksburg. He even then intended the deserted Hunting Creek estate as his eldest son's inheritance, and not long before his death he saw Lawrence return in broken health from the Cartagena campaign to marry Anne Fairfax from the neighboring plantation called Belvoir. Lawrence brought his bride to the square eight-room house his father had built on high land overlooking the Potomac at the mouth of the Creek, and named it Mount Vernon, in honor of the British Admiral under whom he had recently served in the Caribbean.

Anne Fairfax's father, like her husband, had seen service in the British Navy, before a spell of Army duty which took him to Spain, and like Augustine Washington he had married twice. The first four of his seven children were by the daughter of a British major stationed in the Bahamas when Fairfax was appointed Chief Justice there in 1723. He had arrived in Virginia by way of a job as Collector of Customs at Salem, Massachusetts, where his first wife died, and he married his second. When his friend the elder Washington died on the Rappahannock in 1743, Colonel William Fairfax of Belvoir on the Potomac became the natural counselor as well as the father-in-law of Lawrence, who at twenty-three was resigning from the Navy in favor of a major's commission in the colonial militia, in order to settle down on his 2500 acres and become a tobacco planter like his neighbors.

Augustine Washington's second son, called Austin, was also a recent bridegroom, and he inherited the plantation to be known as

Wakefield at the mouth of Pope's Creek, farther down the Potomac shore in Westmoreland County, where the family had been living when George was born. The five children of Augustine's second marriage were left at his death to their mother's care at the third Washington homestead, the old Ferry Farm opposite Fredericksburg, which his will named as the portion of her eldest son George, then eleven years old, big for his age, already conscientious and capable.

II

FROM the time of his father's death George Washington lived at Wakefield and Mount Vernon more than he did in his mother's household. Austin was in easy circumstances, having married into the wealthy Aylett family. Lawrence's failing health made welcome at Mount Vernon the helpful presence of his devoted half-brother George in an atmosphere always damped by the inability of Anne's babies to survive more than a few months after their birth.

The substantial story-and-a-half house with its four rooms and a central hall on the ground floor, from which a sturdy staircase mounted to the four dormered chambers above, was not so grand as the red brick mansion a few miles down the River where Anne had grown up as the eldest daughter of the lively, prosperous, and handsome Fairfax family. Colonel Fairfax, who was said to have the happy faculty of treating boys like grown men, received young George into his cheerful circle as another son, and his second wife until her death gave the boy a more indulgent maternal affection than he had got from his own undemonstrative and humorless mother.

Three years after her marriage to Lawrence, Anne's brother George William Fairfax returned to Virginia from his schooling in England. Between Lawrence and George Washington in age, he was then twenty-one, and like Lawrence he was gilded with a sophistication beyond the experience of the admiring young colonial, but he gave himself no airs, and on his side had much to learn of half-forgotten plantation ways.

Colonel William Fairfax had come to Virginia from Massachusetts as agent for his cousin, the eccentric sixth Lord Fairfax, who it was said had never been the same since in his remote youth a heartless English girl had jilted him to marry a duke. Possessed of some six million acres in twenty-one counties in Virginia as an inheritance from his grandmother, who was a Culpeper, Lord Fairfax had turned over his English estate, including Leeds Castle, to his brother Robert, and himself retreated across the Atlantic to the western wilderness to brood. He built the rustic mansion he called Greenway Court on the near side of the frontier town of Winchester in the Shenandoah Valley, from where he erupted periodically into Tidewater society as a guest at Belvoir, maintaining perhaps with some difficulty his chosen attitude of woman-hater amid his cousin William's attractive female belongings. He was a massive, swarthy man, aggressively plain in his dress, moody, lonely, autocratic, and capable of great kindness, along with his majestic manners.

Young George Washington had already begun to use his father's surveyor's instruments in little jobs for Lawrence at Mount Vernon, running lines and marking boundaries, mapping turnip-fields and wood-lots, when George William Fairfax came home from England. Colonel Fairfax encouraged his son to join in George's occupation and himself learn to use a compass, sextant, and chain. In a benevolent mood Lord Fairfax gave the boys a real job, laying out lands for leaseholders on the vast Fairfax tracts in the Valley. In this way George first met the frontier which was to claim the rest of his youth. He camped out, foraged for his food, tended his horses, endured bad weather and small alarms and saddle fatigue, and encountered at first hand the unpredictable, elusive, dangerous riddle called Indian. And there his boyhood ended.

When he returned from this first surveying expedition for Lord Fairfax, he had already chosen a profession apart from farming his small inheritance on the Rappahannock. Before he reached his eighteenth birthday he had taken the usual oaths and received his commission as public county surveyor, and earned his first payment in actual cash (not tobacco). He made several more trips westward into the rough but beautiful Valley country, and invested his earnings in some land on Bullskin Creek in Frederick County to the extent of 1500 acres. Lawrence believed firmly in the value of the frontier land, once the Indians could be brought to terms.

Young George William Fairfax was soon elected to the Virginia Assembly, of which Lawrence was also a member, and during his attendance at Williamsburg in 1748 George William met and married Sally Cary, eldest of the four well-educated, well-dowered, and beautiful daughters of Willson Cary of Ceelys on the James. George Washington, who at first might have regarded his friend's new wife as an intruder, succumbed to Sally's tact and good nature, and the visits of her sisters Mary, Anne, and Betsy Cary to Belvoir certainly enlivened the Potomac scene. At seventeen, George was not unaccustomed to the society of pretty women. His half-brother had married George William's sister Anne. Colonel Fairfax's second wife had only recently died, and his daughter Sarah had just married a wealthy merchant and ship-master named Carlyle who was building for her a handsome house, half fortress, in the new town of Alexandria a few miles up the River. The youngest Fairfax daughter, Hannah, was about George's age.

Lawrence Washington was by now aware that his life might be a short one, and that his offspring lacked vitality, and George was tacitly recognized as his favorite brother and the probable heir to Mount Vernon. In the autumn of 1751 George accompanied Lawrence on a voyage to Barbados undertaken in the hope that the West Indian climate might benefit the stubborn complaint of the lungs which Lawrence had brought back from Cartagena. But Lawrence did not improve, and soon after their arrival at Bridgetown George contracted a severe case of small-pox, which left him slightly marked but immune for life.

Lawrence reached home again in the spring of '52, using the last of his strength, and George was with him at Mount Vernon when he died in July. Widowed at twenty-seven, with one baby girl, Anne went home to her father's house. The sickly child soon died like the others, and Anne re-married before the year was out. In accordance with his father's wishes, Lawrence's will named George as his residuary heir, after Anne and the child or her issue. Now that the child was dead, and Anne was living at Mount Pleasant in Westmoreland County with her new husband, who was a Lee, George could not but contemplate Lawrence's house, which he had been taught to regard as his home, with an affectionate and possessive eye. No one seemed to want it any more, and its 2500 acres were already falling into neglect for want of proper managing. He had nearly 2000 acres of his own now, up Winchester way, but that was still a wilderness. Mount Vernon was ready and waiting. Mount Vernon only wanted a master.

He had from Lawrence a more immediate legacy. Already known as a serious and responsible young man, although he was barely twenty-one he was appointed by the Governor to succeed Lawrence as District Adjutant of his Majesty's Colony of Virginia, with the rank of major and pay which came to about £150 a year. The regimental dress of the colonial militia became his tall form and erect, Indian-stepping carriage—a blue coat faced and cuffed with scarlet, and trimmed with silver; a scarlet waistcoat with silver lace; blue breeches, and a cocked silver-laced hat. In November, 1752, he laid aside his surveyor's sextant and chain to study fencing, drill, and tactics, in preparation for active army service on the western frontier, and in the same month he was initiated into the Grand Lodge of the Free Masons at Fredericksburg.

But while as a surveyor he was already acquainted with the hardships and dangers he now encountered as a soldier, he was not prepared for the backstairs criticism, insubordination, and garrison politics of an army career. During the next two years he found his colonial rank and privileges encroached on by arrogant officers of the British establishment. Having risen to a Virginia colonelcy, he resented being overlorded by any King's commission captain who showed up, to the detriment of the discipline and authority he had laboriously achieved over his rugged troops, and he was bitterly disappointed by Governor Dinwiddie's failure to support him in what he considered his well-earned due. Even his pay was £15 a month less than the British commission brought. In the autumn of '54 he resigned from the army in disgust, although he retained the adjutancy of his district—determined to become a planter like the Fairfaxes, stand for election to the Assembly, maybe marry. His friends and contemporaries were getting ahead of him, founding fortunes and families of their own.

His mother and the three youngest boys were still living on the Rappahannock farm, and though by his father's will he might have claimed it when he turned twenty-one, George was already wearing the King's uniform then, and was content that the family should continue to occupy his little property. It kept them under the eye of his sister Betty, who was next to him in age and had recently married Fielding Lewis and was established at Fredericksburg. Betty could get along with their strong-willed, unaccommodating parent, as her brothers could not.

Lewis, who was eight years older than Betty, had been a widower with a small son. He owned a store and warehouses and a seagoing vessel, and acted as justice of the court and vestryman of his church. His first wife Catherine, dead after only three years of marriage, had been a daughter of Augustine Washington's brother John, and his grandmother and Betty's had been sisters, so that in the interlocking Tidewater relationships Betty had known him as one of the family all her life. She stepped easily into the closer association within a year of Catherine's death, though there was a rumor that she had hesitated until he promised her the finest house in Virginia as a wedding present. Perhaps at sixteen Betty had had a brief dream of some more romantic-seeming suitor, which soon gave way to the persuasion of what was for her a brilliant match, with an old friend she could not but admire. They had at once sent for George, with his surveyor's eye, to help them choose a site for the new house, on a green slope which looked eastward towards the Rappahannock, a mile or so back from the river-bank because of mosquitoes and flood water. Hickory trees, gums, and oaks screened the buildings of Fredericksburg to the south. When George returned from Barbados in '52 the house, which they called Millbank, was already well along, under the direction of the Virginia-born architect John Arris, who had recently returned from his studies in England, and was much in demand in the Tidewater country as a disciple of the great William Adam and owner of Adam's famous book of Georgian design.

The bricks for Millbank were made on Lewis's property in his own kilns, and the great beams were cut and weathered there. The window glass, brass and nails, and some of the finely carved woodwork were brought out from England, along with skilled craftsmen to complete the work on the spot. Arris worked slowly and patiently, in loving detail. By the autumn of '54 the Lewises were able to occupy the house, though its interior decoration was still unfinished.

George paid them a visit on his way home from Williamsburg

aftter the unpleasant session there with Governor Dinwiddie which had ended in his resignation from the King's service. He had acquired a certain reputation for bravery and enterprise, although he had suffered defeat and humiliation by the French on the Ohio frontier in July, for which not even the Governor held him to blame. He considered nevertheless that Dinwiddie had let him down in favor of men with British commissions, his youthful pride was raw, and his health had suffered from two years of camp life and campaigning. He paused at Fredericksburg to admire Betty's house and her two babies, and saw that the marriage was a happy one, before he rode on to the place he had always called home.

His old Potomac neighborhood welcomed him cordially, and he enjoyed all the social luxuries so long denied him by his hard wilderness life as a soldier. He won 14/3 at cards at Belvoir, and he rode to hounds. Sally Fairfax and her young sister-in-law Hannah brought him up to date on all the family and county news. Sally's sister Mary Cary, for whom he had long cherished a warm affection, had married Edward Ambler of Jamestown, who was lately returned from England with all the advantages of a Cambridge education and the Grand Tour. Anne Cary was now the wife of Robert Carter Nicholas, a grave Williamsburg lawyer, which left only Betsy, youngest of the four brilliant sisters, unwed. George Mason, another of his boyhood companions, had married a Maryland girl and fathered a son, and was building a house to be called Gunston Hall on the River just below Belvoir. Fine houses were the fashion, extravagant outlay for their adornment was the rule.

George's affection for Mount Vernon reproached him for its present lonely condition and the deterioration which was already setting in. Lawrence's widow, as the wife of George Lee, had no further use for it, though it still stood in her name. Before the year was out, George signed a lease with the Lees, at an annual payment in tobacco which amounted to nearly double his pay as Adjutant, for the term of Anne's life interest. That Christmas season, as the tenant and titular master of Mount Vernon, he entertained guests in a home of his own for the first time and embarked at once on a modest program of improvements and repairs. He did some canny shopping for his immediate household needs, and welcomed the friendly advice of the Belvoir ladies regarding his bachelor establishment. Eighteen resident slaves went with the estate, and he bought three more who came to his notice—paying £52.5 for Jack, £50 for Clio, and £40 for an odd-job fellow. He also acquired John Alton, a white man, to act as steward and overseer.

Then, in the spring of '55, when he had been for only a few months a private citizen, General Braddock arrived in Virginia from England to lead an army of British redcoats against the French on the Ohio, and once more George answered the drum.

III

BRADDOCK had heard about him at Williamsburg on the way to the frontier, and sidestepped the touchy question of colonial rank by offering him a post on the Staff as a volunteer aide, so that George could not resist having another go at the French. He got his favorite brother John Augustine Washington to come up from the Rappahannock and run Mount Vernon for him and carry forward whatever plans could still mature in the absence of its master; dealt firmly with his mother's outspoken objections to a resumption of his soldiering; bought a strong bay horse for £10; and accompanied by John Alton as orderly, was off to the wilderness again with Braddock's redcoats.

The campaign turned out a total disaster for the British. Braddock's men, trained in formal European warfare which had all the flexibility of a minuet, were slaughtered by an unseen enemy who fired from behind rocks and trees into the helpless column which had never been taught to take cover. Braddock got a mortal wound, and was buried in the road during the retreat. Young Colonel Washington, so weakened by dysentery that he rode with a pillow tied in the saddle to enable him to endure the jolting, was the only officer on the Staff who was not either killed or disabled. The wildfire rumors of calamity which ran ahead of the broken army included a report of his death, which afforded him some amusement at the time:

"Dear Jack: [he wrote from Fort Cumberland to his brother at Mount Vernon on July 18th, some ten days after the battle on the Monongahela] As I have heard since my arriv'l at this place, a circumstantial acct. of my death and dying speech, I take this oppertunity of contradicting the first and assuring you that I have not as yet composed the latter. But by the all powerful dispensations of Providence I have been protected beyond all human probability and expectation, for I had 4 Bullets through my Coat and 2 Horses shot under me, and yet escaped unhurt.

"We have been most scandalously beaten by a trifling body of men; but fatigue and want of time prevents me from giving any of the details till I have the happiness of seeing you at home; which I now most ardently wish for, since we are drove in thus far. A Weak and Feeble state of Health obliges me to halt here for 2 or 3 days, to recover a little strength, that I may thereby be enabled to proceed homeward with more ease; You may expect to see me there on Saturday or Sunday Se'night, which is as soon as I can well be down as I shall take my Bullskin Plantation's in my way. Pray give my Complt. to all my F'ds. I am, dr. Jack, y'r most Affect. Broth'r, &c."

For a time, then, he resumed his interrupted domestic program at Mount Vernon, with a peaceful interlude for rest and doctoring, visited by the whole neighborhood and nursed by John Alton and the ladies from Belvoir. But his friends in the Williamsburg Assembly wrote urgently about a new command to be undertaken for a new campaign against the French. His high colonial pride and his youthful, stiff-necked self-respect insisted that he make his own terms this time, although his almost fanatical sense of duty to Virginia compelled him at least to contemplate any reasonable new proposals from the Governor, who was now at sixty-three in irritable bad health and obsessed by a conviction that only the waters at Bath, in England, would cure him.

Although the recent interval at home had much increased George's desire to devote himself wholly to the business of his estate and let the army worry along without him, he still found himself unwilling selfishly to abandon the burden he had carried, to men who daily demonstrated their incapacity to shoulder it for him. Reluctantly therefore, he journeyed to Williamsburg in August, '55, and there found himself regarded as no less than a hero for his part in rallying the British remnants and leading their more or less orderly retreat towards Winchester.

As he might have expected, one thing led to another at Williamsburg. The Assembly expressed their gratitude by a grant of £300, which he had not applied for, to cover his losses of property in the past campaign—losses consisting mainly of horses and baggage; all his complaints and conditions for continued service were cordially met and soothed away, until somewhat to his own surprise he returned to the frontier that autumn as Commander-in-chief of all the Virginia forces, committed once again to the colossal effort of organizing the ill-equipped, half-trained, unruly citizen soldiery who were expected to defend the border settlements against the Indian raids and atrocities which had brought them to the verge of panic.

He went with many misgivings, but mindful that he had much to lose in public esteem by a persistent refusal to undertake a difficult command. "..... I wish, my dear Charles, it was more in my power than it is to answer the favourable opinion my Friends have conceiv'd of my abilitys," he wrote to Fielding Lewis's brother, who aspired to join him as a soldier. "Let them not be deceiv'd, I am unequal to the Task, and do assure you it requires more experience than I am master of to conduct an affair of the importance that this is now risen to......"

He was still two months short of being twenty-four years old.

So the grim grind began again—recruiting, drill, inspection, commissary problems, near mutiny and harsh army discipline—"Any soldier who shall desert, though he returns again, shall be hanged without mercy," read his General Orders for December 25th, 1755, and not one word about Christmas.

Once more, it all went pretty much as it was bound to do, in continued insubordination, hardship beyond imagining by the men in the streets of the tidy little capital where the Assembly met, lack of food and clothing, horrible reports of massacre and flaming homesteads only a few miles beyond the gates of the fort, charge and counter-charge of corruption, drunkenness, and immorality among his hard-bitten troops—everything but adequate funds, supplies, and reinforcements.

Early in 1756, he rode all the way from Fort Cumberland to Boston to consult on the forever explosive matter of rank, pay, and seniority at the frontier forts with the supreme commander of British forces in America, Governor Shirley, whose son William had died with Braddock on the Monongahela. George travelled in some state, accompanied by Captains George Mercer and Robert Stewart as aides, his servant John Alton, and Braddock's orderly, Bishop, who had attached himself as a sort of bequest from the dead general to his colonial aide. He was received all along the way as the hero of the Braddock tragedy, and was respectfully entertained by the Governors in Philadelphia and New York. The Boston *Gazette* made mention of the arrival in town of "the Hon. Colonel Washington, a gentleman who has deservedly a high reputation for military skill and valor. . . . ."

He was impressed by Philadelphia's paved streets, lighted and patrolled at night, and the mansions and shops of the largest city he had ever seen. After months of active service he took the opportunity of renewing his wardrobe, paying a tailor £21.9 and the hatter £2.14–and 16s.11 to the washerwoman. In New York he bought a pair of shoes for 14s. and paid another tailor's bill of £3.3.7, and lost 8s. at cards. Also he was much taken with Mary Philipse, the sister-in-law of Beverley Robinson, his New York host, an ex-Virginian who had married into the wealthy Philipse family.

In Boston he lodged at Cromwell's Head Tavern, on School Street, where the sign still hung so low that every tall passerby had to bow to the Protector. He found the Massachusetts rate of exchange so much in his favor that he was tempted to still more expenditure–gloves, silk stockings, cockades, and a breeches buckle–than 35/9 to the barber, £1.2.6 to the chambermaid, and stockings for Bishop, £1. Not all his purchases were frivolous. £25 went for a new mare, and £10.12.6 for a tent and marquee–just in case he ever took the field again. Doubtless on behalf of his fellow officers at the fort he ran up a tailor's bill of £95.7.3, and what must have been a bale of silver lace cost him £94.17.1.

He had now seen the world, but although he seemed to have won his point with Governor Shirley, he discovered too late that he was still subordinate to a previous Crown appointment. Proceeding straight to Williamsburg again in a mood to resign, he was again dissuaded by such dreadful news from the frontier that he could only hurry back to his tragic responsibilities there: "Not an hour, nay, scarcely a minute passes, that does not produce fresh alarms and melancholy accounts, so that I am distracted what to do!" he reported to Governor Dinwiddie, with one of his rare exclamation points, after his arrival at Winchester. "..... Three families were murdered the night before last, at the distance of less than twelve miles from this place; and every day we have accounts of such cruelties and barbarities, as are shocking to human nature. Nor is it possible to conceive the situation and danger of this miserable country. Such numbers of French and Indians are all around, no road is safe to travel, and *here* we know not the hour how soon we may be attacked....."

The Assembly had authorized the construction of a new fort near Winchester, and had left the design and engineering to him. It was to be one in a proposed chain of defence points running southward almost to the Carolina boundary, in an attempt to link up the isolated stockades which for lack of communications and reinforcements had become ineffective in the long game of defensive warfare which was all the army's resources would permit. Lacking tools and conviction, the work proceeded slowly. George relieved the summer monotony by taking fencing lessons from a Sergeant Wood, at a cost of £3.4.6 for three months' instruction.

Even his Potomac affairs were heavy on his mind. Lawrence's will had left room for discord on the division of his property. Anne's second husband was making difficulties, and it was hard to assemble all the interested parties at one time. John Augustine Washington had married Hannah Bushrod of Westmoreland County, and there was some uncertainty about his continued residence at Mount Vernon. Hannah would inherit her father's handsome house called Bushfield at the mouth of Nomini Creek, and while she had consented to come to Mount Vernon for an extended honeymoon, it was natural that they should wish to establish themselves permanently. Meanwhile, Mount Vernon had been too long under the hit-or-miss management of bachelor males. During a brief midsummer stop-over there on his way north from Williamsburg back to the fort, George was able to map out some domestic rearrangements which were to be got under way before Jack and his wife departed for her home and left his plantation without a resident manager.

In September, '56, George got leave from the Governor for another ride to Mount Vernon to participate in the adjustment of Lawrence's muddled estate, and he spent a valuable week at home with what he regarded as his family. Sally Fairfax offered him the services of her seamstress to make him some new shirts, and he sent her a sample garment and some material, accompanied by directions of a military thoroughness.

"Dear Madam: John [Alton] informs me that you told him Miss Nancy West was to be at your House in a day or two; and that you wou'd, if I sent my Linnen over, give it to Miss Nancy to make; I shall readily embrace the oppertunity of doing this, tho' I am at the same time sorry to give you the trouble of directing about the making.

"I have sent a piece of Irish Linnen, a piece of Cambrick, and a shirt to measure by. The Shirt Fits tolerably well, yet I wou'd have the others made with somewhat narrower Wrist bands; Ruffles deeper by half an Inch; and the Collars by three quarters of an Inch, which is in other respects of proper bigness. If Miss Nancy will do me the favour to get thread and button's suitable it will oblige me much, I have really forget to procure them myself. Please make my Compts. to Miss Fairfax and Miss West when you see her. I am, dr. Madam, etc."

As for the persistent dreary superstition that he never really loved anybody but Sally Fairfax, Douglas Southall Freeman in the first of his seven authoritative volumes on Washington's life points out that "there survives not one echo of the gossip that would have been audible all along the Potomac had there been anything amiss in their relations," while the proof of an ever deepening devotion between Washington and his wife is very plain to see.

It is not, of course, reasonable to suppose that a man who did not marry until he was turning twenty-seven had never been in love before. The tall militia colonel was a striking figure on the Williamsburg social scene, and soon after he had come of age he had a wide reputation as a soldier and a man of substance. Magnificent on horseback, accomplished in the minuet, sociable if a little shy and untalkative, he was not to be overlooked in Tidewater society. A letter quoted in Paul Leicester Ford's *The True George Wash-*

ington (1896), the original of which did not come to light during Dr. Fitzpatrick's Bicentennial research, indicated that Washington once offered for Betsy Fauntleroy's hand and was refused, which would hardly have broken his heart at the age of twenty. Miss Fauntleroy is always mentioned as one of several supposed early loves of Washington's who performed the legendary swoon during his triumphal arrival at Williamsburg in 1781 on the way to Yorktown—any one of whom would by then have been a matron if not a widow in her forties.

Without much doubt he was for a time attracted to Sally Fairfax, as he may well have been to her three sisters and a dozen other Tidewater beauties before his marriage in 1759 to the young widow Custis; but some ten years earlier when Sally arrived at Belvoir as the bride of George William Fairfax she would have been no particular revelation to a boy of sixteen who was already accustomed to the propinquity of the Fairfax girls and their friends. The few surviving letters from him to Sally which are of undoubted authenticity—the original of the one written in September, '56, is in the Morgan Library—are as formal as if, says Dr. Freeman, she were no nearer or dearer than any other woman. There are only two of those often cited, somewhat naive and confused avowals which are supposed to convict him of a secret passion for his best friend's wife, and they have not been seen for half a century, if they ever did exist as anything but forgeries. The knowing myth of a lifelong hopeless love affair is dismissed by Dr. Fitzpatrick as "the product of a type of mind." The subtle absence of a qualifying adjective is inspired.

IV

ON his return to the fort from Mount Vernon in the autumn of 1756 George undertook a long and hazardous inspection tour of the stockade posts, narrowly escaping ambuscade and murder like any border settler. Arriving back at Winchester late in the year, he found his officers bored and quarrelsome, grumbling about back pay and overdue leave. The political press was blasting the lack of discipline and achievement among the troops, and the Governor and Assembly were again critical of his conduct, and implied that he should have had more to show for his time.

Saddle-weary and sick at heart, he once more contemplated retirement from the army in order to look after his own interests on the land which he loved as he might have loved a woman. He could see nothing ahead where he was, beyond the dull garrison existence, subject always to ignorant interference and contradictory orders from the capital, his position forever complicated by the domineering behavior of officers fresh from England who were without any comprehension whatever of the Indian problem.

The impending arrival of Lord Loudoun, Governor Shirley's successor as commander of the British forces in America, and the urgent protests of his friends and fellow officers once more deterred him until the impulse to lay his resignation before the irascible Dinwiddie was absorbed again into the pressing emergencies close at hand. He seemed to have very little choice but to sit out another army Christmas. He bought a puppy for 2s.6d. and took it with him to Fort Cumberland. "..... My strongest representations of matters relative to the peace of the frontiers are disregarded as idle and frivolous; my propositions and measures, as partial and selfish; and all my sincerest endeavors for the service of my country perverted to the worst purposes," he wrote angrily to his good friend Speaker Robinson at Williamsburg. "My orders are dark, doubtful, and uncertain; *today approved, tomorrow condemned.* Left to act and proceed at hazard, accountable for the consequence, and blamed without the benefit of defense! . . . . . However, I am determined to bear up under all the embarrassments some time longer, in hope of better regulation on the arrival of Lord Loudoun, to whom I look for the future of Virginia. . . . . . ."

But he might as well have saved himself the trouble of Lord Loudoun. The new commander at a March conference of Governors at Philadelphia, which Colonel Washington attended on leave from the still unfinished fort to be named for his lordship, only handed down a decision that no offensive against the French at Fort Duquesne would be possible in the immediate future. In his frustration and despair, Washington fell back on the Mount Vernon dream, and got out the lists and notations he had collected during his autumn visit there. John Augustine had made the house weathertight and refinished the walls and woodwork and put the chimneys right. It was now time for a little style and adornment.

The colonies were not allowed to manufacture much of their finished goods, beyond the cobbling, smithing, and carpentering by local workmen, and the homespun weaving and knitting by female slaves. Tools, hardware, table delicacies, fine clothes, even household furniture, china, silver, and ornaments, must all be ordered from England, and the payment was usually made in tobacco shipments from the plantation owners to their chosen agents in London. It was an exasperating system, for however minute the description of the articles desired, the selection of each item was at the mercy of an indifferent or conscientious stranger, as the case might be, while dishonest tradesmen often took advantage of the overseas customer by sending outdated or inferior goods.

On April 15, 1757, Washington sat down at his rough-hewn writing-table in his quarters at Fort Loudoun, to go over his accounts and work out an invoice to his London agents, with whom he had already established a cordial correspondence:

". . . . . I have been posted for twenty Months past upon our cold and Barren Frontiers," he wrote in his free, legible hand with a freshly cut quill, "to perform I think I may say impossibilitys, that is to protect from the cruel incursions of a Crafty Savage Enemy a line of Inhabitants of more than 350 Miles in extent, with a force inadequate to the taske; by this means I am become in a manner an exile, and Seldom inform'd of these oppertunities which I might otherwise embrace, of corrisponding with my friends......

"I have now to add, That I am so little acquainted with the Business relative to my private Affairs that I can scarcely give you any information concerning it. I know that I ought to have some Tobacco and that it ought to be shipp'd; that I have beg'd the favour of Colo. Carlyle on Potomack and Fielding Lewis, Esq., on Rappahannock, to do this for me, and I desir'd them to write to you in my behalf and draw for Sundry things I am in want of; but whether any part, or all of this is done, I know not. I shall therefore desire these two things of you; first that you may put yourself to no real Inconvenience in providing Goods to greater amount than my remittances will fetch, because I by no means intended to be troublesome when I solicited your corrispondence; and secondly, that whatever Goods you may send me where the prices are not absolutely limited you will let them be fashionable, neat, and good in their several kinds. Enclosed is a list of Sundries which I should be glad to receive agreeable to these Directions. I am, etc.

A Marble Chimney piece of the Dimensions of the Inclos'd (given by the workmen) the Cost not to exceed 15 Guineas. N.B. Let it be carefully pack'd.

A Neat Landskip 3 feet by 21½ Inches—1 Inch Margin—for a Chimney

250 panes window glass 11 by 9

Paper for 5 rooms of the following Dimensions (viz) 18 by 12; 16 by 12; 16 by 14; 18 by 15; and 15 by 16, all 8 feet pitch, the Paper differing in their colours; also paper of a very good kind and Colour for a Dining-room 18 by 16 feet above the Chair-boards; the pitch of the room is 11 feet.

Papier Machee for the ceiling of two Rooms, one of them 18 Feet Square, the other 18 by 16 with Corner Chimneys

Two neat Mahogany Tables, 4½ feet square when spread, and to join occasionally

1 Doz'n neat and strong Mahogany Chairs at 21/
Doz'n fashionable Locks for Partition doors and appurtenances
1 Doz'n fash'e Hinges for the said Doors and 2 pr larger"

It was a beginning, though a small one, to bring Mount Vernon up to the mark of Belvoir and the Carlyle mansion at Alexandria, and the fine houses he had seen at Philadelphia, New York, and Boston. He was already learning how insatiable is the appetite of a beloved house for trinkets, which are often disguised as necessities, and how a man can spend and spend, as for a mistress, without satisfying his own dream of perfection for his dwelling place.

Immediately after dispatching the invoice he was summoned back to Williamsburg by the Governor on the matter of arrearages of pay and other grievances of his regiment, and enjoyed a reunion with his family and friends along the way. His sister Betty at Fredericksburg had had another son, named George for her brother and Fielding for his father. His half-brother Austin at Wakefield after three girls had at last got a boy, named William Augustine.

The Assembly was in session, and Williamsburg was gay. Some months had elapsed since his last appearance there, and his welcome was cordial. The Fairfaxes were all in town, except the erratic younger son, Bryan, George William's half-brother, whose unsuccessful courtship of a Miss Turberville, the latest in a semi-comic series of disappointments, had led to his total disappearance, causing his father some anxiety. Daniel Custis of New Kent County was in the Governor's Council now, and with his small, serene wife Martha attended the Assembly balls at the Raleigh Tavern, and the receptions at the Governor's Palace. Martha's sister Nancy Dandridge was about to marry the widower Burwell Bassett of Eltham in New Kent County. John Robinson, one of George's staunchest friends, old enough to be his father, and for twenty years Speaker of the House, was always a faithful defender of his protégé's rights and reputation during the tedious wrangles with the unreasonable Governor Dinwiddie.

On his way back to the fort in May, George visited his mother at the Ferry Farm on the Rappahannock. She was always in want of funds though it was hard to see why, and this time it cost him £5 to pay his respects.

The summer of '57 passed in the usual garrison routine—desertions, recruiting, Indian councils, alarums and excursions. By the first of August the inevitable dysentery was again undermining his health, and his scouting parties had had little success in curbing the Indian depredations. ". . . . The inhabitants of this valuable and very fertile valley are terrified beyond expression," he wrote Dinwiddie from Fort Loudoun. "Some have abandoned their plantations, and many are packing up their most valuable effects in order to follow them. Another iruption into the heart of this settlement will, I am afraid, be of fatal consequence to it. . . . . And I think I may venture to affirm that unless an expedition is carried on against the Ohio next spring, this country will not be another year in our possession. . . . ."

That September brought his second grave bereavement, in the death of Colonel Fairfax, who had always been to him as to Lawrence a kindly, wise, and experienced counselor and friend. George mourned him like a son, and with a double loss, for as President of the Council and a member of the Assembly throughout George's military service, Colonel Fairfax had done all that was humanly possible to smooth the steadily worsening relations between his young friend and the unpredictable Governor.

George's low state of health did not prevent his journeying to Belvoir to be present at the funeral. He found George William Fairfax on the point of departure for England to secure his Yorkshire inheritance by an uncle who was under the delusion that because his birth had taken place in the Bahamas his mother must have been black-skinned. While George William's absence abroad would for a time emphasize the melancholy change at Belvoir, it would not by any means leave Sally alone in the house, as his half-sister Hannah was still unmarried, and young Bryan had turned up safely to transfer his volatile affections from the lost Miss Turberville to Sally's youngest sister Betsy Cary. By his father's will, which gave Belvoir to George William, Bryan inherited an estate in the western part of the county called Towelston after the Yorkshire family seat, which combined with a new religious conversion seemed likely to have a sobering effect.

While George was still at Mount Vernon he heard of the sudden death of Daniel Custis, snatched away from his little family and a useful career as a member of the Council and master of a prosperous plantation on the Pamunkey. His widow was left with two small children and a fortune, and people said she was bound to marry again if only to get an honest manager for so large an estate. Only a few months ago at Williamsburg George had seen her happy and secure in her husband's obvious affection.

He was called upon for a ruling in the matter of his brother Charles's wish to marry Mildred Thornton of Spotsylvania County. Charles was still a minor, and their mother had written to George in some agitation that the careful Mrs. Thornton was concerned for her daughter's inheritance in case Charles died before his twenty-first birthday, which anyway was less than a twelvemonth distant. George replied with an offer to sign an undertaking to secure Mildred's rights, since if her mother "believes I am capable of taking these ungenerous advantages [she] knows little of the principles which govern my conduct; however, I suppose Mrs. Thornton is actuated by prudent motives and therefore would be safe," he concluded philosophically, and went on to what was to him a matter of more importance, for the winter clothing ordered from England for his Mount Vernon Negroes had not arrived. He therefore begged the favor of his mother "to choose me about 250 yds Oznbergs, 200 yds of cotton, 35 pr. Plad Hose and as much thread as is necessary in Mr. Lewis' Store if he has them, if not in Mr. Jackson's, and send them up by John [Alton] who comes down with a Tumbler [tumbril] for that purpose. I set out this afternoon on my return to Winchester. I offer my love to Charles, and am, Hon'd Madam, Yr. most Dutiful and affect'e Son."

His journey to the Potomac for Colonel Fairfax's funeral and back again to the fort had not relieved his internal misery, and the repeated crises of his command reduced him still further, though he refused to give up and stay in bed. By early November he was scarcely able to stand or walk, for weakness, and was in constant pain and high fever.

On the 9th the devoted Captain Stewart undertook to write to the Governor: "...... This complication of Disorders greatly perplexes the Doctr. as what is good for him in one respect hurts him in another, the Doctr. has strongly recommended him immediately changing his air and going some place where he can be kept quiet (a thing impossible here) being the best chance that now remains for his Recovery; the Colo. objected to following this Advice before he could procure Yr. Hons. Liberty, but the Doctr. gave him such reasons as convinc'd him it might then be too late and he has at length with reluctance agreed to it; therefore has Directed me to acquaint Yr. Honr. (as he is not in condition to write himself) of his resolution of leaving this immediately and of his reasons for doing it which I now have the honour to do...."

Dinwiddie's crotchets at once collapsed into his innate goodheartedness, and he expressed concern for Colonel Washington's health. He was on the eve of departure for England and they were never to meet again.

The doctor whose professional orders had finally prevailed over George's sense of duty was James Craik, a Scot who had been a surgeon with the army since 1754, and had shared with George the horrors of the Braddock defeat, which formed the firm foundation of a lifelong friendship between them. He had already a conviction of some great destiny for the tall colonel whose many narrow escapes had created among his comrades an almost mystical sense of divine interference for his protection. Craik nevertheless forwarded to George at Mount Vernon his own reinforcement to the workings of Providence:

"......As nothing is more conducive to a Speedy recovery than a tranquil easy mind, Accompanied by a good flow of Spirits," he wrote, as a postscript to a lecture delivered before George's departure from the fort, "I would beg of you; not as a Physician but as a real friend who has your Speedy recovery Sincerely at heart; that you will keep up your Spirits, and not allow your mind to be disturbed with any part of Publick bussiness that perhaps may not be going on so well as your concern for the Publick would wish.....

"The fate of your Friends and Country are in a manner dependent on your recovery—And as I am sensible of the regard you have for both I make no doubt but that you will use every endeavour that will be in the least conducive to your recovery....As reading and writing must be very troublesome to you in your present Circumstances, I shall only pray God, who is the best of all Physicians, that he in his infinite mercy may restore you to your wonted health, and preserve you in the Command which is so agreeable to so many, and none more so, than to him who has the honour to subscribe himself with the greatest Duty & Esteem, Dr. Sir. Your Most Affec. & Devoted humb. Servt.

JAS. CRAIK

P.S. Please to hint to me in a few lines, if your disorder hath yet taken a turn for the better."

George arrived home by easy stages, stopping at Alexandria to consult Mr. Green, who was a physician as well as a clergyman, and enjoying the hospitality of the Carlyles. George William Fairfax was still abroad, and John Augustine and Hannah Washington had left Mount Vernon for Bushfield. They returned to see him through the Christmas holidays and then, as he seemed for a time to get worse instead of better, they remained to keep him company. Sick and foundered again, feeling solitary and without close human ties of his own, it was inevitable that he should be a little haunted of Lawrence, whom he had loved with a touch of hero-worship, and who had returned home at the same age, shattered in health, to an early death here at Mount Vernon.

V

IT was young Colonel Washington's habit at the end of each year to cast up his accounts and review his situation, his past accomplishment and future prospect. At last, in January of '58, he was able to undertake a little personal business and amuse himself by preparing another invoice for England. The plaid hose ordered by the dozen for the slaves still had not come, nor had scythes, curry combs, and weeding hoes he was awaiting for work on the home farm, though some of his best Mountain Sweet-scented Tobacco had been shipped to the London market in payment. What goods had arrived were unsatisfactory, and the letter he wrote to his London agents about the errors and omissions showed that his interest in life was not entirely lacking:

"I. . . . . can't help complaining of the little care taken in the purchase: Besides leaving out one half, and the most material half too! of the Articles I sent for, I find the Sein is without Leads, Corks, and ropes, which renders it useless; the Crate of Stone ware dont contain a third of the Pieces I am charg'd with, and two things broke, and everything very high Charg'd. . . . . .

"In my last I desir'd two pair of Work'd Ruffles at a guinea each pair; if work'd Ruffles shou'd be out of fashion send such as are not, and to the things wrote for in my last add these following, viz.

A Neat Mahogany Card Table w'ch may serve for a dressing one
2 doz'n Packs of play'g Cards
2 Setts Counters for Quadrille
1 doz'n watch Cristals better than an Inch and a half Diameter

50 lb. best Raisins
50 lb. best Currants
50 lb. Almonds in the Shell
1 Cask best bottled Cyder
½ doz'n deep white Stone Dishes sortd.
½ Doz'n fashbl. China Bowls from a large to Midlg. Size
3 doz'n Plates deep and Shallow

"Your sending these things together with those wrote for in my last by the first Vessel will very much oblige, etc."

Always the best and most fashionable were specified. He appreciated the elegancies of life as it was lived at Belvoir and Wakefield and Fredericksburg, and his Boston journey had impressed on him still further that he was missing a great deal by sticking to the army when with some expenditure, which he was now able to make, and some thought and care, which he knew how to accomplish, Mount Vernon could become as fine a residence as most that he had seen, especially with the addition of an attractive wife. It was in this matter of a wife that he had begun unwillingly to realize a drawback.

His military service had left him little time or opportunity for serious courtship, or even for a normal social life, but recent observation of his brother Jack at Mount Vernon with a sympathetic domestic partner presented a new train of thought. George's own prospects were somewhat barren. The girls with whom he had passed a few pleasant hours at Williamsburg or in the neighborhood gatherings on the Potomac had married someone else while his back was turned. Betsy Fauntleroy, Lucy Grymes, Sally Fairfax's sister Mary—they married the men who were always there, who did not wear the King's uniform and live by the Governor's whims. Furthermore, there would have been a tendency on his part to compare all other women with Sally Fairfax herself—witty, educated, slender as a reed in her childlessness. It would be hard to find a mistress for Mount Vernon who could hold a candle to the mistress of Belvoir. And the solitary game of embellishing his beloved home for his own sketchy bachelor existence there was robbed of some of its savor by the lack of even a prospective family of his own to share it.

Reflections like these hardly made for the tranquil mind recommended by Dr. Craik, and the knowledge that Jack's and Hannah's anxiety about her father's failing health made them impatient to be off again to Westmoreland County obliged him at least to pretend an improvement in his health which he could not maintain from day to day. He engaged an overseer named Knight for the farms and another man named Patterson, to learn what they could from his brother's management routine, and found them both earnest, somewhat ignorant men, but anxious to please. When they had been a little broken in, he encouraged Jack and Hannah to make their own plans, and then found himself left alone with Bishop and John Alton in an echoing, half-furnished house. George William Fairfax's absence from Belvoir curtailed the free and easy come and go in that direction, and George's continued low spirits and limited diet made him poor company, causing him to withdraw still further into himself.

As the soft Virginia spring of '58 came in, a persistent cough and an ill-defined pain in the chest seemed to him all too plainly to resemble Lawrence's fatal affliction. He began again to consider, not in anger or thwarted ambition now, but of hard reality for his health's sake, a permanent retirement from active service and a possibly shortened life of semi-invalidism like Lawrence's, at Mount Vernon—in which case he would not marry at all. Sometimes his natural resilience warred with his melancholia, and after one false start when a new bout of pain and fever forced him to turn back, he set out in March to confer with his friend Speaker Robinson at Pleasant Hill on the Mattapony, to consult a Williamsburg physician, and to report to the acting Governor, President Blair, and wind up his accounts with the army.

When next he saw Mount Vernon, at the end of the same month, it was suddenly a different world.

Dr. Amson, who was considered an authority on the bloody flux and kindred ailments, found no tuberculous symptoms after all, prescribed a new remedy, which at once eased his malady, and promised that he would live. More powerful than the nasty medicine in the bottle, was the change in George's mental attitude towards his future. Reassured about his health, he approached President Blair in a different frame of mind, and found him cordial and candid. Lord Loudoun had failed to give satisfaction. Another commander, General Forbes, had been appointed to lead an expedition against the French at Fort Duquesne, with which Colonel Washington was expected to command his own Virginia regiment in the Line. And a chance meeting with Daniel Custis's widow at the house of a mutual friend led to a visit to her home on the Pamunkey, and the springing hope that at last, when he least expected it, he had found the wife Mount Vernon needed.

She was within a year of his own age, small and kind and motherly, and her two children, Jacky, who was four years old, and Patsy, who was two, were both spoilt and charming. Custis had died without leaving a will, which despite his competent overseers and lawyers laid a heavy responsibility on his widow, and she at once recognized in the master of Mount Vernon an experienced and willing counselor. Tidewater gossip was sure to say that he had an eye to the widow Custis's fortune if he married her, and he was not the only man who was more than willing to assume the protection of the little family. But no man would undertake it with more honest intent than himself, or more tender concern for their future welfare and happiness.

Now that his private affairs had taken a sudden turn upward it seemed for a time after his return to Fort Loudoun that his military prospects would do the same. General Forbes was delayed by illness at Philadelphia, but his quartermaster, Sir John St. Clair, who had served with Braddock and had survived a wound in the Monongahela battle of '55, was in cordial correspondence with Colonel Washington. It was on St. Clair's orders that George set out again for Williamsburg late in May, carrying a list of queries and requests regarding the proposed campaign, which he was to take up with the authorities there pending the arrival of the new Governor, Francis Fauquier.

The Custis house on the Pamunkey lay conveniently along his way. He stopped there briefly on his journey down, promising to return. And a few days later, his mission at the capital completed but with little time to spare, he made his offer to Martha Custis and was accepted.

Where only a few weeks before, the outlook had seemed to him empty and dull and hopeless, he now had both hands full and was much restored in health. This new offensive against the French was too long desired to be foregone, even for the urgent business of preparing Mount Vernon for a wealthy bride with two small children of her own. And while a timid woman might have flinched at the inevitable dangers the campaign would entail for a man who had engaged himself to marry when it was over, and a selfish one might have jibbed at what she could call a wilful risking of her happiness, Martha took it like the soldier's wife she was to prove herself many times over in the years to come. To the veteran militia colonel, jeopardy was always in the day's work, and played no part in his plans.

Although Martha had never visited on the Potomac, everyone knew everyone at the Assembly times in Williamsburg, and she was therefore no stranger to the families of the Northern Neck. Fortunately George William Fairfax had just returned from England, and would be able to take charge of Washington's affairs at Mount Vernon in John Augustine's stead, though Bushfield was not so far away as to prevent him too from looking in on Patterson and Knight without giving warning.

In the limited time at George's disposal, he and Fairfax went over the house together and developed a rather extensive program, which included raising the dormered roof to two and a half stories to provide third-floor rooms for storage and a possible overflow of guests or family. The sudden acquisition of two small children, and the reasonable expectation of more to come, would require additional accommodations. Knight and Patterson seemed to comprehend what was expected of them, and were confident of their ability to have the house ready for occupancy when he had beat the French, which would surely not take long this time.

In pursuit of his renewed determination to retire into private life at the end of this campaign, George arranged to become a candidate in the coming election, and would take his seat in the Assembly at the next session, if he got in. His friends Fairfax and Carlyle, and even the officers at the Winchester headquarters, were to do his electioneering for him, and had no doubt of his success.

A little preoccupied with so much enterprise after months of dismal doldrums, George rode on to Fort Cumberland and his army duties. He was still there when he received a letter which began *Dear Burgess*, and congratulated him on a comfortable majority at the polls. The entertainment, largely of a liquid nature, provided by his friends for the voters on his behalf, had cost him £39.6s. but he did not complain. Already he could see himself, with Martha and her children beside him, driving in a chariot with six horses from Mount Vernon to Williamsburg—no longer a harassed militia colonel with dysentery cramps, but a family man and a law-maker, with perhaps enough influence to improve the lot of his long-suffering ex-comrades who would still hold the frontier.

Meanwhile letters from his Tidewater domain followed him westward from Fort Cumberland along the new road through the wilderness which St. Clair and Forbes insisted upon hacking out for themselves in preference to the Braddock route, against Colonel Washington's advice. Forbes was by now a very sick man, carried in a horse-litter well to the rear, and for St. Clair the Braddock route no doubt held hideous memories. Washington fumed and protested in vain—it was the old story over again; the opinions of colonial officers carried no weight with the men in red coats blessed with the King's commission. Delays and hardships increased as the weather gradually worsened into autumn and the usual shortages of food and ammunition, and the usual army ailments brought grumbling, desertion, and despair to the ranks.

The news from the Potomac when it contrived to overtake him was at least mainly cheerful, and provided some amusement and relief to the bone-weary soldier who read by guttering candlelight in a drafty tent beyond the outer fringe of civilization:

"I shall take ye Roof off ye House, as soon as ye Carpenters gets ye Laths for to shingle on," wrote Patterson, not long after Washington's departure, "having ye chief of ye Work fream'd at this Instant; I shall want two inch plank for to cover ye Balustrade, & am of Opinion that Pine is before Oak for that purpose. But if you think proper to have ye Latter, ye Carpenters can get it.... Depend Sir on my deligence to forward ye Work, & will stick to it early and laite till finish'd....."

"I expect all the rents in next week without fail," Knight reported in his turn, "and I shall act according to your orders in paying Piper &c..... Sir I hope you will not be Doubtfull of my ~~Digles~~ Dilligence in your business, Ile Loose my life before any thing should Go amiss if I can help it, our people has been very sickly which has hurt us and a Great Deal of hinderance in building which I hope your Honr. will Consider; ye freame is all sawd but the Leaths which will soon be done; ye house will be raised next week. ....Please to excuse our making so little Tobacco, I hope we shall make a good Crop this year; I have planted Seventy thousand and shall finish next season; our Corn is very likely and in good order; ye water fails at the mill Very mutch..... All our stock is well and a fine parcell of Lambs, the roan mairs Colt grows very fast....."

"Most honourabel Cornel, this with Great Submisson and i hope with out a fens, and i hope your honour is in good health," ran a blotted screed from Poole the miller at Dogue Run the following month. "i have hear made Bold to let you no the Qualatys of your mill, i have now....... gaind a great Deal of Custum from Meariland as well as heare, and now She fails for want of water By reason of a good Deal of Dry weather which makes me Sorry that i cant grind faster for your Custumers, and by havein so Cloes in ploy with the mill the fore part of the year it has hind ard me from tendin the ground which i was to have...... and have in a Large famalea to maintane i must in Deaver for a maintaneance for them which i hope youre honour wont tak it amiss and that you will be pleast to let me no in time if i am to minde the mill argane and upon what tirms....."

"Upon the receipt of your favor I went to Mount Vernon in order to assist Mr. Patterson with my advice if wanted," George William Fairfax reported briskly. "But I found everything fraimed and prepaired to put up. And when I was last their the roof was raised and they were larthing of it, so that I hope it will soon be coverd, but if anything will prevent it, it will be for want of shingles. ....Triplett has made and burnt the bricks, and intends immediately to set about the underpinning–I propose and shall recommend priming the weather-boards as soon as possible to prevent warping

—and anything else that I see to your interest. I have not time to add more than my best wishes attend you and that you may add sprigs to your laurels and sit down quiet and easy for the future on the banks of the Potomack, which will be the greatest inducement to keep me this side of the water......"

"I have scarcely time to acquaint you That I was Yesterday at Mount Vernon to Visit Mr. Patterson, who consulted me about taking up the upper Floors, as you gave him no orders about them," George William continued in August, "Whereupon I had them clear'd in order to View them the better, and found most of them very uneven and several defective plank, upon which I made Patterson calculate the difference of Expence between New Laying them and intire new, which you'l see is too trifling to hesitate a moment provided you choose either. Undoubtedly they may do with a little plaining, but that cant bring them even, or make them of a piece with the rest of the House. If you prefer a new Floor, their must be new Doors also, So that we beg you'l consider this matter and let us have your directions......I think the Chimneys above are too contracted and would be better were they inlarged. For if you remember they are taken in but whether to prevent Smoaking or for a Stove you perhaps can best tell, and the only one that can direct us. I have the pleasure to acquaint you That you have some of the finest Tobacco & Corn I have seen this Year, and a pritty full crop of both, which I believe is more than any in this or the next County can say......"

"Having consulted Col. Fairfax concerning ye old floors up Stairs, passage floor also," Patterson was next heard from, confirming a slight difference with the gentleman in question, "informs me he would write & have your answer, its just ye Nail holes of ye latter looks but indifferent, but ye Joynts makes amends for that; & in me it would be base to take it up, when I am confident its not in my power to lay a better one, ye Stuff of it being dry, & when playnd over will have a much better look.....In regard to pleacing ye Stairs up to ye Garret, I do not intend to adopt them in ye Room mentioned in ye Last Letter, but opposite to ye head of ye old Stair Caise, takeing them off from ye store room that was; and shall advise with Col. Fairfax on this point, as in every other article. . . . ."

By September, the work on the house had cost him £328.0.5 for Patterson's account alone, which he paid in full. Humphrey Knight took up the chronicle:

"Yesterday your Waggoner came down from your Quartrs. in Frederick [County] with one mair and four colts and Delivered em to John Allton. Colonel Carlyle tells me you mention to him that we Neglect righting to you. I shall Evedently make it appear if I live to see your Honr. that I have lodgd. Severall Letters in Alexandrea to be sent to your Honr. but I find Severall has miscarried. Tuesday last we had a very fine rain which is all the rain we have had this Summer that has bin to mutch acct., we planted our Crop all over but want of rain Causes a Deal to be wanting. We have the best Cornfield I believe in our Parts, our Stock is all well, our people has been sickly and Ned and Ruth is sick now but I hope no danger of Loosing them. I believe we have as good a crop of Tobacco growing as any in ye County. The great house goes on as brisk as Posable, the paintr has bin painting 3 Days, Our Carpenter is now giting leaths to Sheath ye Great House and shall Sheath it. Mr. Petterson tells me he will see it well Dun. . . . . I shall Stick Close to your business and work your people I hope to your Satisfaction. Our mill has been no sarvis to us this 4 or five weeks and more, I Dair say for want of water, ye miller says. . . . ."

Faithful Knight wrote his last letter on September 6th with as much care as usual and two days later was dead:

". . . . As to ye Carpenters I have minded em all I posably could and has whipt em when I could see a fault. Old Kit is a very poor hand at any thing. The great house has took a vast deal of Sawing work besides a vast deal of other work which the Carpenters Did, puling down the old works and Raising the new. . . . . ye Scantlin for the great house is all got out of white oak which made it abundanceye Teadious to get, Searching ye woods to get all white oak.

. . . . I shall Receive all the money I can for you and take cair of it after I Receive it. . . . . ."

Patterson was still at his post. "I shall have ye Old dineing room with ye room adjacent to it finish'd about ye nineth of this inst.," he reported in September. "I will have ye Doors ready at ye same time. The goods from York [River] is not arriv'd, but Col. Fairfax informs me he will do his endeavor to procure them as soon as possible; that Gent. assists me with his advice &c and every other article lyes in his power, for certainly I should be at a stop in laying floor if he had not supply'd me with flooring Boards as there were none to be had here about. . . . . As to my being positive in fixing a time to have ye whole finish'd, its not in my power, but may add without vanity its out of ye power of man to stick more diligent, and take all proper means I am master of to forward ye whole, and shall always make it my study to Oblidge your Honour. . . . . ."

Although the '58 campaign was no better managed by General Forbes than the other Ohio expeditions were, the destiny which played so large a part in young Colonel Washington's philosophy had now decided to end this chapter of his life. When the exhausted, apprehensive, underfed British army at last reached the fort at the junction of the Ohio and the Allegheny Rivers, they found it a deserted, still smoking ruin. The French were gone, without a battle, having destroyed everything they could not take with them. There would be no surrender ceremonies, no captured flags—and no food stores—but the British were in possession, and George could close the book.

From now on, as he saw his own future that November, he would serve his country in other ways than soldiering, as Burgess, churchwarden, magistrate—while he tended his home acres, studied his crops, and raised a family, like his brothers. He welcomed what would be his last orders to ride to Williamsburg to plead and argue for the bare necessities to enable the army to survive another winter at their garrison posts. He himself was again debilitated by dysentery and fatigue; his horses broke down before he reached Winchester on the return journey, and he was forced to lie up there for brief recuperation before he could even go on to the Potomac. From

Winchester on December 9th he addressed Governor Fauquier, to whom he had not yet been presented:

"Reason, nay, common humanity itself points out that some respite should be granted to Troops returning from every toil and hardship that cold, hunger, and fatigue can inflict; and I hope your honors sentiments correspond therein.

"If I easily get the better of my present Disorder I shall hope for the honor of kissing your hand, about the 25th instant. The want of almost every necessary for the journey; and a still greater inducement, if possible, the want of my Papers, requisite to a full and final settlement with the Country, oblige me to take my own house in the way down......"

It was damping, especially in his seedy condition, to find Mount Vernon in such disarray and confusion that he was thankful to accept the hospitality of Belvoir and allow himself to be nursed and encouraged by his old friends. He had hoped, by completing his assignments at Williamsburg before the end of the month, to begin his new life with the new year. But it looked now as though the wedding would have to be postponed until the work on his house, much interrupted by bad weather and the shortage of skilled free labor, could be farther advanced. It was an embarrassing situation in which to find himself as he rode on, accompanied as always by the devoted Bishop, who had been Braddock's orderly, towards the house on the Pamunkey which lay between him and the capital.

But Martha Custis, smiling and serene in her comfortable rooms decked with Christmas greens and lively with the voices of her children, would have had no reproaches for Mount Vernon. He could take his seat as Burgess for the first time early in the coming year, and the Custis house in Williamsburg, now hers, would be his when she became his wife. Meanwhile there was this one on the Pamunkey. They could be married any time, and never lack a house to live in.

When he set out again, to spend Christmas in Williamsburg as the honored guest of the Governor, he had begun to comprehend his good fortune in his choice of a wife.

VI

WASHINGTON'S boyhood copy-book, which ends before he was sixteen, contains the much quoted *Rules of Behaviour*, carefully set down as an exercise in ornamental penmanship. He cannot be credited with inventing this primer for good manners, as it can be traced back through various versions for two generations before him, but it was certainly the foundation of a lifelong habit of courtesy and self-control which was outstanding even in the formal society of the eighteenth century. Almost the last entry in the book is a verse called *True Happiness*, its authorship also unknown, which is equally prophetic of his future character.

"These are the things which once Possess'd
Will make a life that's truly bless'd;
A good Estate on healthy Soil,
Not Got by Vice, nor yet by Toil;
Round a warm Fire, a Pleasant Joke,
With Chimney ever free from Smoke;
A Strength entire, a Sparkling Bowl,
A quiet Wife, a quiet Soul,
A Mind as well as body, whole;
Prudent simplicity, constant Friends,
A Diet which no art Commends;
A Merry night without much Drinking,
A Happy Thought without much Thinking;
Each Night by Quiet Sleep made Short;
A Will to be but what thou art;
Possess'd of these, all else defy,
And neither wish nor fear to Die."

He married the widow Custis at her home in New Kent County in January of '59, and their honeymoon journey was to Williamsburg, where he took his seat as Burgess for the first time. And for the next sixteen years he strove to preserve some such peaceful pattern of life against the encroachments of a relentless destiny. He had entered innocently enough on his career as Burgess, for it was his duty as a land-owner and tax-payer to share with his neighbors and peers the obligations of the twice yearly sessions in the Assembly at Williamsburg. It was also his pleasure to enjoy with Martha the balls and dinner-parties at the Raleigh Tavern and the Governor's Palace, the racing and theatrical entertainments which enlivened the spring and autumn sessions in the little capital.

He was not the only new member in 1759, and his attendance took on the warmth and surprise of reunion with many old friends who had seen too little of him for years, and whose own lives had outgrown his intimate knowledge during his bleak army service on the frontier.

George Mason was now ten years married to his lovely auburn-haired Anne, and the father of four sons and two daughters. His unpretentious new brick house which he called Gunston Hall stood just below Belvoir on a wooded plateau well back from the Potomac shore, and was considered an architectural gem. Its charming Palladian porch, and its interior were executed by an Englishman named Buckland, a skilled carpenter and joiner who had been brought to Virginia under indenture to do the work, at a salary of £20 per year. Buckland had spent a good three years on the design and finish of the woodwork of a dining-room in the fashionable new Chinese style of Chippendale, and a Palladian parlor with arched open cupboards set into the walls and enclosed in fluted pilasters, with intricate broken pediments. There was an elaborate white marble mantelpiece, and fine fabric covered the walls. As a pendant in the middle of the double elliptical archway of the central entrance hall he placed a carved pineapple, the ancient symbol of hospitality. Behind the house boxwood gardens sloped down above the River, and at the sides stood the kitchen, well-house, and basement bulkheads for cool storage.

Mason had the advantage of Washington in age, and was one of the few men to rival him in size, a truly formidable man, grave, swarthy, with luminous dark eyes, and his black hair had begun to show the first threads of gray. His health was already capricious, and he was subject to agonizing attacks of gout, and the mysterious fevers which beset them all. His devotion to his wife and young family was notable, and he grudged every day he spent away from his own domain, where some five hundred people, both black and white, formed an almost self-contained community, wholly prosperous and happy in itself.

Unlike George William Fairfax, and many others of his circle, Mason had not been sent to England to school, but was nevertheless one of the best-read and most respected men in the colony. Unlike George Washington, he had spent his youth at home with his widowed mother, having come early into his large inheritance through the untimely death of his father in 1735, drowned while crossing the River in his barge during a Potomac squall. He had a taste, an appetite for reading, which Washington never entertained even in his later years of relative domestic leisure. Only Mason's daily attention to the plantation affairs at Gunston, which he managed himself without the aid of a steward, and his often impatient concern for his country's future, could draw him away from his books, though he was by no means a recluse, and adorned with wit and grace any social gathering he attended. He soon found legislation tiresome and served only one term as a Burgess. Thereafter, though he gave his opinion and his support freely to his friends like Washington, who continued as members of the Assembly at Williamsburg, he withdrew from the political arena.

From the big red brick mansion called Stratford which stood high above the Potomac between Austin Washington's place at Pope's Creek and John Augustine's Bushfield, two more of the six Lee brothers now joined the Burgesses. While Washington was pursuing his lonely frontier existence, the Lees had kept bachelor hall at Stratford, surrounded by unlimited resources for enjoying themselves. The eldest, Philip Ludwell Lee, who owned Stratford, was truly the heir—arrogant, lordly, hard-riding, and inconsiderate of others, occupying his father's seat in the Council only because it was his right as his father's eldest son. Thomas Ludwell Lee of Belleview was already a member of the House. The newly elected Richard Henry Lee was born within a month and a few miles of

George Washington, but with all the advantages of his tremendous Lee heritage, and had been sent to the academy at Wakefield in Yorkshire while George was still a lad in Lawrence's Mount Vernon household, returning home the year Lawrence died. The second Lee newcomer, Francis Lightfoot, was the charmer of his generation, and had remained at home in Virginia—gentle, urbane, bookish, and lovable, he would have been content only to cultivate his inherited acres in Loudoun County, and he performed his legislative duties more because he considered them duties than by inclination. But Richard Henry, tall, austere, intellectual, undertook the law as a profession, and aspired to statesmanship. There was also their cousin Henry Lee of Leesylvania, who had married Lucy Grymes and had a baby son called Harry.

The House numbered almost as many Carters as Lees, including the spectacular Landon of Sabine Hall, one of the dozen offspring of old "King" Carter of Corotoman; Landon's brother Charles of Cleve, and two more Charles Carters in the next generation. There were two Randolphs—Peyton, the Attorney-General, who had learned his law at the Middle Temple in London and was said to be the most elegant man in Virginia; and his brother John of Williamsburg. John Robinson, the dean of them all at fifty-six, Speaker of the House and Treasurer too, had been George's consistent friend for years, and was the darling of the Assembly times, fashionable, kind-hearted, and gracious. Edmund Pendleton, Robinson's one-time protégé as Washington had been more recently, a serene, contemplative man, had demonstrated that one not born to a Tidewater fortune could by hard work and ability become one of its most effective speakers and lawyers. Richard Bland, a difficult man in debate, tough and wise, was already showing his age on the near side of fifty.

While Washington's colleagues in the Assembly welcomed him to their midst, his former comrades who had remained on the comfortless frontier lamented his departure and many of them wished or prepared to follow their beloved colonel into retirement:

"We are very anxious here to know the fate of the Troops, and who will be Commander," Dr. Craik wrote from Winchester on December 20th. "When the regiment meets with that irreparable Loss of loseing you—the very thought of this lyes heavy on the whole whenever they think of it—and dread the consequence of you resigning—I would gladly be advised by you whether or not you think I had better continue, if they choose to keep me untill my Medecines come from England; or whether I had better resign directly—for I am resolved not to stay in the service when you quit it—The Inhabitants of this place press me much to settle here—I likewise would crave your advice whether or not you think I had better except of their importunities—or settle in Fairfax [County] where you was so kind as to offer me your most friendly assistance—I hope you'll pardon my freedom in giving you this trouble—For as I have experienced so much of your friendship, and received so much friendly countenance from you—I cannot help consulting you on this occasion as my most sincere friend........"

".....Be so good as to offer my Complements in the most respectful and obliging terms to your Lady (a new Stile indeed)," his friend Captain Stewart commented from Fort Loudoun early in January, "and tho' she has robb'd me and many others of the greatest satisfaction we ever had or can enjoy in this Service yet none can be more sollicitous for her happiness—

"The regret, dejection, and grief your Resignation has occasion'd in the whole Corps is too melancholy a Subject to enter on at this Juncture will therefore wave it......"

Impatient to begin his new life at Mount Vernon, George received leave to depart from Williamsburg before the end of the session and with Martha and the children in the Custis coach he took the road which led northward past the Pamunkey towards Fredericksburg, where they paused for a visit to Betty, and to pay their respects to George's mother at Ferry Farm across the Rappahannock.

There was hardly a house in the colony, including Williamsburg, which could now surpass Betty's Millbank, the expensive evidence of Fielding Lewis's devotion and Arris's painstaking genius for decoration. As you entered the front door the wide mahogany stairway swept upward in three flights with a long center run, against the right-hand wall of the hall—the sort of staircase descending which a lady in powder and brocade was seen to great advantage. The motif of its carved ornamentation was the lotus leaf, symbol of sleep. With the dining-room on the left you crossed the spacious hall to the Great

Room, which looked down the garden towards the river, with its own door to a little colonnaded porch. Its notable plasterwork ceiling had a tobacco-leaf centerpiece design, and horns of plenty at the four corners. The library ceiling illustrated the four seasons, and elaborate overmantel plaques were still to come in both rooms. The wood carving everywhere was remarkably fine, and the unpanelled, tinted plaster walls were an innovation intended to set off the still unfinished moulded stucco work.

Near Dumfries the Washingtons stopped at Bel Air to visit the Ewells, who were faintly related to George and had always entertained him on his journeys to and from the capital. Meanwhile a letter to John Alton was preceding them to Mount Vernon.

"Jno: I have sent Miles on to day, to let you know that I expect to be up to Morrow, and to get the Key from Colo. Fairfax's which I desire you will take care of. You must have the House very well cleand, and were you to make Fires in the Rooms below it w'd Air them. You must get two of the best Bedsteads put up, one in the Hall room, and the other in the little dining-room that used to be, and have Beds made on them against we come. You must also get out the Chairs and Tables, and have them very well rubd and Cleand; the Stair case ought also to be polishd in order to make it look well.

"Enquire abt. in the Neighbourhood, and get some Egg's and Chickens, and prepare in the best manner you can for our coming: you need not however take out any more of the Furniture than the Beds and Tables and Chair's in Order that they may be well rubd and cleaned. I am, etc. . . . . . ."

The hasty note seems to bear witness that Colonel Washington had got into something of a flurry as his bride neared Mount Vernon.

They arrived on April 7th, in a Virginia spring—the countryside bloomed, the River sparkled, and the freshly painted white house gleamed through the trees which sheltered its western approach. Martha could find much to admire in her new home. From the west door she entered the hall behind the stairs, which rose above her on the right, with a long first flight against the wall, a carved walnut handrail and simple balusters—a staircase as reticent and dignified as the master himself. The door at the opposite end of the hall gave on to a grassy terrace high above the wide, placid water, for the long, columned piazza had not yet been built. A panelled parlor lay on her left and the dining-room across from it, and the two rooms fronting the River were now bedrooms because of the unfinished state of the upper floor. All the rooms had corner fireplaces, the mantel-piece in the parlor very handsome, with the landscape painting above it as ordered by George from Fort Loudoun in '57.

After the spacious elegance of Millbank perhaps Mount Vernon looked a little small and unadorned, but Gunston too was small, and people said no more perfect house existed in Virginia. Mount Vernon's ceilings and mantel-pieces could always be enriched when a good stucco worker could be found. Some of Martha's furniture from the Pamunkey house was coming round by water to fill in the empty spaces, and more could be ordered from London as soon as they knew what they lacked. As the family grew, the house could be enlarged by adding rooms, balancing each other, at either end.

George William had recently given up burgessing, so the Fairfaxes were at Belvoir to welcome the bride to the Potomac neighborhood. After eleven years of marriage, Sally Fairfax was still childless and slim, and had a vital beauty which might have made other women feel mousy and unfashionable in her presence. But Martha in her matronly bloom, released from mourning into her own handsome wardrobe straight from London, and with two lively children to show for her brief first marriage, had no reason to feel at a disadvantage in the cordial company of the woman who was to be her nearest neighbor in her new life on the Potomac. George William, gallant in his London laces and velvets, was nevertheless admitting to rheumatism at thirty-five. His half-brother Bryan, to whom Washington was always an example, had recently prevailed upon Sally's sister Betsy to marry him, and they were living at Towelston near Alexandria. It was fervently hoped that now Bryan would cease to be a problem.

As the spring mud dried on the roads, the family and neighbors came to Mount Vernon by the coachload. George's brother Sam, already once a widower, was married to his second wife, Mildred Thornton, cousin to Charles's Mildred, and was building a house in Berkeley County to be called Harewood. Charles had an interest in the new tavern he was building on Caroline Street in Fredericksburg, in partnership with his friend George Weedon. The first child of John Augustine and Hannah at Bushfield was a daughter Jane. Austin's felicitations were missing, for his health had begun to fail and he was in England to consult physicians there.

The duties of the mistress of a large plantation were not new to Martha, and George's household soon felt a firm hand on the reins. Her personal maids, who had accompanied her in the baggage-wagon which followed the coach, and the children's nurses had long since learned what was expected of them, for while she might indulge her babies too much for their own good, there was no slackness anywhere else under her eye. George could turn his attention at once to the workmen, the tenants, and the land, where mismanagement and decay had taken toll. The Custis estate on the Pamunkey and York Rivers was left in the hands of a well-trained steward named Valentine, who understood the requirements there, and many of the three hundred Custis slaves remained there to carry on their accustomed labor. Martha's fortune, which was believed to be around £20,000, including some 17,000 acres, now came into Washington's care, as he promptly notified his London agents, desiring them to set up separate accounts for Jack and Patsy Custis, on which he would order for them as occasion arose.

The house staff numbered thirteen. There were Breechy the butler and Mulatto Jack, his assistant; Doll the cook, Beck the scullion, Jenny to wash and Mima to iron; Martha's personal maid, whose name happened to be Sally; Betty the seamstress; Jacky's boy Julius, Patsy's Rose, and nurse Molly to supervise them all; Washington's orderly, Bishop, and John Alton, who would soon be promoted to be overseer on the Dogue Run Farm. There were a weaver, four tanners, and five carpenters with a boy helper. Seven were employed outside on the home plantation, and another two dozen on the various farms. Eleven worked at trades, and seven at the mill. Their clothing was mostly woven and made up on the estate, though materials for the new scarlet and white liveries were to come from England. Their health and their instruction and discipline were the daily concern of their master and mistress.

After an early breakfast, Washington made his daily round of the farms on horseback, returning in time to change out of his riding clothes and put on powder before the three o'clock dinner, when in the fine summer weather there always seemed to be guests. Keeping pace with his sowing and reaping and repairs out of doors, Martha's work went on in the upper floor rooms, which had been freshly finished with the wall-paper ordered at Fort Loudoun in the spring of '57. Even with the addition of her favorite pieces from the Pamunkey house, some of which may have got damaged on the way, such refinements as fire-screens and branching candelabra were in short supply at Mount Vernon, and the upstairs bedroom they would occupy was to be all furnished new, to match its blue and white wall-paper.

By the first of May their separate lists for the London agent had reached formidable proportions, and when George came to write out the invoice, grass seed and books on agriculture jostled sweet-meat stands and dessert-glasses for precedence, following after the tester bedstead with blue and white curtains and coverlid, and matching chair-bottoms, for the bedroom.

In September a much longer invoice went off, including supplies for the Custis plantations and separate lists for each of the children: "I flatter myself that particular care will be taken in choosing them as their directed," Washington wrote in the accompanying letter, "the want of which gives some Tradesmen an oppertunity of Imposing upon us most Vilely. The Coarse Goods for the Estates use are order'd from Liverpool this year, all but the Plaid Hose and these I beg you will cause to be sent from Glasgow in the usual manner and number, directed to the care of Mr. Joseph Valentine or person managing the Estates business York River....."

Again the juxtaposition of the items indicated a comfortable marrying of their separate lists into one invoice in his handwriting. For himself he ordered "a Light Summer Suit made of Duroy or &ca." by his measure at the London tailor, and 2 beaver hats at 21s. each; a piece of black satin ribbon for his queue; a red morocco sword-belt; Irish linen for shirts; and a ream of writing paper.

Martha enclosed a sample of salmon-colored tabby silk with satin flowers, to be made into a negligée sacque and coat, with a cap, handkerchief, tucker, and ruffles of Brussels lace, for which she was willing to pay £20. Her order continued with 2 fine flowered aprons, both silk and cotton hose, both black and white satin shoes ("of the smallest fives") and callimanca shoes for daily wear; a fashionable hat or bonnet; 6 pairs each of kid gloves and mitts; narrow white

Mount Vernon from the South. From a sketch by Benjamin Latrobe, executed in 1796. Courtesy of the Maryland Historical Society.

Mount Vernon from the West. From the aquatint by Parkyns, c. 1797. A rare original, in the possession of the Mount Vernon Ladies' Association, by whose courtesy it is here reproduced.

Perspective Through the Portico at Mount Vernon. From a water-color sketch by Alexander Jackson Davis, c. 1831. Courtesy of the Houghton Library, Harvard University.

"Classical Group at Mount Vernon." By Benjamin Latrobe, 1796. From the collection of the Maryland Historical Society.

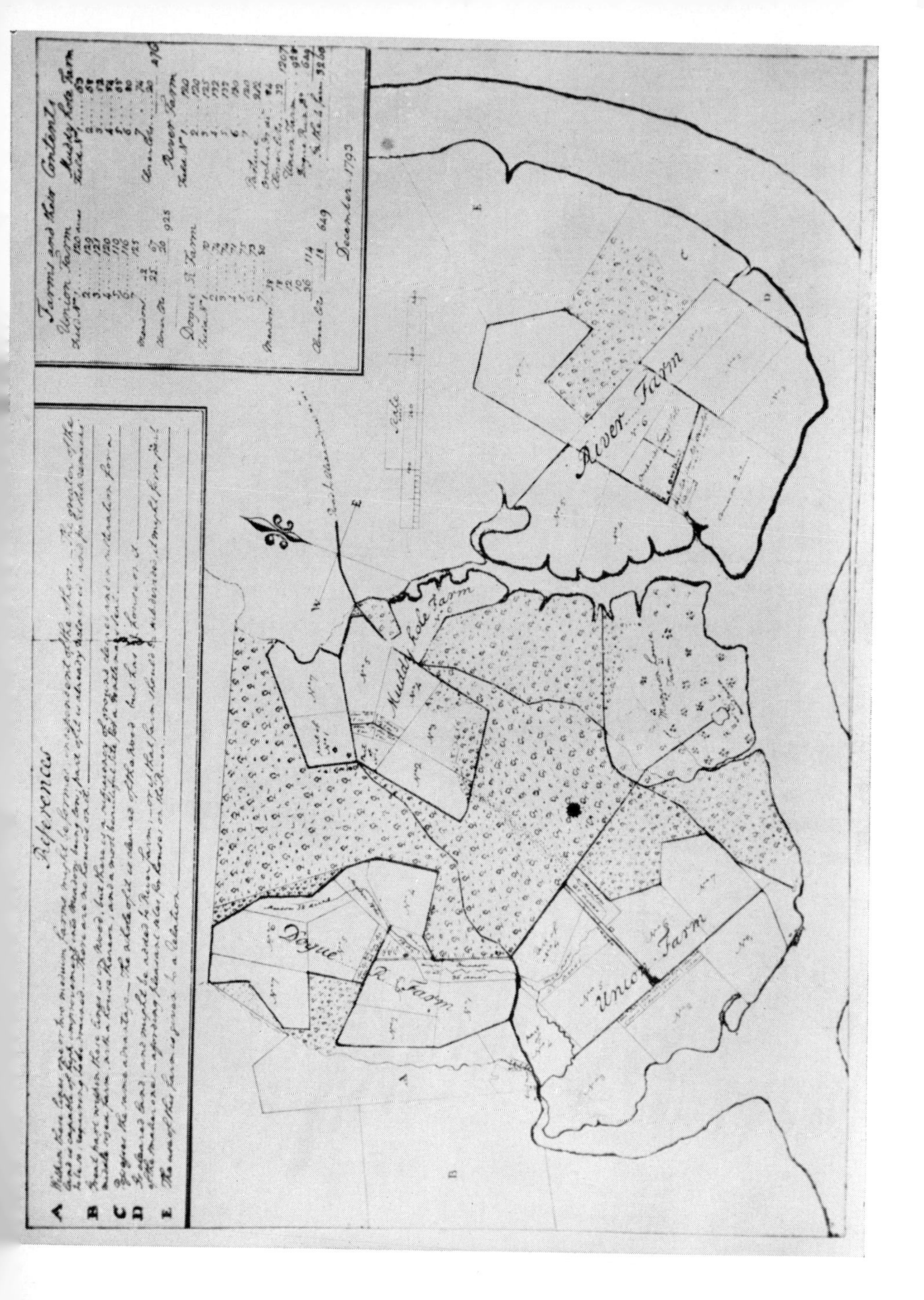

Washington's Own Map of the Five Farms of the Mount Vernon Estate, from his field notes, 1793. Copyright 1931 by the Huntington Library.

The Dining-room at Mount Vernon. Courtesy of the Mount Vernon Ladies' Association.

The ceiling of the Great Room at Kenmore. Courtesy of the Kenmore Association, Fredericksburg, Virginia.

Tobias Lear. From Tobias Lear's *Letters and Recollections of Washington*, 1906.

Fanny Bassett. Painted at Mount Vernon in 1785 by Robert Edge Pine. Courtesy of the Mount Vernon Ladies' Association.

Colonel David Humphreys. By Gilbert Stuart. Courtesy Yale University Art Gallery, Gift of the Widow of General Humphreys.

John Parke Custis ("Jacky'

Eliza Parke Custis. By Gilbert Stuart.

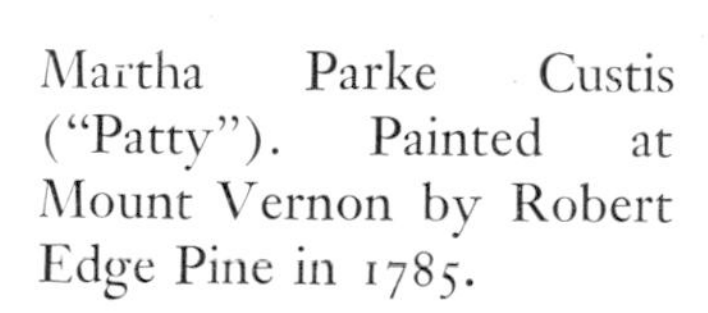

Martha Parke Custis ("Patty"). Painted at Mount Vernon by Robert Edge Pine in 1785.

Portrait of Eleanor Parke Custis Lewis, about the time of her marriage (supposedly a Stuart copy).

Nelly Custis. Supposed by Gilbert Stuart.

August—1785.

The Wheat which had been sowed before the late rains fell was up, and coming up very rich

I observed that Corn, which had been planted under the Persimon trees in the field looked as thriving and well as that which was not shaded—the same thing I had observed before (formerly) in respect to wheat under this sort of trees—and also of corn which proves them to be a valuable tree in Inclosures

Mrs. Washington visited the sick Child of Mr. L. Washington, and returned to dinner—

Finished gravelling the right hand walk leading to the front gate from the Court yard.

Wednesday—31.

Mercury at 70 in the Morning—72 at Noon—and 72 at Night.

Westerly wind and Clouds.

Rid the Plantations in the Neck, at Muddy hole—found the Corn the first as mentioned yesterday at the other places.—

Mrs. Washington rid to see the sick Child of Mr. Lund Washington from whence Doctr. Craik came to Breakfast—after which he visited John Alton, and then returned to Maryland.—

Page from Washington's Diary in August, 1785. From the published text, Mount Vernon Ladies' Association.

George Washington's book plate. Courtesy of the Mount Vernon Ladies' Association.

satin ribbon with a pearl edge; a pound of shaded sewing silks; and a black mask.

Six pounds of perfumed powder for their hair came next; 3 pounds of the best Scotch snuff, though Washington apparently never used either snuff or tobacco himself; a case of pickles (to include anchovies, capers, olives, salad oil, and India mangoes); a large Cheshire cheese; 4 pounds of green tea; 25 pounds each of almonds in the shell and of raisins; a hogshead of the best Porter; 12 pounds of the best mustard, 20 sacks of salt, 5 pounds of white sugar candy and 10 pounds of brown ditto; 10 ounces of hartshorn shavings, 2 quarts of strong cinnamon water, and 4 pounds of anise seeds. Thirty yards of red shalloon, and 25 yards of broadcloth to match an enclosed sample, 20 dozen white washed coat buttons, and a dozen and a half strong coarse thread hose fit for Negro servants, meant new liveries all around—along with a dozen pairs of coarse shoe and knee buckles, 8 dozen assorted plaid hose, and 4 dozen Monmouth caps.

Amongst the items required outside the house were 6 strong halters, 3 girths and 3 snaffle bridles, and 2 sacks of the best English oats; nails by the cask, 6 spades, 2 dozen sickles, 2 dozen pairs HL hinges, 12 chisels, 4 square asticles [astragals], 6 ogees, and 1 moving philester [fillister]. With the farriery medicines were listed 4 pounds of flower of brimstone, 5 pounds of syrup of colt's foot, 5 pounds of black soap, 4 pounds of fenugeek, 5 ounces of liquid laudanum, and 4 ounces of Spanish flies.

For Master Custis, six years old, they ordered a suit of summer clothes "to be made of something light and thin;" a piece of Irish Holland and 2 yards of fine cambric, 4 pairs each of shoes and pumps, silver shoe and knee buckles, "a light duffel coat with silver frogs," a piece of black hair ribbon, 10 shillings worth of toys, and 6 little books "for children beginning to read."

For Miss Custis, four years old, they required 8 yards of printed linen, 2 ells of fine Holland, 8 pairs of kid mitts, 2 pairs of silk shoes, a piece of flowered dimity, 2 yards of fine cambric, 2 caps, 2 pairs of ruffles, 2 tuckers, bibs, and aprons, "if fashionable," 2 masks, 2 fans, and 2 bonnets, a pair of silver sleeve buttons with stones, a fashionably dressed "baby" at 10s. and other toys for 10s.

"......My brother [Austin] is safe arriv'd but little benefitted in point of health by his trip to England," Washington wrote to the agent, who was regarded as almost a family friend. "The longing desire, which for many years I have had of visiting the great Metrapolis of that Kingdom is not in the least abated by his prejudice because I think the small share of Health he enjoy'd while there must have given a Sensible Check to any pleasure he might figure to himself and wou'd render any place Irksome; but I am now tied by the leg and must set Inclination aside......"

In November he ordered for himself "a New Market Great Coat with a loose Hood to it made of Blew Drab or Broad Cloth with straps before according to the present taste; let it be made of such Cloth as will turn a good shower of Rain and made long, and fit in other respects for a Man full 6 feet high and proportionately made...." and 4 pairs of shoes and 2 pairs of Channel Pumps, to be made on Colonel Baylor's last as before, but a bit longer, and with middling high heels.

Among the autumn visitors at Mount Vernon was an English traveller, Andrew Burnaby, vicar of Greenwich, who was writing a book about his experiences in the colonies. After landing at Yorktown he had made quite a stay in Williamsburg, where he was cordially entertained by Governor Fauquier and his wife. "The streets are not paved, and are consequently very dusty, the soil hereabout consisting chiefly of sand," he recorded. "However the situation of Williamsburg has one advantage which few or no places in these lower parts have, that of being free from mosquitoes. Upon the whole it is an agreeable residence; there are ten or twelve gentlemen's families constantly residing in it, besides merchants and tradesmen, and at the time of the assemblies and general courts it is crowded with the gentry of the country: on those occasions there are balls and other amusements; but as soon as the business is finished, they return to their plantations; and the town is in a manner deserted."

Journeying northward through Fredericksburg, which impressed him with its neat layout and parallel streets, Burnaby ferried over the Rappahannock into the Northern Neck and continued through Dumfries and Colchester to Mount Vernon, doubtless recommended to him by everyone from the Governor down. "This place is the property of Colonel Washington, and truly deserving of its owner," he wrote. "The house is most beautifully situated upon a high hill on the banks of the Potomac; and commands a noble prospect of water, of cliffs, of woods, and plantations. The river is nearly two miles broad, though two hundred from the mouth, and divides the dominions of Virginia from Maryland. We rested here one day, and proceeded up the river about twenty miles to take a view of the Great Falls of the Potomac."

Having met Lord Fairfax during his Williamsburg sojourn, Burnaby paid a visit to Greenway Court during his tour of the Shenandoah Valley, travelling the same road which Washington and George William Fairfax had used a dozen years before on their first surveying trip. He wrote down that Lord Fairfax lived there "in the style of a gentleman farmer; or I should rather have said, of an English country gentleman. He kept many servants, white and black; several hunters; a plentiful but plain table, entirely in the English fashion; and his mansion was the mansion of hospitality. His dress corresponded with his mode of life, and notwithstanding he had every year new suits of the most fashionable and expensive kind sent out to him from England, which he never put on, was plain in the extreme. His manners were humble, modest, and unaffected; not tinctured in the smallest degree with arrogance, pride, or self-conceit. He was free from selfish passions, and liberal almost to excess. The produce of his farms, after the deduction of what was necessary for the consumption of his own family, was distributed and given away to the poor planters and settlers in his neighborhood. To these he frequently advanced money, to enable them to go on with their improvements; to clear away the woods, and cultivate the ground; and where the lands proved unfavorable, and not likely to answer the labour and expectation of the planter or husbandman, he usually indemnified him for the expence he had been at in the attempt, and gratuitously granted him fresh lands of a more favorable and promising nature. He was a friend and father to all who held and lived under him; and as the great object of his ambition was the peopling and cultivating of that fine and beautiful country of which he was proprietor, he sacrificed every other pursuit, and made every other consideration subordinate to this great point."

At Winchester, where he doubtless carried reminiscences and credentials from his Mount Vernon host to Colonel William Byrd

III, of Westover on the James, then in command, Burnaby wrote: "Winchester is a small town of about two hundred houses. It is the place of general rendezvous of the Virginia troops, which is the reason of its late rapid increase, and present flourishing condition. The country roundabout it, before the reduction of Fort Duquesne, was greatly exposed to the ravages of the Indians, who daily committed most horrid cruelties; even the town would have been in danger, had not Colonel Washington in order to cover and protect it, erected a fort upon an eminence at one end of it, which proved of the utmost utility; for although the Indians were frequently in sight of the town, they never dared approach within reach of the fort...... During my stay at this place, I was almost induced to make a tour for a fortnight to the southward in Augusta County, for the sake of seeing some natural curiosities, which the officers assured me were well worth visiting; but as the Cherokees had been scalping in those parts only a few days before; and as I feared at the same time that it would detain me too long, and that I should lose my passage to England, I judged it prudent to decline it."

Returning towards Mount Vernon's hospitality, he was belated by being lost for some hours with his guide in the wild and beautiful Occoquan Valley, but was not too apprehensive to notice "the most beautiful of all flowering shrubs," mountain laurel. "At Colonel Washington's I disposed of my horses, and having borrowed his curricle and servant, ... I crossed over the Potomac into Maryland at Clifton's ferry, where the river is something more than a mile broad; and proceeded on my journey to Marlborough, eighteen miles...."

It was the beginning of a long friendship and correspondence, extending even through Burnaby's travels in Italy some years later, when he wrote from Leghorn inviting the Washingtons to join him there, "where we would shew you a new World, with nothing so magnificent as that fine View of the Potomac except a distant prospect of the hoary and indignant Appenines, but still with many beauties and much Welcome."

But Washington was sure that his life had turned a corner into welcome obscurity—"I am now I believe fixd at this Seat with an agreeable Consort for Life and hope to find more happiness in retirement than I ever experienc'd amidst a wide and bustling

World"—and regarded farming as his business and his career henceforth, to be interrupted only by the twice yearly jaunts to Williamsburg with Martha and the children for the frivolities of the Assembly times.

Mount Vernon was not yet self-supporting, though he totalled his year's end receipts as £1839. His war service on the frontier entitled him to large land grants in the Ohio country, whenever the King got around to it, to add to the 4715 acres he now owned in Fairfax County, along with some 49 slaves. He was celebrating his first Christmas with a family of his own, at the age of twenty-seven.

While in Williamsburg for the autumn session, he had acquired the Virginia Almanack for the coming year—a pocket-sized booklet containing the monthly calendars, astronomical tables, receipts—one was "for making Physick as pleasant as a dish of chocolate"—remedies, some rather dubious jokes and aphorisms, and some blank pages where the purchaser might inscribe his own accounts and observations. It seemed to him just the thing for a brief diary of Mount Vernon activities, and on January 1st, 1760, he wrote down his first entry:

"*Tuesday*, 1. Visited my Plantations and received an Instance of Mr. French's great love of Money in disappointing me of some Pork, because the price had risen to 22/6 after he had agreed to let me have it at 20/.

"Calld at Mr. Possey's in my way home and desird him to engage me 100 Bar'ls of Corn upon the best terms he could in Maryland.

"And found Mrs. Washington upon my arrival broke out with the Meazles."

VII

TO make the best use of the insight into life on the plantations of the Northern Neck neighborhood which the closely written pages of the Diary afford, it is convenient to break down the contents into chunks of time, rather than to consider the separate entries day by day. The first year, 1760, Washington recorded in some detail, then lapsed into hardly more than a record of the weather, with long gaps or missing volumes, until 1768, when he resumed a more comprehensive account until the fateful June of 1775. Then, during his attendance at the second Philadelphia Congress, he was appointed Commander-in-chief of the colonial forces, and rode straight out to Boston, without even returning home to put his affairs in order for an indefinite absence. At that point the Diary ceased for six years, and his letters to Lund Washington from the various headquarters, and Lund's weekly reports from Mount Vernon, take over the story.

For sixteen years, however, in spite of the gathering storm of the Revolution, Washington lived the life he most enjoyed, as squire of Mount Vernon. The vexatious interruptions of the Assemblies, Conventions, and Congresses he noted down as an inevitable part of "Where & How My time is Spent," as he headed each new month in the Diary. At the end of the month he usually appended "Remarks of ye Weather," and after that, "Observations," which concerned his ambitious experiments in planting, grafting, sowing, etc.

Taking the pre-war Diary as a whole, it is possible by tedious parallel research to come at some of the lesser known personalities who surrounded him, dined with him, entertained him in their own homes, admired and consulted him—some of whom, like George

Mason, he valued as friends of his own caliber, and some who became an exasperating drain on his patience and hospitality, like the perennial Posey, who had served under Washington in the Forbes campaign. He owned a farm which he called Rover's Delight at the mouth of Dogue Run below Mount Vernon, from where he operated a public ferry to the Maryland side at Marshall Hall. There was good seining along his shore line, and he had built facilities for curing fish, which formed a large part of the slaves' diet. His wife was a Thornton, and his sons and a daughter Milly were about the age of the Custis children and became their nearest playmates.

An obviously happy-go-lucky type, Posey was always in hot water of some kind, improvident and unpenitent, representing everything that the sober, responsible Washington was not. Perhaps for that very reason he became a sort of charge on Mount Vernon's master, who found him always good company for a day's hunting, and was to go far out of his way during the coming years to rescue Posey from his own follies. By '63 Posey was deeply in debt, his wife died, and his dwindling fortunes and doleful correspondence form a recurring theme of Mount Vernon life until shortly before the war began, when he seems simply to have disappeared.

Through the Diary during the whole of the '60's and early '70's runs the bright thread of Washington's vital interest in everything that grew, blossomed, and bore fruit; his benevolent watchfulness over the dependent, irresponsible children of all ages he called his "people" (for the word *slave* was seldom used); and his occasional very human testiness with characters like Daniel French.

French was a well-to-do planter and contractor who lived at Rose Hill, just west of Alexandria, and the controversy over his hogs ran on for some days. On the 2d of January Washington wrote: "Fearing a disappointment elsewhere in Pork I was fain to take Mr. French's upon his own terms, and engaged them to be deliv'd at my House on Monday next." And on the Monday—"In the Evening 8 of Mr. French's Hogs from his Ravensworth Quarter came down, one being lost on the way—as the others might as well have been for their goodness," he grumbled in the Diary, and added—"Nothing but the disappointments in this Article of Pork which he himself had causd and my necessities could possibly have obligd me to take them." And then, the last straw to his day—"Carpenter Sam was taken with the Meazles."

Killed and dressed, French's hogs came to 751 pounds neat, 719 of which were at once required, cut out and salted, for the year's provisions for two of the overseers—"Which accounts for Mr. French's 8 hogs," Washington commented bitterly, "showing the loss of weighing meat so soon killed, which cannot be less than 5 pr. Ct." As late as the 22d, Mr. French's behavior still rankled. "Killed 17 more Hogs which were bought of Mr. French, who was here ready to see them weighed and receive his money," runs the record.

When the new brick church at Pohick was to be built in 1769, the vestry included Daniel French, George Washington, George William Fairfax, and John Posey. George Mason was on the building committee. Mr. French was the contractor, and the Articles of Agreement stipulated that "the said Daniel French doth agree to build two Horse Blocks with each two flights of Steps, and to fix Six Benches for the People to sit on under the Trees. . . . . ."

Washington himself surveyed the land, and had a hand in drawing up the ground plan and the south elevation for the charming square brick building which still stands beside the busy highway which runs to Fredericksburg. One third of the cost of the church was obtained from the sale of the pews above the cross aisle. Mason bought two—his family grew yearly—and Washington, beginning with Number 28 in front of the chancel, also acquired Number 29 for the accommodation of his cousin Lund. The Fairfaxes had Number 21 and Number 15 was reserved for the Rector "and his successors forever." The eight pews below and adjoining the cross aisle were assigned "to the use of the most respectable Inhabitants and House Keepers of the Parish, the Men to sit in the four Pews next to the South Wall, and the Women in the other four Pews next to the North Wall."

Mr. French died in '71, before the church was completed, and George Mason as his executor finished the job. Washington paid his respects by attending the funeral, and French's widow continued to visit Mount Vernon. Their only child, Elizabeth, was a member of the dancing-school which met periodically at the various houses in the neighborhood, and which included the Custis children. When she married in '73 Washington took note of it in a letter to his brother-in-law Burwell Bassett of New Kent County: "Our celebrated fortune, Miss French, whom half the world was in pursuit of, bestowed her hand on Wednesday last, being her birthday (you perceive I think myself under a necessity of accounting for the choice) upon Mr. Ben Dulany, who is to take her to Maryland in a month from this time. Mentioning of one wedding puts me in mind of another, though of less dignity: this is the marriage of Mr. Henderson (of Colchester) to a Miss More (of the same place) remarkable for a very frizzled head and good singing, the latter of which I shall presume it was that captivated our merchant. . . . ."

The rector of the old church of Truro Parish, which Pohick was to replace, did not live to conduct a service in the new building, but it was he whom Washington called in to attend Martha in her 1760 attack of the measles, which threatened to prove serious. Green had practiced medicine before being ordained, and Washington (or Martha) apparently preferred him to Dr. Laurie at Alexandria, who was retained on a yearly fee of £15 to doctor the servants on the estate, and who came the same day, perhaps on his regular rounds, as recorded in the Diary:

"*Friday, 4th.* The Weather continued Drisling and Warm, and I kept the House all day. Mrs. Washington seemg. to be very ill wrote to Mr. Green this afternoon desiring his Company to visit her in the Morng.

"*Saturday, 5th.* Mrs. Washington appeared to be something better. Mr. Green however came to see her at 11 oclock and in an hour Mrs. Fairfax arrivd. Mr. Green prescribd the needful, and just as we were going to Dinnr. Capt. Walter Stewart appeard with Doctr. Laurie.

"The Evening being very cold, and the wind high, Mrs. Fairfax went home in the Chariot. Soon afterwards Mulatto Jack arrivd from Fredk. [County] with 4 beeves.

"*Sunday, 6th.* The Chariot not returng. time enough from Colo. Fairfax's we were prevented from Church.

"Mrs. Washington was a good deal better today. . . ."

Besides Sally Fairfax's friendly visit, Martha had also the comfort of her sister Nancy Bassett's presence at Mount Vernon during her illness. Nancy had come to spend the Christmas season on the Potomac, and although pregnant with her second child, enjoyed a trip to Alexandria with George on the 7th, of which Martha was deprived by her illness, and dined at Belvoir on the 10th. On January 12th Nancy and George set out in the chariot for Port Royal, below Fredericksburg, where her husband was to meet her for the rest of the journey home to New Kent County. ".....The morning was clear and fine, but soon clouded and promised much rain or other falling weather, which is generally the case after remarkable white Frosts as it was today," he wrote with his unfailing interest in the vagaries of the weather. "We passed Occoquan without any great difficulty, notwithstanding the wind was something high, and lodged at Mr. McCraes in Dumfries, sending the Horses to the Tavern....."

Having spent a cheerful evening with the Bassetts at Fox's Inn, he recrossed the Rappahannock the following day to dine with Charles Carter at Cleve, which was one of the great houses built by the many children of old "King" Carter of Corotoman as they grew up and established their families. Cleve was almost identical in plan with the magnificent Carter's Grove on the James, which was the home of Charles's elder sister Elizabeth, who had married Nathaniel Burwell. Although proportionately smaller, Cleve was equally rich in execution, and had been built by the same architect, a Williamsburg man named Minitree and his assistant Richard Bayliss, who had been brought out from England to do the carving.

At Cleve the visitor entered from the river side above the terraces to a large panelled salon, one of the most beautiful rooms in the colony, where a soaring elliptical arch framed the stairway's superb first flight, with its swirled balustrade and inlaid landings. Matching panelled rooms opened off either side of the entrance salon, which with the stairs was two rooms deep, and these two parlors had centered marble mantel-pieces set in carved pilastered woodwork and overmantels. Even the two smaller north rooms were panelled, and both of these were shortened by a service lobby partitioned off with an outside entrance to each. One was the dining-room, and the advantages in bringing hot food to the table were obvious. Washington, always with an eye to Mount Vernon's future improvements, doubtless observed even the finer points of the Cleve layout, with generous admiration of the workmanship.

There was a saying that the Carters married everybody, and there were almost enough of them to do so. This Charles was some thirty years older than Washington, and his youngest daughter, Anne, whose mother was William Byrd III's sister Anne, was about to marry the younger John Champe, brother to Sam Washington's first wife. Colonel Champe Senior's house was Washington's next stop on his homeward journey: "..... Several Gentlemen dind with us at Colo. Carter's (neighbours of his), but we spent a very lonesome Evening at Colo. Champe's, not any Body favouring us with their Company but himself," he complained in the Diary. "The Morning of this day was exceeding cold, the Wind still continuing at No. West; but in the Evening it died away and grew something more moderate, and promised falling weather but no appearance of a thaw."

He breakfasted with his mother at the Rappahannock farm the next day, finding his brother Sam already there, and proceeded across the River in Sam's company to Fredericksburg, where they were entertained at their brother Charles's new tavern near the water front. Betty and Fielding Lewis were away, and it began to snow. "Returnd in the Evening to Mother's–all alone with her," he wrote without comment. He spent the next night at Dumfries, which was still a new town at the head of the Potomac tidewater, with a good brick tavern, founded by thrifty Scotch tobacco merchants who were building their fine mansions in its vicinity. Continuing through an unexpected thaw on Friday, he arrived back at Mount Vernon to find his old friend Dr. Craik awaiting him there.

Craik had carried out his threat to follow Washington into retirement from the army, and was looking for a place to settle into a civilian practice. He was taken as an honored guest to dine at Belvoir on the Sunday, though it rained "without intermission," and was urged to become a member of the Fairfax County circle. In December of this year he married Marianna Ewell of Bel Air near Dumfries–Marianna seems not to have hesitated–and after a brief residence at Port Tobacco on the Maryland side, he set up a prosperous practice in a narrow brick house on Duke Street in Alexandria, which still stands in that picturesque town. Soon after his one-time colonel was appointed Commander-in-chief in 1775, Craik also returned to the army, as chief physician and surgeon-general.

Two of his six sons were educated at Washington's expense, one was named for him and served for a time as his secretary during the Presidency. A stout, hearty man with a Scotch burr to his tongue, Craik was frequently at Mount Vernon as the peaceful days on the Potomac ran out, and after the war he continued to be a welcome visitor for the rest of Washington's lifetime.

Washington's concern for his Negroes was constant, and nothing his white overseers did or didn't do escaped him. On January 28th a small catalogue of disaster and discipline began in the Diary: "Visited my Plantation. Severely reprimanded young Stephens for his Indolence, and his father for suffering of it. Found the new Negroe Cupid ill of a Pleurisy at Dogue Run Quarter and had him brot. home in a cart for better care of him." On the following day: "Darcus, daughter to Phillis, died, which makes four Negroes lost this Winter: viz, 3 Dower Negroes, namely—Beck—appraisd to £50, Doll's Child born since, and Darcus—appd. at—, and Belinda, a Wench of mine, in Frederick County." On Wednesday he wrote: "Cupid was extreame Ill all this day and at night when I went to Bed I thought him within a few hours of breathing his last." But Cupid was mentioned as better next day, and survived to be listed as a laborer at the River Farm in the 1786 inventory. One of the small detached buildings near the Mansion House was used as a hospital for sick Negroes.

On February 3d, "Breechy [the butler] was laid up this Morning with pains in his breast and head attended with a fever." On the 4th—"Breechy's pains Increased and he appeared extremely ill all the day, in Suspense whether to send for Doctr. Laurie or not." On the 5th—"Breechy's Pain increasg. and he appearing worse in other respects inducd me to send for Dr. Laurie." On the 6th, Dr. Laurie sent his servant down "with things to Breechy," and the man was back the next day also. Breechy was saved, and appears in the 1786 inventory demoted from house service to labor at the Ferry [Union] Farm. On February 8th Lucy was ordered "down to the Home House to be Physicked"—a chore which was doubtless carried out by Martha herself. There were at least three Lucy's in '86, all laboring women.

In April, while he was at Williamsburg, Washington received

letters from Winchester that small-pox had invaded his Bullskin plantation, and within a few days, having completed the leasing of the Custis town house to Martha's brother Bartholomew Dandridge, he hurried back to Mount Vernon. Pausing briefly there to inspect the sowing of his clover and lucerne, and to provide a stallion for the great bay mare, he rode on through Winchester to Frederick County, where things had got into a bad way.

"*Wednesday, May* 7. After taking the Doct'rs Directions in regard to my People, I set out for my Quarters and got there abt. 12 oclock –time enough to go over them and find everything in the utmost confusion disorder and backwardness, my Overseer [Hardwick] lying upon his back of a broken leg, and not half a Crop, especially of Corn Ground, prepared.

"Engagd Val Crawford to go in pursuit of a Nurse to be ready in case more of my People should be seizd with the same disorder.

"*Thursday, 8th.* Got Blankets and every other requisite from Winchester and settld things upon the best footing I coud to prevent the small-pox from spreading, and in case of its spreading, for the care of the Negroes.

"Mr. Val. Crawford agreeing in case any more of the People at the lower Quarter getting it, to take them home in his House, and if any more at the upper Quarter gets it, to have them removd into my Room and the Nurse sent for.

"*Friday, 9th.* Set out on my return home. The morning drizzling a little. . . . . ."

Striding about in his own towering, confident immunity won at Barbados in '51, the master had in two days reduced chaos to discipline, provided necessities and care, and ridden out again, leaving the objects of his visitation no doubt a bit shaken up but comforted. Later that month there arrived at Mount Vernon one of overseer Hardwicke's epistolary masterpieces which showed him in his usual form.

"Sir–

"We are disapinted in sending two Waggings down Magnis Talt has declind coming down & Mr Craford's waginner Refus'd to carey the two mars [mares] down So that I was fosed to send down nat with them which I Cud very elley Spare I am in hops I shall soon be able to see about my beseness We have no more people taken with the Small pox as yet nor am I in hops I have prepared them according to your orders & the doctors structions & are all well but the two that had the Small pox & Fortin & Wing & they seame to be very mulch amnded. I beg you till Disspach nat as soon as posable—I am your most obednt Humble servant

CHRISTOPHER HARDWICK"

Only a few days after his return home in May, Washington records that "Lightning wch. had attended a good deal of rain has struck my Quarter and near 10 Negroes in it, some very bad; but with letting Blood they recoverd."

The Stephens family at the Mansion House farm were not let off Washington's oblique irony, even after the severe reprimand of January 28th produced results. "*February 2d* ..... Found Richd. Stephen's hard at Work with an ax—very extraordinary, this; Desird him to see after Wm. Nation's Rent, who died t'other day..... *February 5th* ...... Visited my Plantation and found to my great surprise Stephens constantly at Work...." And then, on February 9th—"Visited my Plantation before Sunrise and forbid Stephen's keeping any horses upon my Expense."

Mount Vernon social life was not confined to the Williamsburg Assembly season. The river port town of Alexandria was capable of providing its own entertainment, such as balls, ship-launchings, barbecues, and the opening of new stores. One of these occasions in 1760 was ticked off by Washington in a way to indicate that he could plague his friends with an almost schoolboy humor.

"*Friday*, [*February*] *15th*...... Went to a Ball at Alexandria, where Musick and Dancing was the chief Entertainment. However in a convenient Room detachd for the purpose abounded great plenty of Bread and Butter, some Biscuits with Tea, and Coffee which the Drinkers of coud not Distinguish from Hot Water sweetened. Be it remembered that pocket handkerchiefs servd the purpose of Table Cloths and Napkins and that no Apologies were made for either.

"The Proprietors of this Ball were Messrs. Carlyle, Laurie, and

Robt. Wilson, but the Doctr. not getting it conducted agreeable to his own taste woud claim no share of the merit of it.

"I shall therefore distinguish this Ball by the Stile and title of the Bread and Butter Ball.

"We lodged at Colo. Carlyle's."

Poor Colonel Carlyle, who was probably subjected to more of the same by his amused guest at breakfast the next day, was the prosperous merchant who had married George William Fairfax's sister Sarah in '48. They had only two surviving children, both girls. Their house, the finest in Alexandria, had in its cellar the foundations of the stone fort which was built by the first settlers in the 1640's, and its broad, shady lawns ran down to the River. Enclosed now by Alexandria's streets, the house remains much in its original state, except for sad deterioration. Arris, who was also Millbank's architect, had designed the famous Blue Room with its comfortable window-seats, its grand corniced ceilings, pedimented doors, and fluted mantelpieces—familiar to Washington since his first meeting there with Braddock in what must have seemed to him a lifetime ago. Braddock was only one of its many important guests in the '50's, and there would be more in the years to come. Now, during the lull between the Indian wars and the Revolution, the house was a glittering center of Potomac society, and how Carlyle, for all his Scotch blood, came to be involved in so meager an affair as the 1760 ball there is no clue. His wife, who had only another year to live, certainly brought with her from Belvoir a knowledge of the way such things should be done. Perhaps her influence did not extend as far as the City Tavern, later known as Gadsby's, where the regrettable affair probably took place.

Dr. Laurie, who claimed no share of it, had nevertheless a weakness, and as a consequence owns the most famous entry in Washington's laconic Diary, which occurs on April 9, 1760: "Dr. Laurie came here. I may add Drunk." The next day he had sobered up sufficiently to bleed Mrs. Washington, who was still suffering from the after-effects of the measles. He is not mentioned again in the Diary, though the Ledger shows that his account ran on for several more years. By 1768, when the Diary entries once more become detailed, Dr. William Rumney was in charge of the plantation ailments, and thereafter his name recurs for years as he made his almost weekly rounds.

As for Mr. Wilson, the third proprietor of the Alexandria ball, this is his sole appearance in history, except for a vote cast against Washington in the 1758 election.

VIII

BECAUSE the Diary for the year 1760 set the pattern for the next dozen, despite his brooding destiny, it is worth while to dip in almost at random, as the weeks flow past him.

In February Washington succeeded in buying William Clifton's land above Little Hunting Creek, after considerable dickering. The purchase was complicated by Clifton's belated qualms as to his wife's dower rights, and an offer from George Mason's brother Thomson of £50 more than Washington's £1150—which offer when it came to light "fully unravelled" what Washington had considered "very shuffling behavior" and convinced him that Clifton was "nothing less than a thorough pacd. Rascall, disregardful of any engagements of words or oaths not bound by Penalties." Nothing so roused the ire of the master of Mount Vernon as a suspicion of sharp dealing against him, and he brought Clifton to court. "Much discourse happend between him and I concerning his ungenerous treatment of me, the whole turning to little acct.," says the Diary. " 'Tis not worth reciting here. Thc result of which was that for £50 more than Mr. Mason offerd him he undertook, if possible, to disengage himself from that Gentleman and to let me have his Land. I did not think myself restrain'd by any Rules of Honour, Conscience, or etca. from mak'g him this offer, as his Lands were first engagd to me by the most Solemn assurances that any Man coud give."

The 1806 acres of the Clifton land, which Washington finally got for £1250, formed the Mount Vernon River Farm or Neck, which with the Dogue Run, Muddy Hole, Union, and Mansion House farms composed the five divisions of the estate.

On his birthday, which the Diary steadfastly ignores, he began laying the worm of a fence around his peach orchard, and rode to Belvoir to pay his respects to Lord Fairfax, who was on one of his visits there, and invite him to dinner on the Sunday.

"Upon my return," he wrote in the Diary, "found one of my best Waggon horses (namely Jolly) with his right foreleg smashed to pieces, which I suppose happend in the Storm last Night by means of a Limb of a tree or something of that sort falling upon him. Did it up as well as I coud this night.

"*Saturday, 23d.* Had the Horse slung upon Canvas and his leg freshly set, following Markham's directions as near as I could. [Markham was a century-old authority on horse-breeding, racing, and doctoring, with many publications on the subject.]

"*Monday, 25th.* . . . The Broken Legd horse fell out of his Sling and by that means and struggling together hurt himself so much that I orderd him to be killed."

Plowing had started as early as February 26th, with the field by the stable which was being prepared for oats and clover by two plows under the care of Mulatto Jack, who was a constant worker indoors and out, along with his team-mate called Cook Jack, who was often found doing field work between meals. Kate, Doll, George, and Little George were set to work grubbing the field by the garden, where Washington intended to plant lucerne, which a century later would be called alfalfa. There was more trouble with horses, and he had a plow harness made for those which drew his chariot.

"*Wednesday, 5th.* [March] . . . . Put in the great bay mare, and horse King. Latter coud not be prevaild upon to plow, the other did very well, but the Plows run very badly.

"Finishd Plow harness for my Chariot Horses.

"*Thursday, 6th.* Fitted a two Eyed Plow Instead of a Duck Bill Plow and with much difficulty made my Chariot wheel Horses plow. . . .

"*Friday, 7th.* . . . . . Put the Poll end Horses into the Plow in the Morng. and the Postillion and hand Horse in, in the afternoon, but the Ground being well swarded over and very heavy plowing I repented putting them in at all, for fear it shoud give them a Habit of Stopping in the Chariot. . . . . ."

Finally he despatched Mulatto Jack to Bullskin to fetch down some mares from there to plow at Mount Vernon. Even then there was disappointment: "Mulatto Jack returnd home with the Mares he was sent for, but so poorly were they, and so much abused had they been by my Rascally Overseer Hardwick that they were scarce able to go highlone, much less to assist in the business of the Plantations."

At this point Washington really took a hand. "Peter (my Smith) and I after several efforts to make a plow after a new model—partly of my own contriving—was feign to give it out, at least for the present." But only for a week. "Spent the greatest part of the day making a new plow of my own Invention," he wrote on the 26th of March. And on the following day, which was warm and fine, with a southerly wind: "Sat my Plow to work and found she answered very well in the Field in the lower Pasture wch. I this day began Plowing with the large Bay Mare and Rankin—Mulatto Jack contin'g to Plow the Field below the Garden." But he was still not satisfied. On the 5th of April—"Made another Plow the same as my former, excepting that it has two eyes and the other one." Even that did not suit, and on the 10th Val Crawford, who a month later was to be called upon to see the Bullskin people through their epidemic of small-pox, came down to Mount Vernon with four hogsheads of Mountain Tobacco for the warehouses at Alexandria, and brought with him "a Plow such as they use mostly in Frederick County." When it was tried, "found She did good work and run Very true but heavy, rather too much for two Horses, especially while the Ground was moist."

The weather that March was unusually bad, and by the 15th a new anxiety had set in. "The Vast quantity of Rain which had fallen in the last two days had Swelled the Waters so high that Dogue Run [Creek] carried off the Tumbling Dam of my Mill and was near to carrying off the House too," he wrote.

The story of the Dogue Run mill became a minor epic complete with a distressed heroine, for the mill, like the plows, was always "she," whether in Miller Poole's helter-skelter written reports or in the master's private Diary. In July, '58, when Washington was absent on the Forbes campaign, she had failed Miller Poole for want of water. Only the week before she lost her dam in this present spring, Washington had been discussing with a millwright a rebuilding job to be done when the mill should have run dry again in the coming summer. But she didn't wait for that, and on March 15th the dam went.

The next day—"In the morning early began Snowing with a strong No. Et. Wind and continud without the least Intermission, or Remission till dark, and how long after I know not." The day after that it was still snowing and had drifted to considerable depth, but he could wait no longer. "Went to my Mill and took a view of the Ruins the Fresh had causd; determined however to rep'r it with all expedition and accordingly set my carpenters to making Wheel and Handbarrows." On the 24th, the weather had cleared. "Began repairing my Mill Dam with hands from all my Quarters carpenters included. In digging Earth for this purpose great Quantities of Marle or Fullers Earth appeard." And on the 25th—"All hands being employd on the Dam again the water was stopd and the work in a fair way of receiving a finish by tomorrow night."

Less than a month later, on the day after the Easter holiday, she was in trouble again.

"*Tuesday, 8th.* [April] What time it began raining in the night I can't say, but at day break it was pouring very hard, and continued so, till 7 oclock, when a messenger came to inform me that my Mill was in great danger of blowing. I immediately hurried off all hands with shovels etca. to her assistance, and got there myself just time enough to give her a reprieve for this time by wheeling dirt into the place which the water had washd.

"While I was there a very heavy Thunder Shower came on which lasted upwards of an hour.

"Here also I tried what time the Mill requird to grind a Bushel of Corn, and to my Surprize found she was within 5 minutes of an hour about it. This old Anthony attributed to the low head of Water, but whether it was so or not I can't say; her Works all decayd and out of Order, wch. I rather take to be the cause. . . ."

She was not, of course, in her first youth, having been built by Augustine Washington during Lawrence's minority. But there were too many other demands in this year of 1760 for anything but another stop-gap repair job, which ran to ninety-seven days' work and a cost of £21.16.6, after which she staggered cheerfully along till 1770, grinding meal for the plantation hands and fine flour of a quality to make Washington's name a guarantee for exporting the very best.

A brief sample of his Memorandums on grafting at the end of March shows the infinite attention to detail which must have harassed his easygoing plantation help as it did even the most earnest Headquarters aides in the war years to come.

"*21st.* Grafted 40 Cherrys–viz: 12 Bullock Hearts–(a large black May Cherry); 18 very fine early May Cherry; 10 Carnation Cherry. And planted them as followeth; the Bullock Hearts in the first Row next the Quarter beginning at the furthest part thereof and ending at a stick. The early May next to them in the same Row and ending at another Stick, the Carnation finishing the said Row.

"*Also on March 21st.* Grafted 12 Magnum Bonum Plums beginning at the farthest part of the Second Row.

"*Also on March 21.* Planted 4 Nuts of the Mediterranean Pine in the Pen where the Chestnut grows–sticks by each.

"Note the Cherrys and Plums came from Colo. Mason's, Nuts from Mr. Green's."

George Mason was famous for his black heart cherries, which on the landward side of Gunston Hall formed an avenue some twelve hundred feet long through an extensive lawn and embodied one of his intellectual jokes. The cherry trees were grown from seed planted in four rows, two on each side of the drive, beginning about two hundred feet from the house, and were so carefully aligned in oblique perspective and controlled growth that from the north doorway of the house one saw only the first tree of each row. Mason's son John, who loved Gunston with his heart's blood, in his old age set down his vivid memories of life as it was lived there in his father's prime:

"More than once I have known my father, under whose special care this singular and beautiful display of trees had been arranged and preserved, and who set great value on them, amuse himself by

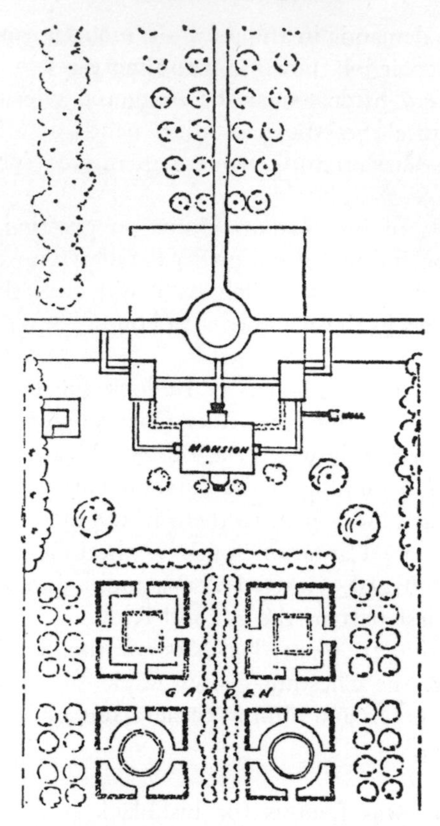

inviting some gentleman or lady (who visiting Gunston for the first time, may have happened to arrive after night, or may have come by way of the river and entered by the other front, and so not have seen the avenue) to the north front to see the grounds, and then by placing them exactly in the middle of the doorway and asking 'How many trees do you see before you?' 'Four' would necessarily be the answer, because the fact was that those at the end of the four rows next the house completely (and especially when in full leaf) concealed from that view, body and top, all the others, though more than fifty in each row. Then came the request, 'Be good enough to place yourself now close to either side of the doorway, and then tell us how many you see.' The answer would now be with delight and surprise, but as necessarily, 'A great number, and to a vast extent, but how many it is impossible to say!' And in truth, to the eye placed at only about two feet to the right or left of the first position, there were presented, as if by magic, four long, and apparently close walls of wood made up of the bodies of the trees, and above, as many of the rich foliage constituted by their boughs stretching, as it seemed to an immeasurable distance."

Day by day, Washington's painstaking record ran, all so tremendously important in the long range view of Mount Vernon produce which he never doubted would absorb and enrich the rest of his life on the land he loved. After May, 1760, the Diary entries begin to fall off into a terse record of planting, reaping, and weather, which even then conveys a sense of unceasing activity:

"*14–18.* [*August*] Cut and made Hay of Clover at River Quarter with part of ye hands—ye rest workg. at Dogue Run.
"*21–22.* Mak'g. do. Rainy.
"*23.* People doing jobs.
"*25–27.* Cutting and Mak'g. Hay at Sein Landing.
"*30.* Doing jobs."

That was Mount Vernon in the '60's. People doing jobs.

During the summer of 1760 George William Fairfax had returned to England on the business of his Yorkshire inheritance, this time taking with him both his wife Sally and his half-sister Hannah. When they came back to Virginia in '63 the old neighborly ways with Mount Vernon were resumed, and Hannah married as a second wife George's cousin Warner Washington, who had bought a handsome grey stone mansion called Fairfield, built by the Millbank architect Arris, overlooking the Shenandoah River.

The summer of '61 found Washington's health bad again, with a recurrence of the old fevers and pains. In alarm and desperation he made a sojourn at Berkeley Springs in Frederick County, leaving Martha and the children at home. He lived in a tent with Bishop and a colored boy to look after him, and was not much taken with his surroundings, but at least it did him no harm and his natural vitality again asserted itself. After his return home to Mount Vernon he wrote in October to his London agent:

"Since my last of the 14th July I have in appearance been very near my last gasp; the Indisposition then spoke of Increased upon me and I fell into a very low and dangerous State. I once thought the grim King would certainly master my utmost efforts and that I must sink in spite of a noble struggle, but thank God I have now got the better of the disorder and shall soon be restored I hope to perfect health again.

"I don't know that I can Muster up one tittle of News to communicate, in short the occurrences of this part of the World are at present scarce worth reciting, for we live in a state of peaceful tranquility ourselves, so we are at very little trouble to inquire after the operations against the Cherokees who are the only People that disturbs the repose of this great Continent......

"On the other side is an Invoice of Cloathes which I beg the favour of you to purchase for me and send them by the first Ship bound to this River. As they are designed for Wearing Apparel for myself I have committed the choice of them to your fancy, having the best opinion of your taste. I want neither Lace nor Embroidery; plain Cloathes with a gold or Silver Button (if worn in genteel Dress) is all I desire......"

The invoice for the children that autumn was not so modest.

For Jacky, who was now eight years old, some of the items were: a handsome suit of winter clothes; a suit of summer ditto, very light; a silver-laced hat; 6 pairs of gloves, and 8 pairs of shoes and pumps; 2 hair-bags and a piece of black hair-ribbon; silver shoe and knee buckles; and a suit of livery, "suited to the Custis arms," for his colored boy attendant, who was fourteen.

For Miss Custis, now six years old, there was to be a stiffened coat made of fashionable silk; 2 fine cambric frocks; a satin Capuchin hat and neckatees; a "persion" quilted coat; a pair of pack-thread stays, and 12 pairs of shoes in callimanca, leather, and satin, with flat heels; 12 pairs of mitts and 6 pairs of gloves in white kid; a fashionably dressed doll to cost a guinea; and a very good spinet, to be made by Mr. Plinius, harpsichord maker in South Audley Street, Grosvenor Square.

The children were each to have a Bible and Prayer Book with their names in gilt letters inside the cover, and their tutor, recently acquired from Maryland, presented a list of books for their use which included Sallust, Horace in Usum Delphini, Terence ditto, Ainsworth's Latin and English Dictionary and 2 copies each of Phaedrus' Fables. Phaedrus had made a Latin versification of Aesop, which had not yet been rendered into English. Sallust's *History of the Jugurthine War* (106 B.C.), Horace's Odes, and Terence's comedies from the Greek must have been fairly heavy going for Jacky, even with a dictionary.

Six years later, when the children were fourteen and twelve, there was an order for Jacky for fiddle strings, a blank book ruled proper for both spinet and fiddle music, a case of surveyor's plotting instruments, a watch chain and seal, and a silver-mounted fowling-piece to be three feet two inches in the barrel and ¾ of an inch in the bore. Patsy, by then almost a young lady, was to have a lutestring corderobe, a handsome suit of gauze, a black silk apron, a black Barcelona handkerchief, 3 pairs of colored kid mitts, a neat fan, 3 fine ivory combs, and a book with the new version of Psalms and Hymns set for the spinet.

There was the usual difficulty about carelessly filled orders which occasioned for the most part remarkably restrained remonstrances from Washington to the agent:

"Among the Goods sent in for Miss Custis there came a black Callimanca Petticoat and full trimmed Night Gown of a straw-colored Lustring marked MPC, but as they were of women's size and not charged to her Account we concluded they must be packed by mistake....."

"Since mine of the 18th the *Laetitia* is arrived, and the box of Shoes for Miss Custis come to hand; of so small a size as not to fit her....."

"My Goods by Captain Johnstown came in good order but Miss Custis looses a Trunk No. 2 containing Linnen and other things to the amount of £25.2.8.....I do not doubt but you will have this matter enquired into and see that Miss Custis is no looser; but disappointed she greatly is....."

"Miss Custis's Trunk which was missing last year is at length received; the contents in good order...."

"The Shoes you sent me last were made with the Grain side out and very narrow Toed, neither of wch I again woud choose, preferring the flesh side outwards and not over narrow in the Toes. . . ."

"I have now to inform you of a very great mistake which you have committed in sending me 2 dozn. Whipsaws, when I only wanted, and wrote for, two; what I shall do with the abundant overplus I really know not, as I apprehend it will be a difficult matter to dispose of such a quantity in this part of the Country. . . . . ."

"There must likewise have been a mistake in Shipping the Plows, for many of the most material parts being wanting, the rest, according to the Bill of Parcells, is entirely useless, and lye upon my hands a dead charge. . . . . ."

Still, he never stopped trying to add to Mount Vernon's equipment the latest improvements in farm machinery, and in February, '64, though times were hard after three bad years, he wrote to the London representatives:

"We have been curiously entertained of late with the description of an Engine lately constructed (I believe in Switzerland, and undergone some Improvements since in England) for taking up Trees by the Roots; among other things it is related that Trees of a considerable Diameter are forced up by this Engine, that Six hands working one of them will raise two or three hundred Trees in the space of a day; and that an Acre of Ground may be eased of the Trees and laid fit for Plowing in the same time. How far these assertions have been amply realized by repeated experiments it is impossible for me at this distance to determine, but if the Accounts are not greatly exaggerated such powerful assistance must be of vast utility in many parts of this Wooden Country when it is impossible for our Force (and labourers are not to be hired here) between the finishing of one Crop and preparations for another to clear Ground fast enough to afford the proper changes either in the Planting or Farming business.

"The chief purport of this letter therefore is to beg the favour of you Gentlemen to make minute inquiries into the Tryals that have been made by Order of the Society and if they have proved Satisfaction to send me one of these Engines by the first Ship bound to this River (Potomack). If they are made of different sizes, I shoud prefer one of a middle Size, capable of raising a tree of 15 or 18 inches Diameter. The Costs I am pretty much a stranger to, 15, 20, and 25 Guineas have been spoke of but the Price (were it dble that) I shoud totally disregard provided the Engine is capable of performing what is related of it, and not of that complicated nature to be easily disordered and rendered unfit for use, but constructed upon so plain, simple, and durable a Plan that the common Artificers of this Country may be able to set them to rights if any accidents should happen to them. If you shoud send one be so good as to let me have with it the most ample direction's for the effectual using of it, together with a model of its manner of operating.

"Mrs. Washington would take it as a favour if you woud direct Mr. Shelby to send her a fashionable Summer Cloak and Hatt, a black silk Apron, 1 pr. of penny and one pr. of two penny Ribbon (white) and a pair of French bead Earings and Necklace; and I shoud be obliged to you for sending me a dozen and a half of Water Plates (Pewter with my Crest engraved). I am, Gentn., etc."

Early in 1761, Lawrence's widow died at her Westmoreland home, and her second husband followed within a few months. Two of her children by George Lee survived, but none by Lawrence. There were no longer any strings to Mount Vernon. By the terms of Lawrence's will, however muddled, now indisputable, the estate had passed completely into the possession of George Washington.

IX

HE was turning thirty now, established, respected, imposed upon, a hard-working, early-rising landowner, a Burgess, a family man though still childless, firmly implanted in his chosen rut, desiring nothing more than his methodical daily round afforded him—except more money, and of course more land, and the necessary "people" to work it.

The years of Mount Vernon's neglect were compensated now, the outbuildings were patched up, the slaves and cattle were decently housed, the mill was repaired and running, the orchards and fields were producing, in spite of bad luck with the weather—"a wet Spring, a dry Summer, and early Frosts have quite demolished me," he wrote to London in January, '64.

In 1760 he had made 93,000 pounds of tobacco, which was a fair yield in a bad year. In '61 he increased the total, but not enough. Then it began to drop, year by year, and he was face to face with the unhappy conclusion that Mount Vernon would never produce the best high grade leaf. Tobacco was a demanding crop in labor, and it exhausted the soil. He began to experiment with alternate crops—wheat, flax, and hemp.

He had over-extended, bringing the place up to par, and adding the Clifton acres. He had then to practice what must have been galling little economies, like having his travelling chair relined, instead of buying a new one. He was accumulating workmen, hoping to make the place more self-sufficient, as Gunston was—he rented a Negro brick-layer for £25 a year, hired a white man named Davis to take charge of the weaving-house and increase the output there. He bought in a few slaves, preferring the higher priced native Virginian

Negroes to the unskilled, often demoralized new slaves off the incoming ships. In '62 he laid out £415 for more slaves. In '63 he bought five and immediately re-sold two of them at a profit. He advertised and paid rewards for an occasional runaway brought back, but there is no indication of punishment, except for the incorrigible Tom, who was "both a Rogue and a runaway." Tom was consigned to the care of a sea-captain to be sold "for whatever he will fetch" in the West Indies, where troublesome domestic Negroes usually wound up, although he was "exceedingly healthy, strong, and good at the Hoe..... which gives me reason to hope that he may, with your good management, sell well, if kept clean and trim'd up a little when offerd for Sale." The amount realized for Tom was to be invested on the spot for specified items of rum, molasses, fruits, and "good old spirits." Twenty-five years later, returned home from the war, Washington expressed in a letter to his friend Mercer a resolve never to possess another slave by purchase.

His white workmen were sometimes as exasperating as the black ones. While George William Fairfax was in England in '62 Washington wrote him with some heat and less syntax concerning John Askew, a joiner, whose labor was apparently shared between Belvoir and Mount Vernon: "I shall beg leave to say a little now in regard to Jno. Askew. That he went to Work at your House was not only with my knowledge but by my express desire, and had he stayed there 'till this time it woud have been perfectly agreeable to me; but as you know when he left your Work, so I can assure you that he never came to mine untill Wednesday or Thursday last; I then asked him if he did not think himself one of the most worthless, and ungrateful fellows that lived, for his treatment of me; for you must know, Sir, that so small a job as making the Front Gate in my yard was left him to do when I went to Williamsburg abt. the 10th of May last and was found undone at my return, altho I urged him in the strongest manner I coud to get it finished, for this very prevalent Reason–namely, that I might Inclose my Chariot Horses in a Pasture round the House secured by a Post and Rail Fence and by that means prevent them from breaking into a field where I had about 10 Acres of Pea's, that is now by his Idleness and there letting in my Sheep entirely rooted out.... so that you may partly judge from this of the provocation he has given me, but you will be more convinced of it when I tell you that the Balance he owes me is for Tools Imported for him, and money actually lent to keep him from starving and from a Gaol, from whence I have once or twice redeemed him; and lent him money to Cloath and buy necessaries for his Family. This is the real truth of the case, and it is so far from my wanting to keep him (longer than he will finish the Gate, and repays 7 days Work due to my Carpenters) that I never desire to see his Face again, if he can fall upon any method of paying what he owes me in Money...."

It is hard to see why Fairfax got both barrels in the argument, and after all Askew was not fired, but continued to exasperate for years to come.

Foster, the overseer on the Dogue Run farm, suddenly decamped in '62, apparently to escape his creditors, and the faithful John Alton, who had married and become a fixture on the place, was promoted to fill Foster's place.

In '65 Lund Washington, of the Chotank or down-river branch of the family, came to Mount Vernon as general manager and assistant. Lund was a distant cousin of vague relationship, descended from the younger of the two Washington brothers who had arrived in Virginia from England in the 1600's, and with his own brothers had been a playmate of George's youth when he lived on the Rappahannock. Lund was still unmarried at twenty-eight, and had had some experience of estate management on the large Ravensworth tract owned by the Fitzhughs. With his advent Washington could delegate some of the travelling and responsibility, and have more time for his guests, his family, his public duties at Alexandria where he had become a trustee and magistrate, his burgessing at Williamsburg, and his fox-hunting.

Captain Posey was by now in deep trouble, though he could always find time to go hunting while his debts piled up. In '61 Washington's carpenters under the direction of Turner Crump, a hired white man, had built a barn for Posey at Rover's Delight, at a cost to Washington of £97.18.7 1/2. By '63, when Posey had not paid off this debt, his other creditors were demanding cash, and he somehow succeeded in borrowing £700 from Washington at a time when Mount Vernon itself was running behind with its London bills. In June, '67, he had not even paid the interest on that loan when he asked for another £500, and Washington finally sat down and wrote him a lecture:

"...I was in hopes, and you gave me the strongest assurances to believe, that when I lent you (and very inconvenient it was for me to do it) the first sum of £700, you could therewith not only discharge all your creditors, but in two years time sink the principle, which was lent to effect that end; how it comes to pass, then, that instead of being prepared in twice two years to discharge my claim, you should require £500 more to satisfie others is entirely beyond my comprehension, and leaves but too much cause to apprehend that if you could be supplied with the further Sum required, it would afford but temporary relief...... The only favour therefore that is in my power to shew you, is to be easy and forbearing in my own demands, which I shall endeavour to do as long as I can with any sort of convenience to myself, notwithstanding that I am in want of the money....."

He offered Posey the same advice he would have given to his own brother in the same circumstances–to sell out, discharge his debts, and go westward "where an Enterprising Man with very little Money may lay the foundation of a Noble Estate in the New Settlemts. upon Monongahela for himself and Posterity."

But Posey was not the pioneering type. Instead, he fled to Maryland, from where he wrote to Washington in the midst of a new dilemma: "I could have been able to Satisfied all my old Arrears Some Months Agoe, by marrying an old widow woman in this County, She has Large soms cash by her, and Prittey good Estate.–She is as thick as she is high–And gits drunk at Least three or foure times a weak–which is Disagreeable to me–has Viliant Sperrit when Drunk–its been a Great Dispute in my mind what to Doe–I believe I shu'd run all Resk's–if my Last wife had been an Even temper'd woman, but her Sperrit has Given me such Shock–that I am afraid to Run the Resk Again......"

He brought himself to the sticking point, however, or he had no choice, and in June of '69 Washington wrote from Mount Vernon to Posey in his Maryland retreat:

"Hearing by your son Price, and perceiving by the Maryland Gazette that you are again entered into the Estate of Matrimony

I wish you joy. Your Affairs in this County having now come to a Crisis, I am under a necessity of reminding you of matters as they stand between Us; and hope you will consider them with that attention and care which the Subject deserves.

"You will no doubt be informed by your Sons, that every thing which is not under Security to me hath been attached. Many of them sold, and the rest on the point of selling..... And moreover, by the Deminution of the Goods, which by one means or another are greatly lessen'd, I may, if some speedy steps are not taken to raise money to discharge my demand, be a considerable looser by that forbearance and Indulgence which was meant as a favour to you, without you or yours gaining anything by it.....

"In the first place, then, if you coud with the greatest ease and convenience imaginable Cut your Grain, and pull your Corn, I have but too much reason to believe that both will be attached so soon as it happens; and by this means, and the neglect and waste that consequently follows, the proceeds of either woud turn to very little Acct. In the next place, Hanson [Posey] informs me that in a very few days your People will be without bread, at present the Horses have nothing to eat; and how a Crop is to be made under these Circumstances is beyond my management to discover. Again, if you can dispose of your Crop as it now stands, to any tolarable advantage, the expences and Inconvenience which are here pointed out are avoided, your Negroes and other things will then be sold at once, and but a very little while perhaps before the Court may decree it.... But as the Crop is a matter I am by no means anxious abt., I only proposed it for your consideration; and to shew that by this method you might remove every obstruction to a Sale and dispose of the whole at once...."

More land. He would buy Posey's land to add to his own acres and cut his losses that way. But Posey still hung on—hesitating, postponing the decision, hoping, finagling, falsifying, shilly-shallying—

"What, then, did all these Promises and Protestations mean?" Washington was demanding some weeks later. "Were they intended for no other purpose than to deceive a Man who had discovered by every means in his power an Inclination to serve you and your Family with the best advice he was capable of giving, and with his

Purse also? .... and therefore I woud go further, and recommend it to your Sober and serious reflection whether such treatment is due to a man who has so often saved your Person or Estate from the Officers of Justice, in hopes of your pursuing such measure's as wd. retrieve your Circumstances; and then say whether the appointments of this time, that time, and t'other time for fulfilling your Engagements are right......

"If you propose to redeem your Virginia Estate by the Sale of any part of your Wifes fortune is it not high time that there were some steps taken towards it? ..... But I shall tell you what I have heard, and that is that your Wife not only denies having conveyed her Estate, or any part of it, to you but has declared that She will never do it; Why then do you endeavour to amuse the World with these kind of Tales, which in fact answers no Earthly end or purpose; for People .... are more and more confirmed in a belief that you never intend to part with anything so long as you can hold it. ..... And take notice also that I shall want my own Money at the time it becomes due, having a considerable payment to make between this and Christmas out of that Sum. I am, Sir, etc."

The autumn of '69 found Washington putting the whole affair in the hands of Robert Hanson Harrison, the Alexandria lawyer who was later to serve as confidential aide and secretary during the worst days of the war. Posey had by then returned to Virginia with his new wife in tow, and she was exhibiting some of the valiant spirit he had attributed to drink and was resisting all his attempts to make use of her possessions to save his own.

"Captn. Posey's effects of every kind not Mortgaged are disposed of," Washington wrote in October. "Many of those which were Mortgaged have been seized and sold for Publick Dues. And others disposed of by himself. Some Articles are perishing fast, and the whole wasting and subject to continual deminution. Add to this, that the Mad and distracted manner in which he lives is alone sufficient to create unfavourable Idea's of a foul Intention, but when those Suspicions are corroborated by the Information of a Person whom one would naturally suppose best acquainted with his secret Intentions, it then becomes a matter of serious concern..... Mrs. Posey when she took refuge at Colo. Fairfax's did in the presence of him and his Lady upbraid him (that is, Posey) with a design of Transporting his and her Negroes to Pensacola and there selling them. This she not only did in the course of Altercation, but afterwards in a serious manner assured Mrs. Fairfax that he was fully bent on it. I have taken occasion since of mentioning this matter to Posey who of course denied it but acknowledged that he had made use of such expressions to his Wife in Order to Plague her. . . .

"From a tender concern for Characters you will readily perceive that great part of this Letter is intended for your private information only, for if Captn. Posey's Intention's are honest and upright I shall be sorry even for my Suspicions of him; but should be more so if any thing were propagated through my means that should cast any unjust odioum on His Character, tho' I have some reason's to believe that what I have heard mentioned is pretty generally talked of. . . ."

Certainly Posey's character was no secret along the Potomac, but Washington's indestructible patience with the man still hampered his stern sense of justice. He bought in Posey's farm, Rover's Delight, at the bankruptcy sale at the end of October, '69, and it came to be known as the Ferry Farm, perhaps in memory of his old home on the Rappahannock, where his mother still dwelt—though Posey's ferry proved to be a nuisance as it required a road kept open for its use. This land, joined to a later purchase from French's estate, was eventually called Union Farm.

Posey was allowed to retain a few acres and a house for his family's sake, perhaps out of Mrs. Washington's affection for his hapless daughter Milly, and he continued for a while to haunt Mount Vernon as a periodic diner and overnight lodger. As late as January 9th, 1774, Washington's Diary records his arrival, notes with possible boredom on the 11th, "Captn. Posey still here," on the 13th, "Dind here, nobody but Captn. Posey," and on the 14th, doubtless with a sigh of relief, "Captn. Posey went away to Maryland after Breakfast."

His last appearance in the Diary is in April of '74, when he spent three days at Mount Vernon and "went away after Dinner." What became of him, and his second wife, is a mystery. His sons must have maintained some kind of establishment in the neighborhood, as the one called Price got a job managing Jacky Custis's Pamunkey lands and in '81 was found to have committed all sorts of depredations like selling slaves and putting the money in his own pocket, so that as late as '86 Washington in a letter to Martha's brother Bartholomew Dandridge referred to "that Superlative Villain, Posey." Thomas, on the other hand, went for a soldier in the Revolution, became a colonel at Valley Forge, a Senator in Congress, and wound up Governor of Indiana.

Poor Milly's history remains a blank, except for her association with Patsy Custis. In April, 1770, after her father's fortunes had collapsed into bankruptcy, she accompanied Patsy to the itinerant dancing-school then meeting at Gunston Hall, and Washington paid her fees. In 1772 the Diary says: "*July 16.* Went up in the afternoon with Mrs. Washington, J.P. Custis, Miss Custis, and Milly Posey to a Ball in Alexandria. Lodged at my House in Town." So Milly saw life a little, and even after Patsy's death the following year she remained under Martha's protection. In March of 1781, writing to Lund from the New Windsor Headquarters on the Hudson, Washington sent best wishes from himself and Martha to Mrs. Lund Washington and Milly Posey, so it may be that for a time some place was found for her in the household at Mount Vernon.

Bridging the gap until the detailed '68 Diary takes up the story again, one can still piece together an illuminating record. In the immediate family, George's sister Betty Lewis and Martha's sister Nancy Bassett both brought their nurseries up to six, including the 1767 Bassett baby named Fanny who was to play an important part in the later Mount Vernon annals as the wife and widow of George Augustine Washington, son of George's brother Charles. John Augustine's first son Bushrod was born in '62, the same year that Austin died at Wakefield, survived by his widow, a son, and three girls, well provided for.

Throughout all the political squalls at home and the gathering storm across the Atlantic as the Stamp Act came and went in the mid-'60's, Washington's intense personal interest in the weather as it passed over Mount Vernon day by day never slackened.

"*Jan. 26th.* [1760.] A Very white frost the ground and River hard froze. The wind at Sun Rise at No. Et., in an hour afterwards it got to South, and continued there the whole day. A very remarkable circle round the moon—another indication of Falling Weather.

"*April 1st.* [1760.] Moon at its first rising remarkably red.

"*March 21st.* [1766.] Note.—the latter part of Feby., and all March till the 19th was extreamely wet and disagreeable—scarce two fair days together and sometimes hard Frosts, insomuch that neither Hoe nor Plow coud be stuck into the Ground, which prevented my sowing Hemp till the 21st, as above.

"*February 26.* [1767.] Brisk wind from the southward. Clear, warm and pleasant. According to Colo. West ye greatest part of the next Moon should be as this day, i.e. the same kind of weather that happens upon thursday before the change will continue through ye course of the next Moon, at least the first and 2d quarter of it. quere—is not this an old woman's story?"

Lund had proved a valuable asset to the estate in his quiet efficiency and devotion to George's interests, and when the master was away from home on the business of the Custis estate or attending the Assembly sessions Lund's letters were conscientious and frequent. One of these, written in March of 1767 while George was burgessing at Williamsburg without his womenfolk, carried the usual news of the mill and the plowing and the weather—it had rained on the flax as soon as it was sown—they were trimming the hops and setting up new poles—the family was well—and they had 137 lambs.

At the bottom of Lund's page Martha penned a postscript. As she later burned the whole of the correspondence between her and George, probably during the two years which elapsed between his death and hers, these few lines are the only ones in her hand to him which are known to exist. She began with what was apparently their customary salutation, for it occurs also in the only two letters surviving from him to her—"My Dearest." Everyone was well, and the weather still rainy and wet—she was sorry that he would not be home as soon as she had hoped—it would be better if her sister Nancy did not come up till May, which was pleasanter than April—there was nothing new to tell him since the last post, and she was his most affectionate Martha Washington.

1767 closed peacefully at home, in the west, and abroad. But change was in the air. In March of 1768 the popular Governor

Fauquier died at Williamsburg, and no one could surmise where the new man might stand, in the worsening relations between the colonies and the mother country.

Nearer home, Mr. Green, who had doctored the souls and bodies of the parish ever since the time of George's father, died, and Dr. Rumney of Alexandria was employed at an annual wage to tend the plantation people. An unobtrusive man, he was to continue his almost weekly visits to Mount Vernon right through the war and into the happy interlude which followed, always a willing companion for hunting, fishing, or a fireside bowl of punch when his rounds were completed. Walter Magowan, the children's tutor, departed for England to be ordained as a clergyman, and though he intended to return, it was necessary to find a suitable school for Jacky Custis, aged fourteen.

People were growing older, people were growing up and getting married. It was ten years since Washington had brought home his bride—ten busy, fruitful years, with a great deal to show for hard work and a dream. Give him another ten years—and by 1778 Mount Vernon would have begun to show what it could do....

In Virginia, no one had ever heard of Valley Forge.

X

ALTHOUGH the Stamp Act had been hastily repealed in '66, its aftermath was the Townshend Acts which insisted on the right of the British Government to tax the colonies for the support of their own customs and Crown officials. The death of Governor Fauquier at this point had caused both grief and alarm—though the same acting Governor who had smoothed Washington's way between the departure of Dinwiddie and the arrival of Fauquier in '58 was again in office. President of the Council John Blair was now eighty-one, but quite capable of presiding in the uneasy interval which must elapse before the next Governor took up residence in the capital.

No shadow of the gathering transatlantic cloud lay over the pages of Washington's Diary as he kept his daily catalogue of Mount Vernon doings. Not even its habitual brevities could conceal the cheerful fact that life was various and lively on the Potomac in the spring of '68, and that George Washington was enjoying himself exceedingly in his family and neighborhood society.

On January 1st he went fox hunting with two guests from Alexandria and "catchd nothing." Brother Charles paid a visit, and the Fairfaxes came to dine while he was there, along with more guests from Alexandria. On the 16th it snowed from the northward, and they stayed indoors playing cards all day. Later in the month he went hunting at Towelston with Bryan Fairfax, and after a five-hour run lost the fox. On the plantation, Davy, George, Jupiter, Ned, and Mike were building a new overseer's house at Muddy Hole Farm.

At the end of February he "went a-ducking between breakfast

and dinner and killd 2 Mallards and 5 bald faces," and found Dr. Rumney there when he returned. The carpenters were building a goose pen at the home farm. On March 2d in company with the Alexanders from Alexandria, Posey, George William Fairfax and others he went hunting again and "catchd a fox with a bobd Tail and cut Ears, after 7 hours chase in which most of the Dogs were worsted." He returned home that time "much disordered by a Lax and griping," and Dr. Rumney had to be sent for. By the 10th he was "mending," and Fairfax came to dine and see how he did. On the 16th he was hunting again, with Lund and the perpetual Posey, who was not yet sold up. On the 18th he went with the whole family to dine at Belvoir, where Colonel Carlyle was making a visit, with his second wife and the daughters of his first–and the Washingtons found the children's itinerant music-master awaiting them when they got home.

The first lamb of the year was born on March 25th. In mid-April Miss Tracy Digges and her sister Betty from Warburton Hall in Maryland came to visit Patsy, and a few days later their father spent the night and fetched them home with him. At the end of that month Washington set off for Williamsburg with his family, having skipped the spring session of the Assembly. They stopped at Fredericksburg, where Fielding Lewis joined them, and went on to Eltham, where they collected Mr. Bassett. Proceeding to Williamsburg, they lodged at Mrs. Dawson's fashionable boarding-house and went to the play.

George no doubt found the changes at Williamsburg somewhat sobering. His old friend John Robinson, who was for thirty years both Speaker and Treasurer of the colony, and had supported young Colonel Washington in all the wrangles with Governor and Council during the frontier wars of the '50's, had died in the midst of a financial scandal which rocked the capital for months. Robinson had been the model Virginia gentleman of wealth and fashion, master of the plantation called Pleasant Hill on the Mattapony. Out of the kindness of his heart, and a heedless desire to put things right for his many necessitous friends whose crops had failed and their debts fallen due, he had lent money recklessly with both hands, from his own private purse and from treasury funds, to the extent of over £100,000, much of which could never be recovered except by the forced sale of the estates of the very people he had tried to help. It was the most generous of faults, but it brought ruin on his own family when Pleasant Hill and his other assets had to be sold at auction to help repay the public debt. His successor at the Treasury was the wise and temperate Robert Carter Nicholas, who had married Anne Cary some ten years back, and who now did his experienced best to mitigate the after-effects of Robinson's generosity.

The new Speaker was another great gentleman, Peyton Randolph, whose imperturbable self-possession and imposing façade were to be an asset to the Virginia delegates at the Philadelphia Congress in a few years' time. His brother John stepped into Peyton's former post of Attorney-general, and while Peyton now began to move steadily towards the resolution for colonial independence which he did not live to sign, John hardened into Toryism and fled to England with the last Royal Governor when Dunmore furiously withdrew in '76.

But such a thing as open rupture with the mother country was undreamed-of in this mildly eventful spring of '68, and the Washingtons dined with both the Randolphs in their Williamsburg houses and entertained their womenfolk, and George fished for sturgeon without success and went rabbit hunting with Bassett's dogs. On the 20th of May they set out northward from Williamsburg for Bushfield, to visit John Augustine, whom they found away from home. After a day with Austin's widow and young family at Wakefield, they arrived at Sam's place near Fredericksburg, where they found the John Augustines, as well as Lawrence from Chotank, brother to Lund. The next day Charles turned up with Fielding Lewis, and after a Sunday interval when they attended church and dined together, they all had a day's fishing along the shore on the Monday.

One wonders about the wives and daughters, in this unusual concourse of tall Washingtons, relaxed and jovial in their family reunion, but nevertheless duly observing the Sabbath day. There was George's Martha, small and dignified and blooming in her mid-thirties, with her Jacky, a handsome, over-indulged lad of fourteen, and her beautiful dark-haired Patsy, twelve, but no child of George's after nearly ten years of marriage. John Augustine's Hannah had four, the eldest a daughter Jenny, who only a few years from now at seventeen was to occupy quite a little space in the diary of the Carters' tutor at Nomini Hall, young Mr. Fithian from New Jersey: "She has not a handsome face," he wrote, "but is neat in her Dress, of an agreeable Size, & well proportioned, & has an easy winning Behaviour; She is not forward to begin a conversation, yet when spoken to She is extremely affable, without assuming any Girlish affectation, or pretending to be overcharg'd with Wit; She has but lately had oppertunity of Instruction in Dancing, yet She moves with propriety when she dances a Minuet & without any *Flirts* or vulgar *Capers*, when she dances a Reel or Country-Dance; She plays well on the Harpsichord, & Spinet; understands the principles of Musick, & therefore performs her Tunes in perfect time, a Neglect of which always makes music intolerable, but it is a fault almost universal among young Ladies in the practice; She sings likewise to her instrument, has a strong, full voice, & a well-judging Ear; but most of the Virginia-Girls think it labour quite sufficient to thump the Keys of a Harpsichord into the air of a tune mechanically, & think it would be slavery to submit to the Drudgery of acquiring Vocal Music; Her Dress is rich & well-chosen, but not tawdry, nor yet too plain; She appears today in a Chintz cotton Gown with an elegant blue Stamp, a Sky-Blue silk Quilt, and spotted apron; Her Hair is a light brown, it was crap'd up, with two Rolls at each Side, & on the top a small cap of beautiful Gawze and rich Lace, with an artificial Flower interwoven– Her person & carriage at a small distance resembles not a little my much respected Laura. But on close examination her Features are something masculine, those of Laura are mild and delicate. . . ." And he adds a few days later that after dinner, "when Women were to be toasted, I gave *Miss Jenny Washington*." Mr. Fithian remained faithful to his New Jersey Laura, and Miss Jenny married her cousin William Augustine Washington of Wakefield, being the first of his three wives, and bore him seven children before she died at thirty-three. Her sister Milly, two years younger, was to marry a son of Richard Henry Lee of Chantilly, her brother Corbin a daughter of the same house, and her husband's second wife would be their sister Mary–and while all of these had numerous children, John Augustine's eldest son Bushrod, the heir to Mount Vernon, would have none.

Sam's complicated marital status is not clear at this time, but he had had two sons by his second wife, who was Mildred Thornton, and was probably by now married to Anne Steptoe, his fourth, who would be the mother of three sons and a daughter. Charles's wife and children apparently were not present, and Lawrence was probably not yet married. But it was altogether a notable Washington gathering, one of the last before their new Shenandoah mansions claimed both Sam and Charles away from Tidewater.

When George arrived home at the end of the month, he found two litters of puppies, which were duly entered in the Diary.

"The hound bitch Mopsey brought 8 Puppys–distinguished by the following Names, viz. Tartar, Jupiter, Trueman, and Tipler, (being Dogs) and Truelove, June, Dutchess, and Lady being the Bitches–in all, eight.

"The bitch Chanter brought five Dog Puppies and 3 Bitch Ditto, which were named as follows, viz. Forrester, Sancho, Ringwood, Drunkard, and Sentwell, and Chanter, Singer, and Busy......

"Musick was also in heat and servd promiscuously by all the Dogs; intending to drown her Puppys."

The carpenters and Home House people were at work at the mill again, "repairing of the Dams, hightening of them and opening the Race." And then the frame of the new barn at the Mansion House went up.

The chief concern during the coming year, however, was to be Martha's children–Jacky's schooling, and Patsy's health. Washington took his responsibilities as step-father very seriously, striving to guide the irresponsible Jacky towards manhood, and cherishing frail little Patsy like his own daughter. It was time that Jacky was removed from his mother's coddling and subjected to more discipline than a household tutor like young Magowan had been able to accomplish–to say nothing of his being made to study and to learn.

They had heard during their recent visits of a boarding-school in Caroline County, below Fredericksburg, kept by an English clergyman named Boucher, and on the very day of his arrival at home Washington wrote to Boucher, giving a frank account of Jacky's qualifications, such as they were, and ending briskly: "Now, Sir, if you Incline to take Master Custis I shoud be glad to know what conveniences it may be necessary for him to bring, and how soon he may come, For as to his board and Schooling (provender for his Horses he may lay in himself) I do not think it necessary to inquire into, and will cheerfully pay Ten or Twelve pounds a year extraordinary to engage your particular care of and a watchful eye to him, as he is a promising boy; the last of his Family and will possess a very large Fortune; add to this my anxiety to make him fit for more useful purposes than a horse trader. . . . ."

Boucher was delighted, and almost before Jacky could shake a stick he found himself deposited firmly by his step-father in the midst of two dozen other boys, where for the first time in his pampered life his diet, his stomach-aches, and his fancy whims were of no importance to anybody.

A letter from Boucher to Washington in August indicated that as usual in the circumstances, Jacky's schoolmates took advantage of the new boy: "Master Custis is a boy of so exceedingly mild and meek a temper that I meant no more by my fears than a doubt that possibly he might be made uneasy by ye rougher manners of some of his schoolfellows. I am pleased, however, to find that he seems to be perfectly easy and happy in his new situation; and as the first shock is over, I doubt not he will continue so. . . . . Your son came to me teeming with all the softer virtues; but then I thought, possibly as he was of all the harmlessness of the Dove, he still wanted some of the wisdom of the Serpent; and this by the economy of my family he will undoubtedly sooner acquire than at home. . . . ."

Undoubtedly.

Jonathan Boucher had come out to Virginia in '59 as a tutor in a family at Port Royal, after having started at the bottom as an usher in an English school. Three years later he returned to England briefly for ordination, so that he could take advantage of a good living which was offered to him in Hanover County. When the incumbent of St. Mary's in Caroline County died, Boucher secured that place, and went into debt for stock and slaves to establish at his house in the glebe a small school, with the help of his spinster sister Jinny.

Schools were scarce, and the membership at St. Mary's increased rapidly to something around thirty boys. The place was understaffed, and perhaps underfed, and the water supply was questionable, and Boucher was subject to frequent fevers and mysterious ailments which may have had something to do with drink, but he wrote entertaining letters of remarkable perception and vitality, which appear in S. M. Hamilton's five-volume collection of *Letters to Washington* (1898). The Boucher correspondence with Washington remains one of the few unexploited aspects of Mount Vernon life before the war, and he also left a volume of *Reminiscences* of a very lively nature.

A brief entry in Washington's Diary for June 14, 1768, is the first indication of a new anxiety. "Returned home again [from Belvoir] and found Mr. B. Fairfax here. Sent for Doctr. Rumney to Patcy Custis who was seized with fitts. Mr. M. Campbell lodged here."

Whoever Mr. Campbell was, Mount Vernon hospitality was not denied him, nor Bryan Fairfax, because of the terror which must have pinioned Patsy's mother on that day. It was apparently not a lasting attack, as the Fairfaxes dined at Mount Vernon with other guests the next day, and no further mention of Patsy's health occurs in the Diary until February of the next year, when "Joshua Evans, who came here last Night, put an Iron Ring upon Patcy (for Fits) and went away after breakfast," a ministration which cost £1.10.0. This was the beginning of a tragic ordeal for Patsy, and the first of a succession of desperate remedies and consultations which were undertaken throughout the rest of her short life, when any doctor who would give an opinion was hopefully consulted.

Washington spent the whole day of the 18th of June preparing letters and invoices, and the order to the London agents reveals a continuing attempt to divert Patsy and please her with trinkets and new interests. They ordered for her a smelling-bottle, a pocket mirror, scissors, gloves, "a very handsome and fashl. Woman's Hg. saddle with Bridle & every thg. complete," and a riding-hat with a white feather. For Jacky there were to be more clothes, fiddle-strings, pocket-knives, and a saddle; for Martha "a green satin quilted coat, not to exceed £3," and "a handsome grane Winter Silk (but not yellow) not to exceed £10 to be bought of & made by Mrs. Harris into a sacque & Coat for a middle sized Woman;" for himself a suit of "fashionable coloured cloth," and everything from seeds to rope as plantation supplies, besides—a great venture, this one—a new chariot, to be painted green, a color supposed not to fade, and having preference unless any other color was more in vogue and equally lasting, in which case Washington was as always willing to yield to fashion.

When the chariot arrived in September it was indeed green, and it cost £315.13.6, with transportation charges. The invoice which accompanied it described it as "....made of the best materials, handsomely carvd, carvd anticks to middle of Pillars, and carvd scrowl Corners to top of Pillars and Roof....panneld back and Sides Japannd and Polished, and roof Japand; lined with green Morocco Leather trimmed with Cuffoy Lace, an oval behind, a large Trunk under the seat, the bottom covered with red leather and a handsome carpit to bottom; Plate Glass, diamd. cut, handsomely Painted, the Body and Carridge whls. painted a glazed green; all the framd Work of Body gilt, handsome scrowl, shields, Ornamentd. with flowers all over the Panels......Patent woorm Springs wt. brass sockets;....a handsome seat cloth, embroidered with brd. Lace and 2 rows of hande. Fringe wt. gimp head, all complete; 4 Venetian Pattern Blinds with Mahogy. frames....and a new cover made of Green Bays...."

Within two years of its delivery Washington was writing to complain that the chariot was made of such green wood that the panels had split from one end to the other.

Another important purchase for this year was three mulatto slaves, which along with Adam and Frank brought Billy, sometimes called Will, the best of them all—the body-servant who was to accompany Washington all through the war and share every hardship, softening so far as he was able by his devoted service the fatigue and anxieties of the Commander-in-chief. By the time the Presidency began in '89, Billy was aging and suffered from the effects of two falls which had broken his knees, but he lived on at Mount Vernon, indulged even when he drank too much, long enough to mourn the death of his master. He had cost £61.

July of '68 was spent at the harvesting, with careful observations on the state of the wheat crop, which had now supplanted tobacco as the principal effort at Mount Vernon. The cutting was supervised by Jonathan Palmer, a practical farmer who would hire out, with three other white men and four Negro cradlers, and Palmer was induced to become a permanent member of the Mount Vernon economy. The terms were explicit.

"*Memm.* On the 30th of this Month I agreed with Jonathan Palmer to come and Work with my Carpenters; either at their Trade–Coopering–or in short at anything that he may be set about. In consideration of which, I am to pay him £40 pr. Ann; allow him 400 lbs. of Meat and 20 Bushels of Indian Corn. I am also to allow him to keep two Milch Cows (one half of whose Increase I am to have) and to have Wheat for which he is to pay. He is to be allowed a Garden, and I am also to take his Waggon at £17, if he brings it free from damage, and it is no older than he says–that is about a 12 Month. Note, he is to be here as early as possible in April–if not in March."

But it was the end of June, '69, before Palmer "who came to the House that was provided for him last Night, began Working with my People this day." It proved to be a lucky move for Palmer, as less than a year later, when Rover's Delight had come by the bankruptcy sale into the Mount Vernon fold–"Jonathan Palmer and his Family moved to Posey's to live." He apparently gave satisfaction, as during the harvest of July, '72, "old Palmer" had been promoted. "At Muddy Hole, Palmer (who did not work himself, but only acted as an Instructor) and Six of the youngest Cradlers began."

In August Washington travelled down to brother Sam's near Fredericksburg again, alone this time, for the christening of a child –one of those that did not live long. Brother Charles and Fielding Lewis turned up too, and they all went on to John Augustine at Bushfield, collecting Lawrence of Chotank on the way, for another fishing trip, during which they seined for sheepsheads without success. On his way home he stopped to dine at Eagle's Nest, an immense frame house bowered in myrtle and mulberry trees at the mouth of Potomac Creek, which had been built by one of the many Fitzhughs, whose widow was living there with her second husband, Nat Harrison of Brandon on the James.

Washington's love of the theater took the whole family to Alexandria to see the melodramatic comedy *The Inconstant, or Way to Win Him*, performed. Then they remained another day to see the tragedy of *Douglas*, which must have been over-exciting for Patsy in its sustained catastrophe. This was the controversial piece by the Reverend John Home, based on a lachrymose Scottish ballad, which so inflamed its Edinburgh audience on the first night in '56 that there was a cry from the pit of "Where's yer Wully Shakespeare noo?" Both Peg Woffington and Sarah Siddons appeared in it in many revivals in England, and it was a favorite with the travelling troupes which found their way to America to play in barns, warehouses, and taverns in towns where there was no theater. One wonders what the Custis children made of the complicated agonies of the lost Douglas heir, brought up as a foundling and recognized in his young manhood by his still grieving mother, who since the death of his father had been forced into a hateful marriage—and who, having seen him slain in a duel with the villain who also died by the sword, herself committed suicide in a plunge over a cliff as described by her devoted maid servant—

> "Upon the brink she stood, and cast her eyes
> Down on the deep; then lifting up her eyes
> And her white hands to heaven seeming to say
> 'Why are I forc'd to this?' she plunged herself
> Into the empty air. . . . . ."

—which was immediately followed by her blundering second husband's frenzied final exit to certain death in another battle. Shakespeare was just where he always was, but no doubt in Alexandria he was hardly missed.

In the Diary's sparse entries for that autumn there are unexpected word pictures of the Morland type:

"*6.* [*September.*] My Ox Cart finished drawing in the Wheat at Doeg Run, but during this time it was employd in getting home the Cyder from all Plantations.
"*16.* Anointed all my Hounds (as well as puppies) which appeared to have the Mange with Hogs Lard and Brimstone.
"*22.* Spread my Flax for Rotting at the Home House."

In October the new Governor arrived at Williamsburg, and Washington set out, alone except for the way Fielding Lewis, Burwell Bassett, and others adhered to him as he went, to make His Excellency's acquaintance, and learn what the King and his Ministers had thought up now.

XI

THE first thing Governor Botetourt did was to dissolve the Assembly, which meant all the trouble and expense of another election for the Burgesses. While in Williamsburg, where his stay was brief, Washington dined with both the Randolphs and there met the Governor informally—a likable seeming man, who kept great state at the Palace, a bachelor with an eye for the ladies—and his attitude as representative of the Crown was affable and conciliatory.

On his return journey to Mount Vernon Washington was accompanied by Martha's sister Betsy Dandridge, who was just turning twenty, for a visit on the Potomac. They lodged the first night at William Aylett's house on Mattapony, and as everyone knew everyone in the Tidewater this would hardly have been Betsy's first meeting with William's son John. But it is interesting to note that she married him a few years later.

There was a certain amount of bustle after George's arrival at home, in anticipation of the coming election and out of curiosity about the new Governor. People who had not attended in Williamsburg rode in to Mount Vernon from Alexandria and their houses roundabout to hear the latest news. Besides the regular visitors like Dr. Rumney and the Fairfaxes and the Washington brothers, were William Grayson, Dumfries' most witty and distinguished citizen, who had studied law at the Middle Temple in London and was to serve as Washington's aide and colonel of his own regiment in the war, and as senator from Virginia during the first administration; and George Mason, accompanied by his closest friend and neighbor, Martin Cockburn, who was the hero of one of the great Virginia romances of his time.

Travelling in Virginia with his father at the age of eighteen, Cockburn had fallen in love with Anne Bronaugh of New Town, on Pohick Bay. His father owned estates in Jamaica, and as there was a baronetcy in the family, he doubtless had other plans for young Martin, who had been educated in England, but it was agreed that if after three years when the boy had come of age he still wanted to marry Miss Bronaugh there would be no further objections. His father lost what was certainly a reasonable gamble, for Martin returned to the Potomac to claim his bride at the end of that time. But Anne was a Virginia girl, and had a sister to whom she was much attached, and Jamaica seemed as remote as England–so it was the bridegroom who forsook all others. He bought land adjoining George Mason's Gunston Hall and built Springfield overlooking Pohick Bay not far from New Town; an unusual house for Virginia, as it was in the West Indies style, long and low and rambling, most of its rooms communicating with each other and all on one floor for fear of earthquakes. The Reverend Lee Massey, a man of great wit and humor, and of course truthfulness, said that to his own knowledge after fifty years the Cockburn marriage was still so idyllic that there had never been one word, look, or act to disturb its harmony for a moment. Massey had taken Anne's sister Betsy Bronaugh as his third wife, and lived at Bradley on Occoquan Bay just the other side of Gunston. For all its mutual devotion, the Cockburn marriage remained childless, and they made Springfield a second home for the many Mason children, especially after Anne Mason's early death in '73, which left her youngest a child of three.

"Went to the Election of Burgesses for this County and there with Colo. West was chosen," Washington recorded in his Diary in December, 1768. "Stayd all night to a Ball wch. I had given." Cake and sundries cost him £7.13.3, the fiddler for the ball only £1. When it was over, they all went back to Mount Vernon for several days' hunting, in which Lord Fairfax, on another visit to Belvoir, joined them, and on the 10th they catched a fox.

Jacky Custis came home from Mr. Boucher's school for Christmas, and the Diary for that day read simply: "At home all day." The only *Observation* for all December is "Killd Hogs." On the 2d of January, '69, the whole Mount Vernon family went to Belvoir to dine and spend the night, bringing Colonel Carlyle and Mr. Ramsay of Alexandria back with them for more hunting, in which Jacky was now man enough to take a part, and he did not return to school until the 26th.

In spite of a "spewing frost," Washington's workmen were opening an avenue from the front of the house (on the west) to the Accotink Road to Alexandria, leading across the swampy ravine he called Hell Hole, which was a breeding place for the malaria-carrying mosquitoes from which no one was immune. Visits from the Bassetts and the Warner Washingtons enlivened the early spring, and George made an inspection tour of his Bullskin property. In April another ominous entry occurs in the Diary: "Mr. Fairfax and Mr. Washington went away, and we set out to Captn. McCarthy's, but Patsy being taken ill with a fit on the Road by the Mill, we turnd back." Perhaps because of these alarming seizures, Martha and Patsy remained at home when Washington went down to Williamsburg to attend the spring session of the Assembly, which met in an atmosphere of growing tension and uncertainty.

He left Mount Vernon on April 30th, escorting Betsy Dandridge back home, and he carried in his pocket a document drafted by George Mason, who was in poor health and unwilling to leave Gunston; a well-reasoned argument urging a policy of non-importation, already practiced by some of the northern colonies as a means of colonial resistance to the hated Townshend Acts–including a list of articles which Mason believed that Virginia could do without. "Our All is at stake and the little conveniences and comforts of life when set in competition with our liberty ought to be rejected not with reluctance but with pleasure," Mason had written in an accompanying letter to Washington. "..... We may retrench all manner of superfluities, and confine ourselves to linens, woolens, etc., not exceeding a certain price; it is amazing how much this (if adopted in all the colonies) would lessen the American imports and distress the various traders and manufacturers in Great Britain." Among the superfluities he included everything from clocks to carriages, shoes to saddles, and candles to spirits and wines. Then he weakened: "P.S. I shall take it as a particular Favour if you'll be kind enough to get me two pair Gold snaps made at Williamsburg for my little Girls; they are small rings with a joint in them, to wear in the Ears, instead of Earrings. Also a pair of toupee tongs."

The Diary for May, 1769, records the usual dinners with old friends in the capital, evenings at the Raleigh Tavern where Anthony Hay was now the landlord, and side trips to inspect Martha's dower lands in York County. It makes no mention of the dramatic scene in the Council Chamber when the hitherto amiable Governor Botetourt stunned them all with a curt announcement that their carefully worded address of protest and appeal to the Crown made it his duty to dissolve them. It reduces to "a Committee at Hay's" the momentous meeting in the Apollo Room of the Raleigh, presided over by Peyton Randolph, when the rebellious Burgesses voted Mason's drafted non-importation agreement into a binding Association which would exclude from purchase in Virginia all the so-called luxury tax-free items as listed by Mason, and certain other taxed articles such as paint and tea. And it ignores the presence of a new Burgess from Albemarle County named Thomas Jefferson. The signatures represented a three-fourths majority of the House, and bound Virginia to stand beside the more aggressive northern colonies like Massachusetts.

But there were no hard feelings in this gentlemanly era. The next night but one was the Governor's ball at the Palace in honor of the Queen's birthday, and most of the dismissed Burgesses who had convened in the Apollo Room, including George Washington, attended in full dress and powder.

He made a quick journey back to the Potomac and arrived there on May 22d with not a feather out of place, to find his house full of company. Jacky was there with his schoolmaster, Boucher, as well as his former tutor Walter Magowan in the new dignity of his clericals and a good living in Maryland; Mrs. Bushrod—John Augustine's mother-in-law—and Mrs. Warner Washington, the former Hannah Fairfax; and a couple of stray neighbors anxious to hear the latest news from Williamsburg. Once it was told and discussed, the talk could drift comfortably on to the racing at Cameron nearby, and an impending barbecue at Alexandria.

Communications were so slow that everyone settled back to the summer hiatus, knowing that the King's next move would not be known until the autumn Assembly time. The wheat was doing well this year and was remarkably free from rust. Bryan Fairfax had another son and everyone went up to Towelston for the christening, where Washington stood godfather for the name Ferdinando. Mopsey had puppies again. There was the usual exchange of dinners with the Belvoir Fairfaxes and the Maryland Diggeses. The doctor and the music-master made their routine visits. Milly Posey rode with Martha and Patsy round the harvest fields, doubtless on a horse supplied by Mount Vernon. Brother Charles arrived in July with his little son George Augustine, who was to play a daily part in his uncle George's later life.

Returning from a day on the bench at the Alexandria court, Washington was accompanied by that laconic character "Squier" Lee, Richard of Lee Hall, who sat as Burgess for nineteen years in almost total silence. Most of the Lee spark and crackle resided in his uncle Thomas's Stratford line, a mile or so away, until it shone brightest of all in his nephew Harry. Richard was one of the in-between Lees, still a bachelor at forty-three, but at the ripe age of sixty he was to marry his young cousin Sally Poythress—they had the same grandfather—and father three daughters, the last of whom was named, in desperation, Richarda.

An otherwise happy summer at Mount Vernon was overhung by the dark cloud of Patsy's growing affliction. In July, when the harvest was mostly in, the Washingtons set out for their second visit to the Berkeley Springs in Frederick County, where everyone in poor health seemed to go sooner or later, often as a last resort. They had spent August of '67 there, in a cottage rented from the Mercers—George Mercer had been with Washington on the frontier and had accompanied him on the Boston tour—and while still primitive by Tidewater standards, living conditions were now much improved over what George had found in '61. Again this year they had the use of the Mercer cottage, and carried with them their own cook from Mount Vernon, along with other servants, and their own wine. A butcher and baker and blacksmith were resident at the Springs these days, and there were plenty of eggs and vegetables to be had.

With many last minute things on his mind, Washington in his systematic way made a list headed *Packing Memorandum*:

Blew Coat
Buff Vest and Breeches
1 pair Nankeen Breeches
Old riding Ditto
2 White Vests
1 Worked Nankn Ditto
3 pair drawers
9 shirts
9 stocks
5 White Handkerchfs
5 Silk "
1 Pair Boot Stockings
2 pair Shoe "
Shoes, Slippers, Buckles
Dressing gown, Razors, &ca &ca

The above is besides what I have on.

On the way they spent a night at Warner Washington's Fairfield, the plan of which was similar to Betty Lewis's Millbank at Fredericksburg, with a wide staircase flaring up the right-hand wall just inside the front door, and a large parlor at the back, across a spacious entrance hall. The grey stone house was two full stories high, and stood among fine trees on a knoll above the Shenandoah River, facing the Blue Ridge hills. Everything about it was still rather new, but box trees and a terraced garden were being planted, and beautiful mantel-pieces gave a finish to rooms still without their ornamental plaster-work.

Washington's wagon-horses got loose and caused a day's delay at Fairfield, as he could not with his womenfolk proceed a step without his luggage and servants. They all reached the Springs at midday on August 9th—ninety miles from Mount Vernon as the crow flies, but much farther by the road. George William Fairfax was already there, after a visit to his Lordship at Greenway Court nearby, and they gratefully accepted his invitation to dine with him at his own quarters that afternoon.

The next day Washington rode out personally to select the pasturage for his horses, which were sent there in charge of the coachman. Martha meanwhile had made her arrangements for supplies of food from the local people, and had found the cottage fallen into some disrepair since their last stay in it. Washington ordered an outside arbor built, which served as both dining-room and parlor on fine days. It was surprising, the amount of discomfort and inconvenience people were willing to endure out of a forlorn-hope faith in the insipid, lukewarm, weakly mineral waters, which had been known even to the Indians, and were now dispensed in dripping goblets by an attendant—goblets which went from hand to mouth through a variety of complaints with only a rinsing in the basin of the spring between customers.

There was of course a certain society to be found there—but indisposed neighbors and acquaintances were mingled indiscriminately with invalid strangers suffering from any disease under the sun, and a depressing assemblage of cripples, many of them old habitués, shabby and ill-housed. The Washingtons had their own circle which included the male Fairfaxes, the grown sons of Fielding Lewis and Warner Washington by their first wives, the Crawford brothers from out Bullskin way, some old comrades at arms from the frontier days, the inevitable clergymen, and a sprinkling of new names. They made an excursion picnic to the Mountain, to see the silver thread of the upper Potomac gleaming far below. They went to church, and dined out, and entertained guests to dinner. And then there would be a day when Washington made the stoic entry in his Diary: "Dined alone—Patsy unwell."

By mid-September they were at home again, none the better or the worse for the effort, in time for the election—which saw every single one of the Burgesses of the dissolved Assembly returned for the next session. While the Court was sitting at Alexandria Washington paid 4s.6d. "to see slight of hand performd." He was building a small frame house in the town, on a little eminence at the corner of Pitt and Cameron Streets, for the accommodation of the family during elections, courts, and social occasions. He and Martha became much attached to it, and made themselves more comfortable there than they had ever been at the tavern or as guests in the homes of their Alexandria friends. The only two letters from George to Martha which she allowed to survive were written from Philadelphia in June of '75, to convey to his wife at Mount Vernon the news of his appointment as Commander-in-chief and his departure northward to Boston without returning home to say Good-bye. At that time he thought of the little house in Alexandria, and suggested that she might prefer to live there while he was away—like other wars since then, the Revolution was supposed to be all over by Christmas—perhaps with an idea that she might feel less lonely and more in touch with events in a busy post town than on a Potomac plantation. But except for the time she spent with him at winter Headquarters each year, and a visit to Eltham, Martha never left the place he loved best, even when British raiding parties were in the River and there was a general alarm that they might intend the capture of the American General's wife.

The autumn exchange of dinners and calls and hunting parties in the Potomac neighborhood was resumed—"Catchd a Rakoon, but never found a Fox."—until interrupted by the opening of the Assembly session in November, '69. It promised to be a lively time in the capital, and Martha and Patsy were going with him to consult a Williamsburg doctor. Jacky somehow contrived to escape from school and add himself to the party for an unscheduled holiday. They travelled in the new green coach, which was making its first appearance in Williamsburg, and reached Leesylvania, near Dumfries, the first day in time for a late dinner with Colonel Henry Lee. It was a modest Lee house compared to Stratford and Chantilly, but it had a delightful mistress, who had been Lucy Grymes, and there were four little boys, the oldest of whom, called Harry, was just Patsy's age.

They spent two days at Fredericksburg, breakfasting with George's mother at the Ferry Farm and dining with the Lewises across the river at Millbank. Washington left the family at Eltham and continued to Williamsburg, where the first night he dined with Lord Botetourt and the new Governor of Maryland, Mr. Eden, among others, in an atmosphere of great cordiality.

To everyone's surprise, on the opening of the General Assembly Governor Botetourt's speech ignored the recent dissolution and announced that Parliament was now prepared to remove most of the unpopular Townshend duties in the interests of commerce—except the tax on tea. Delivered with a lot of personal charm and polished words, it sounded very well—but very little afterthought was needed to see that the principle of taxation, the *right* of Parliament to tax the colonies, had been obstinately maintained.

The specious tranquillity produced by the conciliatory shift in the Ministerial position, and Botetourt's professional tact, made it a very gay season in Williamsburg, with everyone pretending that the crisis was well past. Washington's Diary after Martha and the children joined him there is a cheerful chronicle of social events in which young Jacky Custis had now begun to take a part as Washington's own son might have done, and without doubt his stepfather felt real pride in the handsome, well-dressed boy.

"*22.* [*November.*] Dined at Mrs. Dawson's all of us. I and J.P. Custis suppd at Mrs. Campbell's.
"*23.* Dind with Mrs. Washington &ca. at the Speaker's by Candlelight and spent the Evg. there also.
"*24.* J.P. Custis and I dind with others at the Govr's. I spent the Evening at Haye's. [the Raleigh Tavern] ......
"*1.* [*December*] Dind at Mrs. Campbell's with the Speaker, Treasurer, and other Company. Mrs. Washington and Childn. Dined at the Attorney's. Myself and J.P. Custis supped at Mrs. Campbell's.
"*17.* Dined at the Palace and went up in the Afternoon to Colonel Bassett's."

They left Williamsburg, perhaps by design, before the Burgesses' ball for the Governor, at which the patriotic wives of the members had pledged themselves to wear homespun gowns instead of their best silks and laces, to demonstrate their willingness to forego imported luxuries in aid of the tussle over taxation. It had probably been planned that way before the Assembly convened, and must have seemed a little excessive now in view of the amiable compromise speech delivered by the Governor. In any case, Martha took no part in it, and by the 23d of December the Washingtons were again at Millbank in Fredericksburg, where they spent Christmas Day. Doubtless Mrs. Washington, Senior, was fetched over the River to join the family, and Washington entered in his accounts that he gave her £6.

On the last day of December he wrote with an almost audible satisfaction, "At Home all day." Winding up his year, he found his bookkeeping a little out, which almost always happened, no matter how he tried to jot things down. Philosophically he wrote in the Ledger, "By Cash lost, Stolen, or paid away without charging, £143.15.2," and closed the book. It was the best year Mount Vernon had had yet in point of accomplishment and future prospects.

He was definitely through with tobacco as a crop, and intended to rely henceforth on his wheat—which had increased its yield six times over in five years. He was going to build a new mill and grind his own fine flour for export. The fishing showed a small profit, above what had been salted down for home consumption. The weaving-house would never really pay, consuming as it did the time of one white woman and five Negroes, but if they were ever reduced to using all American cloth for clothes it would suffice for their needs. He had acquired a new blacksmith, a Dutchman with the name of Domenicus Gubner, who after probation at 3s. a day settled in at a yearly wage of £32, "he to be found when at work here, and to have the Plantatn. on which John Crook lived (to settle his Family at) and work in anything he pleases, Rent free."

When next George went to Williamsburg, for the spring session of 1770, there had been a riot in Boston, and British troops had fired into a crowd of civilians on the Common, killing three of them. The wind was blowing cold from the North.

XII

IN the winter of 1770 Washington engaged a millwright, John Ball, to build a new mill on Dogue Run to replace the one so laboriously repaired ten years before, and this project occupied his daily interest, along with the fox-hunting. Frequent entries in the Diary trace the growth of the mill from its earliest stages, which brought out the well-worn surveyor's tools which Washington had used since his teens.

"*February 2d.* Agreed with Joseph Goart [a stone-cutter] to come and raise Stone of my Quarry for my Mill at the Rate of Three pounds pr. Month, 26 days to the Month, and lost time to be made up. . . . .
"*March 19.* Went to the Mill with Jno. Ball to take the Level of the Run on the other side; did not get home till Night. . . . . .
"*March 22.* Rid to the Mill and laid off with the Millwright the foundation for the new Mill House. . . . . .
"*April 19.* The Masons began to Dig the foundation of my Mill at 2/6 pr day. . . . .
"*April 30.* The Doctr. [Rumney] stayed till after dinner and then returned to Alexandria. I rid to the Mill and my usual rounds before dinner, and to the Mill after dinner. . . . . .
"*May 2.* The Mason's went to laying Stone in the walls of the water Pit (dry stone) . . . .
"*May 3.* Thomas Emmerson set into ditchg. on my Mill Race on the same terms as above, that is, 1/3 pr. Rod, and finding himself. . . .
"*May 17.* 10 hands at work [on the Mill race] to day. The House frame and Mill beam were put up to day. Began to raise Scaffolds for the Masons this day. . . . . .

"*May 18.* Mr. Ball and his People went into the Woods again to get Scantling to carry on his work, there not being sufft. for that purpose. . . ."

On the 19th of May, with what reluctance, he left the fascinating new toy and set out for the Assembly at Williamsburg. It was not until December of that year that he was able to write: "Began to grind Sand in my Mill, the Water being let in upon the Fore Bay. . . ."

Returning to February of 1770 when the mill work was begun, on the 22d there was apparently a birthday gathering at Mount Vernon, almost the only indication ever found of any such observance. He arrived home from Court at Alexandria as usual to find his brothers John Augustine and Sam, and cousin Lawrence of Chotank, with various female belongings, awaiting him, as well as the Chotank neighborhood clergyman, who often joined the fishing parties along that shore. A whole week's holiday ensued, when Washington did little but enjoy his visitors' company—"At home all day," he wrote, and "Ditto—ditto," though they went fox-hunting, and gunning for ducks, and of course visited the mill. The brief diversion over, his usual routine was resumed.

In March Colonel Mason rode in from Gunston accompanied by the new dancing-master, Mr. Christian, perhaps to secure the Mount Vernon children as pupils in the classes which were to be held in rotation at the big houses of the Northern Neck, the first meeting to take place at Gunston. Patsy attended, with Milly Posey as her companion in case she felt shy, and Washington paid—£2 for both. A fortnight later the dancing-school met at Mount Vernon, and again in July and in September. It must have been a delightful occasion, as the children were brought in from miles around, and the accompanying grown-ups stayed to dinner and had dancing of their own when the lessons were over.

Three years later when the New Jersey tutor Mr. Fithian had taken up his duties at Robert Carter's Nomini Hall in Westmoreland County near Bushfield (where the school also met) he described in his diary several sessions of Mr. Christian's dancing school:

"After Breakfast, we all retired into the Dancing-Room, & after the Scholars had their Lesson singly round Mr. Christian [he] very politely requested me to step a minuet; I excused myself however, but signified my peculiar pleasure in the Accuracy of their performance— There were several Minuets danced with great ease and propriety; after which the whole company Joined in country-dances, and it was indeed beautiful to admiration, to see such a number of young persons, set off by dress to the best Advantage, moving easily to the sound of well performed Music, and with perfect regularity, tho' apparently in the utmost Disorder— The Dancing continued til two, we dined at half after three—soon after Dinner we repaired to the Dancing-Room again; I observe in the course of the lessons, that Mr. Christian is punctual, and rigid in his discipline, so strict indeed that he struck two of the young Misses for a fault in the course of their performance, even in the presence of the Mother of one of them! And he rebuked one of the young Fellows so highly as to tell him he must alter his manner, which he had observed through the Course of the Dance, to be insolent, and wanton, or absent himself from the School— I thought this a sharp reproof to a young Gentleman of seventeen, before a large number of Ladies!— When it grew too dark to dance, the young Gentlemen walked over to my Room, we conversed till half after six. . . . . .

"When the candles were lighted we all repaired, for the last time, into the Dancing-Room; first each couple danced a Minuet; then all joined as before in the country Dances, these continued till half after Seven, when Mr. Christian retired; and at the proposal of several (with Mr. Carters approbation) we played *Button,* to get Pauns for redemption; here I could join with them, and indeed it was carried on with sprightliness and Decency; in the course of redeeming my Pauns, I had several Kisses of the Ladies! . . . . ."

Again somewhat to everyone's surprise the May Assembly, which Washington attended without his family, passed off uneventfully, except for the rising concern caused by what was now called the "Boston Massacre" in the past spring—the total dead being three —and the realization that the non-importation attempt had failed of its desired effect on English commerce. By the end of June he was home again, after the usual Fredericksburg visits on the way.

The removal of Boucher's school from the Caroline County countryside to Annapolis presented new complications as the summer waned. The ambitious and amusing clergyman had secured the living of St. Anne's, which made him chaplain to the Maryland lower House and launched him in a political and social environment where his gift of telling a story and quoting an apt tag brought him to the notice of the easygoing and hospitable Governor Eden.

Perhaps stimulated by his new environment, Boucher conceived the idea that Jacky's education required a trip abroad and a leisurely tour of the Continent (conducted of course by his schoolmaster as companion) and painted a dark picture of Jacky's character as it was then developing: "The chief failings of his Character are that He is constitutionally somewhat too warm, indolent, & voluptuous. As yet these propensities are but in Embrio; Ere long, however, They will discover themselves, & if not duly and carefully regulated, it is Easy to see to what They will lead. At best He will soon lose all Relish for mental Excellence– He will unwillingly apply to any Improvements either in Arts or Sciences– Sunk in unmanly Sloth, his Estate will be left to ye Managemt. of some worthless Overseer; & Himself soon be entangled in some matrimonial Adventure, in wch. as Passion will have much to say, it is not very likely that Reason will be much listened to. I appeal to You, Sir, if this Acct. be exaggerated, & if it be not sadly verified by many living Instances yt. have fallen under yr. own Observation. . . . . ."

While the European project was coolly received and finally vetoed by Washington, out of it arose the discussion of Jacky's inoculation for small-pox, pursued by Boucher in his usual flood of wordage. Washington felt that an inoculation was a precaution which should be taken whether Jacky travelled abroad or not, in preparation for his entry into the world as a young man. Martha agreed in principle, but added to her anxiety over Patsy's health the small risk involved in the inoculation of her son seemed almost too much to be borne. Washington's correspondence with Boucher at this time shows his unfailing concern for her peace of mind, and at the same time his firmness for the welfare of her children.

In the end, by kind connivance between Jacky's schoolmaster and his step-father it was kept from his mother until all danger was past, and Boucher wrote that the inoculation had left hardly a mark to tell that Jacky had ever had it and the boy was as well as he ever was in his life—"indeed, he has such strong Symptoms of Health as we almost find inconvenient at this scarce Season of the Year, and dear Markets." Jacky had a growing boy's appetite.

The Assembly was not sitting that spring, with the taxation question in temporary abeyance, and the trip to Williamsburg had been undertaken mainly in the interests of Patsy's health and the business affairs of the York River plantations of the Custis estate. With his mind at rest about Jacky, Washington gave his attention to Patsy. A consultation with the new doctor resulted in another prescription for her malady, and some touching items in the expense account:

May 7.	By Mr. Prentis for a piece of silk	£7.0.0
	By 4 boxes of fitt drops pr. Mr. J. Carter	1.5.0
May 8.	By 1 Blewstrand Necklace	3.9
May 11.	By curls from Geo. Lefong	?
	By a song book, the Bullfinch	6.6
	By a parrot bought for her	1.16.0

He had his own usual Williamsburg good time—visiting the Bassetts and the plantations on York River, dining with the Randolphs, the Dandridge brothers, and at the taverns, and going to the play. He seldom entered in his Diary the names of the plays he saw, though he does mention *The Recruiting Officer*, which he had witnessed at Colchester in the spring during a sojourn there at the Court with his friend Colonel Mason of Gunston, and which must have amused him particularly with its broad military humor and the improbable masquerade of its spirited heroine in her brother's clothes.

David Douglass's famous American Company was playing in '71 at Williamsburg, which with Philadelphia and New York was one of the few towns in the colonies which owned a real theater. Douglass had married the beautiful widow of Lewis Hallam, who had died in Jamaica when both companies were touring there, and Douglass then combined the two companies under his competent management, including Lewis Hallam, Jr., and his wife and sister Sarah, who later retired from the stage and established a finishing school for young ladies at Williamsburg. Along with many plays now forgotten, the Washingtons must have enjoyed at this time Gay's enchanting musical melodrama, *The Beggar's Opera*, and gone away humming

"How happy could I be with either, Were t'other dear charmer away!"

Moreover, Washington made himself a present. Governor Botetourt having died the previous autumn, his spectacular cream-white Hanoverian chariot horses had come up for sale. By selling four of his own and trading two more, Washington seems to have acquired six of Botetourt's animals, and he drove them home via John Augustine's Bushfield and Robert Carter's Nomini Hall nearby, where he paused to inspect Mr. Carter's mill. As Philip Fithian had not yet arrived to tutor the little Carters, no account of Washington's visit remains beyond the brief entry in his Diary. The homeward journey was broken again at Wakefield to call on Austin's widow and her married daughter, and at Lawrence of Chotank's—"a good deal of company dining there," says the Diary, so doubtless the new Hanoverian horses and green chariot were duly admired.

In September, '71, the Diary opens a new chapter in Washington's social life.

"*21.* Set out with Mr. Wormeley for the Annapolis Races. Dind at Mr. William Digge's and lodgd at Mr. Ignatius Digges.
"*22.* Dind at Mr. Sam Galloway's and lodged with Mr. Boucher in Annapolis.
"*24.* Dined with the Govr. [Eden] and went to the Play and Ball afterwards."

All the Wormeleys of Rosegill on the lower Rappahannock were named Ralph, beginning with the one who had arrived in America in 1649, and the family rivalled the Carters in splendor and influence. The lawns of Rosegill stretched for some thirty acres above the river, and there were thirty guest-rooms in the house, besides an attic chamber with fourteen beds for bachelors. The dining-room was panelled in mahogany, the immense library in oak, and there was a double stair. It was probably the fifth Ralph, though his father was still very much alive, who went racing and playgoing with Washington, who was twelve years his senior. A younger Wormeley brother, John, turned Tory and rode with Simcoe's Loyalists, but was restored to American citizenship at the end of the war.

From now on, Annapolis where Jacky had accompanied Mr. Boucher's school began to rival Williamsburg and Alexandria as an attraction for Washington's holidays. His Maryland friendships already included the Diggeses of Warburton Hall, a handsome mansion at the mouth of Piscataway Creek, and as it now became a convenient stop on the way to Annapolis a closer association resulted. The house stood directly opposite Mount Vernon, so that communications were carried on by light or flag signals from shore to shore. At the start of a journey Washington often sent his horses and chariot over the River the day before, and followed the next morning in his barge, with liveried slaves to row it, to get an early start.

His neighborhood now expanded to include the Galloways of Tulip Hill, a fine brick house commanding a view of the Chesapeake, with terraced gardens falling away to the eastward, a wainscoted library with window-seats, and a double arched stairway with wide, easy risers because Mrs. Galloway was an invalid; and in fact she died almost before she could enjoy the house which was built for her. She left two spirited children—a son who rode his horse up the staircase to his bedroom after a gay evening in town, leaving the print of its shoe in the mahogany tread—and a pretty daughter who was at this time infatuated with Jacky Custis. Mr. Galloway was a wealthy Quaker who owned a racing stable, and there seems to be little justification for the suspicion of fortune-hunting which marks a letter to Washington from Mr. Boucher on the attachment.

And, as it proved, it was not Miss Galloway who ensnared Jacky and his fortune, but a daughter of Benedict Calvert of Mount Airy in Maryland, who did not enter the picture till the following year; while Washington seems by no means to have avoided the Galloways as a result of Boucher's allegations.

Robert Eden was the last and best-loved of Maryland's Royal Governors, a handsome, lively man, so extravagant as to be always in debt, which troubled him not at all. His wife was a sister of the sixth Lord Baltimore, and their house in Annapolis was the scene of lavish dinners and balls. Eden was never a good politician, and his sympathies veered openly to the side of the colonies as the breach with England widened. By some quirk in his character he cultivated the ineffable Boucher, perhaps as a sort of court jester.

Annapolis was an old town, older than Baltimore—and according to Boucher "the genteelest town in North America"—and it kept its traditions green with some of the best racing, theatrical performances, and Assembly balls to be found anywhere in the colonies. The autumn of '71 saw the opening of its new theater. The famous Homony Club, of which Boucher was the current President, held its larkish meetings at the Coffee House, where Washington on this first visit dined with its distinguished membership. The sole object of the club was "to promote innocent mirth and ingenious humor," and its members were bound to contribute verse or prose to its proceedings, which were recorded in fat folios by the Secretary. His Annapolis visits must have been an illuminating experience for the rather serious-minded master of Mount Vernon. Jacky was given £8 to spend at the race-track.

It was not long after his return to Mount Vernon that Washington set off again, this time with his womenfolk, for Williamsburg, where the new Governor, Lord Dunmore, had now arrived amid the usual speculation and curiosity. As Dunmore's first act was to dissolve the Assembly, necessitating a new election, there were fewer demands on Washington's time in the capital and he was able to indulge his growing weakness for the theater by going to the play four days running. He dined as usual with Speaker Randolph, with the Council and the Governor, and formed who knows what estimate of the choleric, domineering Earl who four years later was to see the end of the King's rule in Virginia.

XIII

THE year 1772 opened with the worst weather on his record. "At home all day alone–that is with the Family," he wrote on January 26th, for in a house given over to such continuous hospitality as Mount Vernon was required to dispense, days without any guests at all seemed to him as good as solitary. On the 27th–"At home by ourselves, the day being dreadfully bad." On the 28th –"Just such a day as the former and at home alone." On the 29th–"With much difficulty rid as far as the Mill, the Snow being up to the breast of a Tall Horse everywhere." On the 30th–"At home all day, it being almost impracticable to get out." And on the last day of the month–"Still at home for the Causes above."

February brought no improvement. On the 1st he attempted to ride as far as the Ferry Plantation, but "found it so tiresome and disagreeable" that he turned back half way. A week later he had begun to get bored– "At home all day."– "Ditto–ditto." On the 11th, he went out to do some surveying and "was much fatigued by the deepness and toughness of the snow." On the 17th, he managed to get to the Mill "to see a Negro Man sick of the pleurisy." On the 22d they were back to normal, with guests from Alexandria, who doubtless drank his health and wished him many happy returns. He had turned forty.

Boucher's account for the year and a half of Jacky's school charges in Annapolis had got through before the snows came. "Undoubtedly, it makes a formidable Appearance, and at first View may go nigh to Scare You," the clergyman had written, perhaps a little scared himself. "I cannot, however, believe that when You come to descend to Particulars, You will think it very extravagant, unless it be in the Article of Clothes, which He got by your Permission. . . ."

Washington had a month of bad weather to go over the charges, and took occasion to point out some errors, and some unexplained extravagances, but it was not until the 21st of February that he was able to send off his reply: "Little did I expect when I was writing the Inclosed Letter, in order to dispatch it to you the next Morning, that the Communication between this, My Mill, and the Plantations round about me would be shut up for ten or twelve days, by the deepest Snow which I suppose the oldest Man living ever remembers to have seen in this Country. I embrace this, as the first day the Boat cou'd pass in safety, of sending Bishop over to you with the Money...... I purpose to set off for Williamsburg on Monday next, though I expect to find dreadful Roads (at least between this and Fredericksburg)......."

Boucher's explanations and apologies and elaborations ran to several pages, leading off with one of his most amusing flights of fancy: "I congratulate You, & the World with Us, on our Restoration to a temperate Zone," he wrote, "for in Truth we have had a kind of Greenland Winter. And for my own Part, I own to You, I now have a much stronger Idea of the Nature of a Winter pass'd in a Cave, than I could ever have learn'd from Books alone. I sometimes almost regretted, We could not become quite torpid & sleep out the whole dreary Season, as snakes and some other Animals are said to do: or that as, like Bears, We were shut up in our Dens, We could not, like Them also, live without Fire, & by sucking our Paws; for I had some Cause to imagine, if the Weather had held much longer, We should have had some Temptation to try......"

The abnormal snow was followed by heavy rains, which flooded Accotink Creek and forced Washington to turn back on his first attempt to reach Williamsburg for the spring Assembly. On March 1st, accompanied by Martha and Patsy, he arrived at Eltham, and the next day in Williamsburg he dined with Peyton Randolph and supped with Robert Nicholas. On the 3d, he both dined and supped with Governor Dunmore. The social surface still held firm.

While in Williamsburg he paid a surgeon dentist £4—probably for extractions, as his lifelong dental woes gained on him—and Patsy's doctor's bill was £14. But they attended a concert and the theater, and when they set out for Mount Vernon they were accompanied by the Bassetts with their three little girls. As usual, they found the house full of company when they arrived, and during the rest of the month Washington had Burwell Bassett's companionship on his rounds to the fishing landing, the mill, and the Alexandria court, and the ladies joined them for church.

It had been an unimportant session of the Assembly, and led to another delusively quiet interlude at Mount Vernon. In May Jacky arrived with Charles Willson Peale, an Annapolis saddle-maker who had studied painting in Boston under Copley and in London with Benjamin West, whence he had recently returned to become the fashion in his native Maryland and in Philadelphia, where he found wealthy sitters aplenty. A boyish, soft-mannered man of thirty, with unpowdered hair and a nice taste in dress, he had married young and acquired a small family, along with several influential patrons. He brought to Mount Vernon, besides Jacky's ardent admiration, a letter from Mr. Boucher, expressing confidence that Colonel Washington would require portraits of all his family from Peale's talented brush.

Apart from the unexpected expense, which was not welcome, Washington had no inclination to spare the time himself to sit to an artist, though miniatures of Martha and the children had an obvious appeal, to which he at once succumbed. He was apparently overruled on his own account, as the May 20th entry in his Diary indicates: "I sat to have my picture drawn." And his letter to Boucher the following day fills in the story: "Inclination having yielded to Importunity, I am now contrary to all expectations under the hands of Mr. Peale; but in so grave—so sullen a mood—and now and then under the influence of Morpheus, when some critical strokes are making, that I fancy the skill of this Gentleman's pencil will be put to it in describing to the World what manner of man I am. I have no doubt of Mr. Peale's meeting with very good Incouragement in a Tour to Williamsburg; for having mentioned him to some Gentlemen at our Court, they seem desirous of employing him on his way down. . . . . ."

The picture turned out to be a three-quarters length oil portrait of some size, for which he wore his Virginia militia colonel's uniform—blue with red facings and gold lace, diagonal purple sash, gorget, and sword, with the three-cornered cocked "Wolfe" hat. It was hung up on the wall of the parlor, and cost him £18.4.0, besides three miniatures at £13 each. The expression of the unexpectedly youthful face is neither sleepy nor sullen, though in some of his later portraits boredom is certainly visible, however hard the artist may have tried to paint it out.

Young Mr. Peale thoroughly enjoyed his visit to Mount Vernon and left his own record of its leisure moments:

"One afternoon, several young gentlemen, visitors at Mount Vernon, and myself were engaged in pitching the bar, one of the athletic sports common in those times, when suddenly the Colonel appeared among us. He requested to be shown the pegs that marked the bounds of our effort; then, smiling, and without putting off his coat, held out his hand for the missile. No sooner did the heavy iron bar feel the grasp of his mighty hand than it lost the power of gravitation, and whizzed through the air, striking the ground far, very far, beyond our utmost limits. We were indeed amazed, as we stood around all stripped to the buff, with shirtsleeves rolled up, and having thought ourselves very clever fellows, while the Colonel on retiring, pleasantly observed, 'When you beat my pitch, young gentlemen, I'll try again.'. . . ."

This rare instance of Washington's showing off deserves preservation, though his strength became a legend in the army a few years later, where it was noticed that he lifted single-handed the field marquee rolled around its poles and tossed it into the vehicle which awaited it—a task which normally bent the backs of two men.

1772 was a happy year at Mount Vernon, the best for a long time to come. Little family excursions were made to neighborhood dinners, to Alexandria to see a new store, to witness a ship-launching, or to attend some balls, which Patsy was well enough to enjoy. The Washington brothers made their usual visits accompanied by their wives and children; George rode out to his western lands; Lord Fairfax came down to Belvoir and was duly entertained. New names appeared in the Diary, among the regulars. Mrs. Cox, the seamstress, came to stay in the house, making and altering gowns for Martha and Patsy, at a cost of over £12. Jacky was in and out, spreading his particular brand of sunshine and anxiety.

In July Washington penned an exasperated letter to a London milliner which was obviously dictated, as it was signed, by Martha:

"Madam: I can't help writing to you in behalf of my daughter, Miss Custis, who together with myself, Imported some very hard bargains from you last year. Messrs' Cary & Co. was wrote to for a handsome Suit of Brussells Lace to Cost £20; in conseq. of w'ch, she recd. from you a pr. of triple Ruffles, a Tucker, and Ruff set on plain join'g Nett (such as can be bought in the Milliners Shops here at 3/6 pr. yard.) When, if you had even sent a Tippet and Cap with the other things I sh'd have thot. them Dear. These things have been shewn to sev. Ladies who are accustomd to such kind of Import'ns, and all agree that they are most extravagantly high chargd.

"I now send for a Suit at the price of £40; wth. Lappets &ca., but if you can't afford to sell a much better bargain in these than you did in the last I sh'd hope that Mr. Cary will try elsewhere, as I think her Cust'm added to my own is worth a little pains. Am'g the other things sent last y'r for myself &ca. were 5 Gauze Caps w' Blond Lace bord'rs at a Guinea each, when the same kind might have been bo't in the Country at a much less price. I have now sent for 2 Caps for Miss Custis, and 2 for myself of Min't Lace and w'd have them genteel but not expensive; hers to Suit a Person of 16 yrs old, mine one of 40, and I can't help add'g that I think it neces'y that the last y'rs Suit (w'ch ought to be ret'd if she c'd do without it in the meanwhile) sh'd be complet'd with a Tippet and Cap as it is scarce more than 1/2 a Suit without."

Washington too still had his troubles with carelessly filled orders, the wheat riddles being useless, as he had required them "made open enough to let everything smaller than the broken heads of Wheat and Straw through—in Short to have had the Wire 5/8th of an Inch apart, and thought my directions on this head would have been expressive enough of my meaning to have obtaind my desire..."

The ineffectual non-importation agreement having been mostly dropped, except in the matter of tea, which had been banished from patriotic colonial tables until its tax was removed, the invoice which accompanied the complaint about the wheat riddles was on an unusually large scale, and included such items as:

"1 piece of best India Paduasoy, of a fine Mazarine blew
A White Sattin quilted Coat, £3
A piece of fine and well fancied India Chintz of the bordered kind
2 handsome Caps of Minionet Lace, one to wear in dress, the other with a Nightgown
4 handkerchfs of Jackanot Muslin with borders to them
15 yards of fash'ble ribbon, difft; sorts
a Blew Sattin Bonnet
20/ worth of Paste and Garnet Pins for the hair
A Small neat gold Seal proper for a Lady's Watch
white kid Mitts, purple ditto, white silk gloves, white kid gloves, and mitts ditto
1 pr. Toed Clogs, to be made by Shoe sent (having Martha Washington wrote therein) by Gresham at the Crown in Covent Garden, who is desired to keep the Shoe by him to save the trouble of send'g a Measure Ev'ry yr
8 Damask Table Cloths, 10/4 long and abt. 7/4 wide at abt. 25/ each
30 lbs. best Jordan Almonds
4 lbs. White Ginger
1 1/2 dozn. pr. strong Dog Couples, with Rings, Swivels, and straps
2 dozn. prs. large Chinese great Ivory Table Knives and Forks to suit those sent last year by Thos. Squire and charged at 36/ a dozn.
4 Hair House Brooms
4 Neat and fash'ble Cut glass Decanters w' broad bott'm, that they may stand firm on the table
6 neat and fash'ble Cut glass Beer Glasses to suit ditto
2 1/2 doz'n. ditto Wine ditto to suit ditto, to be rather low, and strong, as well as neat
1 pr. of best Buck Breeches pr. Measure sent last year to J. Coleman, to have a side Pocket, and a Buckle behind
A Gentleman's hunt'g Cap, covered with black Velvet, to fit a pretty large head, cushioned round or stuffed to make it sit easy there on, a Silk Band, and handsome Silv'r Buckle to it
1 pr. of Silv'r Spurs of the new'r Fashion

1 Neat and Fash'ble Silver Pencil Case
1 doz'n spare Pencils for ditto, some of them red, some black, and pretty hard, at least not too soft
1 best whole hunting Whip, pretty stout and strong, cap'd with Silver and my name and the y'r engravd thereon
30 yards of yard wide Floor Matting
1 Doz'n large Breakfast Tea Cups and 1 Doz'n Saucers, with 8 Coffee Cups and 8 Saucers
Also 1 doz'n smaller Tea Cups and the like number of saucers together with 8 Coffee Cups and Saucers to them, with a Tea Pot, Milk Pot, Sugar Dish, and slop Bowl to each Set, the whole to be of the same kind of China, of a fash'ble but not of a costly sort. . . . ."

So the embargo on tea was not expected to last, or the Mount Vernon stock was adequate for a while to come. A growing prosperity is reflected in the items—he had sold 273 barrels of his flour to the West Indies, and the fishing and wheat harvest were increasing under his watchful eye.

Besides the re-order on the lace gown for Patsy, some of her other requirements were: "A handsome Suit of Tambour Worked Muslin; A Tambour Frame to Work Muslin in with proper needles and Thread; A Black Silk Apron; A String of Amber Beads; A Guinea's worth of Hair Pins set with Paste and Garnett; a pair of Fash'ble and handsome Garnett Shoe Buckles; 1 Small Silver Thimble with a steel top; A Powder Box and Puff; 2 pieces of fine cordid Dimoty; A handsme. Fan at a Guinea; 2 pr of fashe. Silk Shoes with Shapes, one of gold, the other of Silver; the Ladys Magazine. . . . ."

Patsy was growing up.

Washington's order for several suits of clothes of different weights, and Jacky's, were almost duplicates, and included "a Waistcoat of Superfine Scarlet Cloth with a Neat light gold Embroidery (if Embroidery is in the Fashion, if not then to have a gold Lace on it.)"

There was a flurry of excitement during the summer over the marriage of Mr. Boucher to Eleanor Addison of Oxon Hill in Maryland. The courtship had been open and eventful, and could hardly have escaped the notice of Jacky Custis before he arrived at Mount Vernon in June, bursting with the latest developments in a story which in all its teapot drama is exposed, if not flaunted, in Boucher's own *Reminiscences*. The bride was the elder of two sisters, spinsters in years, fatherless nieces of Henry Addison who had two sons at Boucher's school. She had been courted unsuccessfully by that Dr. Rumney of Alexandria who was retained on a yearly fee by Washington to attend the plantation people at Mount Vernon, and Boucher after a reprehensible involvement with his housekeeper, during his sister's absence on a visit to England, had been refused by one of the Miss Fitzhughs, who was later discovered to be subject to fits, so that he was able to congratulate himself on a lucky escape there. Then one day he happened to accompany Mr. Addison to Oxon Hill, where a rather Gothic episode occurred which is best conveyed in Mr. Boucher's own unfettered prose:

"About a year before she saw me at Oxon Hill, she had had a remarkable dream, in which she fancied she saw the man to whom she was afterwards to be married. And the dream made so strong an impression on her that she related it to her mother and sister, and described the person. What made this the more extraordinary, was that at this time she was courted by a Dr. Rumney, whom she then thought of marrying, and whom she would have married had she not reason afterwards to think very differently of him.

"When I went there with Mr. Addison, the servants through a mistake had told them that I was Mr. Brooks, a clergyman who was their relation. Miss Addison came out, expecting to see her uncle, only and Mr. Brooks. But on seeing me she started, and was with difficulty kept from fainting. When, without her having been able to speak a word to us, she was carried back to her mother and sister, 'Good God,' she said, as soon as she could speak, 'Yonder is the man I dreamed of that I was to marry!'

"Of this story, which is literally and strictly true, all the remark I have to make is, that its being extraordinary and unaccountable is no argument against its reality. On her coming into company again the blame of what had happened so oddly was laid on a bat that was said suddenly to have flown across her face. At that time her attachments were to another person, as mine also were. I knew nothing of her dream; it was years before I saw her again; and when I resolved to pay my addresses to her it was much opposed both by her uncle and her mother; and had she not possessed an uncommonly independent mind it is certain we never could have come together. Mr. Addison's true objection was that he wished her to marry a near and opulent relation of his wife's who had long courted her; and Mrs. Addison wished her (merely through a false tenderness and want of resolution to part with her) not to marry at all. . . . . ."

Mr. Boucher had only just settled into a new house in the center of his Maryland parish when the deep snowfall of '72 which isolated Mount Vernon brought his courtship plans to a standstill for three weeks. But he was now so situated that he felt he had something worth while to offer a young woman of Miss Addison's station and as was suitable he first disclosed his intentions to her uncle, who attempted to discourage him.

"I then wrote to the lady herself, apprising her of my wishes and my pretensions. This letter, I afterwards learned, she immediately shewed to her mother who on seeing it instantly burst into tears, saying, 'I know, Nelly, you will have Mr. Boucher.' Her reply was, 'I think so myself; yet never him, nor anybody else, with out your consent and approbation.'

"Her conduct to me when I first waited on her was equally frank, honest, and generous. I told her with the most perfect unreserve, as well as I could, everything that made against as well as for me. And she was won, though not unwooed, yet with such a generous contempt of all the little idle tricks of teasing, too common on such occasions, as greatly endeared the conquest to me. Four or five months now passed in courtship and preparations, by far the happiest of my life. Her mother was soon reconciled; and I have the great comfort to reflect that she often declared, and repeated it almost in her last moments, how resigned and happy she was to leave her daughters under my care.

"And here before I come to that happy day which made me the happiest of men, I wish to draw something like a character of a woman to whom I owe not only the chief happiness I have ever enjoyed in this world, but to whom also I owe almost all my hopes of happiness in the world to come. . . . .

"At the time I married her she was just turned of thirty-three years of age, as I was of thirty-four. She was of middling stature, and her person was genteel. She had been exquisitely handsome, but a long series of ill health had much impaired her beauty; yet her eyes still retained an uncommon degree of animation and lustre. Her hair was jet black, and her complexion somewhat of the brunette. With a constitution naturally good, she had long been sickly; and this entirely owing to the ingenious mismanagement of a Dr. Brooks, a relation of her family; a man of worth and abilities but too apt to speculate, and in his practice to indulge in ingenious whims. Her fortune in money was two thousand pounds currency, which together with sundry slaves, etc. I used to estimate in all at twenty-five hundred sterling. And at the time of our marriage, besides my Preferment, I was worth about one thousand pounds. . . . ."

Governor Eden and his wife came to the wedding, which took place at the home of the bride on a very hot day, and she settled down to help her sister-in-law with the school housekeeping. It was, according to Boucher, a singularly happy marriage, although after an early miscarriage his wife relapsed into permanent invalidism. When his violent and tactless Tory sentiments forced his departure from America to England in '75, she had the courage to uproot and go with him. Boucher secured a good living at Epsom, where his wife died ten years later, and he married twice again. From the time that Washington assumed the leadership of the colonial army, all Boucher's professed admiration turned to spleen and bitterness, and he never thereafter ceased to disparage the man whom he had so long flooded with sycophantic esteem.

But in this golden autumn of 1772 there were few signs of the tempest to come, and the usual September visit to Annapolis cast no shadow ahead, though the new portent was there in the Diary, for anyone with second sight:

"*4.* Set out with Mrs. Washington and Miss Custis (attended by Mr. Custis) on a visit to Mr. Boucher &ca. Breakfasted at Mr. Wm. Digges's (the Horses and Carriage being got over the day before) and dined at Mr. Boucher's with Governor Eden and Mr. Calvert, and his two Daughters. . . . . .

"*7.* Dined at Mr. Calvert's (going with the Govr. in his Phaeton and calling at Mr. Sprig's.) Mr. Igns. Digges and Family dind there also. We lodgd, they retd.

"*8.* At Mr. Calvert's all day and night. The Govr. returned to Annapolis this morning.

"*9.* Mr. Boucher, who came to this place with us, returned home early this morning. We dined at Mr. Ign. Digges with a good deal of Company, among whom Mr. Calvert's Daughters, he himself going to Annapolis.

"*10.* At Mr. Digges's all day. The Miss Calverts came, and returned in the Afternoon......

"*11.* Returnd home by way of Mr. William Digges's, where we Dind and where my Boats met us ...."

Mr. Calvert's daughters, Nelly and Betsy, only two out of his handsome brood of ten children, were introduced to Jacky's family so casually, in a swirl of carriages and dinner-parties and new acquaintances that even Martha's doting eyes apparently failed to detect Jacky's romantic attachment to Miss Nelly. Six months later the Washingtons could look back on that Maryland holiday in dismay and incredulity. If only they had noticed—and what could they have done, while there was still time....

Meanwhile at Fredericksburg it had been necessary to take his mother's affairs in hand. After consultation with the Lewises, Washington had bought two lots in the town, only a garden away from Betty's Millbank, including a simple frame house in which he made alterations and improvements, and some time during the summer Betty got her moved across the River into the new home.

So relaxed was the general atmosphere of 1772 that Jacky was allowed to escape again from his studies in Annapolis to accompany the family to Williamsburg in late October, perhaps because the overseer of the York River plantations had died, and it was proper that the heir and prospective owner should make the acquaintance of the new man already installed. There was to be no autumn session of the Assembly, but Washington was still engaged on behalf of the soldiers' bounty lands in the West—a settlement would add materially to his own acreage there as well—and Patsy was well enough to enjoy a holiday.

This year they attended a ball in the Apollo Room at the Raleigh

Tavern, lodged in Williamsburg with the widowed Mrs. Ambler (who had been Mary Cary in the old days at Belvoir), took Patsy to see the waxworks and the puppet show, and bought her a new music book and two bottles of Norris's Drops, in the endless search for a remedy for fits. On the way home they spent several days at Fredericksburg with the Lewises, which cost Washington £15 as a gift to his mother in her new home, and stopped again at Leesylvania —young Harry Lee was now a student at Princeton.

It was a mild winter, compared to the ferocious snows of last year. During December, when the hunting was good, there is mention in the Diary of Mr. John Fitzhugh of Marmion as a guest at Mount Vernon—son of William, Washington's friend, whose courtship of John's mother must have caused laughter of one kind or another all along the Potomac. The widow Anne Rousby had been still young enough to hesitate over a second marriage, at least long enough to look about her, and she had a baby daughter. William Fitzhugh was a widower, and apparently an impatient man. In the course of what had become a heated argument between them during one of his visits to her at Rousby Hall on the Patuxent, he snatched the infant girl from the arms of her nurse and holding her over the waters of the river declared his intention of dropping her in if her mother did not at once consent to marry him. There is no indication of whether Anne gave way in terror or in anger or with indulgent amusement at a monumental bluff, but she did surrender, to become the mistress of Marmion, one of the most beautiful houses in the Northern Neck. It overlooked the Potomac in King George County, its elaborate carved woodwork and the pilastered black walnut panelling of its elegant drawing-room coming as a surprise after the informal white weather-board of its exterior.

The Christmas season was uneventful at Mount Vernon—the last they were to have together as a complete family, and one lingers over minutiae as the time runs out. Washington relatives and old friends like Dr. Rumney, Mr. Magowan, and the Fairfaxes made their usual visits, besides the Bouchers who all three came to dinner, and assorted Diggeses, Dulanys, and other Marylanders. Martha and Patsy went with him to Williamsburg for the spring Assembly of 1773, which again produced no fireworks in the transatlantic deadlock, and it was not until after their return home late in March that things began to go to pieces.

XIV

WASHINGTON had felt an increasing dissatisfaction with Jacky's schooling, for as Mr. Boucher's social and political ambitions increased, his attention to the discipline and instruction of his few remaining pupils diminished. The choice of a higher institution such as Princeton or William and Mary College had been discussed at some length in his correspondence with Washington. He was against Princeton, as being tainted with the new colonial ideas of resistance to the home government in England—though young Harry Lee and two of Fielding Lewis's sons were there. William and Mary College was believed to be in a general decline of standards under mismanagement since Thomas Jefferson's student days. King's College in New York seemed on the whole the most desirable, and its President was known to be a zealous supporter of the King's rule in America.

Perhaps because he got rattled by the prospect of a northern exile subject to increased restraint, or perhaps as a natural result of his habitual irresponsible behavior, Jacky at this point suddenly announced that he and Nelly Calvert considered themselves engaged to be married, and that he had finished going to school. He was just eighteen, she was not yet sixteen.

The news exploded at Mount Vernon with shattering effect, apparently during a visit Jacky made there when the house was full of hunting guests at the end of March. Washington sat down at once and wrote a long, severe letter to Mr. Calvert, suggesting that in view of Jacky's youthful instability it would be as well if he went to college before the marriage took place. Mr. Calvert replied with ill-concealed satisfaction that a match with the Custis fortune was "much superior to the sanguine hopes which a parents fondness may have at any time encouraged me to indulge—" and pointed out that Jacky's circumstances made his wife's dowry a secondary consideration, which was lucky, as from the largeness of his family Calvert would not be able to provide a very substantial portion for Nelly. And Boucher wrote to Washington in exclamatory astonishment that such a thing had happened (under his very nose) and maintained that he had been under the impression anyhow that it was Miss Betsy Calvert, and not Nelly, that Jacky had always favored, though not of course seriously, and that he had not advised Washington of the affair, as on previous occasions he had seen fit to do, simply because he had been unaware of it—and added the philosophic reflection that marriage to such an amiable young woman would be sufficient advantage to Jacky's morals to compensate for the damage to his intellectual pursuits.

It was an easy conclusion to come to. But Nelly's lack of dowry was not the only drawback Washington saw to the alliance, though it was true that the accident of her father's birth—he was the illegitimate but acknowledged son of the fifth Lord Baltimore—had never told against him in Maryland. He had been provided with a suitable post as Collector of Customs and member of the Council, and had even married the daughter of Governor Charles Calvert, who was his cousin in the legitimate line. His family was well-reared and handsome. His house, called Mount Airy, was nothing like the Virginia mansion of the same name belonging to the Tayloe family, but it was a rambling, comfortable hodge-podge, with a columned entrance and an artificial lake. Even Martha, whose weakness was always that Jacky must have whatever he wanted whether it was good for him or not, must have felt a secret qualm that he might have done much better than Nelly Calvert. But it was too late, without an undignified situation, to do anything but accept his choice and invite the Calverts into the Mount Vernon circle as graciously as though nothing could have pleased his family more. This was done, with the understanding that the marriage would at least not take place until after Jacky had attended King's College where he was already enrolled.

At the end of April Washington was writing to Burwell Bassett, who had recently lost his eldest daughter Betsy at fifteen:

"That we sympathize in the misfortune, and lament the decree which has deprived you of so dutiful a child, and the world of so promising a young lady, stands in no need, I hope, of argument to prove; but the ways of Providence being inscrutable, and the justice of it not to be scanned by the shallow eye of humanity, nor to be counteracted by the utmost efforts of human power or wisdom, resignation, and as far as the strength of our reason and religion can carry us, a cheerful acquiescence to the Divine Will, is what we are to aim; . . . . .

"Mrs. Washington, in her letter to Mrs. Bassett, informs her of Jack Custis's engagement with Nelly Calvert, second daughter of Benedict Calvert, Esq., of Maryland. I shall say nothing further therefore on the subject than that I could have wished he had postponed entering into that engagement till his studies were finished. Not that I have any objection to the match, as she is a girl of exceeding good character; but because I fear, as he has discovered much fickleness already, that he may either change, and therefore injure the young lady; or that it may precipitate him into a marriage before, I am certain, he has ever bestowed a serious thought of the consequences; by which means his education is interrupted and he perhaps wishing to be at liberty again before he is fairly embarked on those important duties. . . ."

Jacky was firmly escorted to New York by his step-father, who renewed acquaintance along the way with old friends in Philadelphia, where hospitality overflowed, and made some new ones. In New York he was in time to join the farewell ceremonies for General Gage, an old frontier comrade who was now the departing Commander-in-chief of the British forces in America. He had a satisfactory interview with President Cooper of the College, saw Jacky comfortably installed, with a parlor and two bedrooms for himself and his Negro body-servant, and the privilege of keeping two horses and dining with the faculty—deposited £100 sterling against the cost, and returned home by the fastest possible route.

Only a few days later Nelly Calvert arrived at Mount Vernon with a friend for a visit, to become better acquainted with her future in-laws, and while she was still there John Augustine Washington drove in with his wife Hannah and one of their children, perhaps to inspect Jacky's fiancée. On the 19th of June, after what would have been one of the most harrowing days of his life so far, Washington wrote two lines in the Diary: "At home all day. About five o'clock poor Patsy Custis Died suddenly."

The letter which he wrote to Burwell and Nancy Bassett, so recently bereft of a daughter about the same age, told the story: "She rose from Dinner about four o'clock in better health and spirits than she appeared to have been in for some time; soon after which she was seized with one of usual Fits, and expired in it, in less than two minutes without her uttering a word, a groan, or scarce a sigh. This sudden and unexpected blow, I scarce need add, has almost reduced my poor Wife to the lowest ebb of Misery; which is encreas'd by the absence of her son (whom I have just fixed at the College in New York from whence I returned the 8th Inst) and want of the balmy consolation of her Relations. . . ."

The result was inevitable. Before the year was out Jacky would be back at Mount Vernon, his higher education at an end.

Everything was done for Patsy correctly, and with dispatch, in the midst of devastating grief. Besides the young visitors from Maryland, and the Bushfield Washingtons, the Fairfaxes came over from Belvoir to attend the funeral, which was conducted the following day by the Reverend Lee Massey, of the new Pohick Church. Massey was a beloved lifelong friend of Washington and George Mason, and it was at their request at the time of the venerable Mr. Green's death in '68 that Massey had relinquished his Alexandria law practice and gone to England to be ordained, so that he could take charge of the parish of his neighbors. Tall, learned, compassionate, with remarkable deep blue eyes and a rich speaking voice, Massey by his mere presence would have brought comfort and support in a time of need like this.

The clothes for first mourning were ordered sent by post from Williamsburg. The second mourning came from London by a July invoice which required for Martha: "A Black Silk Sacque and Coat prop'r for Second Mourning; a suit of fash'e Linnen to wear with it (containg. 2 Caps); a White Silk Bonnet; 8 pr. Women's White kid Mitts, to fit a small hand and a pretty large Arm; . . . . 1 Handsome Fan, prop'r for Second Mourning; . . . . 1/2 Ream best large Folio Pap'r Mourning; . . . . ." For Washington: "A genteel Suit of

Second Mourning, such as is worn by Gentlemen of taste, not those who are for running into the extreme of every fashion," and "a genteel Mourning Sword, with Belt, Swivels, etc."

The letter of condolence written by Fielding Lewis from Fredericksburg shows that Patsy's condition had been recognized as hopeless before the event: "Poor Patsy's death must have distressed Mrs. Washington very much, but when she considers the unhappy situation she was in and the little probability of ever getting well, she must conclude that it's better as it is, as there was little appearance of her ever being able to enjoy life with any satisfaction......"

It was the first death in the Mount Vernon household since Lawrence's twenty years before. But death had struck at Gunston nearby, carrying off George Mason's lovely red-haired Anne after a long illness with a slow fever which Dr. Craik, who prescribed a "weak milk punch" to be taken in bed every morning before rising, had been powerless to arrest. Mason was left a widower after twenty-three years of marriage, with nine children, the oldest a boy of twenty, the youngest only three. He himself was not yet fifty, and his loss produced in him "a settled melancholy from which I never expect or desire to recover."

The same son John who wrote of his father's cherry-tree avenue was only seven years old at the time of his mother's death, but he left a loving account of her household arrangements and her own chamber:

"There stood, among other things, a large old chest of drawers so-called, which held the children's clothes, to which, little fellow as I was, I was often carried to get something, or would run there to rummage in it without leave. The lower tier consisted of three drawers.... [illegible]..... Next above, and the whole length of the case was the cap drawer, next above that, a deep one also and of the whole length, was the gown drawer. Next above that was the shirt drawer, and next to that the jacket drawer. Then above all came the drawers, each of half length, which were kept locked. They were devoted to my mother's more private use and for matters of greater value. The other drawers were always unlocked and each was devoted to the purpose its name designated, and by that name it was known and used by all the family.

"There were also two large, deep closets, one on each side of the deep recess afforded by a spacious stack of chimneys. The one on the right of the chimney contained the current part of my mother's wardrobe and was called her closet, or, as the case might be by children or servants, 'mama's closet' or 'mistress's closet.' The other, on the left, was emphatically designated *the* closet. It held the smaller or more precious stores for the table, and would now, I suppose, be called an upper pantry. I can't forget one of the articles deposited in my mother's closet. It was a small green horsewhip, with a silver head and ring by which it was hung there against one of the walls, and which my mother used to carry when she rode on horseback, as she often did when in health. This little instrument was applied sometimes to other purposes as discipline required among the children, and we used to call it 'the green doctor.' "

Sixteen at her marriage, Anne Mason was dead at thirty-nine. "I remember well her funeral," John Mason further recorded, "that the whole family went into deep mourning suddenly prepared, that I was led clothed in black to her grave, that I saw her coffin lowered down into it by cords covered with black cloth, and that there was a large assemblage of friends and neighbors of every class and of the slaves of the estate present; that the house was in a state of desolation for a good while, that the children and servants passed each other in tears and silence, or spoke in whispers, and that my father for some days paced the rooms, or from the house to the grave (it was not far) alone." Although his health was always bad, Mason outlived his wife for some twenty years, and married again in 1780.

Nelly Calvert and her sister Betsy were encouraged to become a part of the Mount Vernon family, and accompanied Martha to church, to Alexandria, and on rides around the farms as the harvest began. Their youthful spirits and companionship helped to sustain the Washingtons through another grave change in the accustomed daily round, when the Fairfaxes again sailed for England in July.

The affairs of George William's English inheritance were still tangled, and both he and Sally were in failing health at a comparatively early age—George William was already a martyr to rheumatism and gout, and Sally was often confined to her bed with an obscure disability which they hoped English physicians could cure. On the 8th they dined for the last time at Mount Vernon, and the next day the Washingtons went to Belvoir to see them take shipping there. George was charged with the rental of Belvoir to a suitable tenant during their absence.

Uncertain as the times were, and relentless as were the years, they probably parted in the brave conviction that it was only for a year or two, as it had been in the '60's—and that George William and Sally would return, as they had done before, even though everyone was ten years older now. It was mercifully hidden from them all on that summer day that the ship in which the Fairfaxes sailed would pass as it neared England other ships bound for Boston harbor with a cargo of tea—and that before English remedies could work, or English courts could rule on George William's business, the pace of colonial resistance to Ministerial tyranny would have quickened on a downhill slide into war. The Fairfaxes would never come home to Belvoir again.

XV

IN their effort to go on as usual in the emptiness caused by Patsy's death and the echoes at Belvoir, the Washingtons kept up the neighborhood and Maryland visits and the Mount Vernon hospitality throughout the summer of '73. Sam and his current wife, the fourth, and two children came to dinner; Charles spent several days of brotherly companionship in October; and Washington attended the Annapolis races, the theater, and the balls. Jacky Custis joined him there on leave from the New York college, and they returned to Mount Vernon together—Washington having lost £3.16 "By Cards and Racing," and doubtless not regretting a penny of it.

Jacky had been shocked and sobered by his sister's death, and had clothed both himself and his Negro boy in New York mourning. His inheritance had been enlarged by some £8,000, and the other half of Patsy's portion, being Martha's, came into Washington's possession. Some of it went at once to clear up outstanding indebtedness to his London agents and to back up large new orders for materials to be used in improvements at Mount Vernon. New bricks, scantling, and shingles were ordered locally by the thousands, and he wrote to London for window glass, paint and oil, lead and hardware. His knowledge of tools and materials was extensive, as demonstrated by a letter to an English maker of scythes:

"Sir: Please to make me a dozen Scythes for Cradling Grain exactly as follows—viz.

"All of them to be exactly three feet 10 Inches in the Cut; pretty straight in the Back for the greater ease in delivering the Grain out of the Cradle; all to have the same bend, the Plate, or Rim at the back to be short and strong; otherwise in the rough and stumpy ground we often use them in, they are constantly breaking; and the blade where it joins this Rim at the Back, to be of good substance altho the Scythe is made the heavier by it. The whole to be well tempered, that is, not so hard as to be always gapping, nor yet so soft as not to keep an edge; to have Nibs, Rings, and Wedges. Robt. Cary Esqr. & Company will pay you the cost and I am, etc . . ."

Jacky was still at Mount Vernon when the time came to set out for Williamsburg, where the veterans' bounty lands were still an unsettled issue. He would soon come of age, and it was time he was further acquainted with his responsibilities on the York River plantations, so he won another stay from college to accompany his family. Perhaps at his own instigation, or with Martha's connivance, it was also arranged for Nelly Calvert to go along in Patsy's place.

They spent the first night at Colonel Blackburn's Rippon Lodge on Neabsco Bay near Dumfries—one of the little Blackburn daughters would grow up to be the wife of John Augustine Washington's son Bushrod, himself at present ten years old—and proceeded via Fredericksburg to Eltham, where everyone but Washington remained while he went on alone to Williamsburg. Martha's sister Nancy Bassett had only four surviving children; the youngest, called Fanny, was now six years old and a particular favorite of her aunt's. During the following week they visited Martha's brother, "Bat" Dandridge, and his family of five, and then Washington took Jack on a tour of visits to the James River mansions, beginning with magnificent Westover, a long brick house facing on a wide green lawn which sloped to the very edge of the placid River, shaded by mighty tulip poplars.

Westover was owned by William Byrd III, who had served on the frontier with Washington in the '50's, had married as his second wife Mary Willing of Philadelphia, and was raising a family of beautiful daughters. Byrd had a weakness for gambling and race horses, and kept a fine stable. His shaky financial condition, which led to his suicide in '77, was not apparent in the superb rooms of the house. It was this William's lovely half-sister Evelyn Byrd who had been prevented by her tyrannical father, William II, from marrying the man of her choice during a visit to England, when at the age of eighteen she was presented at the Court of George I. The King himself, not notable for chivalry, had made a rather Hanoverian jest about the beautiful Byrds produced by his American colonies. Evelyn was the sensation of the 1725 Season in London, and had her portrait painted by Kneller. Her father, who kept a daily diary and was a crank about his food, astonished the Town as a civilized grandee from the transatlantic wilderness, and refused Evelyn's hand to the son of an English peer, perhaps because the suitor was a Catholic. He hurried her back to Westover, where for the next ten years she steadfastly declined every offer of marriage. "Either our young fellows are not smart eno' for her or she seems too smart for them," he reported cynically to an English correspondent. She died at Westover, "a disconsolate spinster," before she was thirty, and her father, having got his way at a stiff price, made amends with a handsome tomb near the river. It was said that the rustle of her taffeta skirts could still be heard on the staircase, though by '73 she had been in her grave more than thirty years.

From Westover Washington and Jack, accompanied by Bassett and Byrd, rode up the river to Benjamin Harrison's Berkeley, another fine brick house which stood high above the shore and was famous for its interior woodwork, hand-tooled and painted chalk white against tinted plaster walls. Berkeley had a long central hall with an elliptical arch midway, fluted and pilastered, and on the second landing of the staircase was the only musicians' gallery in Virginia. The present owner, the fifth Benjamin, was a few years Washington's senior, and had come into his magnificent inheritance at eighteen. He was a large, candid, Falstaffian man of great dignity, who nevertheless loved a joke and preferred it broad, and bought his liquor by the gallon. He had married Burwell Bassett's elder sister Elizabeth, which made him in a fashion kin to Martha Washington, and his own sister was the wife of Peyton Randolph. In the still unforeseen future, which was now only three years away, he would attend the Congress in Philadelphia, where his convivial ways and gamy humor annoyed John Adams of Boston. There was a story that Harrison was so unimpressed by his Philadelphia surroundings that he offered a guinea for every handsome face to be seen there if anyone else would give a copper for every face that was not comely. He signed the document to be known as the Declaration of Independence, and was twice governor of Virginia in the '80's. He joined the opposition to the Constitution in '88, although once it was adopted he gave it loyal support.

Washington's visit to Berkeley included an inspection of the mill. Being so near, they then went on to Shirley, the next house above, which had passed into the possession of the Carter family by the marriage of its heiress Elizabeth Hill to a son of "King" Carter of Corotoman. It was now the property of their son Charles, who had married his cousin Mary Carter of Cleve. His infant daughter Anne, whose earliest cries may have been audible to her father's guests that day, would at the age of twenty become the second wife of Harry Lee of Leesylvania—to her father's distress, for the spectacular "Lighthorse Harry" of the Revolution, seventeen years older than his infatuated bride, had then begun his long decline into debt and tragedy, which was to overshadow the childhood of their son Robert E. Lee.

Shirley was in many ways the most beautiful house in Virginia. A unique two-story columned portico painted white rose against the red brick of its outer walls, with a dormered third story above. From the drive on the garden side one entered a spacious hall in which the famous "flying staircase" soared without visible support to the third floor, in carved walnut. All the interior woodwork was remarkable, and its recurring motif was the pineapple, symbol of welcome to guests. Shirley remains intact today, in the possession of the ninth generation of Carters, and has never been on the market.

It was young Nelly Calvert's first visit to Williamsburg, and Jack was given up to £20 to do the honors of the capital for his fiancée, who lodged with Martha at Charlton's Tavern in the town. They did not reach Mount Vernon again till December 9th, and on the 15th Washington acknowledged defeat in a letter to President Cooper at King's College: ". . . . . and at length I have yielded, contrary to my judgment, and much against my wishes, to his quitting College; in order that he may enter soon into a new scene of Life, which I think he would be much fitter for some years hence, than now; but having his own inclination, the desires of his mother, and the acquiescence of almost all his relatives, to encounter, I did not care, as he is the last of the family, to push my opposition too far; and therefore have submitted to a Kind of necessity. . . . . ."

The furniture of Jack's rooms in New York was sold at auction and his clothes and belongings were packed up for him and sent home. A tailor's bill of £58.3.10 1/2 came to light during the settlement of his New York accounts. He had been in residence there only from June till October. "Graham's Bill is an *heavy* one; but You know best what Articles You had of him," Dr. Cooper wrote to Jack when he mailed the statements. "I always heard him reckoned a Dear Fellow—as I once told you;—whether he is *honest* or not, is another Question; But it is certain he is a violent Presbyterian."

When Washington sent money to President Cooper for a final settlement, early in '74, the whole New York affair still rankled. He enclosed a draft for £65 to "discharge the several claims which you have taken the trouble to collect, against Mr. Custis; whose residence at King's College I little expected would have been of such short duration; otherwise, I shou'd not (as his Guardian) have thought myself justifyed in incurring so great an expense," he wrote. ".... However, as his discontinuance at it is an act of his own, and much against my judgment, he can only blame me (if he blames at all) for yielding too easily to his importunities, supported by the concurrence of his relations....."

This year when Washington came to balance his books he was again some £144 short. His charities during the year had included a loan to the white man Davis who oversaw the weaving-house, to pay for the passage of his mother and sister from England—a sum which was never returned; a contribution to the schooling of his old friend Craik's son; and a substantial payment to keep the sheriff off Captain Posey, who was about to disappear from the neighborhood, so far as the record goes.

The news of another Boston crisis during the past December had no place in the Diary as 1774 opened—some Massachusetts hotheads disguised as Indians had dumped a cargo of tea into Boston harbor in protest over the tax. But besides the usual hunting and family guests, Jacky's marriage was uppermost at Mount Vernon. The wedding took place at Mount Airy in Maryland early in February, and Washington attended with Lund, though Martha in her recent sorrow for Patsy and her mourning clothes remained at home with Nancy Carlyle down from Alexandria for company—one of the two daughters of the late Sarah Fairfax Carlyle, now grown to companionable young womanhood. A month later Jack made his first visit to Mount Vernon as a married man, accompanied by his wife and her parents, and a large party came from Alexandria to dinner to meet them. In April the Bassetts made a long visit with their little Fanny and Billy, and again there was a great deal of company.

On the 1st of May the Washingtons were "at home all day—alone." On the 2d, he wrote: "Rid in the forenoon with Mrs. Washington to Belvoir." Perhaps it was something to do with the rental of the house, which did not take place till later in the year. But it must have been a sad occasion for both of them, with the new year coming into bloom, and the once welcoming house closed and empty.

The May Assembly at Williamsburg found itself confronted by repercussions to the action at Boston harbor. Both Parliament and public opinion in England had reacted with a violence which took the colonies by surprise. The port of Boston was ordered closed to all shipping until the tea was paid for and the town had expressed its submission to the King and his revenue officers—or until Boston starved. Boston rallied angrily and called on its sister colonies for support. Quite suddenly the air of Williamsburg was crisp with alarm.

Washington had travelled down with Martha as usual, with leisurely stop-overs at Fredericksburg and Eltham. He arrived at Williamsburg on the 16th and dined with Governor Dunmore the same evening, when the Boston Port Bill was still only a rumor. But on the 24th the Assembly, where Patrick Henry and Thomas Jefferson held the floor, passed a resolution—which was read by Treasurer Nicholas in his grave, measured tones—setting the 1st of June as a day of fasting and prayer in sympathy with Boston, and "to implore the divine interposition, for averting the heavy calamity which threatens destruction to our civil rights and the evils of civil war. . . . ." The next day in the middle of their afternoon business the Burgesses received notice from the Governor that they were dissolved.

They had expected that, of course, but not so soon. Most of them had been members in '69, when after dissolution by Governor Botetourt they had simply reassembled at the Raleigh Tavern and voted on George Mason's non-importation resolutions. Now, almost exactly five years later, they returned to the Apollo Room at the Tavern and voted approval of proposals by Richard Henry Lee which called for a meeting of deputies from all the colonies "to consider means of stopping exports and of securing the constitutional rights of America." An attack on one of the colonies was to be regarded by the rest as an attack on all thirteen. For the first time Virginia, who had no British troops on her soil and whose ports were so far unmolested, stood up shoulder to shoulder with New England where the trouble was.

But it was still a very remote trouble, and Virginia good manners were such that Washington was able to dine at the Palace, wearing powder and his blue and scarlet militia uniform, on the very evening after the dissolution, and to ride round the Governor's farm with him the following morning. The night after that most of the dismissed Burgesses attended a subscription ball given by the members of the Assembly for the Governor's wife, lately arrived with his family from New York. On Sunday, however, which was the 1st of June: "Went to Church and fasted all day," the Diary reads simply.

George Mason was no longer a member of the House, but private business had taken him to Williamsburg just at this critical time, where his presence was much appreciated by the men at the helm. He wrote to Martin Cockburn of Springfield, who with Mrs. Cockburn acted as guardian of the little Masons during their father's absence from home:

"At the request of the gentlemen concerned, I have spent an evening with them upon the subject, where I had an opportunity of conversing with Mr. Henry, and knowing his sentiments; as well as hearing him speak in the House since, on different occasions. He is by far the most powerful Speaker I ever heard. Every word he says not only engages but commands the attention; and your passions are no longer your own when he addresses them....

"Mr. Massie [the minister at Fairfax] will receive a copy of the resolve from Col. Washington; and, should a day of prayer and fasting be appointed in our county, please to tell my dear little family that I charge them to pay a strict attention to it, and that I desire my three eldest sons and my two eldest daughters may attend church in mourning, if they have it, and I believe they have.

"I begin to grow heartily tired of this town, and hope to be able to leave it some time next week, but of this I can't yet be certain. I beg to be tenderly remembered to my children, and am, etc., etc. . . . . ."

The dissolution of course required another election, and Mason again declined the most urgent requests, including one from Washington, to stand for election in the place of Washington's present colleague who had decided not to serve again.

Bryan Fairfax also refused to offer himself at the polls, as his convictions were largely on the side of the King, and certainly were against any such open defiance as Massachusetts was exhibiting. Washington's reply to a lengthy appeal from Bryan recommending conciliation and petition instead of the dangerous course indicated by Patrick Henry, shows the trend of thought behind the considered reticence of the master of Mount Vernon: "What hope then from petitioning, when they tell us that now or never is the time to fix the matter? Shall we, after this, whine and cry for relief when we have already tried it in vain? Or shall we supinely sit and see one province after another fall a prey to despotism? . . . . ."

When he arrived home at the end of June Washington was already committed to return to Williamsburg to an August 1st convention of the Burgesses, meeting without the Governor's blessing, to determine Virginia's future course and choose the delegates to the proposed Congress of representatives from all the colonies.

Meanwhile a general meeting and election had been called for July 18th at Alexandria, and George Mason had consented to draw up another of his eloquent, closely reasoned resolutions as a guide to Virginia's future action. He brought it to Mount Vernon on the 17th, and spent the night, and on the 18th Washington carried it to Alexandria, where it became the famous Fairfax Resolves, forerunner of the Declaration of Independence, which was not yet even a gleam in Thomas Jefferson's eye. At this meeting Washington was again elected Burgess, along with a Major Broadwater who had served with him on the frontier, but of whom, compared to Mason and his kind, he had no very high opinion. "Staid all Night to a Ball," the Diary remarks.

On the 28th Washington took the road from Mount Vernon southward again, to attend the convention at Williamsburg. This time he was accompanied by Jacky Custis, who was there with Nelly on a visit, and whose curiosity over political affairs was awakened by the grave faces and closed doors and late conferences he found at his once uneventful home.

They were away less than a fortnight. But in that short time Washington's life reached a crossroads and turned a corner, and his destiny began. He was chosen one of seven delegates to represent Virginia at the Congress which was to meet in Philadelphia on September 5th, along with Richard Henry Lee, Patrick Henry, Richard Bland, Benjamin Harrison, and Edmund Pendleton–and Peyton Randolph, the Speaker. Amongst them all, Washington was the only soldier. Amongst the men from all the other colonies, he would be the colonel from Virginia, who had ridden with Braddock, encountered Indians and French troops in combat, who was initiated in matters of drill and discipline and commissary, who had already heard the whine of bullets and the clash of arms. And he was young –forty-two–and born to the saddle. When at Philadelphia in the days to come they would recognize their need of a man to lead an army, there he sat, one of them, yet apart from them by the hard experience of his frontier youth.

Without doubt he felt already the rising pressure of events, but most of what was to come of that Williamsburg fortnight had still never crossed his mind as he went methodically about his interrupted Mount Vernon affairs during that summer of '74. The conventions were a nuisance, in that they took him away from home, and consumed time which he wanted for other things. But it would not have occurred to him to shut himself away from his growing responsibilities as George Mason did at Gunston. Washington had no such good reasons as Mason–his house had a capable mistress, he had no children, and his health was good. Moreover, his conviction that the colonies had a cause to defend was growing daily.

Belvoir had been advertised for rental, and it was Washington's melancholy duty to attend the sale of its contents, held to clear the house for its new tenant, a clergyman named Morton. George

William's gift to the Washingtons of the Blue Room furniture suite and his orders to sell the rest of the house's contents made plain that his return to Virginia was indefinitely postponed if not entirely relinquished. Riding over on the 15th of August with Jack Custis and Dr. Craik and some other gentlemen from Alexandria, Washington bid in a number of items outside the Blue Room—including a mahogany shaving-desk at £4; an oval looking-glass with a gilt frame from the Green Room at £4.5.0; twelve mahogany chairs and three crimson window curtains from the dining-room, £31; two candlesticks and a bust of Shakespeare, £1.6.0; a mahogany spider-leg tea-table, £11.11.0; two mahogany card tables, £4; carpets and bedding, and in what was probably a mixed lot, a Japan bread-tray, bellows, tongs, and a toasting-fork. Perhaps it was some form of comfort at Mount Vernon to give safe-keeping to the abandoned belongings which had known and served the Fairfaxes in happier days. Besides, there would soon be room for more furniture at Mount Vernon when his long-planned additions to the house took form, as they were now about to do.

Even with Patsy gone and Jack married, the house overflowed, and there was insufficient privacy for its master—as with Jack's marriage came more visits from the Calverts and their Maryland friends as well as the Virginia regulars and relatives. It was Washington's intention to build an addition at each end, containing on the south a ground-floor library with a little private stair leading up to a bedchamber above it for his and Martha's use; and on the north a handsome two-story reception or banquet room for entertaining his many guests. A master joiner named Lanphier had been engaged to carry out the work, beginning with the south end first, and he was now laying out the library, which would be ready to raise before the year was out. When the house was being rebuilt in '58 Washington had been away with Forbes on the campaign which took Fort Duquesne, and George William Fairfax was left to do the daily supervision and make the daily decisions which are so essential even with capable workmen. Now that he was at last able to embark on his cherished design for enlarging the house again, there were these tiresome committees and conventions demanding his presence, so that much of the responsibility—and the fun—of directing the work must be left to Lund.

On the 30th of August Colonel Pendleton, Patrick Henry, and George Mason arrived at Mount Vernon, as had been arranged at Williamsburg earlier that month, and the candles burned late at night—so late that Mason slept there, returning home in the morning when the other three rode north towards Philadelphia. It would not be Washington's way to cast a lingering look behind him at the home he loved so much, but he may have envied Mason, even his gout and his motherless children, which bound him snugly to Gunston while other, less handicapped men strove to carry out the ideas which flowed so clearly and easily from Mason's pen. In any case, none of them was yet aware that this Philadelphia meeting was the thin end of the wedge, and that now there would be no turning back, for anyone.

XVI

HE was exactly two months at Philadelphia. And then it seemed as though not much had been accomplished—non-importation again, non-consumption of tea and other taxed articles—a long address to the King—so inconclusive a session, in fact, that it adjourned committed to meet again at the same place the following May.

Peyton Randolph had been the outstanding Virginian at the Congress, and had presided in the chair, before hurrying back to resume as Speaker of the Assembly at Williamsburg. Washington had made no speeches and attracted no particular notice, beyond his height and military carriage. He brought back presents—a pocketbook for Martha, a bed with furnishings, a riding-chair for his mother, (£40) a sword-chain and watch-key. The neighborhood came in to dine and hear the story.

He appraised the progress made by Lanphier on the library addition and found it wanting, rode to the mill as usual, went to church at Pohick and brought back guests to dinner—soon it was almost as though he had not been away from home at all, except that in the interval Virginia had changed. The young men were forming companies for drill, buying uniforms, drums and colors, demanding arms. Even George Mason, after presiding at the establishment of the Fairfax County Independent Company of Volunteers, had acquired its uniform—a blue coat, "turned up with buff, with plain yellow metal buttons, buff waistcoat and breeches, and white stockings.... a good flintlock and bayonet, slung cartouche box and tomahawk"—and it is probable that Washington adopted the same at about this time, which may have established what came to be recognized as the Continental colors.

Once he had been Commander-in-chief of the Virginia forces, and they appeared to expect him to serve again, if it came to that. Reviewing the alternatives, even Washington's modesty could not find a likely rival candidate for the post. William Byrd's sympathies were Loyalist, and he was known to be tragically in debt. Men like Patrick Henry, however fiery on the floor of the Congress, had had no experience whatever in the field. There was, of course, that raffish character who called himself a general of the British Army, and professed sympathy with the colonies and a desire to serve their cause—Charles Lee, of no blood connection with any Virginia Lees, though he was buying land in Berkeley County and intended to live there, a bachelor, with a troupe of ill-trained, pampered dogs. After hanging around the Congress at Philadelphia, he turned up at Mount Vernon at the end of December in the company of one of Washington's more eccentric neighbors, Mr. Ballendine of Occoquan, remained over the New Year, and borrowed £15 of his host before he left. It was the beginning of a long, unhappy acquaintance which came to a spectacular climax on the battlefield at Monmouth in '78, and ended in court martial for Lee.

Meanwhile the house swarmed with young people, as Jack's and Nelly's friends joined them on their frequent visits to what Jack still called home. Nelly's sister Betsy Calvert usually accompanied them from Mount Airy, and there were numerous Diggeses from Warburton in the younger generation, the three young Carlyles from Alexandria, including a son by Carlyle's second marriage, who at seventeen was to die on a Carolina battlefield at the very end of the war—Betsy Ramsay, Molly Manley, Nancy Peake, and the McCarthy girls from Longwood and Cedar Grove. It was gay and noisy and it kept Martha from missing Patsy so much, and it seemed to have no connection with the grimmer gatherings of their elders, when Mason and Cockburn and the elder Dulany, Craik and Grayson and Nat Harrison, remained closeted with Washington after dinner until an overnight stay was often obligatory. Where to purchase ammunition, and the weapons to fire it.... at what point in the organization and officering of independent companies could the charge of treason be lodged.... it was only militia, after all....

In March, 1775, Washington went to Richmond for the meeting in the little white church where the delegates for the second Philadelphia Congress were to be chosen. There was not much hope that he would escape another tour of duty as one of the Virginia representatives–which would call him away from home just as the south addition to the house was being enclosed, but Lund would have to see to all that. What no one anticipated at Richmond was an impassioned call to arms by Patrick Henry, who electrified them all with a blistering speech against the Throne, and demanded liberty or death. Even the more conservative members were stirred by Henry's eloquence, and Washington was named to a committee for putting the colony into "a posture of defence." All the delegates to the first Congress were re-elected for the second, which would leave Washington barely a month at home between Richmond and Philadelphia. That he was resigned to whatever further demands might be made on him was apparent in a letter written before he left Richmond, to his brother John Augustine at Bushfield:

"Dear Brother: Mr. Smith deliverd me your Letter of the 16th, but as one is generally in a hurry and bustle in such places, and at such times as these I have only time to acknowledge it, and add that it would have given me pleasure to have met you here. I shall refer you to Mr. Smith for an Acct. of our proceedings up to this day, and you cannot fail of learning the rest from the Squire [Lee] who delights in the Minutiae of a Tale. I am in doubt whether we shall finish here this week, but as I shall delay little time on the Road in returning, I shall hope to see you on your way up, or down, from Berkeley. I am much obliged to you for the Holly Berries and Cotton Seed. My love to my Sister and the Children. I had like to have forgotten to express my entire approbation of the laudable pursuit you are engaged in of Training an Independent Company. I have promised to review the Independent Company of Richmond [County] sometime this Summer, they having made me a tender of the Command of it; at the same time I could review yours and shall very cheerfully accept the honr. of Commanding it if occasion requires it to be drawn out, as it is my full intention to devote my Life and Fortune in the cause we are engaged in, if need be. I remain, Dr. Sir. Yr. most affect. Brother....."

The Diary's record of his homeward journey shows the usual stop-overs, including what must have been a very talkative evening at the Fredericksburg tavern which was now known by the name of his brother's partner in the original enterprise, since Charles had taken to spending much of his time at his new, unfinished house called Happy Retreat in the Shenandoah country near Sam's Harewood. Washington's host, George Weedon, was to be with him as an officer off and on throughout the war which was now drawing very near—Weedon was always independent about his furloughs, but he stuck it out through the Valley Forge winter, as his Orderly Book bears witness. (In the spring of '77, when they were all still breathless from that narrow squeak at Trenton before the tide turned, Weedon wrote home his opinion of his one-time customer who had become the Commander-in chief: ". . . . no other man but our present General, who is the greatest that ever did or ever will adorn the earth, could have supported himself under the many disappointments and disgraces he was subjected to from this singular system of carrying on a war against the most formidable army in the world. . . .")

The Scotch apothecary Hugh Mercer would have been present at Weedon's that evening too, to discuss the Richmond news. Like Craik, Mercer had served on the frontier with Washington, and as a result of the friendship formed then he had chosen to establish a medical practice at Fredericksburg, where he set up a shop in his house in Princess Anne Street which is still to be seen today. He married a Fredericksburg girl, and Washington's mother was one of his patients until in '76 he turned soldier again, and distinguished himself as an officer, before receiving a fatal wound at Princeton only a few days after the Trenton victory.

Fielding Lewis probably strolled round through the spring evening from Millbank, to join the company at Weedon's, though Washington was to spend the following day at Betty's house, with a visit across the garden to his mother—"By Cash paid my Mother part of her Income, £30.0.0"—and after he had dined with the Lewises on the 30th, the entry for the 31st reads: "Set off from thence. Dined at Dumfries and reachd home about Sun Set."

That April at Mount Vernon saw many visitors, some new names, and the same familiar ones. The day after Washington returned from a long day at Alexandria at the muster of the Independent Company there, Harry Lee of Leesylvania, recently graduated from Princeton, arrived with the English General Lee and his obnoxious dogs, in a state of boyish hero-worship, for Lee's stories of his exploits in the Continental wars abroad were tall and handsome. Harry was already wavering in his intention to study law at the Middle Temple in London—in case there should be more fun nearer home. The following year, he would be given a captaincy in the cavalry, and before the war was over Lighthorse Harry Lee's Legion of daredevil riders was famous for its hit-and-run raids; his *Memoirs* are still a glowing chronicle of the hard-fought Carolina campaign where the Legion provided invaluable support and comfort to the always hard-pressed General Greene.

Within a fortnight of General Charles Lee's welcome departure there appeared at Mount Vernon the man who next to Lee did more than any other to make Washington's life a burden to him during the war years ahead—Horatio Gates, accompanied by Bryan Fairfax, who would never willingly have done Washington a disservice, though his views remained obstinately Loyalist as Washington's swung hard against Ministerial tyranny. Gates had been somewhere in the Braddock army, serving without distinction and, judging by his later conduct, retiring with discretion and alacrity before it was time. Instead of returning to England, he had married an Englishwoman who had somehow emigrated from Liverpool to America with a fortune of £10,000—General Charles Lee's acid tongue was to label her "Medusa" and "daemoness" during the first war winter at Cambridge. The Gateses had bought an estate in Berkeley County and established themselves there to rear an idolized only son, until Gates was impelled—everyone came to wonder why—to offer himself for a commission in the colonial army. He and Bryan Fairfax dined and lodged at Mount Vernon on May 2d, and although Fairfax departed on the morning of the 3d, Washington noted grimly that Gates "stayd all day," overlapping what was probably a confidential meeting of old friends when Richard Henry Lee, his brother Thomas of Belleview, and Charles Carter of Cleve came to dine on the last day before Washington was to set out for the Congress at Philadelphia.

If he went. It had almost seemed, at the end of April, that his presence at Williamsburg would be more imperative. Governor Dunmore, alarmed at all the mustering and drilling, had suddenly sent a party of British marines from an armed schooner to seize the powder stored in the Williamsburg magazine, and excited patriot volunteers gathered all along the Tidewater, ready to march on the capital, occupy the magazine, and demand the powder back. Peyton Randolph and Treasurer Nicholas, acting with presence of mind and authority, had personally averted an assault by the Williamsburg citizens on the Palace itself, where Dunmore and his family were living behind barricades.

Simultaneously, alarm had spread southward from Massachusetts, where trouble always seemed to originate. A party of British infantry from Boston had been ordered out to Concord to seize military stores belonging to the colonial companies there. Volunteers had rushed to arms to bar the way, there had been shooting and casualties, and in a running fight the British had retreated into Boston. The colonial force had chased them all the way, gathering strength and confidence as it went, and now in a manner of speaking were besieging their own town of Boston in which the redcoats were billeted.

It was not surprising that Virginians took the road to Mount Vernon. This business at Concord was not just a street mob against soldiers, as the other shooting at Boston had been a few months back. This was an affair between British Regulars and an armed force of Massachusetts farmers who considered themselves part of an army. This was war. Who, then, but Colonel Washington was the man to consult?

The long, grave counsels took place against the noise of hammers and saws and workmen's uninhibited voices, as the framework of the library went up on the south end of the house beyond the dining-room. It is unlikely that Washington's attention strayed from the matter at hand, but in spite of Lund's capabilities there must have been interruptions, questions, quick decisions, which had nothing to do with Boston—and always the tug of his own suppressed desire to watch the work progress under his own eyes.

News from the North—news from the South—but the latter was soon reassuring, as under Peyton Randolph's deft management the crisis at Williamsburg subsided without bloodshed. The Governor

—who had had a fright—agreed to pay for the powder, some £300 worth, and the volunteers dispersed to their homes. It would be Philadelphia, then. Not for long, of course—two months last time—that would make it July, before he got home again....

It was eight years.

XVII

THE Diary stops short in Philadelphia on the 19th of June, 1775, and does not resume until May of 1781, when Washington was at the New Windsor Headquarters on the Hudson, some weeks before the march on Yorktown began. He had been notified by Congress of his appointment as Commander-in-chief on June 15th, but there is no mention of that in the four ensuing entries of a few lines each before he closed the book and rode towards Cambridge, where the disorganized but enthusiastic colonial army was assembling around the beleaguered British in Boston. He was already in uniform—he had worn it to the Congress, perhaps because he often used uniform as dress clothes in Williamsburg, perhaps with some idea of signifying his readiness to serve again in some way for Virginia, but certainly not with any intention of securing the supreme command.

"Spent the evening at my lodgings," he wrote on three of those four days which elapsed between his acceptance of the command and the last entry, which read simply: "Dined at Colo. Ried's. Spent the evening at Mr. Lynch's." Joseph Reed of Philadelphia was to be a close friend and trusted aide during the first year of the war, after which his loyalty to Washington was undermined by his naif admiration for the aggressive General Charles Lee, and although Reed soon realized his mistake the damage was done, and he did not remain in Washington's military family. Lynch was one of the delegates from South Carolina.

On Sunday the 18th Washington composed the difficult letter to Martha which broke the news to her that he was not even coming back to Mount Vernon before riding north to take command. It was in this letter that he took thought for her with the suggestion that she might prefer to live in the little Alexandria house while he was away, in which case she was to direct Lund to have a kitchen built there for her use—apparently they had hitherto dined out when they used the house, without transporting servants from Mount Vernon for the preparation of meals. He enclosed his will, which he had had drawn by Colonel Pendleton in Philadelphia, asked to be remembered to Milly Posey and all his friends, and added a postscript: "Since writing the above, I have received your letter of the 15th and have got two suits of what I was told was the prettiest muslin. I wish it may please you. It cost 50/ a suit, that is 20/ a yard."

Two days later he allowed some of his inner doubt and desolation to show on the pages of a letter to his brother John Augustine at Bushfield:

"Dear Brother:

"I am now to bid adieu to you, and to every kind of domestic ease for a while. I am Imbarked on a wide Ocean, boundless in its prospect, and from whence, perhaps no safe harbour is to be found. I have been called upon by the Unanimous Voice of the Colonies to take Command of the Continental Army; an Honour I neither sought after nor desired, as I am thoroughly convinced that it requires greater Abilities and much more experience than I am Master of, to conduct a business so extensive in its nature and arduous in the execution; but the partiallity of the Congress, joined to a political motive, really left me without a Choice; and I am now Commissioned a General and Commander in chief of all the Forces now raised or to be raised, for the defence of the United Colonies. That I may discharge the Trust to the Satisfaction of my Imployers is my first wish; that I shall aim to do it, there remains as little doubt of; how far I may succeed is another point.....

"I shall hope that my friends will visit and endeavour to keep up the spirits of my Wife as much as they can, as my departure will, I know, be a cutting stroke upon her; and on this account alone, I have many very disagreeable sensations. I hope you and my sister (though the distance is great) will find as much leisure this Summer as to spend a little time at Mount Vernon.

"My sincere regards attend you both, as also the little ones, and I am yr. most Affect. Br. . . . . ."

On the 23d, in a room full of aides and Congressmen, he sat down to write a last hurried message to Martha, which he signed, "Yr. entire—Geo. Washington," and was gone, with a glittering escort, northwards, towards Boston. The news of Bunker Hill met him on the way.

Even after he arrived at the camp in Cambridge, to find it still seething with the aftermath of the fight at Bunker Hill, even when the full enormity of the undertaking before him was becoming evident, Washington could not relinquish the hope, if not the conviction, that at the worst he would not be long away from Mount Vernon. Lund was to send him weekly reports, to which he would devote a part of each Sunday for his replies. In this way he hoped to keep in touch with his beloved projects at home, while giving all his daily energies, as during the campaign of '58, to the business at hand.

Many of the letters from Lund have been lost or destroyed. Enough of them remain, a considerable number still unpublished, to form an illuminating chronicle if linked with those of Washington which are also available. There are of course disastrous gaps—but it is possible to follow in some degree the work which was carried out in Washington's absence, and to experience his own frustration and anxiety as the months and years crept by with only a deputy to supervise the estate affairs which were so dear and so immediate to him, even in the midst of a war.

Alarmed at his unpopularity since his attempt to get possession of the Williamsburg powder, Governor Dunmore had taken refuge with his family on board a British man-o'-war in York River, from where he proclaimed martial law and threatened devastation by fire and shot to all the great river houses whose owners dared to attend the Philadelphia Congress or take up arms against the King. Within two months of Washington's appointment as Commander-in-chief there were wild rumors that the British Navy would come up the Potomac to burn Mount Vernon and carry off the General's wife as a prisoner. The Independent Companies roundabout the neighborhood declared their intention of defending her, and Martha expressed a serene determination to remain at home undisturbed. Lund wrote for instructions, and on August 20th Washington replied:

"I can hardly think that Lord Dunmore can act so low, and unmanly a part, as to think of siezing Mrs. Washington by way of revenge upon me; howev'r, as I suppose she is, before this time, gone over to Mr. Calvert's, and will soon after returning go down to New Kent, she will be out of his reach for 2 or 3 months to come, in which time matters may, and probably will, make such a turn as to render her removal either absolutely necessary, or quite useless. I am nevertheless exceedingly thankful to the Gentlemen of Alexandria for their friendly attention to this point, and desire you will if there is any sort of reason to suspect a thing of this kind provide a Kitchen for her in Alexandria, or some other place of safety elsewhere for her and my Papers. . . . . .

"I wish you would quicken Lanphire and Sears about the Dining-room Chimney Piece (to be executed as mentioned in one of my last Letters) as I could wish to have that end of the House completely finished before I return.—I wish you had done the end of the New Kitchen next to the Garden as also the Old Kitchen with rusticated Boards; however, as it is not, I would have the Corners done so in the manner of our new Church. (those especially which Fronts the Quarter.) What have you done with the Well?—is that walled up? . . . . . ."

By Lund's reply to this letter, written September 29th, Washington learned that Martha would set out for Mr. Calvert's the following day, apparently to fetch Nelly back to make the journey with her for the New Kent visit. On October 5th, when she had returned to Mount Vernon with both the young Custises, Lund wrote: " 'Tis true that many people made a stir about Mrs. Washington continuing at Mount Vernon, but I cannot think her in any sort of danger. The thought I believe first originated in Alexandria. From thence it got to Loudoun County. I am told the people of Loudoun talked of sending a guard to conduct her up into Berkeley, with some of their principle men to persuade her to leave this and accept their offer. Mr. John Augustine Washington wrote to her, pressing her to leave Mount Vernon. She does not believe herself in danger, nor do I, without they attempt to take her in the dead of night, they would fail, for ten minutes notice would be sufficient for her to get out of the way. Lord Dunmore will hardly venture himself up this River, nor can I think he will send up on that errand. Surely her old acquaintance the Attorney [John Randolph] who with his family are aboard his ship, would put him off doing an act of that kind. I have never advised her to stay, nor indeed to go. Col. Bassett thinks her in no danger. You may depend I will be watchful, & upon the least alarm persuade her to move. She sets off next week with her son and daughter down the country......"

The estrangement of old friends had begun as much as a year before, when Washington's views on colonial rights became apparent to his circle. The presence of John Randolph and his womenfolk in Dunmore's party was the result of a tragic breakaway from his brother Peyton and his own son Edmund, when he elected to join forces with the Royal Governor instead of supporting the colonial cause. Edmund Randolph at twenty-two, handsome and unmarried, had for some time felt himself under a cloud because of his father's militant Toryism, and had gone to live as the adopted son of his childless uncle Peyton. During the summer of '75 he rode to Cambridge and was welcomed into Washington's military family as a very useful social secretary-aide, where he remained till the sudden death of Peyton in Philadelphia in the autumn called him back to Williamsburg and the entangled Randolph inheritance. He soon married and was seen no more at the war.

His place was filled by Washington's lawyer friend Robert Hanson Harrison of Maryland and Alexandria, who was now a widower with small children. Leaving his family in the care of his father-in-law, George Johnston of Belvale, Harrison responded at once to an appeal from Washington and although he had taken a major's commission in the home militia he joined the Headquarters family at Cambridge in October. At the advanced age of thirty, Harrison was senior to most of the striplings in uniform who clanked about the comfortable but crowded mansion where the Commander-in-chief spent the first winter of the war, and as time went on he became known affectionately as the Old Secretary. He was also the longest in service at the Headquarters post, as it was the spring of '81 before he resigned and returned to Maryland, to an appointment as chief justice, broken in health and under heavy family and financial obligations after the death of his father.

Washington's army was soon stiff with Virginians, most of whom wrote Junior after their names. Harrison's brother-in-law, George Johnston, Betty's son George Lewis, Baylor from the Valley, Grayson of Dumfries, Fitzgerald of Alexandria, Dick Meade of Coggins Point on the James, all served at one time or another on the Headquarters staff. Harry Lee of Leesylvania at the age of nineteen was a captain of cavalry in the regiment of Light Dragoons raised by his cousin Theodoric Bland of Cawsons. Weedon of Fredericksburg was a lieutenant-colonel. Muhlenberg, the Lutheran pastor at Woodstock in the Valley, was said to have preached a final sermon wearing his clerical gown over his uniform, and then casting it aside beat the recruiting drum himself. Woodford of Caroline County got into the first real shooting fight with Dunmore's ragtag and bobtail army, which besides a small force of British regulars was composed largely of runaway indentured servants and bewildered fugitive slaves—and Woodford won it, in December of '75.

Mr. Boucher, Jacky's one-time schoolmaster, always more of a Tory than his friend Eden, the Royal Governor of Maryland, ever was, wrote fiery letters for publication, and preached his sermons with a theatrical pair of loaded pistols lying on the cushion in the pulpit beside him, to intimidate his patriot parishioners. But finally, after an undignified scene at the church, during which Boucher considered that his life had been threatened, he took passage for England, at about a week's notice, with his wife and her uncle Mr. Addison, though his sister Jinny elected to remain in America. Before he went he gave himself the satisfaction of composing a long diatribe to Washington, which arrived at Cambridge in mid-August, not long before Boucher looked his last on the American shoreline—certainly only a fleabite among the colossal consequences of Washington's shouldering of his burden, but its flamboyant egotism must have caused him the wryest of smiles: "You are no longer worthy of my friendship," wrote Mr. Boucher to the Commander-in-chief. "A man of honour can no longer without dishonour be connected with you. With your Cause I renounce you; and now for the last time, subscribe myself, Sir, Your humble servant, J.B." Boucher thought enough of it, however, to preserve a copy for his published *Reminiscences*.

With Dunmore still at large in the rivers, on October 15th the General's wife was still at Mount Vernon: "Mrs. Washington I believe was under no apprehension of Lord Dunmore's doing her an injury, until your mentioning it in several of your last letters," Lund wrote to Cambridge. "She intended to set off tomorrow down the Country. I propose to her to put whatever she thought most valuable into trunks, & should there be a necessity to move them it will be sooner done. She will stay tomorrow & do it. Your papers are among the things which will be put up & I think to send them from home at all events......"

Soon after Washington rode to Cambridge his friend George Mason reluctantly consented to fill the soldier's vacant legislative post in the impending Convention at Richmond, leaving his children again in the neighborly care of the Cockburns of Springfield. In October he reported to Washington his dissatisfaction with the fumbling Convention, which had made him actually ill with vexation, so that he returned home without fulfilling his additional duties with the Committee of Safety. He mentioned at the same time the state of alarm which prevailed in Tidewater Virginia in that autumn of '75: "Many of the principle families are removing from Norfolk, Hampton, York, and Williamsburg, occasioned by the behavior of Lord Dunmore, and the commanders of the King's ships and tenders upon this station," he wrote.

Lund wrote Washington that Mason had been ill ever since he came from the Convention, and added with a gloomy fatalism which fortunately proved to be unjustified: "He looks very badly and he is quite worn out in appearance. He seems to be much disturbed that he is not able to attend the Committee of Safety. I wish he was well. We want him much, and shall miss him if it pleases God to take him out of this world."

Washington's hope of getting back to Mount Vernon before Christmas soon evaporated and in mid-October he was writing to John Augustine from Cambridge about their effort to put the troops under cover for the New England winter, and reminding him that in the manufacture of arms for public use care should be taken to make bores of the same size so that the same balls could answer, lest trouble arise from the mixture of cartridges. The enemy, he added, did not come out, though the advanced works were within musket shot of each other; and the American lines received a daily cannonrade without returning a shot, from scarcity of powder. "I am obliged to you for your advice to My wife, and for your Intention of visiting her," he wrote. "Seeing no great prospect of returning to my Family and Friends this Winter, I have sent an Invitation to Mrs. Washington to come to me, altho' I fear the Season is too far advanc'd (especially if she should, when my Letters get home, be in New Kent, as I believe the case will be) to admit this with any tolerable degree of convenience. I have laid a state of the difficulties, however, which must attend the journey before her, and left it to her own choice. My love to my Sister and the little ones are sincerely tendered, and I am, with true regard, yr. most Affecte. Brother."

Lund had at once forwarded the "invitation" to Martha at Eltham. "I expect her home immediately, as she has often declared she would go to the camp if you would permit her," he assured Washington on the 29th of October. "In my last letter as I told you Mrs. Washington had packed all your papers with your Books of Accts. in a trunk the day before she left home . . . . . I told her she should be careful to tie the papers in bundles and put them carefully in, so that they might not be in any great confusion hereafter when they came to be opened. I suppose they are so. She chose to put them up herself. Whether she has put the whole of your papers in that trunk or not I cannot say. She left me the key of your study, that I might eventually if necessary secure whatever was left there, but whether that desk contains papers of consequence or not I cannot tell nor shall I look into any part of it or in any other part of the study without her being present, unless I find it absolutely necessary to do it. But as soon as she returns, I will endeavour with her to put everything in the best order I can, and take some method of having them secured—I will do everything in my power to not only secure your papers, but every other valuable thing that can be saved even at the risque of my life if necessary . . . . . . From the accounts I get from you, and what we are daily hearing here, it looks like lost labour to keep on with our building, for should they get burned, it would be provoking. But I shall keep on until I am directed to the contrary by you . . . . . I think 50 men well armed might prevent 200 from burning Mount Vernon, situated as it is—no way to get to it but up a steep hill, and if I remember right General Gates told me it couldn't be done by the shipping. I wish I had the muskets, I would endeavour to find the men, black or white, that would at least make them pay dear for the attempt......"

For a home-keeping man who unlike his cousin George had never heard a shot fired in anger, Lund took a surprisingly bellicose stand on the matter of Dunmore. For months to come, once Martha was safely off to Cambridge, accompanied in the coach by Jack and Nelly Custis, Lund's mind ran upon the likelihood of an attempt being made on the American Commander-in-chief's property, and the means of its defence and the safe preservation of its contents, in which determination he was supported by half of Virginia.

On November 12th he wrote: "I imagine Lord Dunmore will now put off sending up this river until the spring, the northerly winds, frost, etc., will make it troublesome, and he will find enough to do below. If he comes here I shall endeavour to destroy a few of his men, before the House is fired, and if I get notice of his coming I think he, or any other, will be disappointed. I shall not think myself so secure as not to take care of what household goods can be saved......"

And on the 14th of the same month: "I have been some time thinking, if you think it is not too near the River, to Build a strong house at Morrises, [overseer at Dogue Run] & put your wine, rum, & other goods in it. I am at a loss to know where to move them. I wish you would tell me in your first letter after this comes to hand whether you approve of it. Perhaps I may be obliged to move them before. If so, I cannot tell where I shall send them to...... I believe that we must defend our plantations upon the Potomac with our muskets. I believe the gentlemen are ready & willing to turn out and defend any man's property, but the common people are most hellishly frightened......"

There was a project to blockade the Potomac and fortify it in some way to prevent the British ships from coming up the River as far as Alexandria, but it got nowhere, to Lund's disgust. "I am apt to believe nothing will be done towards a battery on the Potomac," he wrote on December 10th. "I have said all I can about it, & urged the matter in every company, but I fear to very little purpose. The cry is all that All the Estates that would be immediately benefitted by it would not be able to pay the expense of it. . . . . . If things do not change for the better I shall move your furniture somewhere or other in the spring. I wish I had 12 or 15 good muskets on tender should they burn your houses, and as it is, they may possibly lose some men in doing it. I think your corn houses are too near the water, but I know not how to remedy it. Suppose the corn should get burned next spring. It would be bad. . . . . ."

XVIII

WITH Martha on her way to join him for the winter in Massachusetts, Washington's anxiety for his Potomac property increasingly occupied his mind, crowding in on the daily perplexities of the command, where casualties still constituted a smaller part of his responsibility than food, clothing, and shelter for his army. Late in November he wrote a long letter to Lund, and kept among his papers a memorandum which preserved its content:

"What follows is a part of a Letter wrote to Mr. Lund Washington 26th day of November, 1775. A Copy is taken to remind me of my engagements and the exact purpose of them. These paragraphs follow an earnest request to employ a good part of my force in cleaning up Swamps, Hell Hole Ditching, Hedging, etc.

"I well know where the difficulty of accomplishing these things will lie. Overseers are already engaged (upon shares) to look after my business. Remote advantages to me, however manifest and beneficial, are nothing to them; and to engage standing Wages, when I do not know that anything I have, or can raise, will command Cash, is attended with hazard; for which reason I hardly know what more to say than to discover my wishes. The same reason, although it may in appearance have the same tendency in respect to you, shall not be the same in its operation. For I will engage for the Year coming, and the year following, that if these troubles, and my absence continues, that your Wages shall be standing and certain, at the highest amount that any one Year's Crop has produced to you yet. I do not offer this as any temptation to induce *you* to go on more chearfully in prosecuting *these* schemes of *mine*. I should do injustice to you, were I not to acknowledge that your conduct has ever appeard to me above everything sordid; but I offer it in consideration of the great charge you have upon your hands, and my entire dependance upon your fidelity and industry.

"It is the greatest, indeed it is the only comfortable reflexion I enjoy on this score, to think that my business is in the hands of a person in whose integrity I have not a doubt, and on whose care I can rely. Was it not for this, I should feel very unhappy on Account of the situation of my affairs; but I am persuaded you will do for me as you would for yourself, and more than this I cannot expect.

"Let the Hospitality of the House, with respect to the Poor, be kept up; Let no one go hungry away—if any of these kind of People should be in want of Corn, supply their necessities, provided it does not encourage them in Idleness; and I have no objections to your giving my Money in Charity, to the Amount of Forty or Fifty Pounds a Year, when you think it well bestowd.—What I mean by having no objection is, that it is my desire that it should be done.—you are to consider that neither myself or Wife are now in the way to do these good Offices.—In all other respects, I recommend it to you, and have no doubts of your observing the greatest economy and frugality; as I suppose you know that I do not get a farthing for my Services here any more than my Expenses; and it becomes necessary, therefore, for me to be saving at home.—

"The above is copied, not only to remind myself of my promises and requests; but others also, if any mischance happens to G. Washington."

Lund's first reply to this important communication either went astray or in his concern for immediate plantation affairs was somehow inadequate, so that Washington wrote again, insisting upon some further comment, which drew from Lund on February 15th one of several eloquent testimonials of his loyalty:

"If I neglected to answer your letter of the 26th of November relative to my wages it was not intentionally. I should be very sorry if you should believe that I would exact more of you now than when you lived at home. Had you not offered to pay me equal to what I had in any former year I should not have murmured, but cheerfully endeavoured to have executed your orders with regard to hedging, meadowing, &ca. If my mind had been set upon riches, I very probably should have been trying every year that I have lived with you to get more of you. You will do me the justice to say that I have made no such attempt. God forbid I should at this time do it when you have it scarcely in your power to refuse me.

"I never expect to be rich. My only wish or ambition has been to save so much out of my wages during the time I have served you and others as would be sufficient to purchase a small farm in some part of the country where the produce of it would enable me to live and give a Neighbour Beef and Toddy. But that I now despair of ever accomplishing on this side the Allegheny Mountains, for my own employment is such that I cannot do you justice and run about the country to look where such a purchase may be made. But no more. My affairs are to myself, and why should I pester you with them. You may be assured my whole time and thoughts shall be devoted to your service, and as to any extraordinary care or trouble I am at, I think nothing of it, for it is a maxim with me that he who receives the wages of another hath no time in right he can call his own..."

Within seven years of expressing this modest wish, Lund was building a handsome brick house on a tract of land probably purchased from Washington, west of Mount Vernon, which he called Hayfield. His affection for his absent relative is evident in every letter he wrote during the war. When the Commander-in-chief sent for his wife instead of coming home for that first winter of '75—"I should have been happy to see you this winter, but as fate has ordered otherwise, it must be so. God grant you health and success," wrote Lund.

It was not just that he missed their company, for he found some of his duties quite overwhelming. Washington had suggested, perhaps in some ignorant masculine blunder, that a Mrs. Barnes who lived somewhere near Falls Church and was frequently mentioned but remains an anomaly, should come and stay at Mount Vernon as a sort of housekeeper while its lady was away at camp, but Martha seemed, as Lund reported ruefully, "to think it will not answer," so that he himself was forced to "encounter the housekeeping." This caused many a plaintive note in his correspondence, as in the case of the 247 barrels of salt pork and beef laid in for the first winter: "You will ask me what we are going to do with so much meat," he surmised unhappily. "I cannot tell. When I put it up I expected Mrs. Washington would have lived at home, if you did not, and was I to judge the future from the past consumption there would have been a use for it, for I believe Mrs. Washington's charitable disposition increases in the same proportion with her meat house. I thought last year there was a sufficient supply put up to supply our laborers in harvest, but we got scarcely any, and she can tell you there was very little salt provision in the house for the servants all this fall past. Besides, I am by no means fit for a housekeeper. I am afraid I shall consume more than ever, for I am not a judge of how much should be given out each day. I am vexed when called upon to give out provisions for the day. God send you were both at home, and an end to these troublesome times!"

On January 1, 1776, Dunmore justified everyone's fears by shelling and burning Norfolk at the mouth of the James, and again a thrill of alarm ran up the Tidewater rivers, as Lund reported by the middle of the month: "The Alexandrians expect to have their town burned by the enemy soon. They do not take any steps to prevent it. They put their trust in the Convention, and the Convention, I believe, in God, for I cannot learn what they are about. We are not well represented in Convention. Colonel Mason's indisposition has prevented his attendance this winter. Our other delegate you may remember is no conjuror. I intended if I was drove to the necessity of moving any of your goods to carry them to Mrs. Barnes, she often having pressed me to do it. But without I begin very soon, she will have very little room to spare. She has offered her house to everyone in Alexandria. . . . ."

Two weeks later he wrote: "Alexandria is much alarmd, & indeed the whole Neighbourhood—a report prevails that there are 5 large Ships laying off the mouth of Cone [River] and express county to county brings the Information—altho the River is block'd up with Ice—The Women & Children are leaving Alexandria & stowg themselves into every little Hut they can get, out of reach of the Enemy's Canon as they think; every Waggon, Cart, & Pack Horse that can be got, are employ'd in moveg the goods out of Town—the Militia are all up (but not in arms) for Indeed they have none, or at least very few. I expect the 5 large Ships will prove to be 5 oister Boats—I cou'd wish if we are to have our Neighbourhood invaded soon, they [the British] wou'd first send a Tender or two among us, I want much to see how the people would behave upon the occasion......

"I am about packg up your China, Glass, &c., into Barrels, & shall continue to pack into Casks Whatever I think shou'd be put up that way, & other things into Chests, Trunks, Bundles, &c., and I then shall be able at the shortest notice to move your things out of harms way (at least for a while) some to Mrs. Barnes & the Rest into Morrises Barn; and if they are found not to be safe there, move them farther after—I fear the destruction will be great, altho the greatest care be taken......

"As yet I have mov'd nothing but your papers—every Body I see tells me if they cou'd have notice they woud immediately come and defend your property so long as they had life..... One hundred men in my opinion wou'd prevent 1000 from Landg here to do mischief.... These are dreadfull times to give people so much trouble & vexation. Fightg and being killed is the least troublesome part.—I wish you had said how large you would have the Negroe Houses you speak of in your Letter, and whether you woud have them Built with or without sheds......"

It was of course another false alarm, for the British never got to Alexandria, though no one was sure they wouldn't until well into the summer of 1776. At the end of February Lund wrote again: "I think if you could be of the opinion that your buildings would not be destroyed this summer it would be best to have the other addition to the end of your house raised, the chimney pulled down and put up again, that being the most troublesome part of the work. But this cannot be done without a master workman, unless you choose to try Lanphier again....."

Turning back to Lund's letters written during the weeks immediately after Washington's departure from Philadelphia for Cambridge in answer to his questions about the work he had seen begun on the south end, its daily progress can be followed, along with the homely news of the household and neighbors. The dining-room, whose ceiling and corner chimney-piece were undergoing alterations as the new library next to it went up and a new chimney flue was added, was still in the hands of the workmen—a plasterer from Fredericksburg who had worked for Fielding Lewis at Millbank, and the man named Sears who worked alongside the master-builder Lanphier from Alexandria.

"Sears is still here about the chimney-piece," Lund wrote on September 29th. "No doubt you think him long about it, so do I, but I can assure you he is constantly at work. I think you never intended such a one and must have been mistaken in the look of the draught of the chimney-piece." In Lund's next, Sears was absent with a week's work still to do—"I am told he is sick at home," Lund added with some skepticism. Sears stayed away a month, and then returned to put two coats of paint on the dining-room and one on the room which would be the library. "Since Mrs. Washington went away we have been trying to cure the chimney from smoking," Lund wrote in December, "and I am in hopes we have done it, after doing and undoing it twenty times. The celler, new room, and dining-room—they really smoked so bad that the walls looked as bad as any Negro quarter and the smoke from the cellar came up into the rooms."

The "stucco man" had still four weeks work ahead in September by his own estimate, and Washington may have suggested that he might be overdoing it. "The ceiling is not clumsy," Lund reassured him on October 15th. "I think it is light and handsome. It is altogether worked by hand, which makes it tedious." On November 5th—"I believe you will not be displeased by the heaviness of the work in the dining-room when you come to see it. It does not look heavy but is the kind of work that goes on slow. The man is still at it, and will be for a fortnight." On November 12th—"The dining-room will, I expect, be finished this week now come in. It is, I think, very pretty. The stucco man agrees the ceiling is a handsomer one than any at Colonel Lewis's, although not half the work in it." On November 24th, when Martha was on the road to Cambridge, Lund wrote—"I have not yet got rid of the plasterer. Perhaps my next letter will tell you he is done. Mrs. Washington concluded to leave the room intended for her chamber done quite plain, no ornaments upon the ceiling, the sides plain stucco. He is now about it, but has yet something to do to the dining-room." It was not till

December 10th that Lund was able to report that he had sent the plasterer back to Colonel Lewis.

Lanphier, who undertook everything from mending old spinning-wheels because new ones could not be got hold of, to building the covered ways which were to link the outside buildings like the kitchen to the mansion house, was a constant trial. "I intended to have the stuff aired up for the palisadoes this winter," Lund wrote in November, "but I am unwilling to put them up, for I really am at a loss for the just proportions of each particular post, nor have I anybody to direct me. I have once or twice talked to Lanphier about it, but he mouths and talks in such a way that I do not understand him. I mean as to the dimensions of the palisades, sills, rails, posts, and different heights, but I cannot see that it will make any difference whether that work is first or last done."

As to the well, which Washington had inquired about in August, it was December before Lund was able to engage a man named Skilling to work on it. "There is a rascal in Alexandria that has promised to come every week for three months past," he explained—but because of cave-ins which made the workmen afraid to go down in it Lund feared for a while that it would have to be filled in and abandoned altogether. "And you must write me whether I must have another dug and where to dig it," he wrote confidently to a man tied down in Massachusetts with an army on his back. Fortunately, by putting down a frame they were able to get the old well bricked up again. "You want the top done with large stones," Lund noted, on February 8th. "We have no stone in our banks that can be got up large enough. Knowles says he can do it with brick, that shall stand much longer than any stone we can get, for the water dissolves most of the stone we have."

Knowles was the brick-layer at work on the chimneys of the new quarter and the garden wall, who had recently got the worst of a skirmish with a bull which had left the grey wagon-horse gored to death in the yard. "If I find sawing his horns pretty close will not prevent his doing mischief, I shall fasten a board across them," Lund wrote, but he left it too long, and a fortnight later had to report: "Knowles has been laid up some time and not yet recovered. They attempted to saw the bull's horns when I was out of the way, and as everything Bishop does is wrong, so that was. Every man, woman, and child I am told upon the plantation assisted, but the bull proved too much for them, and in the scuffle Knowles had like to have lost his life. He will be well, I suppose, in a few days."

The tally of sickness and disaster and death among so large a population as Mount Vernon supported was bound sometimes to play a significant part in Lund's weekly reports. There were always some Negroes sick of fevers and agues. Sometimes the catalogue was lengthy and lugubrious, sometimes terse and callous. "Knowles is well. Webster is sick. John Barry is dead. I am, sir, etc.," Lund put it on October 29th. In November after listing the pressing jobs still to be done, he went on: "Now to do all this we have Cook Jack, who is growing so crazy he scarce works two days in a week—I think he is in a consumption. Old Pete and Schomberg differ but little from the above. Gunner has been laid up 3 months with a sore foot, and when he will get well the Lord knows, for he is still confined to the house with it. Lewis and Guy drive the waggon. Bosun and Webster are sound, Myrtilla, Phoebe, and the 4 boys." On December 3d he mentions that "Doll had a little one this fall, and the other people have been rather sickly." Soon after Christmas—"John Broad in a playing frolic last Sunday got a small wound in the thigh which gives him much pain and is very much swelled and inflamed. He thinks it will kill him, but I am of a different opinion," Lund wrote with his frequent skepticism. But John Broad was right. He died in February, probably of an infection, after a long and miserable illness. At the end of January Gunner was still lame, but was able to card the tow for the women to spin. "I set a parcel of little people to spinning," Lund reported, meaning the pickaninnies. "At first they were rather troublesome, but they begin to do a little better. We have thread enough spun to make piece or 2 of linen, which we are preparing to have wove." And a few weeks later—"Our little people spin three cuts a day and sometimes less. We have 9 wheels at work."

Washington's frustration at long distance farming can well be imagined by the scope and detail of Lund's conscientious effort to consult and follow his employer's wishes and to keep him informed of the difficulties and achievements of his deputy. The sheer man-hours represented by their correspondence as the months roll on is impressive: "You wrote me some time past about breaking up Dogue

Run meadow & sowing it in the spring with oats & timothy," Lund was writing on November 24th. "I gathered all the seed this summer that could be saved, which was not so much as I wanted, for there was very little seed on our grass, whether owing to wet weather or what I cannot tell. The whole of it I sowed in the ground cleared in the mill swamp. I think if we had the seed, it would be an improvement to break up that meadow before you had the one at the mill fit for cutting hay, for the old meadow there will not next crop yield 1000 weight of timothy. Consequently if the Dogue Run meadow was broke up you would be one year without timothy hay, so that upon the whole I think you would better let it stand one year longer. I will have the weeds grubb'd out of it. We got a large crop of hay of it this year....."

Sometimes their views were at variance: "I shall have the cherry trees dug up and transplanted but I believe it will be labor lost to do it for they will not live," was Lund's opinion on November 24th. And a month later—"The cherry trees in the walk, all but the two you desired might stand, are taken up and replanted. They cost us a great deal of labor, I think, for little purpose. I cannot think they will live."

Miscellaneous news items stand out during that first autumn of the war. November 24th—"The people are running mad about salt. You would hardly think it possible there could be such a scarcity. 6/ and 7/ per bushel. Conway's sloop came to Alexandria on Monday last with a load. He saw no British tenders in the bay....." November 5th—"I find myself equally anxious to discharge a debt against you as I am to pay one of my own. I sometimes am asked for small sums which they say you owe them. It may be true or false, I cannot tell, but it distresses me, for I would that you should owe no man. John Low the barber says you owe him 7/6 for a false tail for your hair. If I thought you owed it I would pay it. I told him you would have paid such a wretch as him upon receipt of the bill. But enough of this. In money matters as in all other things, I will do the best I can."

That is a constant refrain. At the end of February, '76, Lund wrote —"I am exceedingly sorry to hear of your troubles and vexations, I hope they are near an end. Let not your affairs in this part of the world add to them. I will do the best I can."

XIX

IN May, '76, when Washington had succeeded in ousting the British from Boston and was in New York awaiting their next move, George Mason returned to the Virginia Convention, now sitting at Williamsburg. Perhaps he felt it was the least he could do in support of his fighting neighbors. Royal rule in Virginia had come to an end with Dunmore's belligerence, which had culminated in the virtual destruction of Norfolk in January, and a new plan of government for Virginia was required. Mason's confreres around the green baize council table were familiar ones—Patrick Henry, Pendleton, Thomas Ludwell Lee, and a youngster named James Madison—many of the others he dismissed as dead wood. Jefferson was in Philadelphia at the Congress.

In mid-June the final draft of the Virginia Declaration of Rights, composed in Mason's own regular, readable hand, was unanimously adopted by the Convention at Williamsburg—"That all men are by nature equally free and independent and have certain inherent rights," it read, ". . . . . namely, the enjoyment of life and liberty, with the means of acquiring and possessing property, and pursuing and obtaining happiness and safety. . . . ." It was not original with Mason. John Locke in his *Treatises of Government* a generation ago had used almost the same words, except for *happiness*. That was added in the New World.

The proceedings of the Convention were published in the Philadelphia papers. Less than a month later, the Congress passed Jefferson's Declaration of Independence by a unanimous vote. Jefferson had read Locke too, and never claimed to have invented its principles single-handed.

Patrick Henry was elected the first native governor of Virginia, the term to run one year, though he could be re-elected twice. Mason was on the committee which notified him, and saw him installed in the elegant brick palace of the Royal Governors—a gaunt, red-haired man from up-country, speaking with a twang and wearing his wig awry, who suddenly took to powder and a scarlet-lined cloak, and acquired a second wife who was a Dandridge.

After March, 1776, all of Lund's letters to Washington are missing until December of 1777, and there are only four to Lund during that period. The first of these was written on August 19th, at the New York Headquarters where Martha had accompanied him from Boston, and from whence she had but recently departed, with reluctance, for Philadelphia, after the British ships, loaded with the trained professional forces of Generals Howe, Clinton, and Burgoyne, in fancy uniforms, appeared in the Bay.

She was still in Philadelphia on that hot July day when the bell of the State House rang for the signing of the Declaration of Independence and the thirteen colonies became the United States of America. She lingered there until the battle of Long Island at the end of August removed any prospect of her rejoining her husband, who was by then committed to a campaign against the whole British Army.

On the 19th of August, however, the British were still assembling their troops, stiffened with hired Hessians, on Staten Island, and Washington could turn his mind to Mount Vernon and ease his many immediate anxieties by discussing with Lund the always fascinating subject of hedges and tree-planting. It is plain that despite the prospect of more British raids in the Tidewater rivers during the summer, the building had gone ahead at Mount Vernon as suggested by Lund in February, so that the addition at the north end was by now well under way. On the south end the upstairs bedroom was finished and ready for Martha's use on her return home, but the new library below it would remain without its shelves and interior decoration until the end of the war.

"There is no doubt that the Honey locust if you could procure Seed enough, and that Seed would come up, will make (if sufficiently thick) a very good hedge," Washington wrote to Lund from New

York on August 19th. "So will the Haw, or Thorn, and if you cannot do better, I wish you to try these, but Cedar or any kind of ever Green would look better; however, if one thing will not do, we must try another, as no time ought to be lost in rearing of Hedges, not only for Ornament, but use. . . . . .

"Your Works abt. the Home House will go on Slowly I fear as your hands are reduced, and especially if Knowles fails. Remember that the New Chimneys are not to smoke. Plant Trees in the room of all dead ones in proper time this Fall, and as I mean to have groves of Trees at each end of the dwelling House, that on the South end to range in a line from the South East Corner to Colonel Fairfax's, extending as low as another line from the Stable to the Dry Well and towards the Coach House, Hen House, and Smoak House as far as it can go for a Lane to be left for Carriages to pass to and from the Stable and Wharf. . . . ." (and so on, minutely, past the smith's shop and the woodpile, to the last foot of ground and the last tree) ". . . . . . . these Trees . . . . . to consist that at the North end of Locusts altogether; and at the South, of all the clever kind of Trees (especially flowering ones) that can be got, such as Crab apple, Poplar, Dogwood, Sasafras, Laurel, Willow (especially yellow and Weeping Willow, twigs of which may be got from Philadelphia) and many others which I do not recollect at present . . . . It will not do to Plant the Locust Trees at the North end of the House till the Framing is up, cover'd in, and the Chimney Built; otherwise it will be labour lost as they will get broke down, defaced and spoil'd, But nothing need prevent planting the Shrubery at the other end of the House. Whenever these are Planted, they should be Inclosed, which may be done in any manner till I return. . . . . .

"As my Greys are almost done, and I have got two or three pretty good Bays here, I do not Incline to make an absolute Sale of the bay horse you mention. But if Mr. Custis wants him, and you and he can fix upon a price, he may take him at such valuation, paying the Money, and using him as his own; subject however to return him to me if I should hereafter want him and will repay him his Money; by this means he will . . . . . have the use of the Horse and I the use of the money.

"Before I conclude I must beg of you to hasten Lanphire about the addition to the No. End of the House, otherwise you will have it open I fear in the cold and wet Weather, and the Brick work to do at an improper Season, neither of which shall I be at all desirous of. My best wishes to Milly Posey, and all our Neighbours and friends. With sincere regards I remain, etc."

Almost as this letter was being written, Dunmore arrived at Staten Island with the remnants of his raffish crew to join the British forces there. Earlier in the summer he or one of his zealous deputies had come up the Potomac as far as Robert Brent's plantation called Woodstock near Aquia, and burnt the house and grain before being driven off by Colonel Grayson's militia. Charles Moore in his book on Washington's family life (1926) quotes a letter from Jacky Custis at Mount Airy to Washington at New York which described the raid on Woodstock with some humor, possibly heightened by hearsay. "A Captain James with 60 militia were stationed there who all got drunk and kept challenging the men-o'-war to come ashore, and upbraiding them with cowardice," Jacky wrote, and added that when the British finally accepted the challenge they found the pot-valiant militia sleeping it off, and Colonel Grayson's little force arrived too late to save Mr. Brent's possessions.

Martha was then still in Philadelphia. Both Mount Vernon and Gunston got off with alarms, but Lund's emotions can be imagined. A month later Dunmore was driven by the militia from his last fortified base at Gwynne's Island below the mouth of the Rappahannock in Gloucester County, and sailed to New York. He did not remain to fight the war, but soon returned to England with a cargo of Loyalists, which included John Randolph of Williamsburg and his family.

Washington's second surviving letter to Lund in 1776 was written from his Harlem Headquarters on the 30th of September, when he had suffered defeat on Long Island and had seen his men break ranks in cowardly flight at Kip's Bay, and then stand to fight at Harlem Heights a few days later. He was angry and uncertain, and felt himself handicapped by an ill-fed, ill-equipped army which he had had no chance to drill and discipline. It was the old story of the '50's again, with the Continental Congress doing no better than the Royal Governor and Council at Williamsburg had done for the men in Washington's care on the western frontier.

By an ironical circumstance which could not have been lost on him, the comfortable house which Washington and his Staff now occupied at Harlem was the confiscated property of the English-born Loyalist Roger Morris, who had been a fellow-aide to Braddock in '55, one of the several who were wounded in the Monongahela battle while Washington went unscathed. Morris had retired from the British service and married the New York heiress Mary Philipse, who even Morris at one time believed had caught young Colonel Washington's fancy during his visit to New York in '56. Two years elapsed before she married Morris, and they built the mansion which now sheltered the military family of the American Commander-in-chief, while Mrs. Morris refuged at the home of her brother-in-law Beverly Robinson near West Point on the Hudson. Twenty years almost to the day lay between her first meeting with Washington and this near miss. The Morrises were to return to England and die there as British subjects still. The house later became forever identified with its most notorious tenant, a certain Mme. Jumel.

There is a noticeable echo of his earlier letters to Speaker Robinson and to John Augustine Washington, as he wrote to Lund on September 30th from Harlem, at such white heat that for once affairs at Mount Vernon took second place, until he had simmered down:

"..... The amazement which you seem to be in at the unaccountable measures which have been adopted by [Congress] would be a good deal increased if I had time to unfold the whole system of their management since this time 12 months. I do not know how to account for the unfortunate steps which have been taken, but from the fatal idea of conciliation which prevailed for so long—fatal, I call it, because from my soul I wish it may [not] prove so, though my fears lead me to think there is too much danger of it..... In short, such is my situation that if I were to wish the bitterest curse to an enemy this side of the grave, I should put him in my stead with my feelings; and yet I do not know what plan of conduct to pursue. ...... In confidence I tell you that I never was in such an unhappy and divided state since I was born. To lose all comfort and happiness on the one hand ...... and to be told on the other that if I leave the service all will be lost, is at the same time I am bereft of every peaceful moment, distressing to a degree. But I will be done with the subject, with the precaution that it is not a fit one to be publicly known or discussed......

"With respect to the chimney, I would not have you for the sake of a little work spoil the look of the fireplaces, tho' that in the parlor must, I should think, stand as it does; not so much on account of the wainscotting, which I think must be altered (on account of the door leading into the new building) as on account of the chimney piece and the manner of fronting into the room..... The chimney in the new room should be exactly in the middle of it—the doors and everything else to be exactly answerable and uniform—in short, I would have the whole executed in a masterly manner. You ought surely to have a window in the gable end of the new cellar (either under the Venetian window, or one on each side of it).....

"Remember me to all our neighbours and friends, particularly to Colonel Mason, to whom I would write if I had time to do it fully and satisfactorily. Without this I think the correspondence on my part would be unavailing. I am, etc."

The third letter to Lund was also written at Harlem, only a week later, on October 6th, just before the battle of White Plains and the beginning of the long retreat across the Delaware which so narrowly missed becoming an American rout and ending the war then and there: "We have been in daily expectation of having our Quarters beat up, but as yet nothing of the kind has been attempted," he wrote. "On Wednesday last I expected to have some pretty warm work, but it turned out otherwise."

That was a raid to bring in some grain, which was accomplished without the expected opposition. Again, Washington sent off a letter with very little but his own war news, which was concerned with the refusal of Congress to allow him to leave the city of New York unfit for the British to use as a snug headquarters—but this was in part accomplished for him by a devastating fire which swept the city on September 20th. "Providence, or some good honest Fellow, has done more for us than we were disposed to do for ourselves, as near one Fourth of the City is supposed to be consumed," he reported to Lund. "However, enough of it remains to answer their purposes." Which was true, as New York was occupied by the British from the autumn of 1776 until long after their defeat at Yorktown in Virginia in '81 had brought an end to the shooting war.

The last letter of the year, dated December 10th at the Headquarters house called Summer Seat in Pennsylvania, Washington wrote at the very nadir of his fortunes, when it seemed that only a miracle could preserve the starving, frost-bitten remnant of his army. That miracle he and his men were to perform at Trenton on Christmas night, when they re-crossed the frozen Delaware in a blizzard and took the town from the Hessians. But the harassed man who led them had no inkling that the turn of the tide was near, when he wrote to Lund on December 10th, "I wish to heaven it was in my power to give you a more favorable account of our situation than it is." Even then, in the midst of disaster, the dear escape to Mount Vernon's peaceful perplexities was made to serve as his balance wheel:

"If you can get some Holly Trees to plant upon the Circular Banks in the manner, or rather thicker than I did a year or two ago, I should be glad of it, or if good and well set Holly cannot be had then young and strait bodied Pines will do. If you have a mind to try Sycamore upon some of the cross Banks in the Neck, or elsewhere, I have no objection to the experiment; but it runs in my head that I have heard of some objection to the Sycamore..... Perhaps Colonel Fielding Lewis (who I think it was told me they did not answer) can tell. The honey locust must, I should think, be better, if to be had.

"If you can get a good match (and a young horse) for the Stallion, I should like it very well; but let the match be good, and the Horse handsome. The hurried situation I am in at present allows me no time, or indeed anybody to spare, to send the Horses as I promis'd. Mrs. Washington must therefore make the old greys serve her a little while longer; I think if there can be any possible makeshift made, without buying Linnen for the Negros at the enormous price you speak of, it ought to be attempted, as the price is too heavy to be borne with, if it be possible to avoid it without making the poor Negros suffer too much; this I would not do to save any expence, as they certainly have a just claim to their Victuals and cloaths, if they make enough to purchase them."

This letter, unfinished and forgotten in his "hurried situation" of falling back faster than General Cornwallis could advance, accompanied him on the withdrawal to Keith's Farm near Newtown in Pennsylvania, "to be more convenient to our great and extensive defences of this river," he wrote to Lund in a postscript on the 17th of December. "Hitherto, by our destruction of the boats, and vigilance in watching the fords of the river above the falls..... we have prevented them from crossing; but how long we shall be able to do it God only knows, as they are still hovering about the river."

Martha was of course then at Mount Vernon, but she was prepared to join him again wherever the winter Headquarters should be established. It was plain that as he wrote this postscript on the 17th his mind turned anxiously towards her personal safety and a possible emergency at Mount Vernon if the British Army could not be headed off, and if he himself became a prisoner or a fugitive:

"Matters to my view, but this I say in confidence to you, as a friend, wears so unfavourable an aspect..... that I would look forward to unfavourable Events, and prepare Accordingly in such a manner however as to give no alarm or suspicion to anyone; as one step towards it, have my Papers in such a Situation as to remove at short notice in case an Enemy's Fleet should come up the River. When they are remov'd, let them go immediately to my Brothers in Berkeley [County].

"Since writing the above I have determined to send Mrs. Washington another Horse for her Chariot, which with the one before mentioned, the one you have, and the one you are to buy, will make a very good set, if you can purchase a good one and likely; the two I send are exceeding good Horses, and young, the lightest of the two Bays is an exceeding tough, hardy Horse as any in the world, but rather lazy, he will do well for the Postilian....."

Martha was thus to be provided with reliable transportation, and perhaps in his letters to her at this time he suggested the home of one or the other of his brothers in the Shenandoah as a refuge for her as well as for his papers. But within a month of the time he wrote these lines, the British had retired in some surprise to winter in New York, retaining only a few outposts in Jersey, and Washington was safely in Headquarters at Arnold's Tavern in Morristown, where Martha joined him in March '77.

XX

THE only surviving letter from either side during 1777 was written by Lund on December 24th, and reached Washington at Valley Forge, where he had led his beaten and exhausted army after the battles at Brandywine and Germantown had given the British possession of Philadelphia. As Martha did not arrive at Valley Forge until February, '78, Lund again expressed their hope that Washington might make a winter visit to Mount Vernon, which must have caused a weary smile in the cramped stone house at the head of the valley where Washington had established his Headquarters, with his army spread out behind him in streets of log huts built along the only road by which the British could, if they had had the ambition, attack.

Lund too was in a gloomy mood. "It gives me real concern that we are making nothing," he wrote. "—all our wheat destroyed, our mills idle, and but a short crop of corn. . . . . You, sir, may think, and everyone would, that in your absence we live at less expense than when you are at home, but it is the reverse. It is seldom that this house is without company, our stables always full of horses. Custis keeps seven here, Mrs. Washington's chariot five, seven mares, the young horse that I cut in the Fall, which I fear will never make more than a wagon horse, the wagon horses, and my one, making in the whole twenty-four. These, added to the visitors' horses, consume no small quantity of corn. . . ."

On the 28th of January, '78, Lund wrote that "Mrs. Washington crosses the River today, in order to go to camp. Captain Thomas Triplett attends her there. I fear she will have a bad journey, the roads being froze. . . . . ." The Triplett brothers of Round Hill near

Alexandria were old hunting neighbors of Washington's and held military commissions until ill health forced both to retire from the service.

Lund also expressed in this letter his intention of coming to camp in March, with a promise to visit all the tenants before then in order to be able to answer Washington's inquiries. But when March came Lund had a sore hip, the weather was cold with snow, and he kept postponing his departure from Mount Vernon on what must have seemed to a sedentary man of forty-seven an arduous journey at best.

He had troubles aplenty where he was. On the 11th he wrote: "It is a matter of doubt whether I shall be able to prevail on Lanphier to come to work this spring or not. If he comes I shall be at a loss how to manage in my absence about victualling him and others about the family. Experience teaches that Bishop is not to be trusted. Milly Posey will be from home. What to do as yet I cannot tell, but I will fall upon some way or other, though indeed I cannot tell what. ...... Bad weather this, for lambs. We have lost more than I could wish......"

Before he wrote his next letter, dated March 18th, Lund had received a letter written at Valley Forge on February 28th in which Washington appeared to anticipate that Lund might be drawn into the army, which raised the old specter of Mount Vernon deserted and untended. Washington offered to provide a substitute for Lund's enlistment, "as nothing but your having the charge of my business and the entire confidence I repose in you could make me tolerably easy from home for such a length of time as I have been and am likely to be," wrote the Commander-in-chief. "This, however, leads me to say, that I hope no motive, however powerful, will induce you to leave my business whilst I in a manner am banished from home; because I should be unhappy to see it in common hands. For this reason, although from accidents and misfortunes, not to be averted by human foresight, I make little or nothing from my estate, I am willing to increase your wages and make it worth your while to continue with me. To go on in the improvement of my estate in the manner heretofore described to you, fulfilling my plans and keeping my property together are the principle objects I have in view during these troubles; and firmly believing that they will be accomplished under your management as far as circumstances and acts of Providence will allow, I feel quite easy under disappointments; which I should not do if my business was in common hands, liable to suspicions......"

To which Lund replied on the 18th of March: "By your letter I should suppose you were apprehensive I intended to leave you. I hope for the future you will entertain a better opinion of me than to believe that while you were encountering every danger and difficulty at the hazard of your life and repose, giving up all domestic happiness to serve the public and me among them, that I should attempt to take advantage of you by screwing up my wages or leaving your estate to the care of a stranger. At my time of life it is time to think of getting a home, and entering into a different state of life, if ever. But all of this I will forego, and endeavour the best I can for you whilst you are away......"

Coming just at the time of the Conway Cabal, when Washington would have begun to wonder who his friends really were, especially since the implication of his lifelong friend Richard Henry Lee in the conspiracy to force him out of the command, so honest an expression of Lund's loyalty must have been very comforting.

It is interesting to find Lee exonerated in a letter from Lund which recounts a conversation he had had with George Mason. Out of his friendship for Washington, Mason had taxed Lee with taking part in the Cabal, which had been instigated by a rank outsider named Conway, an Irish soldier of fortune who considered himself better qualified to run the war than General Washington. Lee had strenuously denied any part in it, declaring to Mason that he would look upon it "as one of the greatest misfortunes that could befall this continent should you by any means whatever give up the command of the army, for fully convinced he was in his own opinion no other man upon this continent was equal to the task," Lund reported, and added that Mason had expressed his own opinion that no friend to America could be an enemy to Washington, "for by God, which was his expression, there was not nor ever was in the world a man who acted from a more laudable and disinterested motive than you do....." Still later, Jacky Custis as a duly elected representative of his county in the Virginia Legislature, heard Lee again declare his innocence before Jefferson, who had resigned from Congress to serve his native state in the Assembly at Williamsburg.

When Lund wrote on the 18th of March, Lanphier was still a problem at Mount Vernon. "After some conversation with him I found he had very little thought of working here much more," Lund wrote. "He said Money would not purchase the necessaries of life, and he must endeavour to make them. Finding I could do nothing with him, I told him if he would stick to his work and endeavour to finish it, I would make him a present at shearing of 40 pounds of wool and next Fall 30 barrels of corn. He has promised that he will be here very shortly, and stick close to the work, and that nothing but sickness shall take him away from it. Had I not made him the above offer he would not have worked for 10/ a day, nor his man for much less."

The first of April, '78, found Washington still at Valley Forge and Lund still detained at Mount Vernon. He had been up in Loudoun County collecting rents, to the sum of £20—and since seining for shad had begun, from which he hoped to realize another £200, he again postponed the journey to camp for another month, when he would still be in time, he surmised, to accompany Mrs. Washington back to Mount Vernon before the summer campaign began. There was again a shortage of salt at Mount Vernon. The weaver had demanded £100 a year, because he said he could get it elsewhere, and Lund had let him go. "With regard to selling the Negros mentioned," he wrote on April 8th, "you have put it out of my power by saying you would not sell them without their consent. I was very near selling Bet, indeed I had sold her for £200 to a man living in Botetourt County, but her mother appeared to be so uneasy about it, and Bet having made such promises of amendment that I could not force her to go with the man."

On April 22d, Lund still intended to set out for Valley Forge next week, accompanied by Jacky Custis. Mr. Bassett had paid them a visit at Mount Vernon after being inoculated for small-pox—"he pretends not to be afraid, yet you may discover he is much alarmed," Lund wrote unkindly. Wet weather all spring had put them behind with the plantation work. The crabs, thorns, and cedars set out for hedges seemed to be all living, as well as the locusts on the north end and the flowering shrubbery on the south. But the house itself was as usual in trouble:

"Of all the worthless men living Lanphier is the greatest," Lund reported. "No act or temptation of mine can prevail upon him to come to work, notwithstanding his repeated promises to do so. I wanted so much to get the windows finished in the pediment, that I might have the garret passage plastered & cleaned out before Mr. Sam Washington's return. Besides this, the scaffolding at the front of the house cannot be taken away before it is finished. This prevents me from putting up the steps to the great front door . . . .

"We have some of our people sick, among them Ariona, a child of Alice's, who I believe must die. Worms I believe is the cause of its illness. The others not so bad.

"Make my compliments to Mrs. Washington and tell her I shall take care to bring or send the cotton she wrote for, and that I received the letter she mentions. The grandchildren are two beauties, and in good health. . . . . ."

Ariona does not appear in the 1786 inventory. The first child born to Jack and Nelly Custis, named Eliza, had arrived during August of '76 after their return to Mount Airy from the winter at Cambridge headquarters. The second, another Martha, always to be called Patty, was born in December, '77.

When Lund wrote again on May 6th he had been prevented from setting out by rain, a cold sore on his lip, and a dose of physic. After that he must really have got off, and there are no more letters until Washington's of August 15th, which makes no mention of Lund's visit to camp, but a letter from Washington to Captain Triplett, written at Valley Forge, and enclosing with his regrets Triplett's discharge from the army, mentions that he had received a letter from Triplett by Lund, so it is apparent that Lund did finally arrive, and escorted Martha home to Mount Vernon.

The August 5th letter from Washington to Lund is largely concerned with a proposed purchase of more land, which dragged on for some time, complicated by the depreciation everywhere—he remarks that a barrel of corn which used to sell for 10/ would now fetch 40/, and that pork had risen from £3 to £15 per barrel. He was willing to give Negroes in barter for the land, if such a deal could be made—"for to be plain, I wish to get quit of Negroes," he wrote. It oppressed him that Mount Vernon was scarcely able to support itself, in his absence—three wheat crops had failed, and he almost contemplated a return to tobacco. He advised Lund to press for the rents—"as a man who finds it difficult to pay one rent will find it infinitely more so to pay two, and his distresses multiply as the rents increase. . . . ."

"Never was there more rain of a summer than this," Lund lamented on the 19th of August. "We have more wet days than fair. No such thing as ploughing, nor is it in the power of people to keep their cornfields in proper order for sowing wheat . . . . . Frequently we have with the rain violent winds, which break the corn off below the ear, which is totally lost and most of it blown down in such a manner that it will be impossible to plough in wheat before the fodder is got; for set it upright one day and it is down the next, the ground being so soft. . . . ."

His letter of September 2d, in reply to Washington's of August 15th, was full of disaster. One of the most valuable slaves, Cooper James, had been drowned while bathing in the mill-race—a mystery, as he could not swim a stroke and was known to be afraid of water. And Carpenter James had so cut his foot and ankle by a stroke of his broad axe that it would be months before he could do his work again. Then Miller Roberts, a white man on wages at the Dogue Run Mill, sat for his portrait by Lund's uncompromising pen:

"Wm. Roberts and myself have had some talk about his continuing here longer. He, like most of the others, said his wages will not purchase him clothes, I in return tell him his services are not worth his wages. . . . . . Roberts has faults. He is fond of Drinking too much, and when in liquor is apt to be ill-natured, and at times neglects his duties by being absent drinking; although an excellent workman, yet he seldom lays his hands on anything more than the immediately and absolutely necessary repairs in the mill. There are many things he might do that is not done. They are put off from time to time until the year is expired, and then they are mentioned as necessary to be done next year, and made use of as an argument why it would be more to your advantage to employ him than another. . . . He is fond of horse-swapping, and new objects generally draw the attention more than the old. Consequently his time is taken up in that way when he might be doing something or other of more service to you. He has now 2 or 3 horses which he has picked up this summer, by chaffering one way or another. I believe by what he said to me he wants to winter two of them at your expense & be permitted to let them run in your pastures & to raise colts from them. Roberts is very clever provided the mill is always kept in wheat. I believe there are few millers as good as he is. He is active and industrious and keeps everything in order. But we have had little done by him since you left us except what little flour we have made. He has made 1 new water-wheel and done some other repairs in the mill, and has assisted in making and repairing the tumbling dam at Piney and Dogue Run, made a gate and dome in the race, frequently attended the mending of the race and so on. Indeed, I should do him injustice not to say that he is not only very clever in all such repairs, but very ready to attend to them. Whether these perfections or imperfections predominate I cannot say. I leave you to determine and say whether you will employ him or provide another, for I suppose one must be had. I am of the opinion if you and Roberts part he will repent it and be anxious after one year's experience to come home again, should you want him on your own terms. He now lives comfortably and well at your expense for provisions, except a few luxuries. He raises great quantities of fowl, rather more than he consumes. These he sells, although contrary to his agreement, for by that he was to raise for his own consumption only. But he says it is very hard, after taking the pains his wife does, that they should not be permitted to dispose of the overplus for the purpose of getting sugar, coffee, etc. You perhaps may expect me to give my opinions with respect to keeping Roberts. If a miller could be got of a more happy disposition than Roberts, for he is a strange-tempered man, for less wages—I think he is too high—it certainly would be preferable, for a miller being a millwright, cooper, or anything, if he does not work at these things when not employed in the mill, signifies nothing. Should you make a parting with him, would it not be well for you to write to some of your Pennsylvania acquaintances to look out for a miller for you? . . . . .

"I fear I shall not be able to get any workmen to assist Lanphier;

if so the covered ways will not get done. Our people are sickly, many of them having agues and fevers. We have so much wet weather, that we are overrun with grass, weeds, etc. Never was there in my remembrance in the month of August such pasturage, but whether it will fatten cattle etc. or not is by some a doubt. It rained all yesterday and looks likely to do the same today.

"I shall conclude this long epistle by assuring you that I always have been and still am anxious to do everything in my power for your interest. . . . .

"P.S. I robbed your trunk of this quire of paper; at the time I did, which was about ten days past, there was none to be got in Alexandria. . . . . ."

That is the last of Lund's letters which were preserved, until one dated in May, 1782, almost four years later. But this year of 1778 ended with two from Washington to Lund written from the Middlebrook Headquarters in New Jersey in December.

XXI

THE war had ground to a standstill again for another winter, and so far no one was in a position to foresee that compared to the last one at Valley Forge this winter would be a respite. The French alliance promised much, if Washington could hold out till it began to produce material results in men and supplies. Young Lafayette's arrival in the Headquarters family was stimulating, to say the least, and the German drillmaster Steuben had done wonders for the morale and discipline of the troops. The British had evacuated Philadelphia in June, in dread of the French Fleet, and Admiral D'Estaing actually did establish a base at Newport in Rhode Island during the summer. Clinton replaced Howe in the British command, and after the indecisive battle of Monmouth he had settled down to hold New York City to the bitter end.

Washington had chosen a comfortable white frame house at Middlebrook for his winter Headquarters, but he met Martha at Philadelphia on her way up, to spend a gay Christmas season in the recovered capital before they retired together to the cramped rigors of Headquarters life with the army. Depreciation of Continental currency had become a serious complication to the always harassing problem of feeding and clothing the men under arms.

He was in a low frame of mind when he wrote the December letters to Lund. The deal for the land he wanted to buy from his Maryland neighbor Thomas Marshall, of Marshall Hall opposite the old Posey farm, hung fire on a disagreement over the boundaries and the number of acres involved, which led him to suspect that Marshall was trying to take advantage of Lund in his absence. Jacky Custis had bought the plantation called Abingdon near Alexandria, on a long-term agreement involving compound interest payments, and Washington felt he had been taken advantage of by its former owners, hunting companions who had always been considered friends.

"Jack will have made a delightful hand of it, should the money continue to depreciate as it has lately done, having sold his own land in a manner for a song, and be flown in his purchase of the Alexanders," he wrote, to Lund. "If this should be the case, it will be only adding to the many proofs we daily see, of the folly of leaving bargains unbound by solemn covenants. I see so many instances of the rapacity of mankind, that I am almost out of conceit with my own species, and am convinced that the only way to make men honest is to prevent their being otherwise by tying them firmly to the accomplishment of the contracts....

"Has the meadow at the Ferry plantation, which in some former letter you informed me was much injured by an uncommon rainstorm, recovered the damage it then sustained? Are the bare places repaired? And is the grass well taken over the whole ground that was seeded? ......"

There was trouble over the bargain Lund had made in March with the eternal Lanphier, promising to add wool and corn to his wages in order to secure his services at all. Washington thought that Lanphier ought to receive the additional inducement, but should be obliged to continue at his present wages till the covered ways and other work contemplated at the time of the agreement were finished —however slowly they progressed. The depreciation worried him with regard to Lund's own wages, and he again offered Lund a share in the last crop, to be determined by Lund himself, in accordance with what he thought was right—"This it is my full wish to give, and more I do not think you would ask. Therefore we cannot disagree."

Writing to Lund in February, 1779, from Middlebrook, Washington dwelt again on his wish somehow to dispense with slave labor, though he confessed himself at a loss about how to time the change over, for the best of all concerned.

"The advantages resulting from the sale of my Negroes I have very little doubt of, because as I observed in my last, if we should ultimately prove unsuccessful (of which I am under no apprehension unless it falls on us as a punishment for our want of public, and indeed private, virtue) it would be a matter of very little consequence to me whether my property is in Negroes or loan office certificates, as I shall ask for, nor expect any favor from his most gracious Majesty, nor any person acting under his authority. The only points therefore for me to consider are, first, whether it would be most to my interest in case of a fortunate determination to the present contest to have Negroes and the crops they will make, or the sum they will now fetch and the interest of the money; and second, the critical moment to make this sale.

"With respect to the first point, if a Negro man will sell at or near £1000, and women and children in proportion, I have not the smallest doubt on which side the balance .... will preponderate. My scruples arise from a reluctance in offering these people at public vendue, and on account of the uncertainty of timing the sale well. In the first case, if these poor wretches are to be held in a state of slavery, I do not see that a change of masters will render it more irksome, provided husband and wife, and parents and children are not separated from each other, which is not my intentions to do......"

The slaves were not sold, and his will provided for them to receive their freedom after his and Martha's death.

Braddock's old orderly, Bishop, now an indulged pensioner at Mount Vernon, was feeling the universal pinch, and Washington addressed a letter of curt kindliness to him from Middlebrook on April 10th, assuring him that he would not let Bishop want "while we both live. But with respect to the increase of your wages," he added cautiously, "it is a circumstance that must depend upon the services you render in return." He directed Lund by the same post to furnish Bishop with "a reasonable quantity" of wool and flax for the clothing of Bishop's family, which consisted of a wife and one daughter, and left it to Lund to increase Bishop's wages if he saw fit.

On the 29th of May, '79, he wrote to Lund, still from Middlebrook, to acknowledge "the melancholy account of your prospects for a crop, and a still more melancholy one of the decay of public virtue. The first I submit to with the most perfect resignation and cheerfulness. I look upon every dispensation of Providence as designed to answer some valuable purpose, and hope I shall always possess a sufficient degree of fortitude to bear without murmuring any stroke which may happen, either to my person or estate, from that quarter. But I cannot with any degree of patience behold the infamous practices of speculators, monopolizers, and all that class of gentry, who are preying upon our very vitals, and for the sake of a little dirty pelf are putting the rights and liberties of the country into the most imminent danger, and continuing a war destructive to the lives and property of the most valuable part of this community, which would have ceased last fall as certain as we now exist, but for the encouragements the enemy derived from this source....."

After a winter of mild weather at Middlebrook, where the modest social gaieties of the officers' valiant wives were not quite defeated by the lack of refreshments in the worst food shortage yet encountered, there followed a relatively quiet summer, during which Washington never fought a battle, while the British gathered their forces for an assault on the South, as the war prepared to move away from the Commander-in-chief and fall upon his seconds below the James River.

In November of 1779 Lund married his cousin Elizabeth Foote, and brought her to Mount Vernon. Martha probably attended the wedding, as she did not leave home to join her husband at the Morristown winter Headquarters until late in that month. No letter survives from either Lund or George with a reference to the marriage, and Lund's Betsy remains a shadowy figure, religious and withdrawn, always in frail health though she survived her husband by many years. Unable to rear a child of her own, she apparently had charge of the third daughter born to Jack and Nelly Custis in the year of her marriage to Lund. The birth left the mother very ill, and little Nelly, who was to become the General's darling, was brought to Mount Vernon in her babyhood for nursing, doubtless at her grandmother's wish, to be left in Mrs. Lund's care when Martha set out for the second winter at Morristown.

Other changes were taking place in the Virginia society which Washington had not been free for five years to enjoy. His brother

Sam's fourth wife, Anne Steptoe Washington, died after an inoculation for small-pox, leaving three young sons and a baby daughter, and Sam would marry again. Betty's husband, Fielding Lewis, was in failing health, having recklessly expended his fortune and his strength for the colonial cause at his small-arms factory in Fredericksburg. William Augustine, son of George's half-brother Austin, had married his first cousin Jane of Bushfield, whom Robert Carter's tutor Fithian had so admired in '74, and a son was born. Her brother Bushrod, John Augustine's eldest son, had graduated from William and Mary College and meant to be a lawyer. Bryan Fairfax's outspoken Tory sentiments had got him into hot water more than once since the death of his first wife, who had been Betsy Cary. Mary Cary Ambler had died a widow at Jamestown, and Anne's husband, Robert Carter Nicholas, was dead. The fourth Cary sister, lovely Sally Fairfax, when last heard of was living at Bath in England with George William, in poor health and reduced circumstances, their Virginia estates in danger of confiscation.

The beloved Nancy Bassett was dead at Eltham in her thirty-ninth year, leaving two sons and a daughter—Burwell II, John, and Fanny. Martha's youngest sister Betsy Dandridge Aylett had been left a childless widow at twenty-eight, and soon married again. George Mason at Gunston, seven years a widower and his youngest child still only ten years old, had married Sarah Brent of Woodstock on the Potomac, whom he must have known all his life, as she was only a little younger than his own age of fifty-four—"a lady of amiable and domestic character," who doubtless brought order and comfort into his household as his older children married and left it. Thomas Jefferson was Governor of Virginia now. William Byrd III was a bankrupt suicide, leaving his wife and several beautiful daughters at splendid Westover on the James, where they would entertain the traitor Arnold in the spring of '81, confirming suspicions of their obstinate Tory sympathies—only to enchant the French officers who visited the house after Yorktown.

The second Morristown winter proved to be much worse in many ways than the one at Valley Forge, while the British sat tight in New York and sent out raiding parties which did little damage beyond the alarm and confusion they caused in the American camp.

The Headquarters family was housed in the gracious Ford mansion, where they were however overcrowded, short of food, and suffering from the unprecedented cold and snowstorms.

In the midst of privation, Washington was compelled, probably for the sake of Martha's safety and comfort on the homeward journey, to order a new chariot from Philadelphia. On April 8th he was writing to his friend Mitchell in the commissary department, that the painting of it must be well done, "and in a tasty stile with respect to colour . . . . . Though I prefer a plain chariot, it may not be amiss to ornament the mouldings with light airy gilding; this will add little to the expense and much to the appearance. The harness I would have stout and strong, at the same time neatly made, ornamented, and of good leather." In order to pay for it, he had written to Lund to send specie from Mount Vernon, but he assured his correspondent that the workmen would not be disappointed, as "the pocket money which Mrs. Washington has, and some which I can borrow here, added to what you are kind enough to offer, will enable me to pay the full sum at any hour, even if I should not receive the needful from home by the time the chariot is ready for delivering. . . . ."

Mrs. Washington's pocket money—put towards a new chariot.

In May of 1780, while Washington was still at Morristown, General Lincoln surrendered Charleston in South Carolina to Clinton and Cornwallis, along with his whole army, and it seemed the end of the world, but there was worse to come. Gates lost the battle of Camden in North Carolina to Cornwallis in August, and in September Benedict Arnold's treason was discovered at West Point. By the time Washington went into winter Headquarters at New Windsor on the Hudson, Arnold was actually commanding a British raiding force along the shores of the James River. But a French army had landed at Newport, and Washington held grimly to the prospect of a joint action with them against the British in New York, in the spring.

On March 28th, '81, he wrote one of his homesick letters to Lund from the New Windsor Headquarters, where they were awaiting news from Chesapeake Bay after the French Fleet had contrived by delay and confusion to lose Arnold's raiding force. The British in New York meanwhile were thought to be making an effort to reinforce Arnold in Virginia.

"How many Lambs have you had this Spring?" Washington's wistful queries ran. "How many Colts are you like to have? Is your covered ways done? What are you going about next? Have you any prospect of getting Paint and Oyl? are you going to repair the Pavement of the Piazza? is anything doing, or like to be done, with respect to the Well at the edge of the Hill in front of the House? Have you made good the decayed Trees at the ends of the House and in the Hedges &ca., &ca.? Have you made any attempts to reclaim more Land for meadow &ca., &ca? An account of these things would be satisfactory to me and infinitely amusing in the recital, as I have these kind of improvements very much at heart. As soon as you can conveniently do it after receipt of this letter, give me a list of the number and kind of Mares I possess, the number of Colts, from four years old (inclusive) to those of this spring with the ages, colour, kind, and Sexes. Mrs. Washington (from report only, I believe) has taken a fancy to a Horse belonging to Mr. James Cleveland, brother to the one had from him before (and wch. I think a very fine horse.) If you can get him in the way of barter, provided he is as handsome and as fine a horse as represented, and the color of the set she drives, I shall be very well pleased with your doing it. She joins me in best wishes for you, Mrs. Washington, and Milly Posey. . . . ."

The spring of 1781 brought back to Virginia memories of the first summer of the war and its British raids in the Tidewater Rivers. With the ruthless British cavalry leader, Colonel Tarleton, spearheading Cornwallis's northward thrust into Virginia after his Carolina successes, and Lafayette leading a small American force south to head him off, while Washington remained on the Hudson consolidating his army with the French under Rochambeau at Newport, British armed vessels once more ventured up the Potomac and alarm spread into Alexandria.

Lighthorse Harry Lee's father, at Leesylvania near Dumfries, wrote to Governor Jefferson in April, telling of a raid which was driven off after the crew of a schooner had stolen some Negroes and burned some buildings in the vicinity: "If the enemy had succeeded at Alexandria they intended, one of the prisoners says, to have burnt General Washington's house, plundered Colonel Mason and myself, and endeavoured to have made me a prisoner." In May, George Mason wrote to his friend Chapman in Maryland, near the home of his first wife, that he was sending his valuables there for safe keeping, and expected to follow the next day with his wife and daughters.

Martha was still at Headquarters on the Hudson, and it was from Lafayette that Washington learned the disturbing news that Lund at Mount Vernon, after all his stout prophecies in '75, not only had not driven off a British landing party with gunfire, but had received them civilly and supplied them with provisions from the mansion house–apparently in hope of preserving the property from devastation. In this he was successful, but at least a dozen slaves, both men and women, had been taken away, or had willingly accompanied the British when they departed. Washington was both angry and humiliated at the behaviour of his manager, and wrote a sharp rebuke to Lund from New Windsor on April 30th, in reply to Lund's account of the visit, which apparently had not attempted to conceal the hospitality reported by Lafayette:

"It would have been a less painful circumstance to me, to have heard, that in consequence of your non-compliance with their request they had burnt my House, and laid the Plantation in ruins," Washington wrote. "You ought to have considered yourself as my representative, and should have reflected on the bad example of communicating with the enemy, and making a voluntary offer of refreshments to them with a view to prevent a conflagration.

"It was not in your power, I acknowledge, to prevent them from sending a flag on shore, and you did right to meet it; but you should, in the same instant that the business of it was unfolded, have declared, explicitly, that it was improper for you to yield to the request; after which, if they had proceeded to help themselves, *by force*, you could but have submitted (and being unprovided for defence) this was to be preferred to a feeble opposition which only serves as a pretext to burn and destroy.

"I am thoroughly perswaded that you acted from your best

judgment; and believe that your desire to preserve my property, and rescue the buildings from impending danger, were your governing motives. But to go on board their Vessels; carry them refreshments; commune with a parcel of plundering Scoundrels, and request a favour by asking the surrender of my Negroes, was exceedingly ill-judged, and 'tis to be feared, will be unhappy in its consequences, as it will be a precedent for others, and may become a subject of animadversion.

"I have no doubt of the enemy's intention to prosecute the plundering plan they have begun. And, unless a stop can be put to it by the arrival of a superior naval force, I have as little doubt of its ending in the loss of all my Negroes, and in the destruction of my House; but I am prepared for the event, under the prospect of which if you could deposit in Safety at some convenient distance from the water the most valuable and least bulky articles it might be consistent with policy and prudence, and is a means of preserving them for use hereafter. Such and so many things as are necessary for common and present use must be retained and run their chance through the firy trial of this summer.

"Mrs. Washington joins me in best and affectionate regard for you, Mrs. Washington, and Milly Posey; and does most sincerely regret your loss. I do not know what Negroes they may have left you; and as I have observed before I do not know what number they will have left me by the time they have done; but this I am sure of, that you shall never want assistance while it is in my power to afford it. I am, &ca. . . . ."

On the 31st of May he wrote again to Lund with reference to the removal of his portable valuables from the riverside, while the buildings took their chance—"To hear of their being plundered or burnt will be no surprise to me"—and advised that livestock of all kinds should be driven out of reach of the enemy. There was a P.S: "By your figures in your letter of the 19th I do not know whether the number of your lambs is 118 or 218."

The Diary resumes on May 1, 1781, at his camp on the Hudson, with a rather dreary resumé of the situation as he saw it—"instead of a glorious offensive campaign before us, we have a bewildered and gloomy defensive one—" but the arrival of a French Fleet under

Admiral DeGrasse changed the prospect almost over night. In mid-August the tremendous decision was taken, to abandon New York for the present to its British garrison and march southward with the French against Cornwallis, who was now entrenching himself at Yorktown, crowded into a corner and brought to bay by Lafayette's little army.

On the 19th of August the march of the combined French and American armies from the Hudson began. On the 9th of September, by hard riding in the company of a single aide, the devoted Colonel Humphreys, thus gaining time over the French Staff who did not attempt to keep up with him, Washington arrived at the door of Mount Vernon.

XXII

THE entry in the Diary for that September day in 1781 reads simply: "I reached my own Seat at Mount Vernon (distant 120 Miles from the Hd. of Elk) where I stayed till the 12th, and in three days afterwards that is on the 15th reached Williamsburg."

Three days at home, after six years of war. Martha had returned to Virginia from New Windsor in July, when it was still thought that the next campaign would be fought around New York. The excitement, the rejoicing, the satisfaction, at Mount Vernon must all be imagined. The house still stood, perhaps thanks only to Lund's unhappy compromise at the time of the spring raids up the River. The improvements must have been gratifying, for all the hitches, shortages, and delay they had encountered. Washington had never seen any one of Jack's four children, who were brought down from Abingdon to be displayed, the youngest, the boy named George Washington Parke Custis, only a few months old.

Jack caught fire from the uniforms and the chargers and the military bustle, determined belatedly to see something of the war, and joined his step-father's Staff as a volunteer aide-de-camp. There was for Washington the pride of entertaining the French Allies, Rochambeau and his Staff, at the American Commander-in-chief's home, and they expressed themselves as enchanted with everything, from their gracious hostess right down to the humming-birds which whirred about the blossoms in the flower-garden. But the knowledge that the end was now in sight was hidden from them all, as Washington rode out again determined to finish the job at whatever cost, however long it might take.

Cornwallis surrendered at Yorktown seven weeks later, on October 17th. Even then, they had no idea that the fighting war was over. The British still held New York, Charleston, and Savannah, and the triumph over Cornwallis was dimmed by family tragedy. Jack Custis was taken ill with camp-fever during the Yorktown siege, and Washington had him conveyed to Burwell Bassett's house for nursing. He died there on November 5th, a few hours after Washington had been summoned from his Williamsburg Headquarters to join Jack's frantic wife and mother at his bedside.

The Diary breaks off again here, on an unfinished sentence, as though he had laid down his pen to mount a horse for the ride to Eltham, and it was not resumed, or is missing, until the autumn of 1784, after he had been nearly a year at home.

When they had seen Jack buried in the garden at Eltham, Washington escorted Martha and the young widow back to Mount Vernon, where the children had been left when news of their father's illness hurried their mother and grandmother down to Eltham. Nelly, the mother of four, was still only twenty-three years old.

The few days Washington could spend at Mount Vernon then were devoted to Jack's affairs and not his own. It was arranged for the children's uncle, Bartholomew Dandridge, to take their guardianship, as the Commander-in-chief must at once accompany his army back to the Hudson for another war winter. When he set out northward from Mount Vernon on November 20th, Martha had conquered her grief sufficiently to be beside him in the coach. After another Christmas in Philadelphia, entertained by Congress and their many friends, they journeyed on together to the bleak little stone house at Newburgh which was to be the 1781-2 Headquarters.

Not much is known now about the fire which that winter destroyed the stable at Mount Vernon which had been built in 1768, and ten valuable horses. Lund's account of the disaster, which reached Washington while he was still in Philadelphia in January, 1782, has not survived, but Washington wrote to him from there in the usual detail with regard to the rebuilding of the stable, approving Lund's plan on the whole, "provided the Coach house can be placed in the middle; without which, the House, with large and dble. doors at one end would have an uncouth appearance. . . ."

George's brother Sam, of Harewood in the Valley, died that winter, leaving his fifth wife a widow, and four surviving children; and almost at the same time the news reached them at Newburgh of the death of Betty's husband, Fielding Lewis, at Fredericksburg. His estate was hopelessly impoverished by the small-arms factory he had operated there, and his other contributions to the war effort, which had sapped his never robust health. Their only daughter, among five surviving sons, another Betty, had married at sixteen the previous year, Charles Carter of Blenheim in Albemarle County, and the three younger boys were still at home. In the same month, Bryan Fairfax wrote of the death of old Lord Fairfax at ninety-one, a ramping Tory to the end, unable to forgive his one-time protégé for conquering Cornwallis.

On August 7th, Washington at Newburgh addressed a blistering dressing-down to Price Posey, much in the tone of his letters to Price's ne'er-do-well father almost twenty years before: "With a mixture of surprise, concern, and even horror, have I heard of your treatment of the deceased Mr. Custis—in the abuse and misapplication of the estate which he had committed with much confidence, I am sure, and I believe personal regard, to your management......"

In the autumn of 1782 his concern for the health of his nephew, George Augustine Washington, son of Charles, began to be evident, and from then until his death in '93 George Augustine occupied almost the place of a son in the General's life. He had served as a writing-aide at Headquarters for several years, despite bouts of fever and debility caused by his weak chest and chronic colds. During the summer of '82 he left the Staff for a rest at Mount Vernon, and when Martha went north for the second winter at the Newburgh Headquarters George Augustine had retired to his father's house in Berkeley County, where he seemed not to improve.

Lund's surviving correspondence during the summer of '82 was concerned largely with the complicated Custis estate, and further purchases of land adjacent to Mount Vernon—even now, Washington could not resist adding to his acres. On the 4th of December Lund wrote that Colonel Mason had sent a haunch of venison and a basket of white apples and pippins to Mrs. Washington with his and Mrs. Mason's compliments—just too late to be included in the supply of delicacies she always stowed in the chariot to enliven the spartan fare at Headquarters.

The letter from Lund on December 11th, '82, returns again to the fascinating minutiae at Mount Vernon, in response to inquiries from Washington.

"The trees in the pasture were trimmed last winter, and shall again be gone over this winter. They were trimmed of equal height. They shall be done in the way you direct. I planted the flowering shrubs at the north end of the house among the locust which were first directed to be put there, and most of them died. I planted them again, but few of them lived, and I will again plant them as you seem to wish them to grow at that end of the house, but I think you will never cut away the locust, which now flourish there, for little ill thriving trees that perhaps may be many years before they look well....

"My compliments to Mrs. Washington, and tell her Washington [George Washington Parke Custis, now aged less than two years] and Nelly were yesterday at Abingdon in perfect health and spirits. Betty [Mrs. Lund] presents her very respectful compliments to you both. She was on Saturday night delivered of a dead child. She is now very well, and I hope will continue so. I have heard nothing from G.W. [George Augustine Washington] He is not yet, I believe come from Berkeley [County]. I fear he is very ill......"

Washington's letter written at Newburgh on Christmas Day, 1782, is in direct reply to this one of Lund's.

"I observe what you say respecting the Flowering Shrubs and other Ornamental Trees at the No. end of the House, and as the locusts by the goodness of their growth may lay claim to an establishment there, I wish that the afore-mentioned shrubs and curious trees may be planted at both ends that I may determine hereafter from circumstances and appearances which shall be the grove and which the wilderness. It is easy to extirpate Trees from any spot, but time only can bring them to maturity.

"In a drawer in the locker of the desk which stands in my study you will find two small (fore) teeth; which I beg of you to wrap up carefully and send enclosed in your next letter to me. I am positive I left them there, or in the secret drawer in the locker of the same desk......

"P.S. When the case will admit of it, the trees and flowering shrubs that are transplanted to the ends of the House have a better chance of living if taken from the open fields than the woods. In the first case they have been more accustomed to bear drought, and are hardier than those taken from the woods, where sun, winds, frosts, nor drought has had much power on them. And besides, are handsomer."

In January, '83, he wrote a letter of sound and even humorous advice to his nephew Bushrod, who was then embarking on the study of law in Philadelphia, and the following day he exploded to Bushrod's father, John Augustine Washington, in one of his rare fits of exasperation, as everything was coming at him at once and the peace treaty which would release him to deal with his family affairs still hung fire.

"In Gods name how did my brothr. Saml. contrive to get himself so enormously in debt?" he exclaimed. "Was it by purchase? By misfortunes? or shear indolence and inattention to business? From whatever cause it proceeded, the matter is now the same, and curiosity only prompts the inquiry, as it does to know what will be saved, and how it is disposed of......

"I have lately received a letter from my Mother in which she complains *much* of the knavery of the overseer at the Little Falls quarter; that she says she can get nothing from him..... *The whole profit of the plantation according to her acct. is applied to his own use*, which is rather hard upon me, as I had no earthly inducement to meddle with it, but to comply with her wish and to free her from care. This, like every other matter of private concern with me has been totally neglected; but it is too much while I am suffering in every other way (and hardly able to keep my own Estate from Sale) to be saddled with all the expenses of hers and not be able to derive the smallest return from it. She has requested that I would get somebody to attend to it...... I must therefore desire the favour of you to take it under your care......

"While I am talking of my Mother, and her concerns, I am impelled to mention some things which have given and still continue to give me pain. About two years ago a gentleman of my acquaintance [Benjamin Harrison] informed me that it was in contemplation to move for a pension for her in the Virginia Assembly; that he did not suppose I knew of the measure or that it would be agreeable to me to have it done; but wished to know my sentiments on it. I instantly wrote to him that it was new and astonishing to me, and begged that he would prevent the motion if possible, or oppose it if made; for I was sure she had not a child that would not share the last farthing with her, and that would not be hurt at the idea of her becoming a Pensioner, or in other words receiving charity. Since *then*, I have heard nothing of *that* matter; but I learn from very good authority that she is upon all occasions and in all Companies complaining of the hardness of the times, of her wants and distresses; and if not in direct terms at least by strong innuendoes inviting favours which not only make *her* appear in an unfavourable point of view, but those who are connected with her. That she can have no *real* wants that may not be supplied I am sure of; imaginary wants are indefinite and oftentimes insatiable, because they are boundless, and always changing. the reason of my mentioning these matters to you is that you may inquire into her real wants and see what is necessary to make her comfortable; ..... at the same time, I wish you to represent to her in delicate terms the impropriety of her complaints and acceptance of favours, even where they are voluntarily offered, from any but relations. It will not do to touch upon this subject in a letter to her, and therefore I have avoided it. . . . ."

Lund's letters of January, 1783, contained some meager figures on the corn and wheat crop, and a confession that the fly had got into what was stored in the barn. "I generally put off writing from one day to another," he added ingenuously. "I had rather be employed in the most laborious way than copying any writing whatever, and this it is that makes me often neglect the work of that kind and causes me often to keep irregular accounts. At present I believe I shall send it by the next post. . . . . ."

Again we have Washington's direct reaction, in a roll of thunder.

"Delicacy hitherto and a hope that you long ago would have seen into the propriety of the measure, without a hint of it from me, has restrained me from telling you that annual Accts. of my Crops, together with the receipts and expenditures of my money, state of my stock, &ca., ought to have been sent to me as regularly as the year came about. It is not to be supposed that all the avocations of my public duties, great and laborious as they have been, could render me totally insensible to the *only means* by which myself and family; and the character I am to maintain in life hereafter, is to be supported; or that a previous account of these things would not have been exceedingly satisfactory to me. Instead of this, except the acct. rendered at Valley forge in the year 1778, I have received none since I left home; and not till 2 or 3 applications in the course of last year could I get any acct. of the Crop of the preceding one; and then only of the Corn, by the Post on Sunday last. . . . . .

"I have now to beg that you will not only send me the Accounts of your receipts, and expenditures of Specie; but of every kind of money subsequent to the Acct. exhibited at Valley Forge, which ended some time in April 1778.

"I want to know before I come home (as I shall come home with empty pockets whenever Peace shall take place) how affairs stand with me, and what my dependence is. I wish also to know what I have to expect from the wheat of 1781 and '82, as you say the two Crops are so blended that they cannot be rendered separately. How are settlements to be made with and justice done to the several Parties interested under these circumstances? . . . . ."

Lund, of course, was hurt, and both were showing the strain, as his reply went north.

"Be assured I never had the smallest intention or most distant wish to keep you from the knowledge of your private affairs under my care. I do ever desire indeed to have transmitted you an acct. from time to time of what money I have received and in what manner it has been applied; it should have been done when I sent that acct. while you were at Valley Forge. It was unasked. You never hinted you wished a continuation of it. When I told you that I would send an acct. of the receipts and expenditures of hard money you never said it would be agreeable. True it is, I put it off much longer than I intended, but it was owing to ill-luck rather than an unwillingness to do it. It is customary and from long habit

I cannot refrain, for me in all weather to be out, and I cannot sit contented at a table writing when I might be looking after something outside. When it rains I get to that work, and then very probable am prevented by some person at the house. But had I known from you that you expected all those seed accts., nothing would have put me off from sending them. I never have and I hope never shall be happy when I do not do that which seems to give satisfaction......

"It is painful to me to make excuses for bad crops, but owing to one cause or another, we have not made a good one in my remembrance....."

The matter still rankled in Washington in June. Lund had apparently sought to make clumsy amends for his inefficiency by not drawing out his own wages for the past several years, an omission which appeared in the accounts which finally reached Washington at Newburgh. "I shall be more hurt than anything else," he wrote then, "to think that an Estate which I have drawn nothing from for 8 years and which always enabled me to make any purchase I had in view, should not have been able for the last 5 years to pay the manager; and that worse than going home to empty coffers and expensive living, I shall be encumbered with debt. It is disagreeable to me, because I dare say it will be so to you, to make these observations, but as my public business is now drawing to a close I cannot avoid looking towards my private concerns, which do not wear the most smiling countenance......"

Proof that the war with England was over, though the peace had not yet been ratified, came during July of '83 with a letter from George William Fairfax—the first which had come through from him in years. He sent his congratulations on his friend's victory, and remarked that he was now being pestered for introductions to the American Commander-in-chief by intending travellers. Washington's reply was prompt and cordial. Belvoir had suffered from a disastrous fire during its occupation by tenants, and was no longer fit for habitation, and he broke the news with characteristic stoicism. "There was nothing wanting in this letter to give compleat satisfaction to Mrs. Washington and myself but some expression to induce us to believe that you would once more be our neighbours," he wrote. "Your house at Belvoir I am sorry to add is no more, but mine (which is enlarged since you saw it) is most sincerely and heartily at your service till you could rebuild it...... and till you forbid me to indulge the wish I shall not *despair* of seeing you and Mrs. Fairfax once more the inhabitants of Belvoir, and greeting you both there, the intimate companions of our old age as you have been of our younger years....."

But the Fairfaxes, impaired in health and fortune, never saw Virginia again.

During the summer of '83 Lund forwarded the information that a new roof was needed for the mansion—and that Jack Custis's widow was apparently taking an interest in their neighbour Dr. David Stuart, a widower of a certain age, with three grown children by his first wife.

"I am truly unfortunate that after all the expence I have been at about my House I am to encounter the third Edition, with the trouble & inconvenience of another cover to it, after my return," Washington wrote wearily from Newburgh in August. "That there can have been little attention or judgment exercised heretofore in covering it is a fact that cannot admit a doubt; for he must be a miserable artizan or a very great rascal indeed who after one experim't could not tell what kind of shingles were necessary to prevent a common roof from leaking, or how to place them as they ought to be." He then specified exactly what kind of shingle was to be bespoke, and from whom, and gave the measurements, and passed on to the suspected romance. "Mrs. Custis has never suggested in any of her Letters to Mrs. Washington the most distant attachment to Dr. S—t, unless ardent wishes for her speedy return could be so construed.—But if this is the case, & she wants advice upon it, Where is her Father and Mother, those Guardians & advisers pointed out by Nature?—With respect to myself, I am too much acquainted with Women to give advice to any of them, when they are bound for the Port of Matrimony; because I never shall advise *any one* to Marry the Man she does not like—and because I know it is to no purpose to advise them to refrain from the Man they do....."

In August the Washingtons left Newburgh for Princeton, where Congress was in session and a festival spirit prevailed, though the British still gave no indication of their inevitable evacuation of New York. From Princeton Washington wrote to Bushrod at Philadelphia, commissioning various purchases in anticipation of the return to Virginia—"2 dozen strong, neat, and plain, but fashionable Table chairs with strong canvas bottoms"—French wines, imported nuts, fruits, olives, anchovies, etc.—blue and white table china—and he added an inquiry as to the status of French silver plate in fashionable society.

Martha preceded him homeward through Philadelphia in October, purchasing linens and other household goods on the way.

On October 1st Lund wrote to him the last letter which remains before Washington's arrival at Mount Vernon in December—home, as they all thought then, to stay. Spurred by criticism, Lund had made a tour of the western properties, and failed to collect a shilling of the rents. "I know not how it is, but I have been threatened with sickness this summer without being laid up altogether, more than ever I was in my life," he complained, along with his other news. Miller Roberts, whose shortcomings had been gone into as long ago as '78, had refused this year to sign a new contract which he considered placed too much restriction upon his fatal weakness of "abominable drunkenness and quarrelsome frolics." Roberts declared his intention of leaving Mount Vernon and buying a mill for himself, where he might, as it were, get drunk on his own time. (Within the month, however, Roberts thought better of this, gave the strongest promises to Lund of mending his ways, and signed up for another year.) "As to Bateman, the old gardener, I have no expectation of his ever seeking another home," wrote Lund. "Indulge him but in getting drunk now and then, and he will be happy. He is the best kitchen gardener to be met with." Dr. Stuart was purchasing a place in Alexandria—which might have something to do with the supposed attachment between him and Mrs. Custis. Nelly and little Washington continued in perfect health—the two elder girls, Eliza and Patty, were apparently always of less interest to everyone—and had escaped the prevailing fevers and agues which had prostrated everyone else.

On the 25th of November, 1783, the British finally gave up New

York, and Washington entered the city on their heels amid general celebration. There he bade farewell to his officers in an emotional meeting at Fraunce's Tavern, and rode to Philadelphia, where he paused to make more purchases of household goods and presents for the family at Mount Vernon. His next obligation was at Baltimore, where Congress was now sitting, and which required him to endure more congratulations and ceremony before he could escape southward, with three of his aides—including Colonel Humphreys, whose friendship was to endure for many years to come—to accompany him at a hard gallop.

He reached Mount Vernon in time for dinner on Christmas Eve, 1783.

XXIII

THE war was won at last, decisively and without compromise. The colonies were an independent confederation of states, and the weaknesses inherent in their system of government were not immediately apparent.

When a few days after a gay family Christmas with more than enough to eat for everybody, Washington saw his aides off for their respective homes in New York and Connecticut, each with a present of a hundred dollars from his own pocket for travelling expenses, he must have turned indoors with the deepest sigh of relief a man ever drew. He was home again—crippled financially but not physically; he was young enough—fifty-two—to look forward to years of the life he loved best, as the master of Mount Vernon, cherishing his acres, experimenting with new crops and fertilizers and implements, breeding his horses and hounds, grafting his fruit trees, collecting rare plants and shrubs—repairing, building, enlarging, perfecting.

It was in a way like 1759 all over again, when he had retired from the western frontier to marry Martha. Then he had embarked confidently on a similar program, and then there were her two small children, Jacky and Patsy Custis, to enliven the house. Now, almost a quarter of a century later, the two youngest children of Jacky, "little Washington" and Nelly, at practically the same ages, became permanent members of the Mount Vernon household after the marriage of their mother to David Stuart early in 1784.

The Diary for that first year at home is missing, except for a journal of the autumn trip to his western lands which occupied the month of September. But it is possible in his letters to find an almost audible relaxing of tensions as he wrote to the scattered Headquarters friends whose own hardships and homesickness he had shared for the past eight years.

To Lafayette: "At length, my dear Marquis, I am become a private citizen on the banks of the Potomac and under the shadow of my own Vine and my own Fig-tree; free from the bustle of a camp and the busy scenes of public life, I am solacing myself with these tranquil enjoyments of which the Soldier, who is ever in pursuit of fame, the Statesman whose watchful days and sleepless nights are spent in devising schemes to promote the welfare of his own, and the ruin of other countries, as if this globe was insufficient for us all, and the Courtier who is always watching the countenance of his Prince in hopes of catching a gracious smile, can have very little conception. I am not only retired from all public employments, but I am retiring within myself; and shall be able to view the solitary walk, and tread the paths of private life with heartfelt satisfaction. Envious of none, I am determined to be pleased with all; and this, my dear friend, being the order for my march, I will move gently down the stream of life, until I sleep with my Fathers. . . . . ."

And to General Knox, that most dependable of all his officers, still only thirty-three years old, and weighing well over two hundred pounds, who had retired with his stout, jolly Lucy and their brood of children to his Boston home, before assuming the responsibilities of Secretary at War to succeed Lincoln, in '85, Washington wrote in February:

"I am just beginning to experience that ease and freedom from public cares which, however desirable, takes some time to realize; for strange as it may tell, it is nevertheless true, that it was not till lately I could get the better of my usual custom of ruminating as soon as I waked in the Morning, on the business of the ensuing day; and of my surprize, after having revolved many things in my mind, to find that I was no longer a public Man, nor had anything to do with public transactions.

"I feel now however as I conceive a wearied traveller must do who, after treading many a painful step with a heavy burden on his shoulders, is eased of the latter, having reached the Goal to which all the former were directed; and from the Housetop is looking back and tracing with a grateful eye the Meanders by which he escaped the quicksands and Mires which lay in his way; and into which none but the All-powerful guide and great disposer of human Events could have prevented his falling......"

The weather co-operated to emphasize his isolation from the world he had left behind him; in one of the most severe winters in its history Mount Vernon was snowbound until towards the end of February. "The bad weather, and the great care the post riders take of themselves, prevented your letters of the 3d and 9th of last month from getting into my hands till the 10th," he wrote Knox, who shared among other bonds the Spartan memories of Valley Forge.

He made good use of the time he was confined to the house and prevented even from a duty visit to his mother at Fredericksburg, by sitting long hours at his desk in the still unfinished library room, working at his endless correspondence. It was plain that retired or not, he still needed a secretary. He missed his aides, both for their company and their services at the writing-table—he missed Harrison's plodding pen, Hamilton's flashing phrases and beautiful handwriting, Humphreys' good humor, and George Augustine Washington's tireless devotion.

Robert Hanson Harrison, his pre-war neighbor and lawyer, favorite of them all, was now called Judge instead of Colonel, and lived at Port Tobacco in Maryland with his two motherless girls. Harrison would come to dinner when the weather broke, but his health was still affected by the hardships of his war service. He was all of thirty-nine. Hamilton had married wealthy General Schuyler's daughter Betsy, and was practicing law at Albany, after a brief term in Congress—he might never see Hamilton again. Humphreys had to make a living somehow—if Congress had any sense they would make Humphreys Foreign Secretary, and Washington had so recommended, the only suggestion of its kind he ever made to what he called his former masters, and it was doubtful if they would take the slightest notice.

As for George Augustine, they must get him to a milder climate for a while—Barbados had not saved Lawrence, of course—perhaps the Carolinas, where their kinsman, Colonel William Washington, had established himself in a house called Sandy Hill outside Charleston, with a new wife won while he was a prisoner of war during the British occupation. In any case Mount Vernon must foot the bill for George Augustine, as his father had never even found the money properly to finish his odd house in the Valley. Until the time of Charles's death Happy Retreat consisted of the two wings only, connected by an open passageway where the main central section should have been.

Gradually the family story during Washington's long absence filled itself in, and as the current situation of his relations and dependents, as well as his neighbors unfolded, he found in most of it ample cause for worry, arbitration, and assistance in cash. He had sent in his accounts to Congress, for the war years—only his expenses, he had said that June day in Philadelphia in '75 when they named him Commander-in-chief and offered $300 a month in pay—he would take only his expenses, the money he paid out of his own pocket for the privilege of serving his country for what proved to be eight years of hardship, danger, anxiety, criticism, and boredom. (Dr. Fitzpatrick in 1933 estimated the total around $200,000.) He had stuck to it. There would be no compensation now for the greater cost of the lost profits at Mount Vernon, the bad debts and rents not collected, the deterioration and neglect of his property, the precious forfeited years at home. Congress paid up. But it was all spent almost before it reached his hands.

His sister Betty Lewis, widowed at forty-nine, had written to him in August, '83, while he was marking time at Princeton before the Peace Treaty released him: "My Pore Dear Mr. Lewis, and my Brother Sam both lay ill at the same time, and it was the Lords will to take them to Himself, in three weeks, one ofter the other. And with Confinement, and the uneasiness of mind it caus'd me to get into an ill state of health that I expect'd shortly to follow them. It happened at a time when everything Contributed to ad to my uneasiness..... I thank God I am recovering my helth fast, and Please myself with thoughts of shortly Seeing you once more with us; and to Continue in Peace and Quiet for the remainder of our Dayes which is the sincere and ardent Prayer of your affectionate and loving sister......"

As soon as the weather permitted he rode to Fredericksburg.

Betty's three youngest boys were attending the Fredericksburg Academy—Lawrence was seventeen, Robert was fifteen, and Howell thirteen. Fielding Lewis had mortgaged everything he owned to finance his gun factory, and his weapons had played a part at the siege of Yorktown, while his wife and her women friends were said to have joined in making cartridges. Now there were taxes overdue, and a debt of some £7000. But the stucco work had been exquisitely finished at Millbank, and the ceilings and over-mantels were among the finest in Virginia. Betty hoped by selling off some land and establishing a school for small children in the house, with a tutor, that she might keep the place going. Washington, to whom a beautiful house was almost flesh and blood, promised to help her with the necessary payments.

The house he had bought and remodelled for the use of his mother when she left the Rappahannock farm in the early '70's could be reached from Betty's garden by a gravel walk edged with box. Pursuing his always dutiful if reluctant way thither, he listened with his indestructible courtesy to her complaints and what now amounted to hallucinations of fraud and poverty. Betty had engaged a Miss Bensons as companion housekeeper. Washington deposited ten guineas, with an additional gratuity of £2, and escaped back to Millbank.

Brother Sam, always in trouble during his lifetime, had left his family affairs in a very tangled state when he died. Five times married, Sam left four sons and a daughter; the eldest, Thornton, was a married man of twenty-four; the youngest, Harriot, a spirited child about eight years old, in the charge of Thornton's young wife, who had a baby of her own. Sam's offspring, except Thornton, were to harass their long-suffering uncle increasingly as their several characters and destinies developed.

Charles's history remains obscure, except for his unfinished house, which exists today as Mordington in West Virginia, the imposing central section erected by a later owner. His growing tendency to find solace in the bottle was frankly alluded to by his brother George in a letter to Bushrod in '88.

John Augustine, the best loved brother, was finding it difficult to finance his eldest son Bushrod's education in law, which was going forward at Philadelphia. Bushrod had not inherited the tall, bony

Washington frame and fair complexion, but was small, brown-eyed, studious, and relatively steady. He must have been something of a dark horse, for he figured frequently in the mysterious diary of lively Nancy Shippen, cousin to Benedict Arnold's notorious Peggy —as a contant suitor both before Nancy's tragic marriage to the New York Livingston family's black sheep, and again after she had fled with her baby daughter from her husband back to her Philadelphia home. Bushrod was at the time twenty-one—Nancy was married at eighteen—and as an apprentice lawyer with no money to spend, he must have been a little out of his depth in the Shippen circle. When he was recalled to Virginia in the spring of '84—perhaps on the advice of his uncle George, who had recently passed through the city on his way home from the war—Nancy's own account of their farewell is romantic, although she was then still the wife of a man she feared and hated, and was avowedly still in love with another from whom she had been ruthlessly separated by her father's determination to see her married to Henry Beekman Livingston.

It was during Bushrod's Philadelphia sojourn that Washington wrote to him from Newburgh one of those uncondescending, wholly friendly letters of advice which, beginning with Jacky Custis at Boucher's school before the war, he occasionally composed for the guidance of his young people:

"Let the object which carried you to Philadelphia be always before your eyes," he admonished Bushrod. "Remember that it is not the mere study of law, but to become eminent in the profession of it, which is to yield honour and profit.... and that dissipation is incompatible with both; that the company in which you improve most will be the least expensive to you—and yet I am not such a stoic as to suppose you will, or think it right that you ought, always to be in company with Senators and philosophers. But of the young and juvenile kind, let me advise you to be choice..... Be courteous to all, but intimate with few, and let those few be well-tried before you give them your confidence......

"Do not conceive that fine clothes make fine men, any more than fine feathers make fine birds. A plain genteel dress is more admired, and obtains more credit than lace and embroidery in the eyes of the judicious and sensible. The last thing I shall mention is first in importance, and that is to avoid gaming. This is a vice which is productive of every possible evil, equally injurious to the morals and health of its votaries. It is the child of avarice, the brother of inequity, and the father of Mischief. It has been the ruin of many worthy families, the loss of many a man's honour, and the cause of suicide......"

He probably meant *iniquity*. And the lecture on gambling stemmed directly from the recent tragedy of William Byrd III of Westover on the James, who had been a comrade on the frontier in the '50's. Washington's ledgers are full of small losses at cards—usually a matter of shillings—and he dearly loved a game with friends. But Byrd had dissipated a fortune by a gambling obsession indulged at the card-tables of Philadelphia, and had then taken his own life, during the war. His widow, who had then gone to live at Westover with her unmarried daughters, was one of the beautiful Philadelphia Willing girls, and therefore cousin to the Shippens, and Washington doubtless felt an uneasiness over Bushrod's associations.

Amongst his old friends on the Tidewater, George Mason of Gunston was the first to greet him on his return home. Mason was only seven years older than Washington, but the difference in age seemed greater because of Mason's ill health from a chronic gouty condition which plagued his brothers and sons as well as himself, and often left him crippled and in pain, and very irritable, for long periods of time. His mind remained alert, and his general outlook was only a little more cynical than in the old days at the Williamsburg Assembly and the conventions.

Mason had re-established his family life since the death of his wife Anne by marrying a middle-aged spinster of long acquaintance who managed his beautiful house and watched over his younger children. He confined his public service to his immediate community, instead of going in for State politics or Government posts, and was absorbed in the many responsibilities of his large estate and slave population. He had nevertheless lost heavily by the war, to the extent of £10,000 in depreciated money and curtailed profits and labor—"but I think this a cheap purchase of liberty and independence," he had written to Washington at Newburgh in '83.

When after several years in France in quest of health and knowledge, his eldest son, the fifth George Mason, returned to America and married, at the end of the war, Mason gave him an estate fronting on the Potomac above the Occoquan River mouth, where young George built the house to be called Lexington in memory of an April day in '75. The fourth son, John, who was to write those valuable memoirs of life at Gunston in his youth, also spent some years in France with a Bordeaux firm, and while there received enchanting letters from his father, full of advice, neighborhood news, and the satiric Mason viewpoint. Another son, Thomson, established Hollin Hall, north of Mount Vernon, and a daughter named Sally married Daniel McCarthy III of Cedar Grove, a rambling frame house prized for its water views over Pohick Creek.

Thomas Nelson—one of the Signers at Philadelphia in '76, then Governor of Virginia after Jefferson, and a fighting general at the Yorktown siege, where he directed the American artillery on his own handsome brick house because it sheltered the British headquarters—beggared himself like many others by patriotism, and died in unrequited poverty, leaving a large family almost without resources. The Lees were still prosperous, and legislating as usual, in the Virginia Assembly at Richmond, as were Benjamin Harrison, soon to be Governor himself, Patrick Henry, the several Carters, and until his departure to France with a commerce commission, Thomas Jefferson.

During the early part of '84 Washington wrote often to Clement Biddle, a former quartermaster in the army and one of the Philadelphia fighting Quakers. His second wife Rebecca had become one of Martha's friends during the dreadful winter at Valley Forge, when with other heroic wives they had stuck it out at camp beside their men. Before he joined the army Biddle had been a partner in his father's prosperous mercantile importing firm, and had returned to the business when peace came. Washington was accustomed to ordering things from Biddle at Headquarters, and he now considered his former British sources of supply out of bounds for a citizen of the new republic, preferring to buy from American merchants, doubtless at a higher price—"because I do not incline to send to England (from whence formerly I had all my Goods) for anything I can get upon tolerable terms elsewhere," he had written to Lafayette when requesting him to send from France a set of silver-plated tableware.

Seventy yards of livery lace, red and white, three-quarters to an inch wide, sample enclosed; a barrel of good coffee; brass wired sieves of different meshes for cement; burgundy and champagne (if cheap); wall-paper with seventy yards of gilded papier mâché border; a dozen and a half of Windsor chairs; stays for Mrs. Lund Washington; nuts, candles, and even a brick-layer on indenture, all appeared in the Biddle correspondence that spring. The Philadelphian was also called upon in the delicate matter of Billy's wife. Washington's letter to Biddle, written during the summer of '84, shows the rough kindliness cloaked with satire which he often revealed with regard to his dependents, or the young of his family:

"The mulatto fellow William, who has been with me all the war, is attached (married he says) to one of his own colour, a free woman, who during the War was also of my family. She has been in an infirm state of health for some time, and I had conceived that the connection between them had ceased, but I am mistaken; they are both applying to me to get her here, and tho' I never wished to see her more yet I cannot refuse his request (if it can be complied with on reasonable terms) as he has lived with me so long and followed my fortunes through the War with fidility.

"After promising thus much, I have to beg the favour of you to procure her a passage to Alexandria, either by Sea, by the passage Boats (if any there be) from the head of Elk, or in the Stage as you shall think cheapest and best, and circumstances may require. She is called Margaret Thomas also Lee (the name which he has assumed) and lives at Isaac and Hannah Sills, black people who frequently employ themselves in Cooking for families in the City of Phila...."

Washington laid in a stock of new books for his anticipated leisure, and it was his habit sometimes in the evenings to read aloud to the family and guests at the fireside. The list of volumes ordered from New York at the year's end included Arthur Young's *Tour Through Ireland*, lives of Charles XII of Sweden, Louis XIV, Gustavus Adolphus, and Peter the Great; Wildman on *Trees*, and Vertal's *History of the Revolution of Rome*, in three volumes; Goldsmith's *Natural History*, the Campaigns of Marshal Turenne, French-English and English-French dictionaries, Locke on *Human Understanding*, and Thomson's *Seasons*, which latter was doubtless most in demand by the ladies of the family, with its highly stylized imagery.

> "Now when the cheerless empire of the sky
> To Capricorn the Centaur-Archer yields,
> And fierce Aquarius stains the inverted year—
> Hung o'er the farthest verge of heaven, the sun
> Scarce spreads o'er ether the dejected day.
> Faint are his gleams, and ineffectual shoot
> His struggling rays, in horizontal lines,
> Through the thick air; as cloth'd in cloudy storm,
> Weak, wan, and broad, he skirts the southern sky;
> And, soon descending, to the long, dark night,
> Wide-shading all, the prostrate world resigns,"

Washington might have read, perhaps with some difficulty, beside the fire in Mount Vernon's cosy parlor. Or perhaps, anticipating what that winter seemed almost a legendary August heat, he turned the pages to *Summer* and found—

> "Half in a blush of clustering roses lost,
> Dew-dropping coolness to the shade retires,
> There, on the verdant turf or flowering bed,
> By gelid founts and careless rills to muse;
> While tyrant heat, dispreading through the sky,
> With rapid sway, his burning influence darts
> On man, and beast, and herb, and tepid stream."

Small wonder if eyelids began to droop and yawns were smothered under the torrent of Mr. Thomson's rhetoric.

During the General's absence, Lund had raised the unique piazza across the river front of the house, and built the curving colonnades which connect the mansion house to the dependencies on either side—kitchen on the south and lodgings for white servants on the north—and the cupola, which was still without its weather-vane, and was leaking. One of Washington's first concerns was the piazza floor, for which he must order the flagstone from England to replace the native Virginia stone laid by Lund as a temporary flooring.

There was as usual trouble about the ice supply. Writing to his Philadelphia friend the financier Robert Morris in June about finding a position in his counting-house for John Augustine's second son Corbin, who was about to embark in the world, Washington added a postscript: "The house I filled with ice does not answer. It is gone already. Will you do me the favour to cause a description of yours to be taken, the size, the manner of building, mode of management, and forwarded to me. I shall be much obliged. My house was filled chiefly with snow. Have you ever tried snow? Do you think it is owing to this that I am lurched?" The specifications were forthcoming, and Washington with his thanks expressed his intention of building one similar but larger, "if workmen can be obtained."

Several prime projects on the interior awaited his immediate attention, such as designing the shelves in the library to receive his books and the files of his wartime papers, which had arrived safely by the wagon-load before the snows closed in. The banquet room at the north end of the house was still less finished than the library, and lacked even a mantel-piece, which now began to unfold a story of its own.

Samuel Vaughan was a well-to-do London merchant in the West Indies colonial trade, with a large Jamaica plantation and a country house in England. In the course of his travels he had married a Boston girl, and hence entertained a militant sympathy for the colonial cause. At the close of hostilities he emigrated to America, arriving in Philadelphia with his family, including two promising sons, while a third remained in the London business. He expressed a desire to meet General Washington, whom he greatly admired, and accomplished his wish in December of '83, when the Commander-in-chief was on his triumphal way home.

Washington apparently found much to like in the fashionable Englishman, and the talk turned to the ever enlivening subject of Mount Vernon and the additions and improvements there which he was impatient to get at. When Vaughan heard that the New Room still wanted a mantel-piece, he begged the honor of supplying it, as he himself possessed one in England which he considered just the thing—made of brown Siena jasper with three white marble panels carved in high relief in an agricultural motif. Doubtless a little surprised and embarrassed by such excess of good will from a new acquaintance, Washington was persuaded to accept, and a lasting friendship resulted from the first brief meeting.

The mantel-piece, which Washington later learned had been removed bodily from Vaughan's own library at Wanstead by his instructions to his son Benjamin in London, had a roundabout passage, being for a time in the possession of French pirates, and did not reach Alexandria till February of the eventful year 1785, when the Diary again began its daily chronicle of the happy interlude between the war and the Presidency.

On February 5th Washington wrote to Vaughan: "I have the honour to inform you that the Chimney-piece is arrived, and by the number of Cases (ten) too elegant and costly by far I fear for my room and republican stile of living, tho' it encreases the sense of my obligation to you for it. The Ship arrived at her Port just as this second frost set in, so that it has not been in my power to send up for these cases by water; and I would not hazard the transportation of them by land, nine miles. . . . ." It was not until April 6th that the Diary said: "A Mr. Vidler, to whom I had written (an Undertaker at Annapolis) came here and opened the cases wch. contained my marble chimney piece—but for want of workmen could not undertake to finish my New Room. . . . . ."

In November of '86, the gift of the mantel-piece was supplemented by a garniture consisting of three vases of Worcester porcelain with landscape paintings surrounded by a blue and gilt background. Washington's acknowledgment of these repeated a cordial invitation to visit Mount Vernon, and it is surprising that Vaughan seems to have made no move to do so before the autumn of '87, when Washington was absent at the Constitutional Congress. Vaughan's wife had by then returned to England in poor health, and he followed her home in '88, though two of his sons settled in Maine. Washington promised that the "Jarrs" should occupy the place Vaughan intended, and after an interlude they stand again today on the mantelpiece at Mount Vernon where he must have placed them a hundred and seventy-seven years ago.

Meanwhile, the hospitality of the house, always enormous, was increasingly taxed. All the welcome old friends came, like Mason, Craik, the Fitzhughs, the Diggeses, the Carters, the Lees, and the Blackburns from Rippon Lodge—a year from now Bushrod Washington and Julia Ann Blackburn would marry, and visit Mount Vernon on their honeymoon trip. From Abingdon, where Jack Custis's widow was living with her second husband, Dr. Stuart, they brought her two eldest daughters, Eliza and Patty, to visit the two younger children who remained in Martha's care at Mount Vernon. Assorted nephews came–Sam's son, George Steptoe Washington, who with his younger brother Lawrence had been placed at the Georgetown Academy at Washington's expense; Bushrod, about to begin his distinguished career at law; George and John Lewis of Fredericksburg; and from Eltham, the husband and sons and daughter of Nancy Bassett.

Total strangers came, with or without letters of introduction by people already known to Washington. In the Diary he listed the visitors usually without comment, but many of them were characters on their own account, such as the ebullient William Gordon, an English clergyman whose sympathy for the colonies had led him to emigrate to America in 1770, when he settled at Roxbury as pastor of the Congregational Church. In 1775 he was appointed chaplain for both Houses of the Massachusetts Legislature, then sitting at Watertown, and the following year he began collecting material for his ambitious history of the Revolution. He was tireless and even intrusive in his efforts to secure papers, letters, and interviews, travelling through the camps and council rooms and buttonholing officers and men alike for first-hand opinions.

His acquaintance with Washington apparently began at Cambridge in the first winter of the war, and their ensuing correspondence was on such a friendly footing that the General always conveyed Martha's compliments to Mrs. Gordon whe he wrote. As early as 1783, at Newburgh, he invited Gordon to come to Mount Vernon and make use of his own *public* papers *after* Congress should have seen fit to open their archives to him. Gordon had arrived at Mount Vernon in June of '84 and remained nearly three weeks in the most scrupulous diligence, making his own copies of the transcripts of Washington's wartime correspondence and records, which were placed at his disposal. He worked from early morning till late at night, stopping only for meals and making few social demands on his host, though he seems to have established an unlikely *rapport* with Martha's grandson, who was perhaps an uncommonly stout baby to be known affectionately in the family circle as "Mr. Tub." That the childless clergyman had unbent with the nursery set appears in Washington's later correspondence with Gordon. Replying to a letter in November, '84, after his return from the western tour, Washington wrote: "In my absence I had a very sickly family, but no deaths. Mrs. Washington has been very unwell, Miss Custis very ill, and your friend *Tub* a good deal reduced by a diarrhea, he has got perfectly well, and is as fat and saucy as ever. Mrs. Washington is pretty well recovered, but Miss Custis remains in a puny state. the family unite in best wishes for you......" And again in the following spring: "Your young friend is in high health, and as full of spirits as an egg shell is of meat. I informed him I was going to write to you and desired to know if he had any commands; his spontaneous answer, I beg he will make haste and come here again. ......" The child was then barely four years old.

Washington himself unbent in one of his rare flights of facetiousness in writing to Gordon about the recent marriage of a mutual friend, in December, '84.

"I am glad to hear that my old acquaintance Colo. Ward is yet under the influence of vigorous passions. I will not ascribe the intrepidity of his late entreprize to a mere *flash* of desires, because, in his military career he would have learnt how to distinguish between false alarms and a serious movement. Charity therefore induces me to suppose that like a prudent general, he had reviewed his *strength*, his arms, and ammunition before he got involved in an action. But if these have been neglected, and he has been precipitated into the measure, let me advise him to make the *first* onset upon his fair del Toboso, with vigour, that the impression may be deep, if it cannot be lasting, or frequently renewed.

"We are all well at this time except Miss Custis, who still feels the effect, and sometimes the return of her fever. Mrs. Lund Washington has added a daughter to her family. She, Child, and husband are well, and become house-keepers at the distance of about four miles from this place.

"We have a dearth of News, but the fine weather keeps us busy and we have [no?] leisure for cogitation. All join in best wishes for you, Dr. and Mrs. Stuart are of those who do it...."

Washington's casual reference to the "fair del Toboso" is an indication that he was familiar with *Don Quixote,* as Dulcinea del Toboso was the resounding title invented by the self-styled knight for his country-wench lady love. The General may have seen Fielding's dramatization of the book during his theater going, and Smollett's translation was in his library, which in time came to possess such standard favorites as *Gulliver's Travels,* Chesterfield's *Letters, Robinson Crusoe, Peregrine Pickle, Tom Jones,* Shakespeare, Buffon's *Natural History,* Dr. Johnson's *Rasselas,* and at least one Gothic novel called *Children of the Abbey,* by Regina Maria Roche, which Martha ordered and which was therefore always treasured by Nelly; "because my revered & loved Grandmother Mrs. Washington read & liked it," is pencilled on the flyleaf in 1840.

Gordon's published work has been described as rash and devoid of restraint, and his manuscript was subjected to a severe editing process before it was printed, though he had taken it to England in the belief that it would receive fairer treatment there. He had chosen an unfortunate method of presenting his material. The book was composed in the form of letters professing to be written from America to an imaginary correspondent in England at the time of the events they recounted—a clumsy gambol, as by the time of publication there was no longer any suspense as to the next move in the war, or any doubt of the ultimate outcome.

The American edition appeared in three volumes in New York in 1789, the year of Washington's first inauguration as President. He had subscribed for two sets at £1 each, but his thanks to Gordon for the gift of an "elegantly bound" set were written at Philadelphia in '91. He expressed no opinion of the contents.

Gordon died at Ipswich at an advanced age, disappointed and in poverty, having realized only about £300 from the sale of his history.

The most welcome visit of that or almost any other year was the return of Lafayette, which occurred in August, and gave the General infinite pleasure. There would have been long summer evenings on the piazza where Martha's tea-table was set, while the lavender Potomac afterglow from the sunset behind the house lay over the water—and each good-night carried the assurance of another good day tomorrow. Then the Marquis set out for a tour of the north to renew old acquaintances there, promising to return to Mount

Vernon before sailing, and Washington rode out to his western lands, attended by Bushrod and Dr. Craik.

It was November when Lafayette arrived again, full of stories and news of mutual friends. This time Harry Lee was gathered in to share the visit—"come prepared to stay a few days," Washington's invitation read—and the tide of wartime reminiscence round the fireside must have been high and handsome. Martha, after all those winters at Headquarters, sharing the deprivations and the cold and the simple amusements invented to pass the time, could have held her own in the conversation, too.

When Lafayette went home to France he carried letters from Washington to the Marchioness and their little daughter Virginie, who had sent a letter to the General by her father's hand. "Her papa is restored to her with all the good health, paternal affection, and honors her tender heart could wish," Washington wrote to the child. "He will carry a kiss to her from me (which might be more agreeable from a pretty boy) and give her assurance of the affectionate regard with which I have the pleasure of being her well wisher. . . . . ."

The parting from Lafayette, whom he accompanied in his carriage as far as Annapolis, was a sad one, for as though he felt some premonition of the disastrous events of the 1790's in France, Washington was unwillingly convinced that he would never see the young Frenchman again, and sent after him a letter full of affection and foreboding: "I often asked myself, as our carriages distended, whether that was the last sight I ever should have of you? And tho' I wished to say no, my fears answered yes. I called to mind the days of my youth, and found they had long since fled to return no more; that I was now descending the hill that I had been 52 years climbing, and that tho' I was blessed with a good constitution, I was of a short-lived family, and might soon expect to be entombed in the dreary mansion of my fathers. These things darkened the shades and gave a gloom to the picture, consequently to my prospects of seeing you again; but I will not repine, I have had my day. . . . . ."

He did, however, see Lafayette's only son, his namesake, who was sent to him for asylum in 1795, during Lafayette's imprisonment in Austria, and the boy was a welcome guest at Mount Vernon with his tutor for more than a year.

XXIV

MONDAY, 1st. [January, 1785.] Colo. Bassett who brought his daughter Fanny to this place to remain, on the 24th of last Month, set off on his return to the Assembly now sitting at Richmond...."

To remain. This entry in the Diary opens the story of the girl who was to become a second daughter to Martha, filling in some degree the void created by Patsy Custis's death in '73. Fanny Bassett was the youngest child of Martha's favorite sister Nancy, who had died late in '77 when Martha was daily expecting the annual summons to winter Headquarters, which that year were at Valley Forge. She had written at once to Mr. Bassett offering to take the child, who was then ten years old, to bring up as her own, but Fanny did not become a permanent member of the Mount Vernon household till this Christmas of '84, when she was seventeen.

In the meantime, during the family gatherings, she had become very much attached to Charles Washington's son George Augustine, whose frail health continued to cause anxiety. During the past summer letters had arrived at Mount Vernon from George Augustine as he pursued his endless quest for health along the futile route followed by Lawrence a generation ago. Washington's Cash Memorandum book for April, '84, notes "By Cash, gave my Nephew Major George Augustine Washington, to bear his expenses to the West Indies, 100 gns." George Augustine wrote first of a tedious passage of twenty-six days from the Capes to Barbados, which left him very ill, and expressed his sensibility of the obligation he was under "for your unbounded kindness, and how I shall ever be able to acknowledge it I know not." From Bermuda, where next he had gone on an unexpected opportunity for passage, he reported unhappily in August: "I hope the climate will prove salubrious, which is all that can recommend the place. . . . . What I have seen of it is in a perfect state of nature, and appears as little favoured by the hand of Providence as any place I ever saw. . . . ." During the autumn he found his way to Charleston, where he was wintering with his cousin William at Sandy Hill. Washington wrote to him there on January 6, '85, cautioning him to return north, when he came, by water to Philadelphia, and take the twice weekly stage from there to Alexandria, in order to avoid the "dreary roads and bad accommodation" of North Carolina. And he added:

"Since my last, Colonel Bassett has been here and brought up Fanny, who is now with us. She has been unwell all the Fall, as most others in this Country have been; she is not yet recovered, but the change of Air and exercise will soon give her health. . . . .

"If it is not too late in the Season to obtain them, I wish you would procure for me in So. Carolina a few of the Acorns of the Live Oak, and the Seeds of the Evergreen Magnolia; this latter is called in Millers Gardeners Dictionary greater Magnolia, it rises according to his Acct. to the height of Eighty feet or more, flowers early, and is a beautiful tree; there is another Species of the Magnolia of which I wish to get the Seeds, it is called the Umbrella tree; but unless these Seeds grow in cones and the Cones are now on the Trees there is no chance of obtaining them at this Season; in which case prevail on Colo. Washington, or some acquaintance on whom you can depend, to supply me next Seed time.

"The Acorns and Seeds of every kind should be put in dry Sand as soon as they are gathered: and the box which contains them might (if no oppertunity offers to Alexandria) be sent either to Mr. Newton of Norfolk or to Colo. Biddle of Philadelphia, with a request to forward it safely and by the first oppertunity.

"If there are any other trees (not native with us) which would be ornamental in a grove or forest and would stand our climate I should be glad to procure the Seeds of them in the way above mentioned. . . . ."

When George Augustine arrived at Mount Vernon from Charleston the following May, he was accompanied by mahogany seeds, magnolia plants, live oak seeds, some "sower orange trees" in a box, a Palmetto Royal, and as a gift from William Washington some wild geese—all apparently in a thriving state.

The January entries in the Diary for 1785 record again Washington's daily rides around his acres to superintend the plantation work which was always going forward, weather or no, and they show again his perpetual interest in the growth of his long-range plan for the improvement and beautification of Mount Vernon.

"*Friday, 7th.* Road to my Mill, Ferry, Dogue Run and Muddy hole Plantations. Preparing my dry well, and the Well in my New Cellar, for the reception of Ice.
"*Saturday, 8th.* Drawing Ice from the river to my well in the Cellar. Got it ¾ full and well pounded, as it was thrown in....
"*Wednesday, 12th.* Road to my Mill Swamp, where my Dogue Run hands were at Work, and to other places in search of the sort of Trees I shall want for my Walks, groves, and Wildernesses.

"At the Sein Landing and between that and the point at the old Brick Kiln I found about half a dozn. young Elm trees, but not very promising ones. Many thriving Ash trees on high (at least dry) ground of proper size for transplanting, and a great abundance of the Red-bud of all sizes.....
"*Wednesday, 19th.* Employed untill dinner laying out my Serpentine road and shrubberies adjoining.

"Just as we had done dinner a Mr. Watson, late of the House of Watson and Cossoul of Nantes, and a Mr. Swift, Merchant in Alexandria, came in, and stayed all Night."

Here, with the mention of a serpentine road, is an indication of the ambitious design for the west front, which called for a small circular lawn enclosed by a carriage drive studded on the inside verge with posts connected by chains. Curving roads ran from either side of the circle to meet at the white gate on the Alexandria highway, bordering a long bowling-green which was flanked by groups of trees and shrubs—the "wildernesses"—planted to frame the westward view and to screen the low brick walls which enclosed the flower garden on the north and the kitchen garden on the south. The clearing and planting of this western approach occupied his attention and the labor of a large part of the Mansion House population for some time, and the gradual accumulation of unusual trees and shrubs was a favorite pastime.

His unexpected guest, Elkanah Watson, was at this time a precocious young man of twenty-seven. Born "within rifle shot" of Plymouth Rock, he had lived for some time in France as a member of a mercantile firm at Nantes, and had toured Holland and England with letters of introduction to the best people everywhere, from Benjamin Franklin in Paris to John Adams at The Hague. Returning to New York and Philadelphia in '84, he continued to move in the upper circles, and entertained the dinner-tables with amusing stories of his adventures abroad. His *Memoirs,* edited by his son, contain one of the earliest and most graphic descriptions of the Mount Vernon household, as he found it, only a year after Washington's return from the war.

"No pilgrim ever approached Mecca with deeper enthusiasm," he says of his arrival. "I felt an unaccountable diffidence as I came into the presence of this great man. I found him at table with Mrs. Washington and his private family, and was received with the native dignity and urbanity so peculiarly combined in the character of the soldier and eminent private gentleman. He soon put me at ease by unbending in a free and affable conversation......

"I observed a peculiarity in his smile, which seemed to illuminate his eyes, his whole countenance beamed with intelligence, while it commanded confidence and respect. The gentleman who had accompanied me from Alexandria left in the evening, and I remained alone in the society of Washington for two of the richest days of my life. I saw him reaping the reward of his illustrious deeds in the quiet shade of his beloved retirement. He was at the matured age of fifty-three..... To have communed with such a man in the bosom of his family I shall always regard as one of the highest privileges, the most cherished incidents of my life. I found him kind and benignant in the domestic circle, revered and beloved by all around him, agreeably social without ostentation, delighting in anecdote and adventures without assumption, his domestic arrangements harmonious and simple. His servants seemed to watch his eye and to anticipate his every wish. Hence a look was equivalent to a command. His servant Billy, the faithful companion of his military career, was always at his side. Smiling content animated and beamed on every countenance in his presence.

"The first evening I spent under the wing of his hospitality we sat a full hour at table by ourselves without the least interruption after the family had retired. I was extremely oppressed with a severe cold, and excessive coughing, contracted from the exposure of a harsh winter journey. He pressed me to use some remedies, but I declined doing so. As usual after retiring, my coughing increased. When some time had elapsed the door of my room gently opened, and on drawing my bed curtains to my utter astonishment I beheld Washington himself standing at my bedside with a bowl of hot tea in his hand. I was mortified and distressed beyond expression. This little incident occurring in common life with an ordinary man would not have been noticed, but as a trait of the benevolence and private virtue of Washington it deserves to be recorded......"

It is very probable that the Washingtons in their own room had been kept awake by Mr. Watson's cough, and that the tea was brewed by Martha from a kettle on their bedroom hearth, as no servant was on duty at that hour.

"*Thursday, 27th.* [January] Made Mr. and Mrs. Lund Washington a morning's visit. From thence I went to Belvoir and viewed the ruined Buildings of that place. In doing this I passed along the side of Dogue Creek and the River in search of Elm and other Trees for my Shrubberies, etcs......"

The increasingly acrimonious tone of his letters to Lund as the war strain tightened his nerves and thinned his patience, and Lund's well-meant ineptitudes weighed against his undoubted devotion to Washington's best interests, was apparently smoothed away by renewed association at Mount Vernon. Although Lund continued for a time his duties as manager under Washington's supervision, as he had begun in '68, he and his wife Betsy had transferred their household during the past summer to their new house called Hayfield, which stood back from the River on the Alexandria road.

The record is silent as to Lund's actual acquisition of the land which was to fulfill his modest ambition to own a place of his own where he could provide a toddy for his friends. He may have bought it from Washington, or it may have changed hands in lieu of the amount owing him for his services since 1778 when he stopped taking his pay from the proceeds of the estate. He built the house of brick on three different elevations, and it was surrounded by wide lawns which merged into the spreading fields which gave it its name. Following the stillborn child two years previously, Lund's wife had produced another child in August of '84 which was to die at fourteen months.

The mention of a visit to Belvoir leads to one of the most intimate glimpses Washington ever permitted into his personal feelings, and a copy of the letter was preserved by him in his Letterbook. On the 27th of February he wrote to George William Fairfax, who was still at Bath with Sally, both of them in ill health:

"I cannot at this moment recur to the contents of those letters of mine to you which I suspect have miscarried; further than that they were all expressive of an earnest wish to see you and Mrs. Fairfax once more fixed in this country; and to beg that you would consider Mt. Vernon as your home until you could build with convenience, in which request Mrs. Washington joins very sincerely. I never look towards Belvoir without having this uppermost in my mind. But alas! Belvoir is no more! I took a ride there the other day to visit the ruins, and ruins indeed they are. The dwelling house and the two brick buildings in front, underwent the ravages of the fire; the walls of which are very much injured: the other Houses are sinking under the depredation of time and inattention, and I believe are now scarcely worth repairing. In a word, the whole are, or very soon will be a heap of ruin. When I viewed them, when I considered that the happiest moments of my life had been spent there, when I could not trace a room in the house (now all rubbish) that did not bring to my mind the recollection of pleasing scenes, I was obliged to fly from them; and came home with painful sensations, and sorrowing for the contrast.....

"P.S. Do you think it would be in your power, with ease and convenience, to procure for me a male and female Deer or two, the cost of transportation I would gladly be at. If I should ever get relieved from the drudgery of the pen, it would be my wish to engage in these kind of rural amusements, raising of shrubberies, &ca.

"After what I have said in the body of this letter, I will not trouble you with an apology for such a scrawl as it now exhibits, you must receive it, my good Sir, as we have done better things, better for worse....."

He passed the 22d of February that year absorbed in the work which most delighted him, and there is no evidence of any recognition of a birthday.

"*Tuesday, 22.* Removed the pretty large and full green Lilacs to the No. Garden gate, one on each side, taking up as much dirt with the root as cd. be well obtained. Also a mock orange to the walk leading to the No. Necessary.

"I also removed from the Woods and the old fields several young Trees of the Sassafras, Dogwood, and Red Bud, to the shrubbery on the No. side of the grass plat......

"*Monday, 28.* Planted all the Mulberry trees, Maple trees, and Blackgums in my Serpentine Walks, and the Poplars on the right walk, the Sap of which and the Mulberry appeared to be Moving. Also planted 4 trees from Hell Hole, the Name unknown, but of a brittle wood which has the smell of Mulberry......

"*Wednesday, 9th.* [March] A great deal of rain fell last Night and the heaviest sleet I ever recollect to have seen.

"The bows of all the trees were encrusted by tubes of Ice, quite round, at least half an Inch thick, the weight of which was so great that my late transplantations in many instances sunk under it either by bending the bodies of the young trees, breaking the limbs, or weighing up the roots. The largest pines in my outer circle were quite oppressed by the Ice; and bowed to the ground, whilst others were loosened at the roots, and the largest Catalpa trees had some of their principle branches broken. The ground also where the holes had been dug to receive the Trees, and where it had not been rammed, was a mere quagmire.....

"*Thursday, 10th.* Sent my Waggon with the Posts for the Oval in my Courtyard, to be turned by a Mr. Ellis at the Turng. Mill on

Pohick, and to proceed from thence to Occoquan for the Scion [grafting shoot] of the hemlock in my Shrubberies......

"Went to return the visits of Colo. Mason and others in his Neighborhood. Called first at Mr. Lawrence Washington's, who being from home, I proceeded to Colo. Mason's, where I dined and lodged.....

"*Friday, 11th.* Left Colo. Mason's about 12 o'clock, dined with Mr. Martin Cockburn and come home in the afternoon..... Brought 9 Scions of the Portugal Peach from Mr. Cockburn's with me.....

"*Saturday, 19.*.... Received a Swan, 4 wild Geese, and two Barrels of Holly Berries (in Sand) from my brother John, and a Barrel of early corn from New York....."

Everyone contributed, and if they did not it is plain that he did not hesitate to ask—not for himself, but for Mount Vernon.

XXV

ALL this spring of '85 the Diary maintained its careful record of trees planted, staked, pruned, and grafted; of new seeds and plants received, and the laying out of his new roads and ha-ha's—those low, hidden walls which formed terraces to prevent the grazing cattle and sheep from approaching the house; ivy on the garden walls is specified, limes and aspens along the serpentine roads, lilacs and althea trees by the north garden gate, holly, papaws, sassafras, pines, and cedars in the "wildernesses," scarlet honeysuckle ("said to blow all summer") at each column of the covered ways, the gilder rose and Persian jessamine on the walks leading to the two new necessaries.

In April the seining for shad and herring for the Alexandria market began, along with the annual contest between ploughing and rainfall, and before the end of the month he was sowing clover and grass seed. On the 16th they were visited with a great hoar frost, and he wrote: "What injury this may have done to the fruit, and vegetation, will soon be seen. The Buds of every kind of tree and shrub are swelling, the tender leaves of many had unfolded, the Apricot blossoms were putting forth, the Peaches and Cherries were on the point of doing the same....."

There is no further mention of damage, but the entries are studded with loving observation of the small signs of spring:—

"Found what is called the Spice bush (a fragrant aromatic shrub) in bloom. It is a small, greenish flower, growing round the twigs and branches, and will look well in a shrubbery....."

"Perceived the Service tree to be in full bloom. It bears a white flour in clusters but on single stems, and is a tolerable handsome tree in bloom......"

"The blossom of the red bud was just beginning to display; the Dogwood blossom tho' out makes no figure yet, being small and not very white. The flower of the Sassafras was fully out and looks well. An intermixture of this and red bud I conceive would look very pretty—the latter crowned with the former or vice versa...."

"The blossom of the Crab tree is unfolding, and shedding its fragrant perfume. That of the black Haw has been out some days; and is an ornamental flower being in large clusters, tho' individually small upon single foot stems. They are white with a yellowish cast. The flower of the small berry thorn is also good-looking, the tree being full of blossom, which is not much unlike the blossom of the apple tree, but quite white......."

The perennial Roberts again emerges in his usual iniquity in a letter from Washington to his western representative: "My Miller (Wm. Roberts) is now become such an intolerable sot, and when drunk so great a Madman, that however unwilling I am to part with an old Servant, (for he has been with me 15 years) I cannot with propriety or common justice to myself bear with him any longer. I pray you once more therefore to engage and forward a miller for Me as soon as you may have it in your power, & whatever engagement you shall enter into on my behalf I will religiously fulfill. I do not stipulate for the wages; Altho' my mill (being on an indifferent stream & not constant at work) can illy afford high wages.....The House in wch he will live is a very comfortable one within 30 yds of the Mill.....There is a small kitchen convenient thereto, and a good Garden under paling.....I do not object to the man's having a family; a wife I shou'd wish him to have, but I wou'd it not be *too* large......"

On April 12th he wrote again accepting the terms asked by one Joseph Davenport, who took his time about arriving, but in May, '86, Washington reported satisfaction: "Mr. Davenport seems to be a very honest, good kind of man; but as a miller, and as a person skilled in the art of keeping a mill in order, I think him much inferior to Roberts. In these points perhaps Roberts had no superior; but his propensity to liquor and his turbulent temper when under the intoxicating doses of it, were not to be borne. I have no trouble at all with Davenport; he is steady, orderly, and quiet, and does, I believe, as well as he knows how. We have neither of us intimated any inclination to part; and if the reputation of my flour (wch stood very high under Roberts' management) can be maintained, it is all I want. . . . ." Davenport remained at the mill until his death in '96.

The visitors to Mount Vernon that spring and summer of '85 included Generals Stephen Moylan and John Cadwallader, comrades from the war days, and there must have been some free and easy reminiscing over the nuts and wine—it was Moylan who had engaged in an unorthodox feud with the fiery Polish adventurer Pulaski at Valley Forge, and Cadwallader of Philadelphia had called out the malignant, scheming Conway and put a bullet through his jaw in a highly unpermissible duel later in '78.

In April Washington went on a surveying trip in connection with a new purchase of land in the Abingdon district, accompanied by Dr. Stuart, Lund, and black Billy—"And after having run one course and part of another, my Servant William (one of the Chain Carriers) fell, and broke the pan of his knee, wch. put a stop to my Surveying; and with much difficulty I was able to get him to Abingdon, being obliged to carry him on, as he could neither Walk, stand, or ride. at Mr. Adam's Mill I took Lund Washington's horse and came on home. . . . ."

Two days later a double bereavement was tersely recorded: "An Express arrived with the Acct. of the Deaths of Mrs. Dandridge and Mr. B. Dandridge, the Mother and Brother of Mrs. Washington." April was not a fever month, coming before the mosquitoes were hatched, but it was a time for treacherous colds and pneumonia. There is no clue as to why they both went within a week. It left Martha with only one sister, Betsy, who by her second husband, Leonard Henley, was the mother of three boys and a girl, Frances—who was further to entangle the skeins of marriage and relationships after her cousin Fanny Bassett's death by marrying Fanny's second husband, Tobias Lear. "Bat" Dandridge, Martha's last surviving brother, left several children, including a son, Bartholomew II, who would act as secretary to Washington during the still inconceivable Presidential years.

"*Thursday, 28th.* [April] To dinner Mr. Pine, a pretty eminent Portrait and Historical Painter, arrived in order to take my picture from the life and to place it in the Historical pieces he was about to draw. This Gentleman stands in good estimation as a Painter in England; comes recommended to me from Colo. Fairfax, Mr. Morris, Govr. Dickinson, Mr. Hopkinson and others."

In one of his rare expansions on the qualifications of a guest, Washington revealed that he considered Mr. Pine of some consequence. Pine was an R.A., who had devised a grand design of collecting an exhibition of American historical portraits and scenes. He arrived with his family at Philadelphia in '83, and his wife established a drawing-school while Robert Morris, Francis Hopkinson, Generals Gates and Steuben, and Mrs. John Jay were all among her husband's sitters. The Pines were described by Hopkinson as "a family of pygmies," the painter, his wife and two daughters all being of very small stature. It was to Hopkinson, an old Philadelphia friend and one of the Signers, that Washington wrote with his customary straight-faced humor:

"In for a penny, in for a pound, is an old adage. I am so hackneyed to the touches of the Painters pensil, that I am now altogether at their beck, and set like patience on a Monument whilst they are delineating the lines of my face.

"It is a proof among many others of what habit and custom can effect. At first I was as impatient of the request, and as restive under the operation, as a Colt is of the Saddle. The next time, I submitted very reluctantly, but with less flouncing. Now, no dray [horse] moves more readily to the Thill, than I do to the Painters Chair. It may easily be conceived therefore that I yielded a ready obedience to your request, and to the views of Mr. Pine....."

As Pine's early career had been associated with the theater world, when he had painted many of the foremost London players including David Garrick, and had executed a series of scenes from Shakespeare, it is conceivable that Washington found his conversation and reminiscences entertaining. The artist remained three weeks at Mount Vernon and painted all the members of the family, Fanny Bassett and the children, and there may have been some lively sessions with the less docile subjects, as he was said to be a morbidly irritable man.

During his ensuing residence at Philadelphia, where Robert Morris furnished him with a house on Eighth Street, Pine exhibited in a special room at the State House his collection of Shakespeare scenes, his historical subjects such as *Canute Rebuking His Courtiers on the Seashore*, and the portraits more recently painted—probably the first art exhibition to be held in America. He had also brought with him in his luggage one of the first casts of the nude statue of the Venus de Medici, but public opinion in the Quaker city compelled him to keep it enclosed in a box and to show it only in private.

While Mr. Pine was still in residence, there arrived at Mount Vernon a young man named Noah Webster, who held advanced ideas about school books, of which he had prepared several, and the teaching of young children. There was some discussion of his becoming a resident member of the household as a tutor-secretary, but he went away again the following day and except for another visit in November, nothing came of it.

In mid-May George Augustine Washington reached Mount Vernon from his travels, improved in health but still with a weakness in his chest. The reunion between him and Fanny Bassett led to an engagement, if one had not already existed, about which Washington had some reservations, as appeared in a letter to Fanny's father on May 23rd:

"It has ever been a maxim with me thro' life, neither to promote nor to prevent a matrimonial connection, unless there should be something indispensably requiring interference in the latter. I have always considered marriage as the most interesting event of one's life, the foundation of happiness or misery; to be instrumental therefore in bringing two people together who are indifferent to each other, and may soon become the object of hatred; or to prevent a union which is prompted by mutual esteem and affection, is what I never could reconcile to my feelings; and therefore, neither directly nor indirectly have I ever said a syllable to Fanny or George upon the subject of their intended connexion; but as their attachment to each other seems to have been early formed, warm and lasting, it bids fair to be happy; if therefore you have no objection, I think the sooner it is consummated the better.

"I have just now informed them (the former thro' Mrs. Washington) that it is my wish they should live here....."

The following month Charles Washington came in from the Valley to see his son, and Fanny's father and two brothers arrived from Eltham, probably to celebrate the official recognition of her engagement and set the wedding date for the autumn. In the meantime, George Augustine was banished to the Springs for a rest, in the company of his two brothers-in-law to be.

In July Washington wrote with evident misgivings to Lafayette, whose one-time aide George Augustine had been: "George has returned after his peregrination thro' the West Indies, to Bermuda, the Bahama Islands, and Charleston; at the last place he spent the winter. He is in better health than when he set out, but not quite recovered; He is now on a journey to the Sweet Springs, to procure a stock sufficient to fit him for a matrimonial voyage in the Frigate F. Bassett, on board which he means to embark on his return in October; how far his case is desperate I leave you to judge, if it is so, the remedy however pleasing at first will certainly be violent......"

The Washingtons could be pardoned for regarding the literary world with some reservations, after William Gordon was followed in June, '85, by the eccentric bluestocking, Catherine Macauley-Graham, whose controversial *History of England* in eight volumes began to be published in London in 1763. Widowed at thirty-five, Mrs. Macauley had queened it in questionable respectability at Bath, and in Paris—where like everyone else of any consequence she met Benjamin Franklin—and in London, where as "the celebrated female historian" she more than once tilted lances with Dr. Johnson. In her late forties, overdressed and "painted to the eyes," she married William Graham, who was twenty-one, brother of a quack physician. This was too much even for her friends, such as they were, and she found herself cruelly satirized and abused.

She arrived in America in the spring of '85, a tall, vigorous woman of fifty-three, towing her unimpressive young man, and was respectfully received at New York and Philadelphia. Richard Henry Lee, then President of the Congress, gave her a letter of introduction to Mount Vernon, and the ever obliging Colonel Fitzgerald of Alexandria escorted her there. She remained about ten days, and Washington opened his military records "for her perusal and amusement."

Unfortunately Mrs. Macauley-Graham left no record of her visit in her own words. The Diary reveals that Washington's other guests during that week included his brother Charles, Dr. Stuart, Judge Harrison (whom Washington would always call Colonel) and George Digges of Warburton Hall, where she paused on her way back to New York. "I am obliged to you for introducing a Lady to me whose reputation among the literati is high, and whose principles are so much and so justly admired by the friends of liberty and of mankind," Washington wrote gravely to his friend Lee after her departure.

The last two entries in the Diary for June, '85, are typical of the teeming life at Mount Vernon during that summer, when visitors known and unknown flowed through it, and as there was no nearby inn to house their horses and servants these necessarily required hospitality as well.

"*Wednesday, 29th.* Messrs. Philips and Edwards and Mr. Booth and Mr. Hawkins left this after breakfast. Colo. Bassett and his two Sons; Fanny Bassett, and Nelly and Washington Custis, followed soon after for Abingdon.

"Mr. George Lee and Dr. Craik came here to breakfast and soon after returned.

"Discovered the Cayan pepper which was sowed on the 13th to be coming up.

"*Thursday, 30th.* My brother Charles left this after breakfast, and G. Auge. Washington went up to Abingdon.

"Rid to my Hay field at the Meadow, from thence to my Dogue Run, and Muddy Hole Plantations, and dined with only Mrs. Washington, which I believe is the first instance of it since my retirement from public life."

And it was apparently the last, until a similar entry in July, '97. He had established this year what he called his Nursery or Botanical Garden, in a small space back of the Spinning House, as a sort of laboratory where he could experiment with fertilizers, propagation, and the exotic seeds and plants which he received from friends and admirers. The first planting was of Chinese seeds presented by Dr. Craik, with their Chinese names carefully copied out, though they lacked translations, and where names were missing he noted—"like, but larger than Cabbage Seed . . . . . . larger and redder than Clover Seed. . . ."

In August Lund's only child, a daughter a year old, began to ail, as did old John Alton, Washington's faithful servant since the frontier days.

"*Monday, 29th.* Doctr. Craik after visiting John Alton before breakfast went after it to see Lund Washington's child, who had been seized with fits and the family alarmed by it . . . . . .

"*Tuesday, 30th.* . . . . . The Wheat which had been sowed before the late rains fell was up, and coming very well.

"I observed that Corn, wch. had been planted under the Persimon trees in the fields, looked as thriving and well as that which was not shaded. The same thing I had observed before (formerly) with respect to Wheat under these sort of trees, and also of grass, which proves them to be a valuable tree in enclosures.

"Mrs. Washington visited the Sick Child of Mr. L. Washington, and returned to dinner.

"Finished gravelling the right hand Walk leading to the front gate from the Court yard.

"*Wednesday, 31st.* Rid to the Plantation in the Neck, and at Muddy Hole. Found the corn at the first as mentioned yesterday at the other places.

"Mrs. Washington rid to see the sick child of Mr. Lund Washington, from whence Doctr. Craik came here to Breakfast. . . . . . This day I told Doctr. Craik that I would contribute one hundred dollars pr. ann. as long as it was necessary, towards the Education of his Son, George Washington, either in this Country or in Scotland. . . ."

They lost Lund's child in the autumn. George Washington Craik was for a suspiciously short time one of Washington's secretaries during the Presidential years to come.

He had now begun on a cherished project of building a greenhouse, of brick, with big windows facing south, and flanking wings which would contain servants' quarters. There is a notation of the purchase of 28,430 "good Cyprus shingles" for repairs to the Mansion House roof and the piazza, as harvest time began.

On September 10th he wrote: "From the Scarcity of Apples generally this year, and the depredations which were committing every Night upon the few I have, I found it necessary (tho much too early) to gather and put them up for Winter use. Finished the Cieling of the Piazza."

In the autumn Lafayette sent him a present of some French hounds, in the care of John Quincy Adams who was returning from abroad, and who did not take the trouble to announce their arrival to the General, so that they reached him, after inquiry, by other hands.

"*Friday, 30th.* [October] ...... One of the Hound Bitches wch. was sent to me from France brought forth 15 puppies this day; 7 of which (the rest being as many as I thought she could rear) I had drowned.

"Run the ground which I had designed for a Paddock for Deer, and find it contains 18 A. 3 R. 20 P.

"Began again to Smooth the Face of the Lawn, or Bolling Green on the West front of my House—what I had done before the Rains proving abortive....."

On a Sunday night in October after the household was in bed, they were aroused by the belated arrival of the French sculptor Houdon and his party down the River from Alexandria. Houdon brought letters from Franklin, Lafayette, and even Colonel Humphreys, who was then in Paris, as secretary to the Legation. He brought also three young men assistants who spoke no English, and a resident of Alexandria who had volunteered to act as interpreter, and he was commissioned, as Washington had already been notified, to execute a statue of the General for the State House at Richmond.

"Observed the process for preparing the Plaister of Paris, and mixing of it, according to Mr. Houdon," Washington wrote in the

Diary, with his perpetual interest in how things were done. Unhappily there remains no adequate account of what must have been a memorable fortnight at Mount Vernon. M. Houdon was still there on the date of Fanny's wedding and attended the little ceremony, which Washington recorded in the Diary with the unexpected touch which often illuminated his whole page: "After the Candles were lighted, George Auge. Washington and Frances Bassett were married by Mr. Grayson."

Her two brothers John and Burwell II had returned from the Springs with the bridegroom at the end of September, and were still in the house. Burwell Senior wrote from New Kent regretting that an accident prevented him from attending, and promised to send his carriage to bring the young couple to Eltham in time for Christmas. Bushrod had married Julia Ann Blackburn only the week before, and a family party from Rippon Lodge, including the bride and groom, arrived at Mount Vernon the following week. On the 20th they all attended the races at Alexandria, and Washington recorded in his Diary that John Bassett got hurt in a fall on the course and had to be left behind overnight to recover.

Pine's charming portrait of Fanny was delivered at Mount Vernon in December with his congratulations on the marriage, and after an interval it has been returned there by her descendants. The bust of Washington by Houdon has remained at Mount Vernon continuously for some hundred and seventy-six years.

In November Washington began to take stock at all the farms, listing the Working Horses, Working Mares, Unbroke Horses, and Unbroke Mares—each of which had a name: "Kit, a black Mare, 5 yrs.... Punch, grey flea bittn..... Grunt, a Bay..... Betty, White Stocking..... Bonny, Bay, very old...." After them he set down the working Oxen (unnamed), the cows, heifers, steers, bull calves, rams, ewes, and wethers. On the Mansion House list were his three favorite riding horses, Nelson and Blueskin, which had both been at the war with him, and Magnolio. The horses received special notice from a Mr. Hunter, described in the Diary as a London merchant, who came to dinner with a couple of Lees and Colonel Fitzgerald from Alexandria, and stayed the night.

Mr. Hunter kept a diary of his travels, which extended from

Quebec to Carolina while he was on this side of the Atlantic, and he set down a valuable impression of Mount Vernon in its heyday.

"You have a fine view of the Potomac, till you enter a wood," he says of the ride down from Alexandria. "A small rivulet here divides the General's estate from the neighboring farmer's. His seat breaks out beautifully upon you when you little expect, being situated upon a most elegant rising ground on the banks of the Potomac, ten miles from Alexandria......

"When Colonel Fitzgerald introduced me to the General, I was struck with his noble and venerable appearance. It immediately brought to my mind the great part he had acted in the late war. The General is six foot high, perfectly straight and well made, rather inclined to be lusty. His eyes are full and blue and seem to express an air of gravity. His nose inclines to the aquiline; his mouth small; his teeth are yet good; and his cheeks indicate perfect health. His forehead is a noble one, and he wears his hair turned back, without curls (quite in the officer's style) and tied in a long queue behind. Altogether, he makes a most noble, respectable appearance, and I really think him the first man in the world........

"When I was first introduced to him, he was neatly dressed in a plain blue coat, white cassimere waistcoat, and black breeches and boots, as he came from his farm. After having sit with us some time he retired and sent in his lady, a most agreeable woman about fifty, and Major Washington, his nephew, married about three weeks ago to a Miss Bassett. She is Mrs. Washington's niece, and a most charming young woman; she is about nineteen. After chatting with them for half an hour, the General came in again, with his hair neatly powdered, a clean shirt on, a new plain, drab coat, white waistcoat, and white silk stockings.

"At three dinner was on the table, and we were shown by the General into another room, where everything was set off with a peculiar taste and at the same time very neat and plain. The General sent the bottle about pretty freely after dinner, and gave success to the navigation of the Potomac for his toast, which he has very much at heart, and when finished will, I suppose, be the first river in the world......"

The visitors had ordered their horses ready to return to Alexandria after dinner, but Washington pressed them to stay and probably found very little real resistance to his hospitality.

"After tea the General Washington retired to his study and left us with the President, [Richard Henry Lee, President of the Congress] his lady, and the rest of the company. If he had not been anxious to hear the news of Congress from Mr. Lee, most probably he would not have returned to supper but gone to bed at his usual hour, nine o'clock—for he seldom makes any ceremony. We had a very elegant supper about that time.

"The General with a few glasses of champagne got quite merry, and being with his intimate friends laughed and talked a good deal. Before strangers, he is generally very reserved and seldom says a word. I was fortunate in being in his company with his particular acquaintances...... We had a great deal of conversation about the slippery ground, as the General said, that Franklin was on; and also about the Congress, the Potomac, improving their roads, etc. At twelve I had the honor of being lighted up to my bedroom by the General himself."

The next morning Hunter was up early, taking a walk about the grounds, which he found beautifully laid out. "He has about 4,000 acres, well cultivated, and superintends the whole himself," the observant guest continued. "Indeed, his greatest pride now is to be thought the first farmer in America. He is quite a Cincinnatus, and often works with his men himself; strips off his coat and labors like a common man.

"The General has a great turn for mechanics. It's astonishing with what niceness he directs everything in the building way, condescending even to measure the things himself, that all may be perfectly uniform. The style of his house is very elegant, something like the Prince de Condé's at Chantilli near Paris, only not quite so large. But it's a pity he did not build a new one at once, as it has cost him nearly as much repairing his old one. His improvements, I'm told, are very great within this last year. He is making a most delightful bowling green before the house, and cutting a new road through the woods to Alexandria.

"It would be endless to attempt describing his house and grounds. I must content myself with having seen them. The situation is a heavenly one, upon one of the finest rivers in the world. I suppose I saw thousands of wild ducks upon it, all within gunshot. There are also plenty of blackbirds and wild geese and turkeys. After breakfast I went to see his famous racehorse, Magnolia, a most beautiful creature...... I afterwards went into his stables, where among an amazing number of horses I saw old Nelson, now twenty-two years of age, that carried the General almost always during the war. Blueskin, another fine old horse next to him, now and then had that honor..... Blueskin was not the favorite, on account of his not standing fire so well as venerable old Nelson. The General makes no manner of use of them now; he keeps them in a nice stable, where they feed away at their ease for their past services. There is a horse of Major Washington's there that was reckoned the finest figure in the American army.

"It's astonishing what a number of small houses the General has upon his estate for his different workmen and Negroes to live in. He has everything within himself—carpenters, bricklayers, brewers, blacksmiths, bakers, etc., etc.—and even has a well-assorted store for the use of his family and servants. When the General takes his coach out he always drives six horses; to his chariot he only puts four; The General has some fine deer, which he is going to inclose a park for; also some remarkable large foxhounds, made him a present of from England, as he is fond of hunting and there are plenty of foxes in this country.

"I forgot to mention Mrs. Washington's sweet little grandchildren, who I imagine will come in for a share of the General's fortune, with the Major. I fancy he is worth £100,000 sterling, and lives at the rate of three or four thousand a year—always keeping a genteel table for strangers that almost daily visit him, as a thing of course. ..... The General has some hundreds of Negroes on his plantations. He chiefly grows Indian corn, wheat, and tobacco...... The situation of Mount Vernon is by nature one of the sweetest in the world, and what makes it still more pleasing is the amazing number of sloops that are constantly sailing up and down the river. Indeed, all the ships that come to Alexandria or George Town must sail by the General's house....."

When with his friends Hunter took his leave before noon he shook Washington heartily by the hand and wished him all happiness. Lee and his son turned southward towards Chantilly on the Rappahannock, and Hunter with Fitzgerald on their way back to Alexandria fell in with Lund and a foxhunt. Very little is known about this young Mr. Hunter, but we are indebted to him for an intimate view of the man whom, though recently an enemy, Hunter admired "as superior even to the Roman heroes themselves."

A typical day towards the end of November as recorded in the Diary reads: "Colo. Harrison and Doctr. Craik left this after Breakfast, and I went up to Alexandria with G. [Augustine] Washington to meet the Directors of the Potomack Coma. and to a Turtle feast (the Turtle given by myself to the Gentlemen of Alexa.) Returned in the Evening and found the Count Doradour, recommended by, and related to the Marqs. de la Fayette here, as also the Revd. Mr. Magowan."

And on Friday: "Set out after breakfast accompanied by Mr. G. Washington, to make Mr. Mason at Colchester a visit, but hearing on the road that he had removed from thence, I turned into Gunston Hall where we dined and returned in the Evening, and found Colonel Henry Lee and his Lady here. Mr. Shaw returned, having removed George and Lawrence Washington to the Alexandria Academy and fixed them at the Widow Dade's."

Colonel "Lighthorse Harry" Lee, whose campaigns in the Carolinas towards the end of the war in support of General Greene were often spectacular and contributed much to the ultimate victory, had married his cousin Matilda, heiress of Stratford, and settled down, he thought, to the life of a Virginia planter at Stratford, from where he paid frequent visits to Mount Vernon and contributed botanical novelties to its gardens. William Shaw, whom Washington had recently acquired as secretary-tutor, proved to be a light-minded young man who was always running off to Alexandria's social life and remaining away overnight, as was frequently noted with almost audible exasperation in the Diary.

The removal of George Steptoe and Lawrence Washington from the Georgetown Academy to Alexandria followed a tart letter from Washington to their schoolmaster, the Reverend Mr. Balch, very reminiscent of his correspondence with Boucher during Jacky

Custis's school days a dozen years back. Washington had had to pay unexpected bills for them amounting to over £100, and the man with whom they were lodged at Georgetown declined to keep them any longer, Mr. Balch having already found an excuse to transfer them from his house to other care. These two boys, now ten and twelve years old, were to remain a vexation to Washington for years to come, and their younger sister Harriot was soon to be added to his household worries at Mount Vernon.

"*Sunday, December 4th.* Last Night John Alton, an Overseer of mine in the Neck, an old and faithful Servant who had lived with me 30 odd years, died of an imposthume in his thigh after lingering for more than 4 Months with it, and being reduced to a mere skeleton; and this evening the Wife of Thomas Bishop, another old Servant who had lived with me an equal number of years, also died."

Bishop, who was long past military service when the war began in '75, held a sort of honorary post at Mount Vernon with a salary which gradually rose to £25 a year, and as time went on had found consolation in liquor. His wife Susannah was often mentioned in the Ledger as midwife to the people on the place, at 10s. a delivery. After Washington's return home in '83, the old orderly stood every morning in the same place outside the cottage which had been built for him, to see the master pass by on his rounds. He died at an advanced age in '95, when Washington was away at the Presidency. Bishop had an only daughter, Sally, who had married Thomas Green, overseer of the plantation carpenters. John Alton also left one daughter, Anne, who married on the place.

Sally's husband was a chronic drunkard and incompetent, whose services Washington retained only out of compassion for the man's unfortunate wife and several small children. Washington and his managers lectured, threatened, and expostulated with Green for years with no effect, until in '94 he was either dismissed or drifted away, deserting his family, which was left on Washington's charity.

At the end of the year Washington was fox-hunting again, training the French hounds Lafayette had sent him, along with some others. He was often accompanied by Lund and the Dulanys—one of whom had married the wealthy Miss French in '73—and a nephew or two. It must have crossed his mind that two of his former hunting companions, Jacky Custis and George William Fairfax, were no longer riding with him.

Also at the end of the year there arrived from the King of Spain the jackass Royal Gift, attended by a Spanish groom who spoke no English and only wanted to go home as soon as possible. Around Royal Gift the stable humor flowed freely for some time to come, and Washington wrote to Lafayette, who had promised to send him some jacks from Malta:

"..... Your assurances, my dear Marquis, respecting the male and female Asses, are highly pleasing to me, and I shall look for them with much expectation and great satisfaction, as a valuable acquisition and important service.

"The Jack which I have already received from Spain, in appearance is fine; but his late royal master, tho' past his grand climacteric, cannot be less moved by female allurements than he is; or when prompted, can proceed with more deliberation and majestic solemnity to the work of procreation. The other Jack perished at sea....."

It was now arranged, to everyone's satisfaction, that Lund should turn over his managerial duties to George Augustine, who with his wife Fanny would become a permanent member of the Mount Vernon household " 'till the squalling and trouble of children might become disagreeable," Washington added cautiously—intending by that time to provide the young couple with a separate home of their own on nearby land.

Meanwhile, they set off for Eltham in Colonel Bassett's carriage, and did not return until April, when they brought with them as gifts for planting some imported hawthorn, yellow jessamine, and pride of China trees. "The Major," as Washington usually called him, was soon off to Alexandria about the business of the estate.

XXVI

THE year 1786 opened with the usual hospitality. The Lund Washingtons came to dinner and it rained on the hunting. Bushrod, who was already becoming a person of consequence at twenty-four, a practicing lawyer and a member of the Virginia Assembly at Richmond, arrived with his wife in a chariot with four horses and three servants. The Craik family was always welcome, and visited in four's and five's at a time. Bryan Fairfax, once the erratic younger son of the Belvoir household, had married his second wife and was living at his new house called Mount Eagle near Alexandria, and had taken holy orders—"now a Parson," Washington was sufficiently impressed to note in his Diary, whilst jotting down his guests.

The daily demands on his generosity continued to be a cruel drain on his reserves of food and supplies, as well as his time and patience. Besides his numerous family connections on both sides, and his old friends, total strangers were always arriving without even a letter of introduction, and their horses and servants had to be lodged as well. His one-time military comrades also frequently turned up for dinner and an overnight pow-wow which was usually devoted as much to the present uneasy state of affairs in the country as to their mutual memories of anxieties already lived through. Not one of them was yet aware that their separate lives would once again be deflected into a common channel with that of their beloved chief, in another effort to preserve the unity and freedom of their country. But mark well the names as they ride in and out the gates of Mount Vernon in this shortening interlude, for what might seem now the brief reunion of a summer day maintained friendships and mutual confidence which were to endure, or to crack, during many a crisis to come which the most far-sighted of them did not yet anticipate.

A new scene was being set on the American stage. The cast of characters was to shift, enlarge, and regroup itself. More names emerge from the wings—names already familiar to Washington but not hitherto closely linked to his retired life at Mount Vernon. Call them intruders, birds of ill omen, but they did not seem so to him at the time, and they cannot longer be disregarded. And they came always as his friends.

There was swaggering Theodoric Bland, who had brought the first Virginia cavalry troop to Morristown in the winter of '76-7, followed to Headquarters by his lively, letter-writing wife, who was to become a formidable Philadelphia hostess during her husband's subsequent political career in Congress. And there was General Lincoln, still walking lame from his Bemis Heights wound—that benign and temperate man who had served from start to finish of the war, and who at Yorktown, because Cornwallis sent out a deputy with the sword of surrender, acted as Washington's deputy to receive it—and who resigned as Secretary of War in '85 in order to retire to his Connecticut farm and the bosom of a devoted family. There was Edmund Randolph, who had left Washington's military Staff during the first winter of the war to return to Williamsburg and unravel the complicated Randolph estate after the death of his uncle Peyton; he was now Attorney-general, and would soon be Governor of Virginia. There was John Fitzgerald, who as a freshman aide at Princeton in January, '77, had hidden his face with his hat in horror while Washington rode unscathed through a murderous crossfire; he was now a prosperous merchant and shipping agent at Alexandria with one of the Digges girls for his wife. There was James Monroe, who as a raw-boned Westmoreland County lad of eighteen had been in the long retreat of '76 which ended with the Christmas victory at Trenton, where he received a troublesome wound; he had left the army in '78 to study law under Jefferson's wing, and went from there to Congress, and married a reigning belle of New York society. There was that brilliant but unassuming Congressman James Madison, who had never smelled gunpowder, and whose frail appearance masked a tiger's heart—almost a dandy in his dress, he had a mind like a rapier in debate. And always the Lees came—Richard Henry of Chantilly, the aristocratic radical who had triggered the Declaration of Independence, and now in failing health preferred the relative quiet of the Virginia Assembly to the stresses of Congressional leadership in New York; and the fabulous cavalryman, Lighthorse Harry Lee, who found retirement at Stratford too dull and became a member of Congress with a New York residence.

The situation which confronted them was not unexpected. As early as January, '84, Washington had written to his friend Benjamin Harrison, who was then Governor of Virginia: "The disinclination of the individual States to yield competent powers to Congress for the Federal Government, and their unreasonable jealousy of that body and of one another, and the disputes which seem to pervade each, of being all-wise and all powerful within itself, will if there is not a change in the system be our downfall as a nation. This is as clear to me as ABC, and I think we have opposed Great Britain and have arrived at the present state of peace and independency to very little purpose, if we cannot conquer our own prejudices. . . . ."

This amounted to almost frightening second sight, as it was not until two years later that the parade of perplexed legislators began at Mount Vernon, so that it was August of '86 when Washington wrote to John Jay, Secretary for Foreign Affairs:

"Your sentiments, that our affairs are drawing rapidly to a climax, accord with my own. What the event will be, is also beyond the reach of my foresight. We have errors to correct; we have probably had too good an opinion of human nature in forming our confederation. Experience has taught us, that men will not adopt and carry into execution measures the best calculated for their own good, without the intervention of a coercive power. I do not conceive we can exist long as a nation without having lodged somewhere a power, which will pervade the whole Union in as energetic a manner as the authority of the State Governments extends over the several States. . . . . .

"Retired as I am from the world, I frankly acknowledge I cannot feel myself an unconcerned spectator. Yet, having happily assisted in bringing the Ship into Port, and having been fairly discharged; it is not my business to embark again on a sea of troubles. Nor could it be expected that my sentiments and opinions would have much weight in the minds of my Countrymen; they have been neglected tho' given as a last legacy in the most solemn manner. I had then perhaps some claims to public attention. I consider myself as having none at present. . . . ."

Thus he tried to close the door, and his own mind, to the unmistakable trend of thought on the part of his visitors and correspondents—he had done the job once before, and they believed he could do it again. Fresh from the heated debates in Congress or the Assembly, and from the sober dinner-table talk in New York and Richmond, came the younger men, whose task it now was to steer the ship of state—turning by habit and tradition to Mount Vernon still for support and countenance. And it was not in his line any more—he was a soldier, and the fighting was over, and it was time the professional politicians showed what they could do.

Meanwhile the usual work of the plantation proceeded. The ice was got in from the River and packed into the dry well in the cellar. A fruit garden was laid out behind the stables. The same minute record was kept of the transplanting, pruning, grafting, and the gifts of rare shrubs and seeds, while the Diary maintained also its habit of loving observation: "*July 11th*. Perceived as I rode thro' my drilled Corn at Muddy Hole today, that the alternate rows of early corn was Tassling and Spooling;" and the odd, occasional luminous phrase which made unconscious poetry of the terse record: "Finished the harvest at Dogue Run about sundown. In the Night there fell rain."

Harry Lee had sent horse chestnuts and cuttings of both dwarf and tree box, and offered in an affectionate letter to supply cypress and holly and fruit trees, or anything in his power, and was "unalterably your friend and servt;" weeping willows, still a cherished novelty in America, were planted in the artificial mounds by the gate; honey locust seedlings, designed to form a hedge around the vineyard, were coming up; the "scaly bark hiccory nut of Gloucester" [County] was planted in the Botanical Garden; Siberian wheat and Irish potatoes went into wet ground; new fences were being put up of Cypress plank and posts; the octagon-shaped garden houses were moved out to the points of the walls of the formal gardens where they still stand; the bowling-green lawn in front of the house on the west was levelled and sown; an enclosure for tame deer and a paddock for the jackasses were begun; the stone flags for the piazza floor arrived from England and were laid.

Inside the house, the bookshelves were at last being built for a growing library which would finally rival the best in Virginia. And on September 7th an entry occurs in the Diary which presents an amusing domestic image of several possible interpretations: "Began to Paper the yellow room this day—Majr. [George Augustine] Washington and Thos Green the undertakers—by the directions I received with the Paper from England." It is a question whether Washington did actually assist in the paper-hanging, or only heckled from the doorway.

The large banquet-room at the north end was in the hands of a craftsman in decorative plaster-work from Baltimore named Rawlins, who had been recommended by Washington's one-time aide, Tench Tilghman, now a merchant-shipper there. It was ten years since what they called the New Room had been raised and enclosed by Lund, while Washington was embroiled in the disastrous autumn campaign which ended at Trenton, but by the end of '85 it had begun to look as Washington had planned it, with a coved ceiling and handsome moulded cornice, its white stucco ornamentation in an agricultural design picked out on a green background, in harmony with the carved rural motifs on Vaughan's mantel-piece.

In February Washington had taken inventory of his Negroes, which he rarely referred to as slaves, although he wrote to a neighbor, John Francis Mercer, in reply to some inquiry: ". . . . I never mean (unless some particular circumstance should compel me to it) to possess another slave by purchase; it being among my first wishes to see some plan adopted by which slavery in this country may be abolished by slow, sure, and imperceptible degrees. . . . . ." The 1786 list at Mount Vernon included many names which are recognizable from the '60's, and the descriptive comment revealed both a paternal care of the infirm and aged, and an affectionate tolerance of the shortcomings of these irresponsible and costly, but essentially helpless dependents.

At the Home House he leads off rather grandly with the faithful

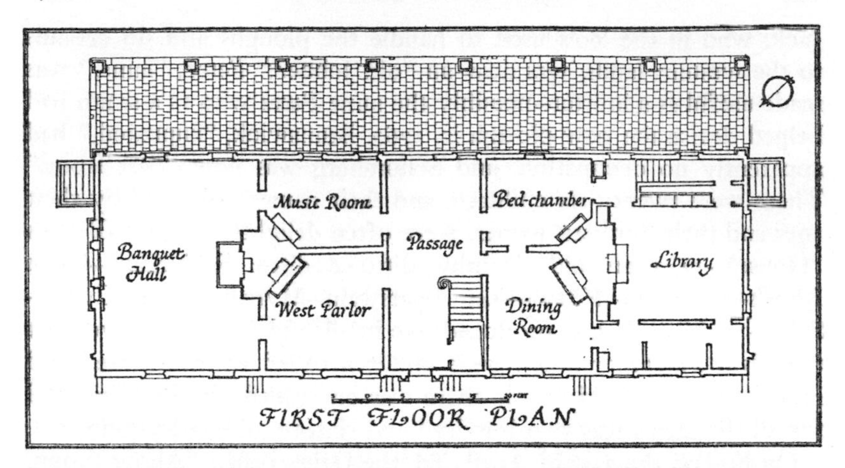

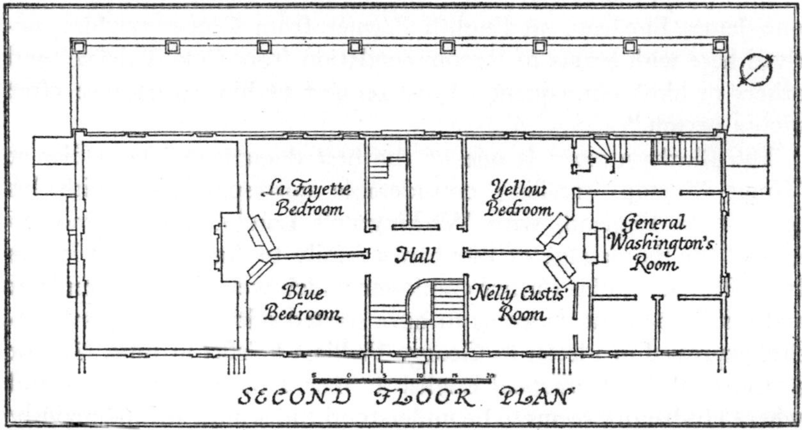

mulatto body-servant Will, or Billy, who is set down as "Val. de Chambre"—perhaps in an echo of Lafayette; Frank and Austin—Waiters in the House; Hercules and Nathan—Cooks; (Hercules went to Philadelphia in '91 to cook for the President, and cut a wide swath there, and came to a bad end.) Giles, Joe, and Paris, "a boy," were Drivers and Stablers; Betty, Charlotte, and Lame Alice—Sempstresses; Sall and Caroline—House Maids; Sall Brass and Dolly—Washers; Bristol—gardener.

Doll and Jenny were bracketed together as "Almost past service." Winny, among the spinners, was "old and almost blind." Cook

Jack, who in the '60's used to handle the ploughs and do errands to the western lands, was now an "old Jobber." Peter, "lame," was made useful as a knitter—possibly the same Peter who as a smith had helped devise the new plough in 1760. Brunswick, "ruptured," had apparently no occupation, and Schomberg was now "past labor." There were twenty-six children, and their names, followed by their ages and their mothers' names, were often delightful; Opey—Betty's (House)—12 years old; Delphy—ditto—6 ditto; Richmond—Lame Alice's—9; Sinah—Kitty's—14; Boatswain—Myrtilla's—11; Cyrus—Sall's—11. Myrtilla had produced five in all, and Kitty had seven. At the River Plantation there were children called Penny, Moses, and Hukey, and at Muddy Hole there was one called Virgin. The total for all the farms was two hundred and sixteen, old and young.

On Friday, the 21st of April, '86, the Dairy reads: "About Noon, one James Bloxham, an English Farmer from Gloucestershire, arrived here with letters of Recommendation from Colo. Fairfax (and others to him) consequent of my request to him to enquire after such a person."

The Bloxham story is one of the best documented comedies at Mount Vernon, entailing considerable correspondence with his sponsors in England, with Washington's London agent, who arranged for the passage of Bloxham's family to America, and letters from Bloxham to his former employer which were full of complaint and disillusionment. It seems to have started with Washington's desire, expressed in a letter to George William Fairfax in June, '85, for a "thorough bred *practical* English farmer, from a part of England where Husbandry seems to be understood and is most advantageously practiced," to take charge of one of the Mount Vernon farms, not upon shares as the Virginia overseers were accustomed to do, but at a standing wage on contract. This document was drawn up for Bloxham on the 29th of May, '86, in Washington's own handwriting, and was to run for one year, renewable at a rise from fifty to sixty guineas wages, and stipulated allowances of provisions, firewood, garden space, stock, a horse to ride, etc.

But Bloxham was accustomed to rich English soil, the mild English climate, and traditional English ways, and he was not a young man, to accommodate easily. He encountered in Virginia a ruinously wet season following on a disastrously dry one, which had already compelled Washington to purchase extra supplies to eke out what he had been able to grow and store for the maintenance of his servants and stock. He also encountered the irresponsible, easy-going, often childish Negro temperament, which he never learned to get along with. Before Bloxham had been three months in Washington's employ, the master of Mount Vernon was writing to William Peacey, whose Gloucestershire estate Bloxham had left to venture to Virginia:

"Excuse the liberty I take in putting the inclosed Letters under cover to you. It is to oblige Mr. James Bloxham, who now lives with me, but who scarcely has sufficient knowledge of his own mind to determine whether to continue more than the present year (for which he is engaged) or not. In a word he seems to have expected to have found well organized farms, than that the end and design of my employing him was to make them so. He makes no allowances for the ravages of a nine year's war from which we are just beginning to emerge, nor does he consider that if our system of Husbandry had been as perfect as it may be found on your Farms, or in some of the best farming Counties in England, that there would have been no occasion for his Services.

"What the old man has written to you respecting the coming over of his wife, sending over plows, seeds, and so forth I know not; because at different times he seems to be of different opinions......"

What Bloxham wrote was far from complimentary. He asked Peacey to get "a Clever Little Deasantt plow which must go without a weeal for the Land is not Level," and added that in Virginia "they have some most Shoking Plows that ever was Seen in the World," and that there was "nothing agreeable about the place," except the terms, which he considered generous enough. While in one paragraph he seemed to think it not worth while for his wife to come over, in the next he wavered again—".... thear is another thing which is very disagreeable tese Black People I am Rather in Danger of being po[i]sind among them which I think I Shall Leave the Country ass Soon ass I Can But the general and I have agreed and articld for one yeare but my Wife may youse [her] one Will about Comming over..... my heart have Yarned for my family A Gret many time and I think of all and like a transport But I hope the Sun will Shine upon me wonce more..... I hope mrs. and all the famly is Well and I have Whent thro a great Dele Since I left England And Lett me have a nanser Imeadetly Remember me to all frends and no more from yr frend and well wisher......"

Bloxham's family did come out to him, and he remained unhappily at Mount Vernon until the summer of 1790, when under George Augustine's management during the Presidency he was encouraged to depart. He then settled, at least temporarily, in a house near Alexandria, while making up his mind whether or not to return to England.

Washington's finances were as usual in a deplorable state, his cash balance at the beginning of this year having fallen to £86—he had overdue debts, and his own debtors were in a similar if not worse condition. He had had to go to the extra expense of finishing the house and undertaking endless repairs, but his orders to Biddle in Philadelphia continued.

In February he wrote for boots and shoes, "a Common Hunting horn of the largest and best sort," Clover and Saint Foin seed, and more books—*The Gentleman Farmer*, by Henry Home, Tull's *Husbandry*, and Arthur Young's *Six Months Tour through England*. In May he acknowledged receipt of the boots and the seed, and required the price of the best Dutch or striped blankets by the piece.

At the end of August he was taken with a fit of the ague, succeeded by "a smart fever," which confined him to the house and caused him to send for Dr. Craik, who prescribed a cathartic and quinine. The indisposition may have provided him with some indoor leisure in which to enjoy his growing library of agricultural publications, and it is possible still to follow him through their pages, which to him were of immediate and no doubt enthralling interest, though he may sometimes have disagreed with what he found there.

Henry Home, Lord Kames, in addition to a distinguished career at the Bar, owned what had been an impoverished estate in Berwickshire, and had no use for book-farmers with no practical experience. In the middle of the century he had first introduced the feeding of turnips to cattle, with marked success, and they were by now in general use, being sown by drills.

Jethro Tull was a practical farmer in Berkshire, who according to the *Gentleman's Magazine*, which Washington often saw, was "the first Englishman, perhaps the first writer, ancient or modern, who had attempted with any tolerable degree of success to reduce agriculture to certain and uniform principles; and it must be confessed that he has done more towards establishing a rational and practical method of husbandry than all the writers who have gone before him." Tull had invented and perfected the seed-drill, and his practice of mechanical sowing and inter-row cultivation created controversy for years, like his theory that tillage reduced if it did not abolish the necessity for manure, of which nobody ever had enough. A retiring man in frail health, he was finally persuaded by his admirers to publish an account of his experiments, which he called *Horse-Hoeing Husbandry*. His book was reprinted in several editions, and was already fifty years old when Washington received it, and drills were in use at Mount Vernon, as were turnips for fodder.

The order for Arthur Young's *Tour* preceded by only a few weeks a letter from Young himself, who had somehow become aware of Washington's search for an English farmer to work at Mount Vernon, opening a correspondence which was to continue into an enduring long-distance friendship, with an offer of assistance. He sent also as a gift the first volumes of his *Annals of Agriculture*, a periodical which was contributed to by many distinguished farmers, including George III in one of his more likable aspects as a country gentleman–signing himself Ralph Robinson–and William Pitt, who offered his views on deep ploughing. Young was said to have written a good third of the text with his own hand, much of it consisting of notes on his little journeys into the rural districts in search of further facts and figures on crop rotation, novel implements in use (including drawings), labor costs, local industries, and the like.

To Washington's alert, inquiring mind the *Annals* would have brought a peculiar joy, and his immediate reply was cordial. "Agriculture has ever been amongst the most favourite amusements of my life," he wrote, "though I never possessed much skill in the art, and nine years total inattention to it has added nothing to a knowledge which is best understood from practice; but with the means you have been so obliging as to furnish me, I shall return to it (though rather late in the day) with hope and confidence." He then ordered two ploughs, with spare shares, colters, and mold; cabbage, turnip, and sainfoin seeds; and several kinds of grass seed, to be paid for by an order on his London agent. Later in the correspondence he wrote: "I think with you that the life of a husbandman is the most delectable. It is honourable, it is amusing, and, with a little judicious management, it is profitable. To see plants rise from the earth and flourish by the superior skill and bounty of the labourer fills a contemplative mind with ideas which are more easy to be conceived than expressed . . . ."

Young lived at Bradfield Hall, Bury St. Edmunds, in Suffolk, and was a popular member of the charmed London circle which surrounded Dr. Johnson and his friend the musician-author Dr. Charles Burney. Young was viewed with favour by Burney's daughter Fanny, whose sharp eyes and sharper pen preserved in pitiless prose her priceless opinions of the exalted company she kept.

The last number of the *Annals* appeared in 1813, when failing eyesight forced Young to bring it to an end. He published his correspondence with Washington in 1801, after the latter's death, and himself lived on into blindness till 1820—which must have been a long martyrdom, for his wife's bad temper was notable, even to the Dictionary of National Biography.

Although Washington's general correspondence continued to be heavy, it was less boring than it had been immediately after the war, when he had complained to David Humphreys: "What with letters (often of unmeaning nature) from foreigners; Enquiries after Dick, Tom, and Harry, who *may have been* in some part, or at *some time*, in the Continental service; Letters, or certificates of service for those who want to go out of their own State; Introductions; applications for copies of Papers; reference of a thousand old matters with which I *ought* not to be troubled, more than the Great Mogul, but which must receive an answer of some kind, deprive me of my usual exercise. . . . ."

As a result of continued inquiry among his friends for a replacement for the inattentive William Shaw, Washington received a letter in January, '86, from General Lincoln, announcing, "I have at last found a Mr. Lear, who supports the character of a gentleman and scholar," and he at once replied to ask Mr. Lear's terms and to state his own requirements:

"Mr. Lear, or any other who may come into my family in the blended characters of preceptor to the Children, and as a Clerk or private Secretary to me, will sit at my Table, will live as I live, will mix with the Company which resort to the Ho., and will be treated in every respect with civility, and proper attention. He will have his washing done in the family, and may have his linnen and Stockings mended by the maids of it. The duties which will be required of him are, generally, such as appertain to the offices before mentioned. The first will be very trifling 'til the Children are a little more advanced; and the latter will be equally so as my correspondencies decline (which I am endeavouring to effect); and after my accts. and other old matters are brought up. To descend more minutely into his avocations I am unable, because occasional matters may require particular Services; nothing however derogatory will be asked, or expected.

"After this explanation of my wants, I request Mr. Lear would mention the annual sum he will expect for these Services, and I will give him a decided answer by the return of the Stages, which now carry the Mail and travel quick; A good hand, as well as proper diction would be a recommendation, on acct of fair entries; and for the benefit of the Children, who will have to copy after it....."

The Diary on May 29th, '86, briefly records the arrival at Mount Vernon of Tobias Lear, "who had been previously engaged on a Salary of 200 dollars, to live with me as a private Secretary and preceptor for Washington Custis"—two dozen words to mark the beginning of an association which was one of the most rewarding and intimate in Washington's reserved affections. After only a few days' acquaintance, he wrote cautiously to Lincoln that Lear appeared to be "a genteel, well-behaved young man."

Lear was twenty-four, the son of a Portsmouth, New Hampshire, shipmaster. He had graduated with honors from Harvard in '83, and then spent a year travelling in Europe, where he learned French. He was a loyal, discreet, industrious, and lovable member of Washington's household for the next eight years, and after an interlude during the latter years of the Presidency, he returned to Mount

Vernon and remained there till the end of Washington's life. When in 1793 he embarked on that brief independent business venture which again carried him abroad, he took with him a letter from Washington to Gouverneur Morris, then the American Ambassador in Paris, which introduced him as "a person who possesses my entire friendship and confidence."

July of 1786 was further enlivened by the return from Europe of Washington's former aide, David Humphreys. A large, handsome, jovial man, Yale, '71, the son of a Connecticut clergyman, Humphreys had come late in the war to Washington's Headquarters family, having already served as aide to old General Putnam and to Nathanael Greene. After Yorktown Washington chose him for the honor of carrying the surrendered British flags to Congress in Philadelphia, and he remained on the Staff till the end of the war, when he was one of the three aides who escorted Washington home to Mount Vernon. He accompanied Jefferson to Paris in '84, acting as secretary to the Commerce Commission, and later to the American Legation. After two years abroad, acquiring under Benjamin Franklin's wing at Paris a sophistication of which he had had no real lack, though he retained his rough diamond manner, Humphreys returned to America via London, where he was presented at Court by the American Ambassador, John Adams, heard Pitt speak, and saw Mrs. Siddons act.

Humphreys had never lost touch with Washington, and more than once urged him to write for posterity his own memoirs, or at least a history of the war compiled from his private papers, but Washington refused to entertain the idea. Aware that Humphreys himself had a nice writing talent, even for poetry, and had recently translated into English de Chastellux's volume on his travels in America, Washington wrote to him in July, '85, while Humphreys was still at Paris: "In a former letter, I informed you, my Dear Humphreys, that if I had *talents* for it, I have not *leisure* to turn my thoughts to commentaries: a consciousness of a defective education, and a certainty of the want of time, unfit me for such an undertaking. . . . . I should be pleased indeed to see you undertake this business . . . . . and I should with great pleasure, not only give you the perusal of all my papers, but any oral information of circumstances, which cannot be obtained from the former, that my memory will furnish, and I can with great truth add that my house would not only be at your service during the period of your preparing this work, but (and without an unmeaning compliment I say it) I should be exceedingly happy if you would make it your home. You might have an apartment to yourself, in which you could command your own time; you wou'd be considered and treated as one of the family; and meet with that cordial reception and entertainment which are characteristic of the sincerest friendship....."

Now that Humphreys was free to undertake some such enterprise, and proposed a visit to Mount Vernon, Washington wrote to him in June: "The only design of this letter is to assure you that you will have *no* occasion for Horses, for mine will always be at your service; and very little for a servant, as your old acquaintance Will (now fit for little else) can whiten your head, & many idlers about the House can blacken your shoes; but in the latter case I entreat you to be governed wholly by your own inclination & convenience....." Humphreys showed his consideration by arriving by the stage to Alexandria, without either servant or horse.

It must have been an altogether delightful summer for the master of Mount Vernon, with Lear, Humphreys, and George Augustine all in the house, one or the other accompanying him on his morning rides around the farms, or to services at Pohick Church, or the Alexandria races and dancing assemblies—bringing youth and fresh vitality to the family dinner parties at Hayfield and Abingdon.

The frivolous Mr. Shaw departed for the West Indies in August and was seen no more. Humphreys' visit was unexpectedly cut short by his election to the Connecticut Assembly, but he promised to return and did so the following year, and from then on remained at Washington's side through the first inauguration. He produced during the summer of '86 his *Ode to Mount Vernon*, which was inscribed to General Washington, and began:

"By broad Potowmack's azure tide,
Where Vernon's mount, in sylvan pride,
Displays its beauties far,
Great Washington to peaceful shades,
Where no unhallow'd wish invades,
Retir'd from fields of war.

"Angels might see, with joy, the sage,
Who taught the battle where to rage,
Or quench'd its spreading flame,
On works of peace employ that hand,
Which wav'd the blade of high command,
And hew'd the path to fame."

and continued for ten more verses. Washington, on receipt of the finished product, wrote cautiously in reply: "The Poem, tho' I profess not to be a connoisseur in these kind of writings, appears pretty in my eye, and has sentiment and elegance which must, I think, render it pleasing to others."

Humphreys had no sooner arrived back in the north than the simmering unrest there boiled over into what became known as Shays' Rebellion, in which a Massachusetts mob intimidated the justices at Concord and roared for the abolition of debts, for common property, and a general insurrection. Rhode Island was in a ferment over paper money, and there were riots in New Hampshire. Washington was unable to believe that his young, brave country could so disgrace itself in the eyes of the world. "For God's sake tell me what is the cause of all these commotions," he wrote Humphreys in October. "Do they proceed from licentiousness, British-influence disseminated by the Tories, or real grievances which admit of redress?" And to Harry Lee in Congress he wrote: "I am mortified beyond expression when I view the clouds that have spread over the brightest morn that ever dawned upon any Country."

Humphreys' reply when it came made heavy reading at Mount Vernon. The Massachusetts troubles were far from resolved, and it was feared that the insurgents might take possession of the Continental magazine at Springfield. Congress was seriously alarmed, and it seemed to Humphreys that only Providence could now prevent "some terrible convulsion." But under Providence there was always George Washington. "In case of civil discord, I have already told you it is seriously my opinion that you could not remain neuter," Humphreys concluded, "and that you would be obliged, in self-defence to take part on one side or the other, or withdraw from the continent. Your friends are of the same opinion....."

His friends. His friends in the Virginia Assembly voted unanimously for a Convention to be held in Philadelphia in the following May, for the purpose of considering a general revision of the federal system—and they placed his name at the head of the list of Virginia delegates, which also included Patrick Henry (who flatly refused to attend), Edmund Randolph (now Governor of Virginia), James Madison, and George Mason, who was now for the first time prevailed upon to extend himself beyond the borders of Virginia.

Washington was again almost incredulous. It was 1775 all over again. It was like living the same life twice. He had answered the bell before, unwillingly even then, and now he was a decade older. They could not ask it of him again. He turned helplessly to the bluff, outspoken Humphreys in this new dilemma. "Should this matter be pressed further, (which I hope it will not, as I have no inclination to go) what had I best do?" he asked miserably, knowing well the answer.

Meanwhile the autumn routine at Mount Vernon proceeded exactly as usual, a tacit denial that it could ever change, or need ever go on without him again. He sent in his orders to Biddle in Philadelphia—blankets, osnabrigs, loaf sugar, best Hyson tea—"Do the Tanners in Philadelphia make Leather which is strong, stout, and well adapted for negroes shoes? If so, what would twenty-five sides of each (unblacked) or as much as would make 150 pair, with three soles, be bought for?"—"Are the Artichokes of Jerusalem to be had in the neighborhood of Philada? Could as much of the root, or the seed be got as would stock an acre? I want to bring it in with my other experiments for the benefit of the stock."—and so on through corn scythes, grass scythes, bramble scythes—two flax spinning wheels . . . . . .

In October he set out in writing in a letter to George Augustine his intention to give to him and Fanny at once what would be their ultimate inheritance—which was the property in the Neck, including the old Clifton farm purchased after the controversy in 1760. Here he suggested they might establish in the buildings which already existed the Negroes which Colonel Bassett had promised them as a wedding present, and at their leisure put up a new house for their own permanent home. "You may say, or think perhaps, that as there is a contingency tacked to this intimation, the offer is too precarious to hazard the expense of building; but if Mrs. Washington should survive me there is a moral certainty of my dying without issue, and should I be the longest liver, the matter in my opinion is almost as certain; for whilst I retain the reasoning faculties I shall never marry a girl; and it is not probable that I should have children by a woman of an age suitable to my own, should I be disposed to enter into a second marriage," he added, doubtless recalling his friend George Mason's prudent alliance with Sarah Brent, for which there had been ample reason in view of his motherless young family.

To clinch it, with his customary generosity he held himself bound to pay the cost of any buildings which George Augustine undertook. "Do not infer from my proposing it to you to build, that I meant it as a hint for you to prepare another home," he went on. "I had no such idea. To point you to a settlement which you might make at leizure, and with convenience, was all I had in view...... But whether you remain in the same house, or at a future day may remove to the place proposed, your services will be convenient and essential to me; because with your aid I shall be able to manage my concerns without having recourse to a Steward, which comports neither with my interest nor inclination to employ....." George Augustine's reply, in his exquisite copy-book handwriting and the formal eighteenth-century phrasing which was never relaxed even within the family circle, revealed a warmth of feeling and gratitude which it is doubtful if Washington received from any other of his many dependents.

He went to Alexandria with Lear and the George Augustines to see the Jockey Club purse run for it—it was won by a Mr. Snickers of Loudoun County—and they brought back with them the two elder Custis children, Eliza and Patty, for a visit. The Diary notes: "Ferry people all gone to race and those at home at Dogue Run all idle—Overseer being gone to the race." He began to set a new brick kiln this autumn. He bought more land, of Daniel French's widow. The Lund Washingtons and the Stuarts came to dine. He bought the indenture of a Dutch family, the Overdoncks, who could ditch, mow, garden, wash, and milk. A hound bitch which appeared to be going mad bit Billy through his coat sleeve but did not draw blood. The annual hog-killing took place.

On December 26th he was writing to Humphreys a fervent hope that heaven would forbid a time should come when he was driven to the necessity of making a choice of the two alternatives presented to him in Humphreys' last—and his regrets that Humphreys had not been present to aid in the attack on the Christmas pies.

XXVII

1787 began badly, with the sudden death in January of Washington's favorite brother and closest companion in youth, John Augustine of Bushfield. He wrote to Bushrod, expressing restrained sorrow and refusing tactfully to act as executor on the grounds that Bushrod's competency as a lawyer was sufficient to deal with his father's estate.

John Augustine's death left unresolved the problem of their mother's future, on which he and George had been in consultation, having arrived at the conclusion that she would be better off to hire out her Negroes and land, retaining for her own use only a man-servant and a maid, the phaeton and two horses, and go to live with one of her children. As Bushfield was now no longer available, having passed to John Augustine's widow and their son Bushrod, only Charles's house in the Valley, Betty's at Fredericksburg, and Mount Vernon remained.

It would appear that Betty's was the obvious choice, but George thought it necessary to rule out Mount Vernon in some detail. On February 15th he wrote to his mother a long letter of advice and explanation, with the recurring defensive note of apology which she seemed always to impose upon him: "......My house is at your service, and I would press you most sincerely and most devoutly to accept it, but I am sure, and candour requires me to say, it will never answer your purposes in any shape whatsoever. For in truth it may be compared to a well resorted tavern, as scarcely any strangers who are going from north to south, or from south to north, do not spend a day or two at it. This would, were you to be an inhabitant of it, oblige you to do one of 3 things; 1st, to be always dressing to appear in company; 2d, to come into [the room] in a dishabille, or 3d, to be as it were a prisoner in your own chamber. The first you'ld not like; indeed, for a person at your time of life it would be too fatiguing. The 2d, I should not like, because those who resort here are, as I observed before, strangers and people of the first distinction. And the 3d, more than probably, would not be pleasing to either of us. Nor indeed could you be retired in any room in my house; for what with the sitting up of company, the noise and bustle of servants, and many other things, you would not be able to enjoy that calmness and serenity of mind, which in my opinion you ought now to prefer to every other consideration in life...... but by the mode I have pointed out, you may reduce your income to a certainty, be eased of all trouble, and if you are so disposed, may be perfectly happy; for happiness depends more upon the internal frame of a person's own mind than on the externals in the world. Of the last, if you will pursue the plan here recommended, I am sure you can want nothing that is essential. The other depends wholly upon yourself, for the riches of the Indies cannot purchase it...."

He was also in correspondence with his brother Charles in an effort to save some portion of Sam's estate from the claims still being made upon it by the creditors. Already sustaining the expense of Sam's sons Lawrence and George Steptoe Washington at the Alexandria Academy, Washington had by now taken their young sister Harriot under his roof—a lively and undisciplined child only a little older than Nelly Custis.

The story of Harriot Washington rests mainly on unpublished letters at Mount Vernon, and has a sort of rueful Cinderella charm. She first appeared in the Diary in August, '86, when at the age of about ten she was brought to Mount Vernon by her maternal aunt, who was the mother of Matilda and Flora Lee of Stratford. After the early death of her husband, Mrs. Lee had married Philip Fendall of Alexandria, leaving Matilda in possession of Stratford when her sister Flora married Ludwell, one of the Chantilly Lees, who had a house called Shooter's Hill near the Fendalls.

It may have been the death of her brother Thornton's first wife which cast Harriot adrift on the somewhat grudging charity of her relatives, most of whom had large enough families of their own.

Probably during some such visit as the one in August, '86, Washington or Martha felt obliged to assume her permanent guardianship, not foreseeing the Presidency, when their enforced absence from Mount Vernon again left Harriot stranded for the better part of eight years. Washington was then compelled to saddle George Augustine's wife Fanny or Betty Lewis with Harriot's upbringing, while the two Custis children accompanied their grandmother. Harriott's letters to her "dear Uncle," which will begin in 1790 while he was at New York, had a bumble-footed eagerness to please and an overflow of affection which can only command heartfelt sympathy.

Washington's involuntary position as tavern-keeper shows in the exasperated entries in the Diary: "A Person calling himself Hugh Patten dined here and returned to Alexandria afterwards."—"A Mr. Rinaldo Johnston dined here yesterday and went away after it."—"A Mr. Van Praddle, and a Mr. Duplaine, and Col. Gilpin dined here and returned in the Afternoon....."

But there were other visitors. Madison came again in January, and Harry Lee, and in their eyes, and in letters from old friends like Knox and Edmund Randolph, Washington read the unwelcome writing on the wall. He would have to attend the Convention which was to open on the 24th of May in Philadelphia as he had done in '75, and though it was still a mystery to him how he could again be of any decisive service now, he knew that whatever they asked of him he would again be unable to refuse.

He had developed—perhaps out of sheer nerves—a rheumatic condition which required him to carry one arm in a sling. Rawlins was still at work on the plaster decoration of the still unfinished New Room. In April a man named Bater was given articles of agreement for the term of one year, in which he promised "that he will, during said time, conduct himself soberly, diligently, and honestly, that he will faithfully and industriously perform all, and every part of his duty as a Gardner, to the best of his knowledge and abilities, and that he will not, at any time, suffer himself to be disguised with liquor, except on the times hereafter mentioned." In consideration of which Washington agreed to provide "a decent suit of clothes," a working jacket and breeches, two white shirts, three check ditto, two pair of yarn stockings and two pair of thread ditto, two linen pocket handkerchiefs, two pair linen overalls, and as many pair of shoes as were actually necessary. In addition to which, Bater was to receive "four Dollars at Christmas, with which he may be drunk 4 days and 4 nights; two Dollars at Easter to effect the same purpose; two Dollars also at Whitsontide, to be drunk two days; A Dram in the morning, and a drink of Grog at Dinner or at noon." This document was drawn up in the handwriting of George Augustine, whose health was again causing anxiety.

In April Fanny's first child was born, a son named Fayette who died a fortnight later. At the end of the month an express arrived from Fredericksburg with news of the serious illness of both his mother and sister, and Washington set off for Millbank at daylight on the 27th. He found their condition less critical than was feared, though Betty was worn out with nursing, and he was able to return to Mount Vernon on the 30th.

The Diary continued obstinately right up to his departure for Philadelphia: "Much fish caught, and no demand for them; Salting them up...... Hoeing up the old road through the Turnip field at home, and otherwise preparing the grnd. for the intended seed by cross-plowing it..... The Oats everywhere in strong and moist land seem to thrive; but appear at a stnd. elsewhere...... Rid to the Fishing landing, and thence to the Ferry, Dogue Run, and Muddy Hole plantations with my nephew G. W. [George Augustine] to explain to him the Nature, and the ordr. of the business at each as I would have it carried on during my absence at the Convention in Philadelphia......"

On the 9th, in bad weather, he started northward again.

His friends the Robert Morrises had invited him to lodge at their handsome house on Market Street and he had declined. "Mrs. Washington is become too domestick, and too attentive to two little Grand Children to leave home," he wrote, "and I can assure you, Sir, that it was not until after a long struggle I could obtain my own consent to appear again in a public theatre. My first remaining wish being to glide gently down the stream of life in tranquil retirement till I shall arrive at the world of Spirits...."

That dream was fading fast, but there was nevertheless a certain satisfaction in the warm reunion at Philadelphia with old friends like Hamilton, whom he had hardly thought to see again, and Benjamin

Franklin, who at seventy-nine had just returned from nearly ten years in France in time to be named a delegate from Pennsylvania to another convention.

Washington was surprised and moved by the reception the whole city accorded him, including a military escort and a chiming of all its bells to greet his arrival, when he had somehow supposed himself to be half forgotten. Even Humphreys was on hand awaiting him, and he was persuaded after all to accept the Morrises' lavish hospitality. Robert Morris was a merchant-banker who had come to America from Liverpool at the age of thirteen in 1747—Washington was two years older—and started his career in the Willing family counting-house. He married well, and rose to a partnership. As a member of the Second Continental Congress he voted against the Declaration of Independence, and then signed it with the rest. He was living now in the stately old Penn house between Sixth and Seventh Streets which had served General Howe as headquarters during the British occupation, and was later occupied by Benedict Arnold during his spectacular courtship of Peggy Shippen. It was a brick house three stories high, and Morris had recently spent money freely to refurbish it. He would surrender it with a gesture to Washington during the Presidency, when it proved to be in many ways inconvenient and inadequate as a Presidential mansion. Morris had also a country house called The Hills, where he entertained his distinguished guests.

By 1798 when Washington had retired for the last time to Mount Vernon, Morris found himself ruined by land speculation in the West and an unscrupulous associate, and he spent some time in the debtors' prison in Prince Street, where Washington visited him, in what must have been a painful nostalgia for them both. During this summer of '87, however, no man's credit was higher than Robert Morris's, and it was freely acknowledged that without his financial aid the victorious Yorktown campaign might not have been accomplished.

The reluctant George Mason was the last of the Virginians to arrive at Philadelphia, where he had engaged rooms at the Indian Queen Tavern. He was accompanied by his son John. It was his first venture beyond the boundaries of Virginia, and would be his last.

Predictably, George Washington was chosen President of the Convention, and the following day when the Diary records that he "Dined, drank Tea, and spent the evening at my lodgings," he wrote one of the same wistful, homesick letters to George Augustine that had gone home to Lund during the war. First, he was concerned that George Augustine might overdo his failing strength in the desire to accomplish too much in his uncle's absence; and he was sorry to hear that they were still in want of rain, with which the countryside around Philadelphia was deluged. "How does the Grass Seeds which were sown with the grain, and flax, seem to come on? How does those which were sown in my little garden advance? And how does the Crops which are planted in drills between the Corn, come up, and progress?...... I send by this conveyance some Pecon nuts; which plant as soon as you can...... I hope the stray doe will not be lost; does any of them appear to be with young?..... Desire Mathew to furnish me with a Memo. for the Hinges wanted for the New-Room, and to which hand they are to rise, that I may endeavor to provide them whilst I am in this place. As I see no prospect of a Speedy return (for contrary to my wish, I am made, by a unanimous vote, President of the Convention) I will, in due time furnish you with a plan for conducting your harvest. In the meantime, send me my last diary which, by mistake, I left behind me. It will be found, I presume, on my writing Table. put it under a good strong paper cover, sealed up as a letter...."

In June he was still hopelessly anchored: "As there is not the smallest prospect of my returning before harvest, and God knows how long it may be after it, I enclose you the observations I made at last harvest, to be practiced on the ensuing one," he wrote, and asked for measurements of the chimney in the New Room, that he might order castings for the back and sides. Later that month he requested them to send "my Blew Coat with the Cremson collar and one of those made of the Cloth sent me by the Spanish Minister, to wit that without lapels and lined with white silk, as I see no end to my staying here," and his umbrella—the new one in his study.

Deep secrecy had at once closed over the debates, with the members enjoined not to repeat in their correspondence or conversation the daily wrangles of this most crucial session. There were of course some leaks, but not many. Mason and Madison were known to have locked horns more than once, though both recognized the danger of a North-South collision of interests.

The exigencies of the often stormy meetings of the Convention devoured Washington's days, but in the evenings his mind would return to Mount Vernon, and the astonishing detail of his letters to his deputy there show how he strove not to lose touch with the daily routine as it would have progressed under his own eyes.

"..... Endeavour to keep the Willow in the Serpentine Walks upright by means of the Stakes, and tow yarn or grass, or something else to tye them thereto that will not rub, or fret the bark; the small, as well as the large trees in these walks should be staked up to give them a proper elevation...."

"In plowing the drilled Corn, it is to be remembered that throwing the furrow always to the plant will leave the land in high ridges; and make it more liable to wash and run into Gullies; to avoid wch, was one of my principle motives for introducing the Hoe and common Iron toothed Harrows....."

"You may inform Thomas Green that if Drunkenness, or idleness constitutes any part of his conduct, that I have directed you to discharge him....."

"Priming the roof of the Greenhouse may be delayed till I return, or till you here from me again on the subject...."

"I desire that the honeysuckles against the Houses and brick walls may be nailed up; and made to spread regularly over them. Should those near the Pillars of the Colonnades, or covered ways, be dead, their place should be supplied with others; as I want them to run up, and Spread over the parts which are painted green...."

He had sent round some articles by boat; "Among them is the top of the Cupula of the House wch has been left so long unfinished. I do not suppose there would have been any difficulty in fixing it without directions but I requested the maker to give them and they are sent accordingly..... The wood part of what is sent must receive a coat of white paint; the spire, if it is not the case already, must have that of black. The bill of the bird is to be black, and the olive branch in the mouth of it must be green. These two last are otherwise by mistake. Great pains (and Mr. Lear understands the compass) must be taken to fix the points truly. Otherwise they will deceive, rather than direct, if they vary from the north, south, east, and west......" (Detailed directions for the use of compass and plumb-line followed.)

"If Mr. Lund Washington wants Dow's money, he must have it; but really I see no more than the Man in the Moon where I am to get the money to pay my Taxes, &ca., &ca., &ca., if I have made no crop, & shall have to buy Corn for my people......"

"I have sent the bust of Commodore Paul Jones, given to me by himself, which I request may be placed opposite my own [by Houdon] in my study, on a similar bracket with that of the latter....."

"......request to be informed of the depth of the well (by the Kitchen door) from the level of the brick pavement, which surrounds it, to the surface of the water within; and the depth of the water. I have some intention of placing a pump in it, instead of drawing the water up in a Bucket as at present, and for this purpose the enquiry is made......"

"P.S. Have you thinned the Carrots which were too thick? ...."

"P.S. Keep the shrubberies clean. What have you done to the Gravel Walks, or rather what remains to be done to them?....."

While in Philadelphia Washington was able to make his own purchases, and these included Venetian blinds for the New Room, the cast iron chimney-backs, and paint. "The Wood part of the New Room may be painted of any tolerably fashionable color, so as to serve present purposes, and this might be a buff," he wrote. "'Tis more than probable it will receive a *finishing* colour hereafter. The buff should be of the lightest kind, inclining to white......It will require small brushes, and considerable attention to paint the carved mouldings, to prevent their filling too much with the paint....." When extensive restoration of this room was begun in the 1950's, layers of paint were carefully scraped away to reveal the buff priming coat requested by the General, and this, with the deep green which was probably his fashionable finishing coat on the pilasters and friezes behind the white plasterwork designs by Rawlins, has been faithfully reproduced.

Samuel Vaughan, after dining with Washington in Philadelphia in June, paid a visit to Mount Vernon in August while the General was still absent. He would have been cordially received by Martha, George Augustine, and Fanny, and had the pleasure of seeing his mantel-piece in place in the New Room, which was just about then receiving its coat of buff paint. He remained for several days, making extensive notes and drawings, and in November he sent to Washington a beautifully executed plan of the grounds. Washington wrote to thank him warmly, and pointed out that he had got the western prospect a little wrong with regard to the two artificial mounds where the weeping willows stood. Vaughan soon after returned to England, where Mrs. Vaughan had preceded him. His beautiful drawing of Mount Vernon as it looked to him in 1787 can be seen there today.

Washington did not reach home again until sunset of September 22d, after an absence of four months and fourteen days at the Philadelphia Convention. On the 23d the Diary resumed again, half the neighborhood having come to dinner.

Then the trouble began. Copies of the Constitution, which must now be ratified by each separate state, were sent to all the Assemblies and legislators, and instantaneous schism developed everywhere. Patrick Henry, having refused to attend the Convention after being named a delegate, wrote to Washington in October: "I have to lament that I cannot bring my Mind to accord with the proposed Constitution." Benjamin Harrison was more tactful: "I feel myself deeply interested in everything you have had a hand in, or that comes from you, and am so well assured of the solidity of your judgment, and the rectitude of your intentions, that I shall never stick at trifles to conform myself to your opinion;"—*(but)*—"If our condition is not very desperate, I have my fears that the remedy will prove worse than the disease."

George Mason, who had attended the Convention unwillingly and was unhappy there, had refused to sign at all, as did Edmund Randolph, one of those who had been most urgent for Washington's attendance at Philadelphia. To the general public, the fact that Washington and Franklin had signed it was almost sufficient recommendation by itself. Washington made no pretense of thinking the Constitution a perfect solution to the young nation's problems—"but I sincerely believe it is the best that could be obtained at this time," he explained to Patrick Henry. While the State Assemblies wrangled over the ratification, and old friendships were strained to the breaking point, Mason went so far as to publish his *Objections* in a pamphlet, of which he sent Washington a copy.

Mason was first, last, and always a Virginian, and after that a Southerner too, and he was inclined, for all his previous astuteness, to hold a short-sighted viewpoint on national affairs. Washington on the contrary was willing to surrender some of the jealous states' rights for the sake of national unity, and was therefore ranked with the younger men, Madison, Hamilton, and Harry Lee, who were best satisfied with the work done at Philadelphia. Edmund Randolph already wavered towards their side.

Mason attended the autumn session of the Virginia Assembly in a bad mood, and joined Patrick Henry and Richard Henry Lee in planning the strategy to defeat ratification of the Constitution in its present form. He often seemed old and weary now, but his characteristic irony still showed in his retort to a heckling opponent who interrupted him by calling out: "Sir, you are an old man, and the public notices that your mind is failing!" To which Mason shot back with something of his accustomed vigor: "Sir, when yours fails no one will ever discover it!"

During the autumn the master of Mount Vernon resumed his daily rides and observations and experiments, dined at Abingdon and Hayfield and the homes of his Alexandria friends, and dispensed his conscientious hospitality at home. October was starred by a visit from the Samuel Powels of Philadelphia, who besides the Robert Morrises were the Washingtons' closest friends there.

Elizabeth Willing Powel was a younger sister of Mrs. William Byrd III, and while not a bluestocking was certainly better read and informed than most women of her time. The marriage was a singularly happy one, of twenty years duration, and had even made an impression on the Marquis de Chastellux, who accompanied Rochambeau to America in 1780 and in his *Memoirs* left a vivid account of the American scene during the last two years of the war. De Chastellux was entertained by the Powels in their handsome brick house in Third Street, and recorded that they lived together "I shall not say as man and wife, which would not convey the idea of perfect equality in America, but as two friends, happily matched in point of understanding, taste, and information." Mr. Powel had travelled abroad, and had twice been mayor of Philadelphia, but in de Chastellux's eyes what distinguished Mrs. Powel was "her taste for conversation and the truly European use she knows how to make of her understanding and information." There is at Mount Vernon a sizable unpublished correspondence between the Powels and the Washingtons which holds a lively interest.

The Pennsylvania Genealogical Society owns the journal which was kept by Mr. Powel during his 1787 visit, which preserved the appearance of Mount Vernon while it was under Washington's hand, before another absence during the eight years of the Presidency again reduced it to slow decay.

"The House has an uniform Appearance, is about an hundred feet in Front, with a Turrett on the Top. The Building is of Wood cut in Squares to resemble Courses of Stone, which is painted & sanded so as to imitate Stone, & may easily be taken for it," he wrote. (Washington described to the architect Thornton in 1799 the unusual outside finish of sanding the wooden siding, which he called "rustication," as an "operation, by dashing, as long as any will stick, the Sand upon a coat of thick paint," designed to answer two purposes, "durability, and presentation of Stone." Like the long piazza, for which no Virginia precedent existed, it was a finish unique even in his time, and the suggestion has been made that he may have seen it during his 1751 visit to Barbados.) "The whole appearance of the Garden front is handsom, tho' not altogether regular as to the Windows under the Pediment having been built at different Times," Powel continued. "It is joined to the Offices by Colonnades with Arches painted green.......

"The View down the River is extensive & most charming,—nearly opposite the House the River Piscataway empties itself into the majestic Patowmack & adds greatly to the beauty of the Scene. In a Word this is altogether the most charming Seat I have seen in America. It is kept with great Neatness & the good Order of its Masters Mind appears extended to every Thing around it. Tradesmen of every kind necessary to a farm are to be found here. This Estate consists of about Eight Thousand Acres......

"After Breakfast I rode with the General over several of his Farms, Mrs. Washington & Mrs. Powel accompanied us to the Mill, which is a very good one. The long & severe Drought which this Country has experienced has rendered the Appearance of these Farms unfavorable. The General informed me that he had about Three Thousand Acres in Tillage...... There is no Tobacco planted on this Estate......"

The Powels were also taken on a pilgrimage to view the ruins of Belvoir.

During the autumn David Humphreys wrote of the death of both his parents, and expressed a wish to return to Mount Vernon. Washington's reply was prompt and cordial. "The only stipulations I shall contend for are, that in all things you shall do as you please; I will do the same; and that no ceremony may be used or any restraint be imposed on any one." Humphreys arrived in mid-November, opportunely to enliven a household which had just been saddened by news of George William Fairfax's death at Bath in England, leaving Sally an aging widow in poor health, far from the friends of her youth and in straitened circumstances. But life went on as usual at Mount Vernon, by the Diary: "In Company with Colo. Humphreys, Majr. Washington and Mr. Lear went a hunting. Found a fox about 11 o'clock near the Pincushion, run him hard for near 3 quarters of an hour and then lost him. Mr. Lund Washington who joined us, came and dined with us and returned afterwards."

There is no Christmas entry in the Diary, but with Humphreys there, and George Augustine, and Lear, and the children, it must have been merry, and Humphreys probably wielded the carving-knife as it was always his special duty in the old days at Headquarters. On the 30th they were descended upon by one of the oddest couples in all Virginia's eccentricities—John and Lucy Paradise, "lately from England but now of Williamsburg," Washington put it in the Diary. The visit lasted four days, during which Washington abandoned his daily routine, which few guests ever succeeded in disrupting, and stayed at home.

A Ludwell and a Grymes by birth, Lucy Paradise was the niece of Lighthorse Harry Lee's mother, and in the interlocking Virginia lines was also cousin to the Stratford Lees. Born at the Ludwell mansion of Green Spring near Williamsburg, then one of the proudest houses in Virginia, she and her two sisters were taken to London by their father in 1760, when Lucy was nine, her mother having died several years before. They lived in a handsome house in Cecil Street, and Benjamin Franklin was their neighbor and a frequent guest, as were Peter and John Paradise, father and son, who had recently arrived in England from Salonika, speaking five languages, cultivated, travelled, well-to-do, and with very little English blood in their veins. The fathers became friends, and when Lucy was eighteen, a small, dynamic girl with a violent temper, she married young John Paradise, who was an Oxford man, studious, inarticulate, gentle, and probably bewildered.

Completely mismatched, they were soon famous in London for their uninhibited domestic storms, and Lucy created embarrassing scenes in London drawing-rooms which were witnessed by the observant Fanny Burney and her circle—making no effort to control her outrageous temper even in "the vast presence of Dr. Johnson," who could never abide her. Her ignorance was surpassed only by her bad manners—complimented on her elegant figure as a "sylph," she thought it an insulting word and flew into a rage. Her unfortunate husband fell rapidly into a hypochondria which permitted him to match symptoms with Boswell. For nearly twenty years the battle had raged between them, while John's health declined and his father's Tory convictions further estranged them and curtailed the inheritance they had counted on from him. Their elder daughter made a scandalous runaway marriage at sixteen with a fortune-hunting Venetian count. After the war Lucy became obsessed with the idea of returning to America to claim her share of the Ludwell property there in the hope of restoring their finances. Her elder sister Hannah had died, leaving her husband in possession of Green Spring, where he was living with two young daughters and a son. In the autumn of '87 the Paradises arrived there in one of their temporary marital truces—it was John's first visit to America, and Lucy had been abroad for twenty-seven years.

Hannah Ludwell's widower, William Lee, of course owed them a certain hospitality at Green Spring. They found him blind and embittered, with acute financial worries of his own; they found the great house in a decaying condition, after having been a battleground during the war; they found Williamsburg no longer the capital and seat of the Assembly, which had moved to Richmond, but a shabby, run-down village, the Governor's Palace burnt down, the Capitol building falling to pieces, the College attended by only eighty students. They had brought letters of introduction—for some reason Jefferson at Paris had befriended them—and in December they set out on the round of visits which brought them to Mount Vernon.

For all the variety of their visitors hitherto, the Washingtons must have been somewhat spellbound by John and Lucy Paradise. Lucy was now only thirty-six, and though overdressed and over-excitable, stubborn, and subject to explosions of fantastic bad temper, she could make herself attractive when she wished. Her husband at forty-four was without doubt one of the most interesting men Washington had ever entertained—the intimate friend of such men as Dr. Johnson, Gibbon, Garrick, Joshua Reynolds, Horace Walpole, and Charles Burney, in whose civilized society he had always taken refuge from his wife's disposition. Moreover, they had known Colonel Humphreys during his recent travels abroad, and were delighted to encounter him again, while he was already prepared to assist Washington in coping with the emotional emergencies which almost certainly occurred during a stay of several days' duration.

Mount Vernon tact obviously withstood the strain, for Lucy departed convinced that Martha was her friend, and in later years nursed a hope that Washington would give John Paradise some lucrative post in the government. Colonel Humphreys and Washington accompanied the Paradises to Alexandria and took leave of them there, probably returning to Mount Vernon a trifle limp, but with a fund of anecdote and reminiscent laughter to last them many a duller day.

Outwardly as usual, and with an unbroken domestic routine, Washington at the year's end was uneasy and in doubt. The Constitution as drawn up in Philadelphia provided for a chief magistrate or head of state to be called President, and there was already little doubt on whom the choice of the people as well as of the Congress would fall, for that office. The term was four long years.

XXVIII

THE Diary resumes its tranquil record through 1788. There was a chimney fire on January 5th, which caused considerable alarm but no damage. The ice was got in. Grubbing and fencing went on. Sam's shadowy third son, Ferdinand, died of a consumption at twenty-one. The unfortunate Billy had another bad fall and damaged his remaining good knee. Fanny's second child was born, a girl named Maria, and Lund's third daughter, whom they called Lucinda II, having lost the first, as they were to lose this one within the year. Sam's small daughter Harriot went with the Mount Vernon family to dinner at Abingdon and was left there for a visit with the two elder Custis girls.

English oats and summer wheat sent by Arthur Young were carefully planted.—"In my Botanical Garden, on thursday morning, before the Rain, I sowed in the Section next the Spinning house, one Row of Rhubarb seed, sent me by Mr. Jay, the Seeds 3 Inches apart," says the Diary on April 4th. And on the 13th—"Went to Church at Alexandria accompanied by Colo. Humphreys, Mr. Lear, and Washington Custis. Brought Hariot Washington home with us who had been left at Abingdon and came to Church with Mrs. Stuart." They caught about 50,000 herrings at a draught one afternoon. A heavy rain washed up the willow cuttings set out by the rail fence near the road, and he had them replaced, so late in the season there was little hope of their living. He sent the two jackasses to the election at Marlborough "that they might be seen." On May 11, which was a Sunday, he was "at home all day," and spent the time counting the number of peas and hominy beans per pint, so that it was possible to gauge how many hills, allowing five to a hill, one bushel of each would plant, of six different kinds. In June, accompanied by Humphreys, he rode out to the Shenandoah, and visited his brother Charles and spent a night at Warner Washington's house called Fairfield.

On nearly every page of the Diary the names of the three young men in his household appear—quiet, attentive, helpful Tobias Lear, expansive Colonel Humphreys, devoted, sickly George Augustine—the sons he might have had, making the morning rounds with him, attending the masculine dinners at Alexandria, escorting the ladies and young of his family on little excursions and to church, riding to hounds with him, stretching out silk-stockinged legs alongside his at the evening fireside when they had all dressed, powdered, and dined—companionable, loyal, affectionate, each in his own way. It was a good life.

In March Mr. Lear wrote to his Harvard classmate William Prescott a letter which he said was on no account to be circulated—an account of Mount Vernon as he knew and loved it. "I have, for a year past, felt myself more attached to this family from affection & love than any pecuniary motive," he wrote. "I am treated in every respect as a child of it, and at the same time feel happy in having placed myself in this point of view without sacrificing a single spark of that independence of mind which ought to govern every man who is worthy to live..... Major Washington, a nephew of the General's about my age, with his Lady, reside here; his business is almost solely upon the farms, but we mutually assist each other in our different employments when anything in either requires immediate dispatch.—our affection for each other is reciprocal & we live in the happiest friendship—His Lady is one of those superior beings who are sent down to bless good men.—Mrs. Washington, the Gen'l's Lady, is everything that is benevolent & good—I honor her as a second mother & receive from her all those attentions which I should look for from her who bore me—A little Grandson of Mrs. Washington's, by a former husband, & his Sister, the one of 6 & the other of 8 years old, afford me no small pleasure & amusement in instructing them, they are, without partiallity, as fine children as were ever seen, I never thought I could be so much attached to children as I am to them...... General Washington is, I believe, almost the only man of an exalted character who does not lose some part of his respectibility by an intimate acquaintance.—I have lived with him near two years, have received as many marks of his affection & esteem as perhaps any young man ever did—and have occasions to be with him in every situation in which a man is placed in his family—have ate & drank with him constantly, and almost every evening play at cards with him, and I declare I have never found a single thing that could lessen my respect for him.—a compleat knowledge of his honesty, uprightness, & candour in all his private transactions have sometimes led me to think him more than a man—His industry is unparalleld—he rises every day before the sun—writes till breakfast (which never exceeds ½ after 7) then mounts his horse & rides round his farms til ½ past 2, sees that everything is in proper order—and if there is no company he writes till dark & in the Evening—plays a game at whist, or, if pressed with business writes till 9 in the Eveng—this is the general round which he pursues with little variation......."

The day on which Olney Winsor paid a visit to Mount Vernon at Washington's invitation is omitted from the Diary, but Winsor in a letter to his wife says that he went with a group of gentlemen from Alexandria on a Sunday at the end of March, arriving about one o'clock—"where we were received by the General & his Family with great freedom and politeness, at the same time without any ceremonious parade.—The general converses with great deliberation, & with ease, except in pronouncing some few words, in which he has a hisitancy of speech—he was dressed in a plain drab Coat, red Jacket, buff Breeches and white Hose.—Mrs. Washington is an elegant figure for a person of her years, perhaps 45.—She is rather fleshy, of good complexion, has a large portly double chin, and an open & engaging Countenance, on which a pleasing smile sets during conversation, in which she bears an agreable part. She was dressed in a plain black Sattin Gown, with long Sleves, figured Lawn Apron & Handkf, guaze french night Cap with black bowes—all very neat—but not gaudy......" Mr. Winsor's letter contains the first mention of a hesitancy in the General's speech, which has gone otherwise almost unnoticed, and his estimate of Martha's age is flattering—she was fifty-six.

In April Washington wrote to Lafayette in that involved playfulness which sometimes overtook his quill: "In answer to the ob-

servations you make on the probability of my election to the Presidency (knowing me as you do) I need only say, that it has no enticing charms, and no fascinating allurements for me. However it might not be decent for me to say I would refuse to accept or even to speak much about an appointment which may never take place; for in so doing, one might possibly incur the application of the moral resulting from that Fable, in which the Fox is represented as inveighing against the sourness of the Grapes, because he cannot reach them. All that it will be necessary to add, my dear Marquis, in order to show my decided predilection, is that (at my time of life and under my circumstances) the increasing infirmities of nature and the growing love of retirement do not permit me to entertain a wish beyond that of living and dying an honest man on my own farm. Let those follow the pursuits of ambition and fame, who have a keener relish for them, or who may have more years in store for the enjoyment....."

James Madison visited Mount Vernon on his way back from Congress in New York to the Convention in Richmond, at which he was to defend the Constitution against such veteran politicians as Patrick Henry, George Mason, and William Grayson–and no doubt he at that time mapped out a course of argument in consultation with Washington. They well knew that he would be a Daniel in the lions' den, for he was himself an unspectacular speaker, his voice was naturally quiet, and he made his most telling points as though they had just occurred to him, though his notes were in the hat he held in his hand. Under Henry's loud and experienced lamentations, Mason's incisive choler, and Grayson's military bluster, Madison should have been swamped. Moreover, as the debates continued into the third week, in Richmond's summer heat, illness overtook him and his always conversational tones sank still lower from sheer weakness. But somehow he wore down the giants by a steady appeal to reason, and was probably the deciding factor in the ultimate ratification by Virginia.

In June the Washingtons set out on a round of visits in the Fredericksburg district, including of course his mother, who was still living in her house at the end of Betty's garden. On June 28th the Diary records: "The Inhabitants of Alexandria having received the News of the Ratification of the proposed Constitution by this

State, and that of New Hampshire, and having determined on public rejoicings, part of which to be in a dinner, to which this family was invited, Colo. Humphreys, my nephew G. A. Washington, and myself went up to it, and returned in the afternoon." The victory had been a narrow one, and it left George Mason bitter and beaten. He compared Edmund Randolph's desertion to the Federalist side with Benedict Arnold's detestable behavior, and retired to Gunston to be ill.

There were other states still to be heard from, but very little doubt remained, even as to what lay ahead for George Washington, though he still refused to consider it inevitable. Perhaps in need of a little buttressing, he wrote inviting Madison to recuperate at Mount Vernon before returning to Congress in New York: "Moderate exercise, and books occasionally, with the mind unbent, will be your best restoratives," he advised. And so, on the afternoon of July 4th, in the company of Dr. Stuart who was now a member of the Assembly, Madison arrived again. The Diary makes no allusion to the date, but there may have been suitable toasts at dinner, and perhaps a few extra ones.

On the 5th Washington remained at home all day with his guest, and not until the 7th did Madison continue his journey northward, travelling in Washington's carriage to Alexandria where he took the New York stage—unmarried, always in frail health, he was certainly able to afford a carriage of his own.

On the same day Washington sent off an order for 100,000 shingles, "distinguishing between what is called bald, and green Cypress," to be delivered at his landing, and a few days later he wrote to Biddle for "12 yards of velvet ribbon of the width and quality of the enclosed sample," to be sent by the post. At the end of the month they began to sink a well at the new barn, and got water which seemed to be good "and in tolerable plenty" in about ten feet digging.

The summer rolled on at Mount Vernon, harvesting much interrupted by frequent showers, in the midst of which the Morrises arrived—Mr. and Mrs. Robert Morris of Philadelphia, their two sons and a daughter, and Gouverneur Morris, who was unrelated, being American born. He had long been associated with Robert, both in politics and business, and was soon to sail for France where Jeffer-

son was still America's Ambassador. Jefferson would be called home to be Secretary of State in the new government, and Gouverneur Morris would succeed him at the Paris post, which he held at some peril to himself during the French Revolution—a big, hearty, genial man, with a wooden leg, which was the result of a carriage accident in the streets of Philadelphia. The tempo of events was picking up speed, but Washington still hoped that they might pass him by in his Potomac backwater.

On July 24th there was a hurricane with a northeast wind accompanied by rain, which blew down some trees in the groves around the house and did "great mischief to the grain, grass, etc., and not a little to my Mill race. In a word, it was violent and severe —more so than has happened for many years...." The following day when he rode out to survey the damage, he found the corn broken off short, the wheat overflowed with the tide, which had risen four feet above normal, driving boats "into fields where no tide had ever been heard of before," and fences carried away so that the stock could get into the grain fields. Damage to the wharves at Alexandria, Norfolk, and Baltimore was extensive.

In August he wrote to Dr. Craik enclosing £30 cash for one year's allowance for the schooling of his godson, George Washington Craik. "I wish it was in my power," he added, "to send the like sum for the other year which is now about, or near due; and that I could discharge your account for attendance and ministrens to the Sick of my family; but it really is not; for with much truth I can say, I never felt the want of money so sensibly since I was a boy of 15 years old as I have done for the last 12 months and probably shall do for 12 Months more to come."

Two days later Sam's incorrigible sons at the Alexandria Academy again drew unfavorable attention to themselves. It appears that Colonel Hanson, under whose roof they lodged, had undertaken to discipline Lawrence, and had been set upon by George Steptoe, who rescued his younger brother from the rod by physical force. Lawrence thereupon fled to Mount Vernon with his story, and although the Diary is silent on the whole affair, being entirely preoccupied with the sowing of turnips and the tilling and weeding of the corn—a letter to Colonel Hanson has survived in the Letterbook copies:

"Sir: On my return home last night I found my Nephew Lawrence here, who said he was afraid to remain at your house, and offered to show me some bruises he had received. Being prepared for it, I was going this morning to correct him; but he begged so earnestly and promised so faithfully that there should be no cause of complaint against him for the future that I have suspended the Punishment.

"The letter which I have written to his Brother on the subject is under this cover and open for your perusal. He is arrived at such an *age* and *size* now as to be a fitter subject to be reasoned with than to receive corporal punishment. As my primary object in placing these boys with you *last*, was that they (at least George) should be treated more on the footing of Friendship, and as companions, than as *mere* School-boys. This I hoped would draw George's attention to objects, and conversations, that would improve, and might contribute in a *degree* to wean him from boyish amusements, the influence of which would extend to Lawrence....."

"Dear George: [the enclosed letter ran] It was with equal pain and surprise that I was informed by Colo. Hanson on Monday last, of your unjustifiable behaviour in rescuing your brother from that chastisement which was due to his improper conduct; and which you know, because you have been told it in explicit language, he was authorized to administer whensoever he should deserve it. Such refractory behaviour on your part, I consider as an insult equally offered to myself after the above communications and I shall continue to view it in that light, till you have made satisfactory acknowledgments to Colo. Hanson for the offence given him....... If the admonitions of friendship are lost other methods must be tried which cannot be more disagreeable to you than it would be to one who wishes to avoid it, who is solicitous to see you and your Brother (the only remaining Sons of your father) turn out well, and who is very desirous of continuing your affectionate uncle."

The boys were at that time fifteen and thirteen years of age. And however straight a face Washington kept, the wise blue eyes were doubtless lit by a gleam of his own once unruly spirit.

But he read with no amusement at all letters from that brilliant,

stormy charmer, Alexander Hamilton, who had so enlivened the darkest days at Headquarters with his good looks, his wit, and his romances. New York's ratification of the Constitution was a personal triumph for Hamilton, and he was certain to hold an important post in the new government. A renewed association with his youngest aide—Hamilton had only now turned thirty—would be for Washington, in spite of some unforgotten fireworks, a welcome one. But Hamilton's insistence that the unanimous wish of the country would call the former Commander-in-Chief to the Presidential chair was not.

Harry Lee continued to urge upon him the same impending duty, as did General Lincoln, to whom in October he replied in a kind of groan: "Every personal consideration conspires to rivet me (if I may use the expression) to retirement. . . . . After all, if I should conceive myself in a manner constrained to accept, I call Heaven to witness that this very act would be the greatest sacrifice of my personal feelings and wishes that ever I have been called upon to make. It would be to forego repose and domestic enjoyment, for trouble, perhaps for public obloquy: for I should consider myself as entering upon an unexplored field, enveloped on every side with clouds and darkness. . . . . ."

Washington's affection for the French, still maintained in his correspondence with Lafayette and several officers like de Chastellux who had served with Rochambeau at Yorktown, was probably subjected to unexpected strain by the visit to Mount Vernon of the new French Minister Plenipotentiary, Count de Moustier, and his "suite" early in November. The Count brought with him his sister-in-law, the Marchioness de Bréhan, whose husband had remained in France on his army duties while his wife acted as hostess for the Minister, with whom her relationship was already a scandal in New York. Jefferson in Paris had written letters of introduction which ignored it—though he was unlikely to be unaware of it—but the fastidious Madison soon complained to him that even in their travels the Minister and his sister-in-law were said "to neglect the most obvious precautions for veiling their intimacy," and added that the ladies of New York society were withdrawing from the Marchioness, the reason for which she recognized and resented.

Whether or not the chaste halls of Mount Vernon took note of the irregularity or remained innocently unaware, Washington invited friends down from Alexandria to dine with his distinguished guests, among them the useful Colonel Fitzgerald, the Ludwell Lees of Shooter's Hill, and Miss Nancy Craik—took them on an excursion to visit the new brick barn at Union Farm and saw them as far as Alexandria on their departure. While there, Madame de Bréhan, who was accompanied everywhere by her young son, executed a charming profile miniature of Nelly Custis, then ten years old and promising great beauty.

They were to encounter de Moustier's eccentricities more than once again, for he remained as the French representative during the first year of Washington's administration. He was a teetotaller—a rarity in the eighteenth century—and was so fussy about his food that he once arrived to dine at Vice-president Adams' house attended by his own cook bearing a special dish of truffles and game. He always dressed in the extreme of fashion, with high red heels to his shoes and jewelled earrings. He had got the finest house in New York, on Broadway below Trinity Church—it became briefly the Presidential mansion after de Moustier returned to France early in 1790—and there he gave elaborate balls and cotillions at which fabulous refreshments were served.

But de Moustier was not a fool. Reporting to his Government on the first President after witnessing the inauguration, he wrote: "He has the soul, look, and figure of a hero united in him. Born to command, he never seems embarrassed at the homage rendered him, and he has the advantage of uniting great dignity with great simplicity of manner."

On the 9th of November, '88, the following entry appears in Washington's Diary, with no sequel: "One of the Bucks in the Paddock having much wounded the Young Woman Dolshy, Doctr. Craik was sent for, who came and stayed all Night." And the following day: "The New Barn would *nearly* if not *quite* have the Rafters go up today."

On the 16th he entertained another of those journalistic visitors to whom we owe glimpses of Mount Vernon life much more intimate than anything the master himself provided. M. Brissot de Warville, a French merchant traveller introduced by Lafayette, was like the de Moustier party taken to view the new barn, which had been constructed after a design sent by Sir Arthur Young with various improvements, of brick made on the spot, and only the joists and shingles purchased. The guest was impressed by Washington's modesty. "He speaks of the American war and of his victories as of things in which he had no direction," he marvelled.

Sam's estate, which Charles was supposed to administrate for the creditors, as his house in the Valley was conveniently close to Harewood, was still giving trouble, and Bushrod, as the family lawyer, had become involved. A sale was now threatened, and he wrote to Mount Vernon for advice. "What the abilities of my deceased Brother Samls Estate towards paying his debts may be, I am unable to say," Washington replied wearily. "But I much fear that the management of it is in very bad hands; as the hours of your Uncle Charles are, I have reason to believe, spent in intoxication. This circumstance, added to a natural indolence, leaves too much to the Steward to expect *industry* and *fair dealing;* unless he differs widely from the generallity of his class. It would seem to me that the best mode for you to pursue, wd. be to go to Berkeley yourself, examine into the debts, the resources of the Estate, and the management of it. . . . . As to writing, *simply*, to your Uncle Charles, unaccompanied by personal application and the investigation here mentioned, I am persuaded it would avail nothing. My Money (tho' it is exceedingly distressing to me to apply it that way) and my credit, is at stake for the board, the Schooling, clothing, &ca. of George and Lawe. Washington, in Alexandria; without being able to receive from the Estate more than a little driblet now and then, entirely inadequate to the demand. My advance for them, at this time, in money and credit, is considerable. . . . . . ."

A few days later he offered Bushrod the use of his little house in Alexandria, rent-free, in which to establish his law practice. In a year's end attempt to bolster up his finances, he wrote to David Stuart about the prospects of receiving any income from Jacky Custis's estate. "The expensive manner in which I live (contrary to my wishes, but really unavoidable); the bad years of late, and my consequent short crops have occasioned me to run into debt, and to feel *more sensibly* the want of money than I have ever done at any period of my whole life; and obliges me to look forward to every source from whence I have a right to expect relief. . . . ."

At about the same time he solaced himself with a long agricultural letter to Arthur Young, inquiring about threshing machines, giving news of the new brick barn, his high opinion of the mules he bred from the imported jackasses—"And indeed, in a few years, I intend to drive no other in my carriage; having appropriated for the sole purpose of breeding them, upwards of 20 of my best Mares."

Disavow it as he might, in his obstinate plans for a quiet future at Mount Vernon, he could no longer have deceived himself into denying that the days of his retirement were numbered. The new government was to convene in New York in the spring of '89. John Adams and John Hancock were ready to contest the post of vice-president—and neither of them would be a particularly welcome choice to the man who had no opponent whatever for the highest office. Madison arrived at Mount Vernon on his way south to win an election to Congress against Monroe, who was Patrick Henry's choice. The weather was very bad, and he remained through Christmas Day, which in spite of Humphreys' always ebullient presence and famous dexterity with the carving knife, must have been overhung by the unwilling conviction that by Christmas of 1789 their host would be again shackled to public duty.

XXIX

A PORTION of the Diary which covered the spring and summer of 1789 is missing. It would contain Washington's own laconic account of his election—by unanimous vote—to the Presidency, his reception at Mount Vernon of the final verdict, and his departure in April for the inauguration in New York. The first man to edit his papers for publication, Jared Sparks, did see this volume, prior to 1836, and quotes the April 16th entry: "About 10 o'clock I bade adieu to Mount Vernon, to private life, and to domestic felicity, and with a mind oppressed with more anxious and painful sensations than I have words to express, set out for New York in company with Mr. Thomson and Colonel Humphreys, with the best disposition to render service to my country in obedience to its calls, but with less hope of answering its expectations."

Sparks is known sometimes to have edited the original text right out of the window, but the wording here is not too far from the tone of a letter to General Knox, then Secretary of War, written only a few days before the arrival at Mount Vernon of the Congressional Secretary Charles Thomson with the official notification: "..... for in confidence I assure *you*, with the *world* it would obtain *little credit*, that my movements to the chair of Government will be accompanied by feelings not unlike those of a culprit who is going to the place of his execution; so unwilling am I, in the evening of a life nearly consumed in public cares, to quit a peaceful abode for an Ocean of difficulties, without that competency of political skill, abilities, and inclination which is necessary to manage the helm......"

Lear, with a substantial rise in salary to $600 a year as senior secretary, had been sent on ahead to New York to put the President's residence on Cherry Street facing Franklin Square (chosen for him by the Congress) in readiness for his arrival, by engaging servants, and so forth. His war-time body-servant Billy was so much disabled by his second knee injury that although he set out with Lear he was unable to proceed past Philadelphia.

Before Washington left home he wrote out a painstaking survey of the work he wanted done in his absence, for the benefit of George Augustine, who would take over the management of the estate as Lund had done during the war. He had ordered a new suit of broadcloth clothes and a cocked hat for himself, and for Martha a riding dress, slippers, and clogs. For his immediate expenses he borrowed £600 ($2000) in cash from Richard Conway, a retired sea-captain who had settled at Alexandria. This debt was apparently repaid in '91.

Washington's chronic lack of available funds has been commented on by the editor of the 1946 Report of the Mount Vernon Association, in connection with a letter from Martha's brother-in-law Leonard Henley, who had recently married the widowed Betsy Dandridge Aylett, and about this time presumed on the connection to ask Washington for the loan of £300 with which to pay Betsy's deceased husband's debts. Washington was not even personally acquainted with the man, and was compelled to refuse. "His inclinations were charitable," says the Report, "and the numerous appeals for financial assistance from relatives, friends, and strangers were, under the circumstances, a continual embarrassment. Then as now he was assumed to be wealthy; a misapprehension which has persisted through the years. The significant fact is that George Washington sacrificed potential wealth to the service of his country. As Commander-in-chief of the Continental Army he received only his expenses in the field; his salary as President did not defray the expenses of the office."

He paid a visit to his ailing mother at Fredericksburg, feeling that it would be the last, as it proved to be. He arranged with his sister Betty for her son Robert, barely twenty-one, to join the household as private secretary under Lear and Humphreys. The latter would accompany him to New York, while Martha remained at Mount Vernon until suitable domestic arrangements had been established, at which time Robert would escort her and the children northward. Harriot was to live at Mount Vernon with Fanny, who was expecting another child, and George Augustine. And he wrote one of his thoughtful letters of advice to the elder of his two nephews at the Alexandria Academy—"I cannot enjoin too strongly upon you a due observance of oeconomy and frugality, as you well know yourself the present state of your property and finances will not admit of any unnecessary expense," he reminded them.

The existing Diary shows long gaps during the Presidential years, when the scene of Washington's daily life shifted to New York and Philadelphia, and the Mount Vernon story depends, except for his brief visits there, on the correspondence with his various managers. George Augustine was a faithful deputy, and his letters are more informative and interesting than Lund's in similar circumstances ten years before. The first of these was written within a few days of Washington's departure in April, '89, and they continued weekly in a conscientious stream, as long as George Augustine's health held out. There was no market for the hay, he wrote, and prices were low, but it would be disposed of—the threshing floor of the new barn was laid, but the work progressed slowly under the habitually lax supervision of Sally Bishop's husband—"I have several times accused Green of sloth, from supposition," wrote George Augustine, "and have done everything in my power to endeavour to detect him in idleness..... and I have been able to fix upon him but a few charges of neglect. I informed him that the slow progress he had made had very highly incurred your displeasure....." The carrots at Muddy Hole had come up thin, but looked pretty good—at River Farm there was hope for a good crop of pumpkins, but the prospects elsewhere were unfavorable—the new Dutch gardener, John Christian Ehler, was at first hard to converse with, but was making progress with his English—the apricot potatoes expected for planting had not come to hand—the fencing operations had come to within fifty yards of the willow pond—the farmer Bloxham's wages were too high for his services, which George Augustine considered anyway inferior to that of American overseers, and he had no capacity for the management of Negroes—and by the end of the year George Augustine was suffering from weakness and an inflammation of the eyes.

Washington himself passed through a harrowing illness during the first summer in New York, when a large painful carbuncle on his thigh had been lanced and kept him in discomfort for weeks. In September he wrote to his old friend Dr. Craik: "Persuaded as I am that the case has been treated with skill, and with as much tenderness as the nature of the complaint would admit, yet I confess I often wished for your inspection of it...... The want of regular exercise, with the cares of office, will, I have no doubt, hasten my departure for that country from whence no Traveller returns; but a faithful discharge of whatever trust I accept, as it ever has, so it will always be, the primary consideration in every transaction of my life, be the consequences what they may. Mrs. Washington has, I think, better health than usual, and the children are well and in the way of improvement...... It gives me pleasure to hear, and I wish you to express it to them, that my Nephews George and Lawrence Washington are attentive to their studies, and obedient to your orders and admonitions......"

The death of his mother that autumn was not unexpected, and while he wrote his sister Betty that it would be impossible for him to attend to the estate, he gave useful advice regarding her accounts, debts, and legacies. "She had had a great deal of money from me at times," he wrote, "as can be made appear by my books and the accounts of Mr. L. Washington during my absence; and over and above this, has not only had all that was ever made from the Plantation but got her provisions and everything else she thought proper from thence. In short, to the best of my recollection I have never in my life received a copper from the estate and have paid many hundred pounds (first and last) to her in cash. However, I want no retribution; I conceived it to be a duty, whenever she asked for money and I had it, to furnish her notwithstanding she got all the crops or the amount of them, and took everything she wanted from the plantation for the support of her family, horses, & besides...."

In October he wrote to Gouverneur Morris in Paris, asking him to send by the first ship "Mirrors for a table, with neat and fashionable but not expensive ornaments for them; such as will do credit to your taste. The mirrors will of course be in pieces, that they may be adapted to the company (the size of it I mean) the aggregate length of them may be ten feet, the breadth two feet. The frames may be plated ware, or anything else more fashionable but not expensive. If I am defective, recur to what you have seen on Mr. Robert Morris's table for my ideas *generally*. Whether these things can be had on better terms in Paris than in London I will not undertake to decide. I recollect however to have had plated ware from both places, and those from the latter came cheapest; but a single instance is no evidence of a general fact. Of plated ware may be made I conceive handsome and useful coolers for wine *at* and *after* dinner. Those I am in need of, viz., *eight* double ones for madeira and claret, (the wines usually drank at dinner) each of the apertures to be sufficient to contain a pint decanter, with an allowance in the depth of it for ice at the bottom so as to raise the neck of the decanter above the cooler; between the apertures a handle is to be placed, by which these double coolers may with convenience be removed from one part of the table to another. For the wine *after* dinner *four* quadruple coolers will be necessary, each aperture of which to be the size of a *quart* decanter or quart bottle, for four sorts of wine......"

In the late autumn instead of turning southward to Mount Vernon for a brief respite from his new duties and for further convalescence, he undertook a strenuous tour of New England as far as Boston, during which as a symbol of the new government he strengthened its influence over a somewhat mixed local opinion. On Christmas Day, 1789, with no doubt a long backward look at the Mount Vernon gathering of the previous year, he attended church at St. Paul's in New York, and noted in the Diary: "The visitors to Mrs. Washington this afternoon were not numerous, but respectable."

At Mount Vernon Fanny's third child, a second Fayette, was born in January, and in April young Harriot, now in her teens, wrote a letter:

"I now set down to write to my dear Uncle as I have not wrote to him since he left this place, I should have done it but I thought you had so much business that I had better write to Aunt Washington, yet I am sure you would be very glad to se me improveing myself by writeing letters to my friends.

"I am a going to ask you My Dear Uncle to do something for me which I hope you will not be against but I am sure if you are it will be for my good, as all the young Ladyes are a learning Musick, I will be very much obleiged to you if you will send me a gettar, there is a man here by the name of Tracy that teaches to play on the harpsicord & gettar; a gettar is so simple an instrument that five or six lessons would be sufficient for any body to learn. If you think it proper to send me a gettar I will thank you if you will send it by the first opportunity. I was informed the other day that you and Aunt Washington were certainly a comeing home this Summer which gave me a great deal of pleasure for I want to se you very much. If you please to give my love to Aunt Washington Nelly and Washington. I am Dear Uncle Your Sincere Neice, Harriot Washington."

But before the summer visit to Mount Vernon could be begun, and the President was looking forward to it more than anyone, he was again in serious danger of his life with illness—this time a pneumonia condition arising from a neglected cold. Lear was away on his honeymoon—he had married his New Hampshire sweetheart in April—but he hurried back with his bride to give what support he could to the stricken household. Although they at one time gave up hope, Washington rallied again, and by the 24th of June, after a six weeks' hiatus, he noted in his Diary that he was exercising on horseback and had resumed his weekly levees and dinner parties.

Writing to Dr. Stuart, he commented wryly on the various inevitable criticisms of his policies and the formalities which he considered due, not to himself but to the office he held: "To please everybody was impossible; I therefore adopted that line of conduct which combined public advantage with private convenience, and which in my judgment was unexceptional in itself. That I have not been able to make bows to the taste of poor Colonel Bland, (who, by the by, I believe never saw one of them) is to be regretted, especially too as (upon these occasions) they were indiscriminately bestowed and the best I was master of; would it not have been better to throw the veil of charity over them, ascribing their stiffness to the effects of age, or to the unskillfulness of my teacher, than to the pride and dignity of office, which God knows has no charms for me? for I can truly say I had rather be at Mount Vernon with a friend or two about me, than to be attended at the Seat of Government by the Officers of State and the Representatives of every Power in Europe. . . . ."

Regarding his recent illness, he took a habitually gloomy outlook, for all his life long he expressed a truly masculine conviction of impending dissolution whenever he ailed: ". . . . I have already had within less than a year, two *severe* attacks; the last worse than the first; a third more than probable, will put me to sleep with my fathers; at what distance this may be I know not. Within the last twelve months I have undergone more, and severer sickness than thirty preceding years afflicted me with, put it all together. I have abundant reason however to be thankful that I am so well recovered; though I still feel the remains of the violent affection of my lungs. The cough, pain in my breast, and shortness in breathing not having entirely left me. I propose in the recess of Congress to visit Mount Vernon; but when this recess will happen is beyond my ken, or the ken I believe of any of its members. . . ."

In July however he was ordering from Biddle tea cups and coffee cups and saucers and slop bowls to match, of blue and white china, "handsome, but not of the highest price, for they are for common use," to be sent to Mount Vernon by the first vessel—along with some patterns of plain India Jaquinett Muslin of the finest kind for Mrs. Washington to choose from. And there was delivered to him about this time as a token from Lafayette the key of the Bastille, the symbol of what was thought to be a bright new dawn in France, before the Terror which turned both the Marquis and his son into exiles. Washington carried the key with him to Mount Vernon when he finally set out with his family in early September, for their first visit home since the inauguration some eighteen months before. It still hangs in the hall at the foot of the staircase where he placed it.

There had been some changes during the long interval at New York, namely the loss of Colonel Humphreys, who was going as a special agent for the new government to Spain and Portugal. Washington's chief aide now was Major William Jackson, a charming, discreet bachelor who had been secretary to the Constitutional Congress in '87, after serving as war-time aide to General Lincoln and then as his assistant Secretary at War in the early 80's.

Bob Lewis and the colored lad Christopher who was already

substituting for Billy in the more menial tasks were sent on ahead to Mount Vernon, and Jackson accompanied the Washingtons on the journey, as did young Thomas Nelson, son of the General, whose brief junior secretaryship now came to an end. As the seat of government was to be changed from New York to Philadelphia beginning with the autumn session, the Lears remained behind to oversee the removal of household goods and some of the servants to the Philadelphia house which Robert Morris now vacated to move into his newly renovated house next door. Polly Lear was an attractive young woman who had begun to fill in for Fanny in Martha's life, and the young couple were to occupy a room in the Presidential mansion as part of the family. A son would be born to them there in the coming spring.

The Diary for that Mount Vernon sojourn in the autumn of 1790 is missing. He found George Augustine's health visibly deteriorated, and there were now two small children, Maria, aged two, and Fayette. A letter from Betty Lewis gave news of the death of her son Lawrence's young wife in childbirth—"Poor thing, it proved fatal to her, she was taken with fits and died in twelve hours without being delivered. He lost a very good wife and with her all the fortune, as she was not of age to make a right to any part," Betty added. In the effort to economize with a family which grew yearly, the Stuarts had moved from Abingdon, which had become involved in litigation with its former owners, the Alexanders, and settled at Hope Park, where Dr. Stuart had lived before his marriage to Jack Custis's widow. This house lay all of twenty miles from Alexandria, and as the Custis girls grew older was considered by them little better than a wilderness outpost.

Bushrod was well established as a lawyer at Richmond, and his marriage was still childless. Sam's two boys, George Steptoe and Lawrence, were, Washington wrote to Lear, neither of them wanting in capacity and both, especially the first, were desirous of improvement, but were accomplishing little at the Alexandria Academy. Their sister Harriot was becoming too much for Fanny's somewhat distracted discipline at Mount Vernon. Little Washington was now nearly ten and showing all the lovable, but feckless, characteristics of his father. Nelly was the President's darling—bright, pretty, and not at all in awe of him.

In October he wrote to Lear from the Potomac to look into the matter of schools: "The easy and quiet temper of Fanny is little fitted I find for the care of my Niece Harriot Washington, who is grown almost, if not quite a Woman; and what to do with her at the advanced *Size* she is arrived at, I am really at a loss. Her age (just turned of fourteen) is not too great for a Boarding School but to enter *now* with any tolerable prospect, the Mistress of it must not only be respectable, but one who establishes and will enforce good rules. She is prone to idleness, and having been under no controul, would create all the difficulty. I have formed no resolution respecting what will be proper for me to do with her; but that I may the better judge, I request that you will enquire whether there be a *proper* School (for her to board at) in Philadelphia. If so, whether there are at it, genteel girls of her size and age. Who the Mistress of it is, what her character; Terms &ca are; The numbers at it, who of the principal families, and how they are entertained and accommodated. I have not yet intimated anything of this matter to Harriot yet; who if it should be, would I dare say be a good deal alarmed as she had, I dare say, rather mix with other company than be at a Boarding School. . . . . ."

Harriot was after all let off going to school, and remained at Mount Vernon when the Washingtons departed for Philadelphia in November, as always taking the Custis children with them. The boys, including young Washington Custis, were sent to the Philadelphia Academy at the first of the year.

The regrettable coolness, born of their differences over the Constitution, between Mason at Gunston and Washington continued to exist. Theodoric Bland and Colonel Grayson, old friends however critical of the new President, were both recently dead. The death of Harry Lee's wife, the lovely Matilda of Stratford, was a loss which although he would be Governor of Virginia in '92 and would marry again, marked the beginning of decline in Lee's once dazzling fortunes. Lund Washington, whose children could not stay alive, was now a martyr to eye trouble, and went in dread of blindness.

Colonel Jackson spent the autumn at Mount Vernon and went to Philadelphia with them. Martha's nephew, Bartholomew Dandridge II, now joined the household as junior secretary in Nelson's place. They were established in the Philadelphia house before Christmas, and Washington did not see Mount Vernon again until March of the next year, when he spent a week there on his way to Charleston during his two months' tour of the South.

He stopped there again on his return journey in June, when a letter to Lear gave a glimpse into his private vexations, even on the road, this time in the conduct of two slaves: "Paris has become so lazy, self-willed and impudent that John (the Coachman) had no sort of government of him; on the contrary Jno. says it was a maxim of Paris to do nothing he was ordered, and everything he was forbid. This conduct, added to the incapacity of Giles for a Postilion, who I believe will never be able to mount a horse again for that purpose, has induced me to find Paris some other employment than in the Stable; of course I shall leave him at home. A boy or two may be necessary there, to assist about the horses, Carriages, and harness, but these (dutch ones) it is possible may be had for their victuals and cloaths; especially if there are large importations from Germany (as some articles in the papers say there will be.) . . . . . ." A few days later he mentioned that Hercules would have to take the wagon box in place of Paris.

Anthony Whiting, whom he had promoted as overseer from one of the farms, to assist George Augustine, appeared to be obliging and active, and as usual Washington left a well thought out memorandum for work to be done in his absence by those left in charge. This included: "Finishing the Well by the New Quarter, that the efficacy of the Rope may be tried in drawing Water. Building a Necessary with two Seats for the use of the New Quarter; Isaac knows where it is to be placed . . . . . . Setting up the new Gates where wanting; and will be pointed out by Mr. Whiting . . . . . Muddy Hole Barn is to be completely repaired . . . . . Frames for Hot beds to be prepared for the Gardener according to his directions if it is not upon an expensive plan. . . . . The Floor and Sleepers of the Ice House should be examined and repaired, if they want it, before the time for filling it shall arrive . . . . . . And I believe I shall lay in materials for building a Barn and treading floor at Dogue Run. But this I shall consider of. New Posts for the circle before the door must be thought of, but of what kind is not absolutely resolved on at present. . . . . . Making gravel Walks in the upper Garden, and in the Pine Labyrinths . . . . Planting Ivy around the ice House and at the No. end of the Lawn East of the House, also on the sides by the front gate. . . . ."

The barn at Dogue Run materialized in '92, as the famous 16-sided structure with the treading-out floor on the second story around center mows, reached by the horses and oxen by an inclined plane from the ground. But it must all be delegated. He could not be there to see it done, and done right. Wearily, in June, '91, he set his face northward again, determined to part with Bob Lewis's services as secretary in order that he might take some of the responsibility at Mount Vernon which was now beyond George Augustine's strength. At Philadelphia he found that the mirrored plateaux ordered through Gouverneur Morris in Paris had arrived—and they are to be seen at Mount Vernon on the dining-room table today.

Martha too found it difficult to carry on her life at second hand, and after Washington's return wrote to Fanny at Mount Vernon: "Your letter of the 25th is come to hand with the ruffles—I wish you'd had them whipp d—it was but little more trouble for Charlot, they cannot be sewed on the wristbands till they are whiped—she is so indolent that she will doe nothing but what she is told, she knows how work should be done—I cannot find how it is possible for her and Caroline to be altogether taken up in makeing the peoples cloths—and if you suffer them to goe on so idele they will in a little time doe nothing but work for themselves—I am sorry for poor Giles & fear he will never be well again. . . . . . The president talks of living this place about the 20th of September to come to Mount Vernon . . . . . . as you know, my dear Fanny that it is probable that we shall have company all the time we stay . . . . . . we bring so many with us that it requires some preparation and I have been so much indisposed my self that I shall leve the House keeping altogether to you—I shall not conscern in the matter at all,—but leve it to you,—make Nathan clean his kitchen and every thing in it and about it very well—I shall bring work for Charlot to doe for me so that she must endeavour to get your family business done as fast as they can—I hope Mrs. Stuart will come to meet us at Mount Vernon. I shall let her know the time I expect to be there—have they got a Carriage or Horses yet—the General has got the better of all his complaints—dear little Wash is quite well and has a very good appetite and gains flesh and strength every day, he is now well enough to goe to school—I hope the Major will be the better for his trip over the mountains, let us know how he is when you hear from him......"

Little Washington had had the measles in July. George Augustine had by now undertaken the journey to Berkeley Springs which so often was the nearly hopeless last resort of the chronic invalid, and Bob Lewis, with Anthony Whiting assisting, was in charge of the estate, though the Major returned in time for the family visit which occurred as hoped for in September. The following month Washington was writing from Mount Vernon to Lear in Philadelphia: "All the family here are well except the Major, who seems to be in a very poor way, and join me in best wishes for you and yours......"

Soon after that he was back in Philadelphia himself, making his third annual address to Congress. In John Watson's *Annals of Philadelphia* there is an eyewitness account of the President's attendance at church: "During the slow movement of the crowd of worshipers issuing from the opened door and the increase of sound from the organ, it was not necessary for the stranger visiting the city, and straining his vision to behold the General for the first time, to inquire of his jostled neighbour—which is he? There could be no mistake in this matter, Washington was to be known at once. His noble height and commanding air, his person enveloped in what was not very common in those days, a rich blue Spanish cloak, faced with red velvet, thrown over the left-shoulder; his easy unconstrained movement; his inimitable expression of countenance, on such occasions beaming with mild dignity and beneficence combined; his patient demeanor in the crowd, emerging from it, to the eye of the beholder, like the bright silvery moon from the edge of a dark cloud; his gentle bendings of the neck, to the right and to the left, parentally, and expressive of delighted feelings on his part; these, with the appearance of the awed, charmed, and silent crowd of spectators, gently falling back on each side as he approached, announced to the gazing stranger —*behold the man!*"

That autumn in reply to a letter from Harriot in which she gave the latest news of Lund's eye trouble—("He is much worse than he was when you saw him," she wrote. "The veal lights which he was informed had made a cure of eyes in his situation has made his much worse.")—Washington got round to her in his recurrent chore of enlightening and advising the younger generation in his care: "Your cousins, with whom you live, are well qualified to give you advice, and I am sure they will if you are disposed to receive it," he wrote Harriot. "But if you are disobliging, self-willed, and untowardly it is hardly to be expected that they will engage themselves in unpleasant disputes with you, especially Fanny whose mild and placid temper will not permit her to exceed the limits of wholesome admonition or gentle rebuke. Think then to what dangers a giddy girl of 15 or 16 must be exposed in circumstances like these. To be under but little or no control may be pleasing to a mind that does not reflect, but this pleasure cannot be of long duration, and reason, too late, perhaps, may convince you of the folly of mis-spending time. You are not to learn, I am certain, that your fortune is small; supply the want of it then with a well cultivated mind; with dispositions to industry and frugality; with gentleness of manners, obliging temper, and such qualifications as will attract notice, and recommend you to a happy establishment for life....."

To which Harriot replied within a fortnight, in the tone of affectionate humility she always adopted towards him; and certainly the harum-scarum reputation which has somehow attached itself to her in the scanty references history has so far made to this most obscure of Washington's charges is not justified by her letters to him—on whose dutiful pages butter wouldn't melt. She was sent to spend the winter of '91-2 with her Lee cousins at Shooter's Hill while Fanny's fourth child, Charles Augustine, was born at her old home in New Kent County in November.

Another Christmas went by for Washington in official duties at Philadelphia, and most of his correspondence on the estate work going forward this winter was carried on with Anthony Whiting, in the absence of George Augustine and Fanny at Eltham. Robert Lewis had taken advantage of his interval at Mount Vernon to marry, and wanted to establish himself in the western lands, where he became Washington's agent.

Whiting's weekly letters were conscientious, especially with the bad news, such as his report of January 22d on sickness among the slaves. "I sent Yesterday for Dr. Craik who promised to Come down this Day, but the Weather being very bad I Guess presented him. I sent him Beck's Case as near as I was able, and he sent some Medicine.

I am fearful she will not recover. Isaac's two girls Minna and Ally are a little better. Delia and Doll continue very poorly, and a great many Children are very bad with the Hooping Cough at every quarter. I have endeavoured to expose the hands as little as possible this Cold Spell, and deep Snow. But Ice we have been gitting all this week and have very near filled the house. It has been a fine time for this Jobb, and I have had it well Rammd and pounded as fine as Snow, which has Occasioned our being so long in filling it. The gitting wood has likewise been an essential Jobb, as well as feeding Stock of every kind. We now find the advantage of having potatoes and turnips. Nothing but raising so large a quantity of these could have saved the Stock from Death, more particularly if this Weather should Continue long. What those will do that has not taken that precaution I know not, as Provender is I believe Scarce almost every Where in this country from the Summers drought......."

An April letter from George Augustine brought nothing but more gloom. Back at Mount Vernon with Fanny and the new baby, he was often so ill that he was unable to leave his bed–the front and ends of the house needed painting–the dining-room chimney smoked so badly that it had destroyed the paint in the room–snow and rain had rotted the roof of the piazza, so that the whole of it must be done over......

At Philadelphia Washington found himself increasingly short-handed. Humphreys was still abroad. Colonel Jackson had fallen in love with one of the Willing girls, and was looking to a trip abroad to increase his fortunes. Robert Lewis would not return to the secretaryship where he was most needed. Washington wrote to Betty offering her youngest boy, Howell, a job in his brother's place as junior secretary along with young Dandridge, at the rate of $300 a year, "provided he is diligent in discharging the duties of it from breakfast until dinner, Sundays excepted..... That I may be enabled to judge of his fitness let him acknowledge the receipt of this letter with his own hand, and say whether he will accept the offer here made him, or not. If he does, and I find him qualified from the specimen he gives me in his letter I will immediately desire him to come on, which he must do without a moment's delay, or I shall be obliged to provide another instead of him." Howell got the job.

But with the spring of 1792, three years of Washington's bondage had passed and he began to look ahead. His view was blocked by the stubborn conviction on the part of almost everyone—even Secretary of State Jefferson—that the country would fall apart unless he accepted a second term.

XXX

As in 1789, when the Presidential cloud first gathered on his horizon, he began to argue, both with himself and his relentless friends. On May 20th he wrote to Madison: "I have not been unmindful of the sentiments expressed by you in the conversations just alluded to; on the contrary I have again, and again revolved them, with thoughtful anxiety; but without being able to dispose my mind to a longer continuation in the Office I now have the honor to hold. I therefore still look forward to the fulfillment of my fondest and most ardent wishes to spend the remainder of my days (which I cannot expect will be many) in ease and tranquillity. . . . . . ."

From there he went into the question of how best to announce his intention to withdraw at the end of his term, which would be in March, '93, and at once found himself in another dilemma: "On the one hand, a previous declaration to retire, not only carries with it the appearance of vanity and self importance, but it may be construed into a maneuver to be invited to remain. And on the other hand, to say nothing, implys consent; or, at any rate, would leave the matter in doubt, and to decline afterwards might be deemed as bad, and uncandid. . . . . ." But he wound up by asking Madison's counsel on the formation of a Valedictory Address.

This letter was written during a brief visit to Mount Vernon on which Martha and the children did not accompany him. George Augustine was now spitting blood and was too ill to accomplish the more strenuous duties of overseeing the work of the estate, which would have to be left more and more to Whiting, and which formed an increasingly urgent reason for Washington's own permanent return. While at Mount Vernon he was joined there by

Howell Lewis, who was to accompany him back to Philadelphia and the formidable prospect of filling in for both his own older brother Robert and the popular Colonel Humphreys.

On their return from Eltham Fanny and George Augustine had reclaimed Harriot from Shooter's Hill, and a letter from her followed Washington to Philadelphia, perhaps to remind him of a conversation during his stay at home: "I now take up my pen to write to my dear Uncle," it began. "I hope you arrived safe in Philadelphia, and at the time you expected. If my dear Uncle finds it convenient to give me a guitar I will thank you if you will direct it to be made with keys and strings both, as they are easier to learn to play on, and not so easy to be out of order, but if one with keys is dearer than without, I shall be much obleiged to you for one with strings; I should not trouble you for a guttar, if I was not certain that I could learn myself, every person that I have asked says that It is the easiest instrument to learn to play on that is, and any body that can turn a tune can play on a guittar, but Mrs. Bushrod Washington has been so kind as to offer to teach me, if I could not learn myself. If you please to give my love to Aunt Washington, Nelly and Washington, I am, My dear Uncle, Your affectionate Neice . . . . ."

She was a persevering child. It was two years and a month since her first request for a guitar. Washington's Cash Memorandum book for June reads: "pd. for a guitar for Miss Harriot Washington —$17." And on July 1st, Martha wrote to Fanny: "The President has given Miss Harriot a guitarre. I have enclosed the key. It is to be sent in the vessel with the other things."

Simultaneously with Harriot's struggle for her guitar, Nelly Custis at thirteen under her grandmother's eye in Philadelphia kept a French exercise book, in the back of which she had copied her daily study schedule, which ran:

Mondays	—Get some French by heart. Rehearse the two last Grammar Lessons
Wednesdays and Fridays	—Get 1 page of Dialogues Get ½ page of Grammar Lesson
Tuesdays and Thursdays	—Get 1 page Dialogues Get 1 verb

Saturday —Be examined on the Dialogue and parse some French
Translate every day but Saturday

Not a back-breaking program. But her brother Washington Custis, writing some sixty years later, recalled Nelly's endless practice of her music—"The poor girl would play and cry, and cry and play, for long hours under the immediate eye of her grandmother, a rigid disciplinarian in all things,"—though according to other accounts he himself seldom encountered any of that discipline himself, and Nelly said that "grandmamma always spoiled Washington."

The President was able to escape with his whole family for a summer visit to Mount Vernon as planned, and before leaving Philadelphia he wrote to Whiting: ". . . . previous to my arrival, I desire you will have the Well by the Kitchen thoroughly cleaned, by some professional people; and while they are about it that they may be well attended, as you know accidents frequently happen in this work, by the noxtious effluvia that some times arises in these places, I would not have any of my own people descend into it; The same persons, or some other skilful one might be employed to sink the Well directly opposite to the centre of the greenhouse, but just within the Brick yard Inclosure so as not to interfere with the Road. . . . . ."

Lear was given leave to visit his New Hampshire home with his wife and baby during the President's absence from Philadelphia, and the two junior secretaries, Howell Lewis and Bartholomew Dandridge, were allowed to go visiting their friends, which left Washington to do his own letter-writing at a time when he longed only to superintend the work outside the house instead of being confined to his desk while the second term pros and cons submerged it. He wrote Lear from Mount Vernon in July, giving news of what was uppermost in his unofficial mind:

"Your letter from New York came duly to hand and I was glad to find that you had got that far in safety. I wish the remainder of your journey may prove equally pleasant and prosperous. My journey was not of this sort, for after I parted with the Coach horses I was plagued with those which succeeded them, the following day; and the sick mare, by a dose of Physic which had been administered the night I reached Chester, was so weakened, and failed so much, that she was unable to carry Austin any farther than Susquehanna: from thence she was led to Harford [Md.] and left, and two days afterwards gave up the ghost.

"I found the face of the Country here, and on the road this side Baltimore, much, very much, indeed, parched by a severe drought, and the Corn in miserable plight; but the day and night we reached home there fell a most delightful and refreshing rain, and the weather since has been as seasonable as the most sanguine farmer could wish; and if continued to us may make our Indian Corn Crop midling, great it is hardly possible to be, so much was it in arrears when the rains set in.

"Great complaints were heard of the Hessian fly, and of the Rust and Mildew, as I travelled on; and in some places I believe the damage had been great; but I conceive more is said than ought to be on this subject; and that the Crop upon the whole will be abundant of Wheat; mine in quantity (and the quality is good) will, I expect, greatly exceed any I have made these several years past....... All here are well, except the Major, whose situation I think is unpromising and precarious, growing worse, they all join me in best wishes for Mrs. Lear, yourself and the Child......"

It was a sickly summer on the Potomac, with the flux and intermittent fevers, and by the time Washington was due to return to Philadelphia in October he had unwillingly recognized that George Augustine was unlikely to survive the winter, which he and Fanny hoped to spend with her father in the supposedly milder air of Eltham near Williamsburg. In the event of another four years' absence on Washington's part, Mount Vernon would have to be abandoned to hired management and slow decay. "As to poor George I shall say nothing," he wrote to Lear, who had returned to the executive mansion from his New England holiday. "His fate is unquestionably fixed, and Fanny's, from prest. appearances, is very unpromising, probably terminating in the same disorder. These occurrences throws my private Affairs into considerable embarrassment; But as they, especially the Major, is not likely to get better, and if they do will spend the Winter at her fathers, I must leave them in it, as there is no remedy at present...... Mrs. Washington went up this Morning to bid Mrs. Stuart (who has lately added a Son to the family) farewell....."

The problem of what to do with Harriot again arose, and a letter from Betty Lewis to her brother in reply to his request that she take charge of Harriot at Fredericksburg for the winter revealed the humiliating conditions which Sam's unfortunate daughter was sometimes reduced to endure: "I shall have no objection to her being with me," Betty wrote rather ungraciously, "if she comes well cloth'd, or provided to get them, that she may appear tolerable, for I can assure you it was not so while she was with me before, by which means she was prevented from appearing in public when it would have been my wish she should. A little money laid out in clothes at this time may be an advantage. I'm sorry it will not appear to be in my power to advance any, having at this time three of my grandchildren to support, and God knows from every account but I may expect as many more shortly. Fielding is so distressed that his children would go naked if it were not for the assistance I give him. I am happy to hear by Howell that you and my sister keep in good health, and I sincerely wish a continuance of it. I never had a more sickly family in my life than I have had this fall...."

Although Betty's letter had made it plain that she intended a visit to her married daughter before receiving Harriot at Millbank, Washington replied at some length, and with the same undertone of exasperated resignation to his responsibility for a hapless girl in her teens:

"As Mrs. Washington and myself expect to set out tomorrow for Philadelphia, and the Major and Fanny the day after, if the vessel which is to carry him to Colo. Bassetts arrives in time, I have taken the advantage of the good opportunity afforded by Mr. Robert Lewis of sending Harriot to Fredericksburg. It is done at this time (notwithstanding your proposed visit to Albemarle) 1st. because it would be improper to leave her here after we are all gone; 2nd, because there would be no person to accompany her down afterwards; and 3d. because it might be inconvenient for her to travel alone.

"She comes, as Mrs. Washington informs me, very well provided with everything proper for a girl in her situation: this much I know, that she costs me enough to place her in it. I do not however want you (or any one else) to do more by her than merely to admit her to your family whilst this House is uninhabited by a female white woman, and thereby rendered an unfit place for her to remain at. I shall continue to do for her what I have done for seven years past; and that is to furnish her with such reasonable and proper necessaries as she may stand in need of, notwithstanding I have had both her brothers upon my hands, and I have been obliged to pay several hundred pounds out of my own pocket for their boards, schooling, clothing, &c. &c. of them, for more than the period aforementioned; their father's estate being unable to discharge the Executions as fast as they are issued against it.

"Harriet has sense enough, but no disposition to industry, nor to be careful of her clothes. Your example and admonition, with proper restraints, may overcome the two last; and to that end I wish you would examine her clothes and direct her in their use and application of them; for without this they will be, I am told, dabbed about in every hole and corner, and her best things always in use. Fanny was too easy, too much of her own indolent disposition and had too little authority to cause, either by precept or example, any change in this for the better and Mrs. Washington's absence has been unjurious to her in many respects; but she is young, and with good advice may yet make a fine woman. If notwithstanding the suggestion that she is well provided with everything (except a Cloak which may not be had in Alexandria, and may be got in Fredericksburg) a deficiency is found and you wish to supply it, there will be no occasion for your laying in advance more than ten days; as I could at any time remit a bank note in a letter to you four days after I was made acquainted with the amount. I do not mean by this to launch into expensiveness; she has no pretensions to it, nor would the state of my finances enable me to indulge her in that if she had. . . . ."

But whether he sent money with Harriot for the cloak, and how she was received at Fredericksburg on the eve of her aunt's intended journey westward, does not appear.

Whiting was again left in charge of the Mansion House, with the long written instructions Washington always made out before his departure—the gravelling of garden walks; the planting of pines in the labyrinths and of willow hedges, and of flowering ever-green ivy around the ice-house; the cleaning of the vineyard enclosure; the sowing and grubbing and trimming which never ceased; potatoes to be dug; buckwheat to be threshed and measured; repairs to the vault, the care of tools, and of the Negroes themselves—"Although it is last mentioned, it is foremost in my thoughts, to desire you will be particularly attentive to my Negros in their sickness; and to order every Overseer *positively* to be so likewise; for I am sorry to observe that the generality of them view these poor creatures in scarcely any other light than they do a draught horse or Ox; neglecting them as much when they are unable to work; instead of comforting and nursing them when they lye on a sick bed. I lost more Negros last winter than I had done in 12 or 15 years before, put them altogether. If their disorders are not common, and the mode of treating them plain, simple, and well understood, send for Dr. Craik in time. In the last stages of the complaint it is unavailing to do it. It is incurring an expense for nothing. I shall now briefly say, that the trust I have reposed in you is great, and my confidence that you will faithfully discharge it is commensurate thereto......"

Whiting's reports continued to be monotonous and gloomy. He had sent for Dr. Craik for Bosun and Charlotte, who had had the flux; the Doctor ordered rice water, which could not be found in the house, and said that a quantity of rice should be kept on hand for the sick, as well as a gallon of honey, but the Major had taken with him to Eltham all the honey from Mount Vernon, as it was proper for his complaint; there were several old horses, lame, or with the pole-evil, not worth keeping after Christmas; and he had received word of the Major's arrival at Eltham in good Spirits.....

Washington got the disquieting news, via the Harewood nephews after a stop they had made at Mount Vernon, that Whiting himself was showing signs of George Augustine's disease. The President wrote to his manager, with no doubt a despairing sensation of having done it all before: "....it is my request that you will not, by attempting more than you are able to undergo with safety and convenience, injure yourself; and thereby render me a disservice, for if this should happen under present circumstances, my affairs in the absence of both the Major and myself, will be thrown into a disagreeable situation. I had therefore rather hear that you had nursed, rather than exposed yourself. And the things which I sent from this place (I mean the Wine, Tea, Coffee, and Sugar) and such other matters as you may lay in by the Doctrs. directions for the use of the Sick, I desire you will make use of, as your own personal occasions may require. I have written, as you will see by the enclosed, long letters both to Thos. Green and the Gardner; in hopes to impress them with the necessity and to stimulate them to the practice of proper exertions during mine, and the absence of my Nephew.... Supply Green and the Gardner with Paper that they may have no excuse for not giving in their Reports and see that they accompany your own every Week..... Doll at the Ferry must be taught to Knit, and *made* to do a sufficient days work of it; otherwise (if suffered to be idle) many more will walk in her Steps. Lame Peter if nobody else will, must teach her, and she must be brought to the house for that purpose. Tell House Frank I expect he will lay up a more plentious store of the black common Walnut than he usually does. Nor ought he to spend his time wholly in idleness....."

In later letters to Whiting that autumn, he wrote: "Desire Thomas Green to date his reports. That of the week before last I send back for explanation of his measurement of the sawing...... Mrs. Washington desires you will order the Ashes to be taken care of, that there may be no want of Soap....... Mrs. Washington expected that two barrels of *good* Shad would have come round with the things which were sent from Mount Vernon; but as this did not happen, take the first opportunity of forwarding them to this place. .... Put long litter against the Cellar Windows; Frank knows how, and should be made to do it, as well as the other things; otherwise he will be ruined by idleness. And can Lucy find sufficient employment in the kitchen? It was expected her leizure hours, of which I conceive she must have very many from Cooking, would be employed in knitting, of which both Peter and Sara do too little. I expected Sinah was one of those who would have been sent to one of the Plantations; whether she remains at the Mansion House or not, it is my desire that when Kitty is unable to attend the Dairy alone, that Anna may be the assistant. The other, besides idling away half the day under that pretence, never failed, I am well convinced, to take a pretty ample toll of both Milk and butter...... I presume Davis has painted the Windows and Cornice of the Green house and New Quarters white. I directed him to do so...... What does the Gardners wife in her report mean by Trowsers? She is not making them longer than common breeches I presume. This wd. be a great consumption of cloth..... If you will send me the size, and length, of the Well rope, I will endeavour to have a proper one made, and sent to you......"

"You ask directions from me respecting your conduct in the building of my poor Nephew, Major Geo. A. Washington's House," he wrote Whiting at the end of the year. "From every Acct. we receive, his disorder is at a crisis, and must soon (if that is not the case already) change for the better, or terminate in his speedy dissolution: and as the latter is most likely to happen, I think you had better not (until further orders) procure any more scantling; especially such as must be cut to waste......"

This was the house George Augustine was building on the Clifton land, in accordance with Washington's letter of the autumn of '86, as a future home for himself and Fanny and the children. Whiting replied: "Poor Major Washington, I believe has never contemplated his disorder as fatal, and his great desire of building his house has been from an intention of retiring from so much business, and the increase of his family being such, as I have often heard him mention, he was fearful might be disagreeable to your Excellency, the having so many children about the house. But according to every account I hear of him it seems almost impossible he can recover. When I mentioned a desire of carrying on his building it was from a wish not to be thought neglectfull in putting into execution what he requested me to do, for in gratitude I know it is my Duty. His treatment was always to me more like a brother than a stranger, which I can never forget, and anything I could do for him would be with the greatest cheerfulness. I shall not, however purchase the scantling while his carpenters have any to work on......"

George Mason died at Gunston Hall in October at the age of sixty-eight. History has a tendency to overlook Mason, who had anticipated the Declaration of Independence in his own writings, with the Fairfax Resolves and the Virginia Declaration of Rights. He had also foreseen the difficulties which led to the first ten amendments to the Constitution, his objections being based on what he considered the lack of a guarantee of individual freedom as he had set it forth, and too much centralization of government which endangered local liberties. Jefferson voiced similar protests, but he lived to see them vindicated.

The last mention of Mason in Washington's Diary is in November of '88, when he came to dinner at Mount Vernon, and the estrangement seems to have remained as a result of the controversy over the Constitution. Only a few months before Mason's death Washington referred to him ruefully in a letter to Hamilton as "my quondam friend." But his sorrow was genuine, for Mason was a link with the old days, the great days before the war, when life in Virginia was easy and secure.

XXXI

GEORGE AUGUSTINE died at Eltham early in February, '93, soon after Burwell Bassett had succumbed to the effects of a fall from his horse. Fanny lost both her husband and father within a month, and the oldest of her three children, Maria, was five. Harry Lee was at Shirley on the James that spring, marrying Ann Hill Carter as his second wife. Having talked with the doctor in attendance at Eltham, Lee wrote Washington that Fanny remained "in a tolerable state of health in the midst of calamity."

Washington sent her an immediate invitation to make her home henceforth at Mount Vernon with her children. "You can go no place where you will be more welcome, nor to anywhere you can live at less expense or trouble," he reminded her. "Matters at Mount Vernon are now so arranged as to be under the care of responsible persons, and so they may continue; which would ease you of that anxiety which the care of so large a family would naturally involve you in..... You might bring my niece, Harriot Washington, with you for a Companion; whose conduct, I hear with pleasure, has given much satisfaction to my sister......"

At the same time he directed Whiting to suspend building operations on the house on the River Farm tract, unless Fanny expressed a wish to the contrary, which she did not.

The death of George Augustine and a noticeable deterioration in Whiting's health came just as Washington found himself unanimously elected for the unwelcome second term. In March he wrote to David Humphreys, who was then Minister to Portugal: "To you, who know my love of retirement and domestic life, it is unnecessary to say that, in accepting this re-appointment, I relinquish those personal enjoyments to which I am peculiarly attached .... and perhaps in no instance of my life have I been more sensible of the sacrifice than in the present; for at my age the love of retirement grows every day more and more powerful, and the death of my nephew, the poor Major, will, I apprehend, cause my private concerns to suffer very much. This melancholy event took place on the 5th of last month at Colo. Bassett's, where he had gone, hoping to benefit from a change of air and situation. Altho' it had been long expected, and indeed, to me, of late appear'd inevitable, yet I have felt it very keenly. . . . . ."

In April he set out, accompanied by Dandridge, to arrange the burial of George Augustine at Mount Vernon and to advise Fanny, who had returned there with her children. His stay was cut short by a letter from Hamilton at Philadelphia reporting the start of a general war in Europe, following the death of Louis XVI on the guillotine, which had aroused horror everywhere, and America's position of neutrality was becoming precarious. Full of anxiety about Lafayette and other old friends from the days when France was a valiant ally, he hurried back to Philadelphia.

His concern for Whiting had been augmented by the man's appearance, and when in June Whiting himself complained of further illness, Washington wrote recommending flannel next the skin, and a milk and vegetable diet with little meat. A letter from Craik about Whiting alarmed him into another flying trip to Mount Vernon to look into the matter of a successor.

An added harassment in his private affairs was Lear's decision to set up some kind of business for himself which would bring in more for his family than the secretarial $800 a year and the cramped quarters of the Presidential mansion, where a small, crying child was no doubt a disturbing factor. Washington could put nothing in the way of Lear's advancement, and it so came about that Lear was in Georgetown on his own affairs when Whiting died. In his usual helpful way Lear sent back word to meet Washington on the road, and himself went on down to Mount Vernon to await the President's arrival on the estate which, with the double loss of both George Augustine and Whiting was left, as Washington put it later to Harry Lee, "a body without a head."

After only a few days at home he returned to Philadelphia and released Howell Lewis from his secretarial duties to act as his uncle's temporary representative at Mount Vernon, until someone more experienced could be found. Howell was then twenty-two, and to lend him some weight, Washington devised one of his comprehensive letters of instructions to the several overseers, which Howell carried with him as an introduction and source of authority. At the end of it was a masterly summing up of what he expected of his employees in his absence: "Tho' last mentioned, it is not of the least importance; because the peace and good government of the negroes depend upon it, and not less so my interest and your own reputation," he wrote, addressing the overseers. "I do therefore in explicit terms enjoin it upon you to remain constantly at home (unless called off by unavoidable business or to attend Divine Worship) and to be constantly with your people when there. There is no other sure way of getting work well done and quietly by negroes; for when an Overseer's back is turned the most of them will slight their work, or be idle altogether. In which correction cannot retrieve either, but often produces evils which are worse than the disease. Nor is there any other mode but this to prevent thieving and other disorders, the consequence of opportunities. You will recollect that your time is paid for by me, and if I am deprived of it, it is worse even than robbing my purse, because it is also a breach of trust, which every honest man ought to hold most sacred......."

Howell tried. His letters were conscientious and detailed, but doubtless his authority was always a little wanting. "At Dogue Run Mr. McCoy has not got more than half his wheat in, if that, and the Shocks in the field are put up in Such a careless manner that they are all tumbling down," he reported in July. "The clover that was Sowen in among the Oats has come up most beautiful...... Thomas Green has been all this week putting up three dormound *Windows* on the Shed of the Stable. He goes on so slowly that it is not in my power to tell when he will finish them...... Since my last letter I have found the machine for gathering the heads of the Clover for seed in the Cellar underneath the room where Mr. Whiting formerly stayed....."

Replying to Burgess Ball, who had married George Augustine's sister Frances, and had written suggesting Howell's older brother Lawrence for the post at Mount Vernon, Washington left open unexpected avenues of speculation in his insistence on a bachelor nephew. Lawrence was now twenty-six, and his wife had died in childbirth three years ago. ". . . . had I known at the time that his brother Lawrence would have undertaken the business, I should have thought him (on account of his age) the most eligible; and would have preferred him accordingly; for possibly if he had chosen to continue there, his conduct might have been found such as to supercede the necessity of employing any other: because, as I could place entire confidence in his integrity, and presume I may do so in his Sobriety, Industry, care and oeconomy, with strict attention to the conduct of the Overseers, and to the plans marked out for their government, my business might progress as well under his auspices as under that of any other I am likely to get; for a married man would not only be inconvenient for me, but (by keeping a separate house) would add considerably to my expenses. Whereas a single man, whether at my first (if from his walk of life he should be entitled to it) or at my second table, would with respect to his board be not more than a drop in the Bucket. But after all, is not Lawrence Lewis on the point of Matrimony? Report says so; and if truly, it would be an effectual bar to a *permanent* establishment in my business as I never again will have two women in my house while I am there myself. . . . . ."

The report proved false, and Lawrence, still single, did come to Mount Vernon in '97, when Washington had returned home after the second term. Two years later Lawrence married—little Nelly Custis.

A letter from Martha to Fanny at Mount Vernon, written in June, '93, showed her resignation to long distance housekeeping—she was used to it by now—and her equal determination not to leave the beleaguered President alone in Philadelphia long enough to superintend herself the work she felt was being neglected. This is one of the few letters in Martha's own hand to survive, and has come safely home to the Mount Vernon archives. "The President thinks that the publick business will keep him at this place all the summer," she wrote, "and it would not be agreable to me to stay at Mount Vernon without him . . . . . . if I could bear the journey I would like to make you a flying visit—but that you know I can not as I am always much fatigued after I get home for several days—that I could not think of setting out again for some time—I do not know what keys you have—it is highly necessary that the beds and bedclothes of all kinds should be aired if you have the keys I beg you will make Caroline put all the things of every kind out to air and brush and clen all the places and rooms that they were in. . . . ."

Washington apparently had hopes of making the flying trip to Mount Vernon which Martha did not feel up to, though nothing came of it before September, in spite of the yellow fever epidemic which swept through the town before then. "When the President comes down," Martha continued to Fanny, "I beg you will get the key of my closet if you have not got it and send me the two bags that has my worked chear Bottoms in, and in [illegible] have them made into something if they are not spoiled and eaten up with the moth if you have the key. . . . . . I have never got the rose water and mint water that was sent to Alexandria to come round hear to me. . . . . ."

The summer of '93 was eventful in several ways. Sam's incorrigible sons, George Steptoc and Lawrence, had been apprenticed at law with the Attorney-General Edmund Randolph the previous year —at a fee of $500 paid by their uncle, who also paid bills for beer at their lodging ($3.88); a watch, with chain and key ($24); a subscription to the Assembly balls which marked their social debut ($16); a music master ($9); and a tailor's bill for the fashionable costumes which were dictated for the Assembly in an article in the *Gazeteer:* "Two yards of black silk ribbon for the shoes and an equal quantity for the knees, are used instead of buckles. The breeches are very tight. Two watch chains and trinkets are worn. The hair is powdered, frosted, and perfumed. The cape is of a different colour from the coat. Muslin and cambric are worn about the neck; and the genteel beau is particularly genteel when he wears a tamboured shirt."—which is to say, embroidered.

At about this time the boys removed from their former lodgings to the boarding-house of a Mrs. Payne, whose elder daughter Dolley had married a Mr. Todd, and had by him a baby son. Dolley would be widowed within the year by the yellow fever, and so stood on the threshold of a long, spectacular career which led to the White House itself. The Paynes were Quakers of the kind called "gay," meaning for one thing that ribbons and curls were allowed, and in this summer of '93 Dolley's younger sister Lucy, aged fifteen, eloped with the President's nephew, George Steptoe Washington, who was almost twenty. To everyone's surprise, they left the extravagances and diversions of Philadelphia and settled down on the neglected Harewood estate to salvage the bridegroom's inheritance.

At the end of July Polly Lear sickened and died within a week. Lear took their small son named Lincoln to his mother in New Hampshire, and then carried out his intention of leaving the Presidential household, perhaps spurred by an added unwillingness to remain in the familiar surroundings after his loss. They missed him acutely after seven years of his unobtrusive, good-natured presence in the family. Young Bartholomew Dandridge moved up a step into increased responsibility, and Martha particularly felt the lack of Polly's companionship.

Soon after her death it became apparent that Philadelphia was in the grip of an epidemic—yellow fever had spread out from the West Indian ships into the filthy streets along the water front and from there into the heart of the city. Late in August Washington wrote to Howell Lewis, who was still at Mount Vernon, "We are all well at present, but the city is very sickly and numbers dying daily." He had intended a visit to Mount Vernon in September, and with his characteristic disregard of precaution for his own health declined to follow the example of most people who had a place to go or could get out of town, and desert his post sooner, even when Hamilton and his wife both contracted the infection—and both recovered. Martha refused to go without him, even for the sake of the children, but business finally became so disrupted by absence and illness that he set his departure up to September 10th.

They tried to persuade the Powels to accompany them to the Potomac sanctuary, but Mr. Powel had no fear of the infection—and was dead of it within the month. His wife escaped by having remained at her brother's house in the suburbs when Samuel returned to their town house to provide for a favorite servant who was stricken, and from whom he was supposed to have contracted the disease. An affectionate correspondence was maintained between Martha Washington and the widowed Elizabeth Powel even after the Washingtons retired permanently to Mount Vernon at the end of the second term.

Late in September Washington wrote from Mount Vernon to Lear, who was about to embark for England in the interests of the mercantile business he intended to establish in Georgetown, that he would have remained longer in Philadelphia, "but as Mrs. Washington was unwilling to leave me surrounded by the malignant fever wch. prevailed, I could not think of hazarding her and the Children any longer by *my* continuance in the City, the house in which we lived being, in a manner blocaded by the disorder and was becoming every day more and more fatal....... Mrs. Washington having decided to let Nelly Custis have her watch and chain, is disposed to receive substitutes in lieu thereof at about 25 guineas price; and leaves the choice of them to you. The plainness of the Watch etc. she will not object to; 120 dollars in Bank Notes are inclosed for the purchase of them...... In whatever place you may be or in whatever walk of life you may move, my best wishes will attend you for I am, and always shall be Your sincere friend &ca...."

He found things at Mount Vernon in an unsatisfactory state. Although Whiting had seemed to give some satisfaction during his actual tenure, his death brought to light his shortcomings, and Howell was too inexperienced to have made his hand felt where it was most needed. The prospect brightened unexpectedly with an application from William Pearce of Maryland, well recommended as an able farmer, a widower of responsible age, with children, and "anxious to be in so distinguished an employ." Pearce came to Mount Vernon for an interview, and signed articles to take charge at the first of the year—at one hundred guineas, with pork and beef provisions, and bread, the use of three cows and three slaves, the privilege of raising poultry (though not to sell) fodder for his horses, a house of his own—and entire control of the overseers with full power to engage and discharge.

Fanny's decision to spend the winter at Eltham with her brother Burwell Bassett II, who had married one of the McCarthy girls of Longwood, altered the arrangements for Pearce's living quarters before he arrived, and Washington wrote him in October that it would be more convenient for them both if Pearce lived in the Mansion House, using the rooms above and below the banquet hall, all of which had fireplaces—"and by being here you will have the use of my Kitchen, the Cook belonging thereto, Frank the House Servant, a boy also in the House; the Stable, Garden, &c. &c. without any additional expense to me...... There are a great number of Negro children at the Quarters belonging to the house people," his instructions continued, "but they have always been forbid (except 2 or 3 young ones belonging to the Cook, and the Mulatto fellow Frank in the house, her husband; both of whom live in the Kitchen) from coming within the Gates of the Inclosures of the Yards, Garden &ct. that they may not be breaking the Shrubs and doing other mischief; but I believe they are often there notwithstanding; but if they could be broke of the practice it would be very agreeable to me, as they have no business within; having their Wood, Water, &ct. at their own doors without....."

Pearce replied from Maryland that he would be very glad to spend the winter in the Mansion House, as it would give him an opportunity to get acquainted with the business there. "But after that," he added, "if it should be agreeable to you, I had Rather Live in the house you intended for me, as I have Several small Children and I should like to keep them at a distance from the Black ones, and I thought I saw a great many at your Mansion house."

Fanny's departure for Eltham left Harriot dangling at Fredericksburg, where Betty Lewis was as usual in distress. "Was it convenient for me to keep her, [Harriot] I know of none that I would sooner have to live with me, but my income is so small, and few servants, that I cannot afford it," Betty wrote to Washington in September. "I am obliged to buy everything that I eat, with the addition of soap, candles, etc.; in short the most trifling things made use of in the house, and my income so small that I find it a hard matter to live and keep out of debt. It is a confinement to me as I have only two horses to my carriage, that I cannot go to visit at any distance, as I have two grandchildren living with me that I am obliged to carry with me....."

Although the worst of the Philadelphia epidemic had passed when the autumn rains and frosts began, it was still a ghost city, with an estimated four to five thousand dead, and only a venturesome few were beginning to trickle back into its deserted streets. Germantown was decided on as a safer place for the government to reassemble in November, and Washington wrote to Edmund Randolph requesting him to hire lodgings there for himself, Secretary Dandridge, two servants, and five horses. Martha and the children were to remain for a while at Mount Vernon, which raised false hopes in Harriot that she might be allowed to return there, but instead she was exiled to Culpeper County with Betty's married daughter, Mrs. Charles Carter, who had recently lost a child and been very ill.

Howell Lewis, fortified by a long letter of instructions, was to await the arrival of Pearce after the new year, though it left Washington shorthanded for his secretarial work. He was also inconvenienced by the further decline of his war-time body-servant Billy, as he wrote to Lear, whose departure abroad had been delayed:

"It gives me sincere pleasure to hear that Lincoln continues well, as I am sure it will do the family at Mount Vernon who must remain there until it is known what Congress will do; for till then I move like a snail, with everything on my back.

"I do not *yet* know whether I shall get a substitute for William; nothing short of excellent qualities and a man of good appearance, would induce me to do it. and under my present view of the matter too, who would employ himself otherwise than as William did; that is, as a Butler as well as a Valette, for my wants of the latter are so trifling that any man (as Willm. was) would soon be ruined by idleness who had only them to attend to. . . . ."

In the end, Billy's substitute, Christopher, qualified for most of his duties, and was among those who waited, weeping, in the bedchamber on the night of Washington's death.

Washington continued to correspond with Arthur Young, to whom he now confided that he entertained an idea of renting all of the Mount Vernon estate except the Mansion House farm, which he would reserve for his own amusement. "No estate in United America is more pleasantly situated than this," he wrote. "It lyes in a high, dry, and healthy Country 300 miles by water from the Sea, and, as you will see by the plan, on one of the finest Rivers in the world. Its margin is washed by more than ten miles of tide water; from the bed of which, and the enumerable coves, inlets, and small marshes with wch. it abounds, an inexhaustible fund of rich mud may be drawn as a manure; either to be used separately, or in a compost, according to the judgment of the farmer. . . . ." Young's reply that it would be necessary for him to publicize Washington's offer, apparently in the press, did not meet with the President's approval, and nothing came of the idea at this time.

In a letter to the incoming manager, Pearce, in December, when the family had all returned to Philadelphia, Washington gave valuable general advice and a shrewd estimate of each of his overseers:

"A steady and firm conduct," he wrote, "with an inquisitive inspection into and a proper arrangement of everything on your part, will, though it may give more trouble at first, save a great deal in the end, and you may rest assured that in everything which is just, and proper to be done on your part shall meet with the fullest support on mine. Nothing will contribute more to effect these desirable purposes than a good example, unhapply this was not set (from what I have learnt lately) by Mr. Whiting, who, it is said, drank freely, kept bad company at my house and in Alexandria, and was a very debauched person; wherever this is the case it is not easy for a man to throw the first stone for fear of having it returned to him; and this I take to be the true cause why Mr. Whiting did not look more scrupulously into the conduct of the Overseers, and more minutely into the smaller matters belonging to the Farms; which, though individually may be trifling, are not found so in the agregate; for there is no addage more true than an old Scotch one, that 'many mickles make a muckle.'

"I have had but little opportunity of forming a correct opinion of my white Overseers, but such observations as I have made I will give..... William Stuart [at River Farm] appears to me to understand the business of a farm very well and seems attentive to it..... His talkativeness and vanity may be humored.–Crow [at Union Farm] is an active man, and not deficient in judgment.... But I am much mistaken in his character if he is not fond of visiting and receiving visits..... I am not clear, either, that he gives that due attention to his Plow horses and other stock which is necessary, though he is very fond of riding the former, not only to Alexandria &ca. but about the farm, which I did not forbid as his house was very inconvenient to the scene of his business.–McKoy [at Dogue Run] appears to me to be a sickly, slothful, and stupid fellow.... If more exertion does not appear in him when he gets into better health he will be found an unfit person to overlook so important a farm, especially as I have my doubts of his care and attention to the horses &ca.—As to Butler, [at the Mansion House farm] you will soon be a judge whether he will be of use to you or not. He may mean well, and for ought I know to the contrary, may in some things have judgment, but I am persuaded he has no more authority over the Negroes he is placed (sic) than an old woman would have.—Davy at Muddy Hole carries on his business as well as the white Overseers, and with more quietness than any of them.

"Thomas Green (Overlooker of the Carpenters) will, I am persuaded, require your closest attention, without which I believe it will be impossible to get any work done by my Negroe Carpenters; in the first place, because it has not been in my power, when I am away from home, to keep either him or them to any settled work; but they will be flying from one trifling thing to another, with no other design, I believe, than to have the better opportunity to be idle, or employed on their own business. . . . . . The Gardener has too great a propensity to drink, and behaves improperly when in liquor; admonish him against it as much as you can, as he behaves well when sober, understands his business, and I believe is not naturally idle. . . . ."

In addition to the instructions to Pearce, Washington spent what must have been nearly the whole of December 23d, '93, in composing individual thunderbolts to each of the overseers personally, which if ever spelled out in full by the recipients must have had at least a temporary effect.

To Crow: ". . . . In a word, I have been so much disturbed by your insufferable neglect that it is with difficulty I have been constrained from ordering you instantly off the Plantation. . . . . And look ye, Mr. Crow, I have too good reasons to believe that your running about, and entertaining company at home, contrary to your agreement, (by which my business is unattended) is the cause of this now irremediable evil in the progress of my business. . . ."

To McKoy: ". . . . . And did you forget moreover that I charged you to have your plows in order, that not a moment might be lost when the ground was in such a state as to admit plowing to advantage? How durst you disobey this order, and instead of bringing the whole force of your plows to this you employ them now and then only, or one or two a week, as if it were for amusement? thereby doing everything which was in your power to derange my whole plan for next year? . . . . . ."

To Ehler, the Dutch gardener: ". . . . . I shall not close this letter without exhorting you to refrain from Spiritous liquors, they will prove your ruin if you do not. Consider how little a drunken Man differs from a beast; the latter is not endowed with reason, the former deprives himself of it; and when that is the case, acts like a brute; annoying and disturbing everyone around him. . . . ."

And to Green: ". . . . . I know full well, that to speak to you is of no more avail, than to speak to a bird that is flying over one's head; first because you are lost to all sense of shame, and to every feeling that ought to govern an honest man, who sets any store by his character; and secondly because you have no more command of the people over whom you are placed, than I have over the beasts of the forists. . . . ."

Jefferson resigned at the end of the year, to return to his little kingdom at Monticello in Albemarle County, and Edmund Randolph replaced him as Secretary of State. Washington must have watched him go with exasperated envy, as his own second term began. Jefferson was free to retire if he chose. The President was his country's bondsman.

XXXII

WHEN Pearce had settled in as manager, he proved to be a man of real integrity. His weekly reports were literate and sensible, if a little dull. "I will do everything in my power to forward the Business of hedging; and hope to Suckseed so as To give you Satisfaction, for I have no wish more at heart than to do your business well, & to Merit your approbation therein," he set down.

Most of Washington's letters to him were preserved by him, and the correspondence between them gives a more detailed picture than any other of the work Washington required to be done in his absence, and the minute interest he took in the separate lives, accomplishments and misdemeanors of his little population. Much space continued to be devoted to the worthlessness of Sally Bishop's husband, Thomas Green, and the small amount of work done by the carpenters he had in charge. Pearce at once labelled him "a very trifling person at best," and in May Washington wrote: "I wish you had discharged Green without any ceremony when you found him drinking and idling his time away..... Nothing but compassion for his helpless family has hitherto induced me to keep him a moment in my service (so bad is the example he sets) but if he has no regard for them himself, it is not to be expected that I am to be a continual sufferer on their account for his misconduct......"

Later in the year Green apparently sealed his own fate, as Washington wrote to Pearce: "Green's quitting my business of his own accord, whatever the pretence may be, is in my opinion a lucky circumstance, as my repugnance to turning him away was on account of his helpless family. These you may suffer to remain where they are until he can provide a place for them; or until you have occasion for the house for his successor; provided this is not unreasonably delayed. Old Bishop must be taken care of whether he goes or stays. . . . . ."

Old Bishop stayed, and Thomas Green's deserted family continued to be a problem throughout the autumn of '94. James Donaldson, an emigrant newly arrived from England, was engaged to replace him, but like Bloxham he was unused to Negro labor, and what Washington called his "easy, simple ways" did not fit him to direct and discipline the irresponsible hands now in his charge, so that in November Washington was writing to Pearce: "If he understands what he professes to have been bred to, and is sober and industrious, he may prove a very useful man to me, although he is unfit to have the care of my Carpenters. But what have you done with him, if Greens family still occupy the house? By my agreement with him, he is entitled to the use of *that* House, and Garden, and may consider it as a breach of contract to be deprived of it. What then is to be done with the other family. I cannot bear the thought of turning them a drift; and it would be as disagreeable to let them come into that part of the Greenhouse adjoining the Shoemakers room; their habits are not good; and to mix them among the Negroes would be attended with many evils as it respected themselves; and no good as it respected me. It would be better on all accounts if they were removed to some other place, even if I was to pay the Rent, provided it was low, or make some allowance towards it. Donaldson and family will get disgusted by living among the Negroes if he is still in the Greenhouse. . . . ."

But Donaldson and his family remained, and early in '95, "I never saw Donaldson's son," Washington wrote, "but from what you have said respecting him, I am very willing to allow him his victuals and course clothing; but ascertain the quantum, and sort of both, to prevent mistakes and grumbling hereafter; I am always ready and willing, to fulfil every engagement I enter into; and hating disputes, I wish always that contracts may be *clearly* understood for this reason also, it is necessary he should know that the boy must work duly, and truly. . . . . ."

Sally Green wanted to go to Alexandria and set up a shop there, which Washington disapproved of on the grounds that it would become "no more than a receptacle for stolen produce, by the Negros," and advised instead that she should take in washing and sewing. At the same time his habitual compassion directed that Pearce should aid her in any way that seemed to him feasible, "to the amount of twenty pounds in the purchase of things or on credit, but not by any advance in money, lest it should be fooled away for unessential things that she can do without...... But if she goes to town you may give her a boatload of Wood, a little flour, and some meat at killing time; besides what is usually allowed her father. If she goes there her eldest son may derive some benefit from the charity school which is established there at my expense."

Sally Green did go to Alexandria and is not mentioned until April, a year later, when she wrote to Washington that she and her children were ill and in distress, and begged for his assistance. He enclosed the letter to Pearce, again with the recommendation that she be given anything but money, "for I very strongly suspect," he added, "that all that has, and perhaps all that will be given to her in that article, is applied more in rigging herself, than in the purchase of real and useful necessaries for her family." She does not appear in the correspondence again, but was remembered in Washington's will, along with John Alton's daughter Anne, for $100, "in consideration of the attachment of their fathers to me, each of whom having lived nearly forty years in my family."

In January of '95 Bishop, whose memories went back to the bloody Monongahela field, died at Mount Vernon in the absence of his master, whose comment, always stoic regarding death, was typical: "Altho' Bishop should never have wanted for victuals or cloaths while he lived," he wrote Pearce on receipt of the news, "yet his death cannot be cause of regret, even to his daughter; to whom, from the imbecility of age, if not when he died, he soon must have become very troublesome to her, and a burthen to all around him."

Among the slaves that year he notes the death of "poor Austin," at a tavern on the way from Philadelphia to visit his family in Maryland, after years of service in the Washington household; of Paris, regarded by Washington as a loss, and of Jupiter as "the reverse." And—"It is happy for old Betty and her children and friends that she is taken off the stage; her life must have been a misery to herself and troublesome to all around her." And—"as that trusty old negro Jack has taken leave of the troubles of this world, you must supply his place at the Stable, or rather at the Provender for it; and I think Allison [new overseer at the Mansion House] had better keep the key of the corn loft; for I know of no black person about the house who is to be trusted."

Pilfering by the slaves of course went on endlessly. "I wish you would find out the thief who robbed the Meat house at Mount Vernon, and bring him to punishment," he wrote Pearce in June, '95. "And at the same time secure the house against future attempts; for our drafts upon it will be pretty large, I expect, when we come home; which probably may be about the middle or 20th of next month. Nathan has been suspected, if not detected, in an attempt of this sort formerly; and is as likely as any one to be guilty of it now. Postilion Joe has been caught in similar practice; and Sam, I am sure, would not be restrained by any qualms of conscience, if he saw an opening to do the same."

The illness and malingering of the slaves, particularly in his absence, was a perpetual exasperation. The duplication of names among them makes continued identification chancy, as the chronicle unfolds. There was a dower slave at the Mansion House named Doll, who was one of the cooks in 1760, and in 1786 she is listed as "almost past service." Another Doll at the Ferry Farm, listed in '86 among the laboring women, appears frequently in the '94-5 correspondence between Washington and Pearce: "I find that Doll at the Ferry is constantly returned sick; the Overseer at that place ought to see that this sickness is not pretence." And the following month: "What chimney has fallen, by wch. negro children were hurt, and how are they now?" he inquired. "Under real, or pretended sickness Doll at the Ferry rarely does any work; it would be well to place her in a situation where her ways can be attended to. If she is really unable to work, none will be required of her; if she is able, deceitful complaints, of which she is very capable of making, ought not to avail her. . . . ."

Every week he checked the sick list with curiosity and care:

"Charlotte at the Mansion House has been reported sick for several weeks. Mrs. Washington desires you will examine her case, and if it appears necessary to request Dr. Craik to attend, and prescribe for her. A fellow Sam also, who under pretense (for I believe this is the greatest part of his complaint) of an Asthmatical complaint never could be got to work more than half his time, has not done a day's work since I left Mount Vernon in October; examine his case also, but not by the Doctor, for he has had Doctors enough already, of all colours and sexes, and to no effect. Laziness Is I believe his principal ailment...."

"What sort of lameness is Dick's (at D. Run) that he should have been confined with it for so many weeks? and what kind of sickness is Betty Davis's, that it should have had a similar effect upon her? If pretended ailments, without apparent causes or visible effects, will screen her from work, I shall get no service at all from her; for a more lazy, deceitful, and impudent huzzy is not to be found in the United States than she is."

"Is it Sarah that was among the Spinners at the Mansion House that is now in childbed? If so, she seems to have begun in time."

"Is there anything peculiar in the case of Ruth, Hannah, and Pegg, that they have been returned sick for several weeks together? Ruth I know is extremely deceitful; she has been aiming for some time past to get into the house exempt from work; but if they are not made to do what their age and strength will enable them, it will be a very bad example to the others, none of whom would work if by pretexts they could avoid it."

In case of actual illness and distress, however, he was compassionate and insisted upon proper care, as in May of '95 when he wrote regarding the death of "a young fellow." "I hope every necessary care and attention was afforded him. I expect little of this from McKoy, or indeed from most of his class; for they seem to consider a Negro much in the same light as they do the brute beasts, on the farms; and often times treat them as inhumanly."

There was need in '93 of an assistant to the gardener, the Dutchman named Ehler who had held that post since '88, and Sam's character came in for further analysis: "Let Sam supply the place of Bristol, until I come home; unless (which does not occur to me at present) a likely and well disposed young fellow of mans growth, or near it, should be found on my estate fit to make a gardener of. If one, not among the Dower Negros, could be selected, it would be preferred. Honesty, with some degree of acuteness, are desirable; but in whom amg. my people these are to be found, I know not. Sam has sense enough, and has had a little experience, but he wants honesty, and every other requisite; particularly industry. Cyrus, besides being a Dower slave, is strongly suspected of roguery and drinking; otherwise he would do very well, as he is likely, young, and smart enough. The children of Daphne at the River farm are among the best disposed Negros I have, but I do not recollect whether there be any of a fit size. . . . ."

"The Gardener complains of the injury which the shrubs (even in the yard) sustain from the Deer," he wrote Pearce that winter. "I am at a loss therefore in determining whether to give up the Shrubs or the Deer! Is there no way of frightening them from these haunts?"

Poor Harriot, born to that patronizing adjective as was poor George Augustine in his frail health, had a very dull winter in the hinterlands of Culpeper County, and was looking forward to the Birthnight Ball at Fredericksburg which she hoped to attend: "I hope my dear Uncle will excuse my troubleing him so soon again," she wrote late in January, "but as he is the only freind on earth that I can apply to, for anything, I am reduced to think that my necessity will apologize for me. I have spent the winter in Culpeper with Cousin Carter in a very retired manner. We have scarcely seen a person since we came up, and as I am just a going to return to Fredericksburg I shall be a thousand times oblieged to my dear Uncle if he will give me as much money as will get me a silk jacket and a pair of shoes to wear to the Birthnight, as that will be the first Ball I shall have been to this winter. . . . ."

Some one in Philadelphia, doubtless Martha, took the trouble to make up a parcel of clothes, and one can only hope they were new and not just this and that from other people's wardrobes, for Harriot was grateful. "She values it more as it comes from Philadelphia, and expects it is more fashionable," Betty Lewis wrote her brother. "Things in this town is scarce and very dear. She seems truly sensible of the many favors received, and says that she will make it her whole duty to deserve them. I can assure you she is truly deserving of the favors received, and I am not acquainted with anyone who takes more care of their things and turns them to greater advantage." So

Harriot at eighteen had changed from the indolent creature whose clothes were once said to be "dabbed about in every hole and corner," and wrote in her letter of thanks that she was sure that nothing could have been procured in Fredericksburg so handsome as what had arrived in her bundle.

But in March she was still in trouble: "It gives me pain to be obleiged to apply to my dear Uncle so soon after his kind present, but embolden'd by your affectionate letter I venture to ask you if it is convenient and you can spare the money to let me have a peice of linnen, some dimmity to make me petticoats, and a great coat. I have not had a great coat since the winter I spent at Shuter's Hill. Mine is not entirely worn out, but it is so small that I can't get it on. I am not in immediate want of the linnen, but Aunt Lewis thinks it will take me a good while to make it up, that if I could get it now it would be better than some time hence. . . . ."

Thoughtlessly, or in haste, they sent her a length of material instead of a coat. At Mount Vernon there would have been seamstresses and tailors, and Martha was accustomed to think in those terms, but Betty's establishment was stripped of all such conveniences. "I received the box which contains the things my dear Uncle was so kind as to send me," Harriot wrote later in the month, with conceivable embarrassment. "How shall I express my gratitude to my beloved Uncle for so much kindness? I hope my dear Uncle will not be displeased if I beg him for as much money as will make my great coat, and will purchase thread and tape to make my linnen. I am afraid you will attribute my not making my great coat to laziness, but I can assure you I would make it with a great deal of pleasure as it wuld save you the trouble of sending money, if I could get it cut out, but there is not a tailor in town that will cut it out unless we will consent to let them make it. I was very much in want of a few things some time ago and was obleiged to borrow 24 shillings from Aunt Lewis. She is in want of money just now and wishes me to pay her. I should be much obleiged to you for as much as will do that. . . . ."

In April Betty wrote to thank her brother for the present of a mule, and said that Harriot had got her money safe. But by now it was May, and Harriot was still growing, and continued in a dilemma: "I hope my dear Uncle will excuse my asking him for some summer dresses, as nothing would induce me to be so troublesome if I was not in absolute want of them. Those that I had last year are almost worn out, I am affraid my dear Uncle will think me careless and extravagant, but indeed I mend and wear them as long as I possibly can. Aunt Lewis says if you will send the money to get them that I shall not have any thing that I am not in real want of, but she says things are very dear here, and if you please to get them there it would be cheaper, as Cousin had told us goods are much lower there than they are here. . . . ."

That was the summer that the Whiskey Rebellion rumbled through the western borderlands, and Harriot's needs were only one small item which suffered from neglect in the disruption it caused. Washington made one of his "flying trips" to Mount Vernon in June without the family, and hurried back to establish Martha and the children in a rented house at Germantown, which was as far from the humid Philadelphia heat as he could allow himself to remain. In answer to a query from the gardener if apricots would be wanted for preserving, he answered no, "for the situation of public business now is, and likely to remain such, that my family will not be able to spend any time at Mount Vernon this Summer, that is, I cannot do it, and Mrs. Washington would not chuse to be there without me."

Tobias Lear returned from abroad in August, '94, to establish his new business at Georgetown, and Washington wrote him from Germantown: "When business or inclination may turn your face towards the Eastward, it will be unnecessary to add, that to see you wd. make this family very happy; and with a little roughing on your part you could be accommodated therein. If you have no accts. later, I have the pleasure to tell you that by a letter from your good mother to Mrs. Washington, that she, and little Lincoln were perfectly well on the 11th of this month, and by her account that he continues to be the fine, sprightly child you left him. . . . . . I had it in contemplation to visit that place [Mount Vernon] about the last of September or beginning of October, but the rebellious conduct of the people in the western counties of this State renders the journey uncertain and may defeat it altogether. . . . ."

Harriot waited a month, and then, having an additional reason to want new clothes, tried again: "I wrote a letter to my honoured

Uncle some time ago and mentioned in it that I was very much in want of some summer dresses, and should be much obleiged to my dear Uncle if he would either send them or send Aunt Lewis the money to purchase them. I hope you will excuse my importuning you with a letter to the same subject, as I concluded by my not receiving an answer from you that my letter has either been mislaid or it had never reached your hand. Mrs. Payne from Philadelphia passed through this town about a fortnight ago, and by her I received an invitation from brother George to return with her and spend the summer and fall. She is to be in this town next week. I thought it better to write to you in the meanwhile to know if you approved of it. I am very anxious to see them, but if my dear Uncle has any objection to it, I will not go. . . . ."

Poor Harriot, who felt herself a burden at Fredericksburg, and yet must beg permission and suitable clothes in order to accept an invitation to what must have looked to her a happy reunion at Harewood, where George Steptoe Washington and his Lucy had settled into a happy marriage and were putting an end to the mismanagement and indebtedness of his father's estate. Lucy's mother, Mrs. Payne, once opposed to the match, had accepted their invitation to live with them instead of running an unprofitable boarding-house in Philadelphia, and Lucy's sister, the widow Todd, lovely, exciting Dolley, had only to choose, rumor said, between Aaron Burr and James Madison for her second husband. . . . .

Washington sent the money, and Harriot got the dresses, and went to Harewood, which she had probably not seen since she was a child —that square stone house, its drawing-room regal with quiet Palladian panelling, built one room deep in a grove of tall trees. And to it in September Madison brought Dolley Todd for her wedding, which Harriot was privileged to attend. Warm-hearted Dolley either recognized a possible friend in Harriot, who was only eight years younger, or took pity on an eager girl without many pleasures, because she arranged for Harriot to accompany them on their visit to Madison's sister, Mrs. Isaac Hite, who had a newly finished house called Belle Grove at Strasburg, the other side of Winchester. Although the trip was a part of the honeymoon, Dolley's sister Anna was also one of the party, but her little son by Todd was left with Lucy Washington at Harewood.

Like everyone else, Harriot was enslaved by Dolley Madison's magnetism, and after their return to Harewood in October she wrote to Washington: "Mr. and Mrs. Madison have given me a very pressing invitation to spend the winter with them in Philadelphia and to return with them to Fredericksburg in the spring. They were very anxious for it, begged me to write to you to ask your consent, and insisted on waiting till I heard from you. But I was afraid it would displease you and so declined it, as my obligations are of such a nature to my dear Uncle that I would not for the world do anything that I thought would offend him, although I should have been much pleased at going with them as I think Mrs. Madison a charming woman. I never saw one that I was more delighted with. I am very much attached to her indeed...."

Most of Washington's letters to Harriot are unfortunately missing, as his advice to his young people was seldom recorded in the letter-press, and there is no knowing what his reply to Harriot's plea may have been. Neither is there any indication that she ever reached Philadelphia during the Presidency, though the two older Custis girls visited their sister Nelly at the Presidential mansion. Harriot's story might have been different if she had been allowed to take advantage of Dolley's friendly impulse to introduce her to Philadelphia society as a guest of the Madisons. The close bond which had existed between Washington and Madison during the fight for the Constitution and the beginning of the first term had been broken, by differences over the policy with regard to France, and Hamilton was in the ascendant. But it hardly seems probable that the estrangement could have extended to blight Harriot's hopes of a season in the capital city under Dolley's wing.

January, '95, found her back at Fredericksburg, writing to ask "for as much money as will purchase me a stuff skirt and a couple of dark calicoes, as I am very much in want of them indeed, and have been ever since the winter commenced, but have postponed plaguing of you until I returned to Fredericksburg." She found her aunt in "a very weak, low state of health," and in need of the cheerful nursing which it was Harriot's duty to provide.

Among the rare autograph letters of Martha Washington belonging to the Mount Vernon Association is the one written in December, '94, from Philadelphia to Fanny, full of family news: "..... Thank god we are all very well—I don't think Nelly so much grown as Mr. Lear describes, he can see the alteration more than I can. the very same clothes fitts her as she had made at Alexandria last fall—Wash has outgrown his cloths that was made since—thank god they are boath very well—and I hope when Nelly has a little more gravitie she will be a good girl—at present—she is I fear half crazey—my love and good wishes to you and the children in which the President joins me, Nelly, Wash, and Mr. Dandridge send their love to you and the children. . . . . ."

Jacky Custis's second daughter, Patty, at seventeen had got engaged to Thomas Peter, son of Washington's friend Judge Peter of Georgetown—a sober and suitable match, between two young people who had had ample opportunity to know each other socially, and their elders approved. A letter from Martha in Philadelphia to Fanny at Eltham gave the news: ". . . . From what I can hear Patty and Mr. Peter is to make a match—The old gentleman will comply with Doctor Stuart's bargain and in the last letter I had from Mrs. Stuart she says Patty had given him leve to visit her as a lover—I suppose by that he is agreeable to all parties—if it is so I shall be very happy to see her setled with a prospect of being happy—I realy believe she is a very deserving girl—I am told that he is cleaver. . . ."

Patty's elder sister Eliza was apparently envious and sighed over her own spinsterhood—she was nineteen—to her uncle, whose reply, written at Germantown during the autumn of '94, has itself survived, treasured somehow through all the misfortunes which later beset this headstrong, star-crossed granddaughter of Martha's, so that it has now come to rest in the Morgan Library. "Do not then in your contemplation of the marriage state, look for perfect felicity before you consent to wed," he wrote, "nor conceive, from the fine tales the Poets and lovers of old have told us, of the transports of mutual love, that heaven has taken its abode on earth: Nor do not deceive yourself in supposing that the only means by which these are to be obtained is to drink deep of the cup, and revel in an ocean of love. Love is a mighty pretty thing; but like all other delicious things, it is cloying; and when the first transports of the passion begins to subside, which it assuredly will do, and yield, oftentimes too late, to more sober reflections, it serves to evince that love is too dainty a food to live upon *alone*, and ought not to be considered farther than as a necessary ingredient for that matrimonial happiness which results from a combination of causes; none of which are of greater importance than that the object on whom it is placed, should possess good sense, good dispositions, and the means of supporting you in the way you have been brought up...... for be assured, and experience will convince you, that there is no truth more certain than that all enjoyments fall short of our expectations; and to none does it apply with more force than to the gratification of the passions. You may believe me to be always and sincerely, your Affectionate uncle...."

It was Eliza who made the disastrous marriage, a year later. Her sister Patty's, which took place in January, '95, at her home at Hope Park, was a happy one.

XXXIII

WASHINGTON'S next homecoming was not till July of '95. "If nothing more than I foresee at present, happens to prevent it, I shall leave this place (with my family) for Mount Vernon on Wednesday next the 15th inst.," he wrote Pearce on the 12th, "but when I shall arrive at it, is more difficult to decide, as the weather is extremely hot, and my horses very fat. These circumstances must, at any rate, cause my movements to be slow; or I shall hazard too much in my horses. . . . ." He arrived on July 20th, and at once sent off an invitation to his sister Betty and Harriot to come up for a visit. Soon after, there occurs an item in the Cash Memorandum: 2 Jaconet Muslins, 20 yds, for Miss Harriot Washington—£12.10."

Fanny Washington was now living in the President's Alexandria house, which had been remodelled for her use, and Lear at Georgetown was not too far away for old friends to resume acquaintance —widow and widower, and Fanny five years the younger, both with small children. An attachment was not surprising, especially in view of Lear's reference to her in his letter to Prescott a year after his arrival at Mount Vernon—"one of those superior beings who are sent down to bless good men," he wrote then of George Augustine's wife. They now planned to marry in August, which was two years after George Augustine's and Polly Lear's deaths, which had occurred within a few weeks of each other. Washington was pleased, and arranged to give them as a wedding present a life lease on the place Lear named Walnut Tree Farm, a part of the River Farm tract once designated for George Augustine and Fanny.

Washington had been at home only a matter of days, when the growing opposition to the unpopular treaty which Mr. Jay had negotiated in London exploded, and letters from the Cabinet and members of Congress rained on Mount Vernon. He returned to Philadelphia on August 6th, leaving Martha and the children behind, and he did not get back till the middle of September. There was a nasty scandal involving Edmund Randolph, who as Secretary of State was accused of having passed secret information to the French Minister, Jean Fauchet, and he had been forced to resign. Proud and bitter, Randolph turned his resentment against the President, whose private feelings could not be allowed to weigh against public opinion in the circumstances.

The Revolution in France had left Lafayette a prisoner in Austria, and Washington sent money and an offer of asylum to Mme. Lafayette, who at once despatched her son in his tutor's charge to America. Feeling was so high against France that it was thought unwise to receive the exiles into the Presidential household at that time, and Washington's personal loyalties were again sacrificed to his office. In September, '95, he wrote to his old friend General Knox, the Secretary at War: "And as his coming to Philadelphia, immediately, at least, might, the French Minister being there, occasion embarrassments and be productive of no essential good, I proposed, until something more eligible could be devised, to have him entered at the University in Cambridge, with his Tutor. I did not write to the youth myself, for reasons which will readily occur to you; but entreated Mr. Cabot to explain them to him in the most affectionate and consoling manner; and to assure him in the strongest terms that I would be to him as a friend and father; and that he might to all intents and purposes count upon me as such."

Almost a year later, young Lafayette and his tutor accompanied the Washingtons to Mount Vernon on a visit, and then remained in the household for some eighteen months.

Patiently Washington at Philadelphia took up his weekly correspondence with Pearce after what must have been only a tantalizing glimpse into his Mount Vernon affairs, that disturbed summer of '95. "I forgot to ask you, what prospect there was of your saving clover seed sufficient for your next year's purposes?" one letter begins. A man named Neale was to replace Donaldson, who had replaced Green, and there was the usual difficulty about securing the incumbent's house for the new man. Overseers were lacking for both Union and Dogue Run farms, and the choice must be left to Pearce, who was suffering from rheumatism.

Back at Mount Vernon for the autumn, Washington exchanged agricultural news with Jefferson, who was rusticating at Monticello: "I am much pleased with the account you have given of the Succory [chicory]," Washington wrote. "This, like all other things of the sort with me, since my absence from home, have come to nothing; for neither my Overseers nor Manager will attend properly to anything but the crops they have usually cultivated; and in spite of all I can say, if there is the smallest discretionary power allowed them, they will fill the land with Indian Corn; altho' they have demonstrable proof, at every step they take, of its destructive effects. I am resolved, however, as soon as it shall be in my power to attend a little more closely to my own concerns, to make this crop yield, in a great degree, to other grain; to pulses, and to grasses. I am beginning again with chiccory from a handful of seed given to me by Mr. Strickland; which, though flourishing at present has not appearance this year. Lucerne [alfalfa] has not succeeded better with me than with you; but I will give it another, and a fairer, trial before it is abandoned altogether. Clover, when I can dress lots well, succeeds with me to my full expectation; but not on the fields in rotation; although I have been at much cost in seeding them...... I shall thank you for the result of your proposed experiment relatively to the winter vetch and Pea when they are made......."

His nephew Robert Lewis was now established with a family of his own on the western lands, where he continued to act as Washington's agent, and he sent in £475.10.2 in rents in October from Washington's tenants around Frederick. This was of course a mere drop in the bucket of Washington's financial necessities.

On their way back to Philadelphia and the winter's grind of Presidential duties, the Washingtons stopped at Mr. Lear's house in Georgetown, where Fanny now reigned as a happy bride of several months, with George Augustine's children growing up in a new home, though little Lincoln Lear remained with his paternal grandmother in New Hampshire. Returning to the crowded, inconvenient executive mansion in Market Street, after the sweeping riverfront peace of Mount Vernon, Washington doubtless found himself counting up time until March, '97—less than eighteen months to go.

As usual, he had forgotten something. "I want a Green Pocket book, which is to be found in the hair trunk, which is usually put on my writing Table in the Study, with my Land papers," he wrote back to Pearce. "The key of this trunk is under the lid of the writing Table. it is tied to a bunch of other keys, by a twine. This Pocket book is of green parchment, and contains the courses and distances of many surveys of the grounds &ca in, and about my farms. let it be put under a cover, and sent to me by the first Post, with the Reports." He continued to exhort his manager on the matter of hedging —"At least 15 years have I been urging my managers to substitute live fences in lieu of dead ones, which, if continued upon the extensive scale my farms require, must exhaust all my timber; and to this moment I have not one that is complete: nor never shall, unless they are attended to in the manner before mentioned; and if plants die to replace them the next season. . . . ." There was so much unfinished when he was forced to depart—"The enclosed small sketch shews the course of the Road from the white gates in Front of the Mansion house to the end of the little old field; and I could be glad, if circumstances would allow it, if a new road was opened along the streight line A B if you can, without a compass, lay it off streight, or if it was to strike the road a little beyond the field. . . . . ."

In February, '96, the affairs of his young people came again to the fore. Eliza Custis announced her intention of marrying an Englishman named Thomas Law, who appeared to be a man of wealth, along with some eccentricities. He lived in great style and luxury in a house he had built on New Jersey Avenue in the new Federal City, and drove the handsomest chariot in town. Arriving in America in '94 via India, where he was said to have made his fortune, he brought with him three Asiatic sons by a former marriage—striking, accomplished boys nearly as old as Eliza, who was turning twenty, while Law admitted to thirty-nine.

The news came as a complete surprise to the Washingtons, although they were acquainted with Law, and Eliza may have met him during a visit to them, when she was described by the vice-president, John Adams, as "a fine, blooming, rosy girl, who I dare say has had more liberty than Nelly." Washington wrote one of his affectionate homilies to Eliza, a short time before her marriage:

"My dear Betsey: I have obeyed your injunction in not acknowledging the receipt of your letter of the first instant until I should hear from Mr. Law. This happened yesterday; I therefore proceed to assure you, if Mr. Law is the man of your choice, of wch. there can be no doubt, as he has merits to engage your affections, and you have declared that he has not only done so, but that you find, after a careful examination of your heart, you cannot be happy without him; that your alliance with him meets my approbation. *Yes*, Betsey, and this approbation is accompanied with my fervent wishes that you may be as happy in this important event as your most Sanguine imagination has ever presented to your view. Along with these wishes, I bestow on you my choicest blessings.

"Nothing contained in your letter, in Mr. Laws, or in any other from our friends, intimates *when* you are to taste the sweets of Matrimony; I therefore call upon *you*, who have more honesty than disguise, to give me the details. Nay more, that you will relate all your feelings to *me* on this occasion; or as a Quaker would say, 'all the workings of the spirit within.'

"This I have a right to expect in return for my blessing, so promptly bestowed, after you had concealed the matter from me so long. Being entitled therefore to this confidence, and to a compliance with my requests, I shall look forward to the fulfilment of it.

"If after marriage Mr. Laws business should call him to this City, the same room which Mr. Peter and your sister occupied will accomodate you too; and it will be equally at your service.

"You know how much I love you, how much I have been gratified by your attentions to those things which you had reason to believe were grateful to my feelings. And having *no* doubt of your continuing the *same* conduct, as the effect will be pleasing to *me*, and unattended with any disadvantages to *yourself*, I shall remain with the sincerest friendship, and the most Affectionate regard, etc."

His letter to Mr. Law, written the same day, was cordial, and mentioned that he hoped that the bridegroom had no intention of separating Eliza from her friends in America, but would remain in this country. This hope was fulfilled, and Washington did not live to see the final breakup of the marriage, which ended in divorce in 1810, with strange stories of Law's mysterious aberrations and Eliza's wild ways and headlong attachments. She married again, a Baltimore man, in 1817, and by him had three children, besides the one daughter which was Law's.

Fanny Lear fell ill at Georgetown in March, as did her daughter Maria, just as Lear was on the point of making a journey to Philadelphia. The child survived, but within a few days Fanny was dead, at twenty-nine, after less than a year of her second marriage. Lear was left with four small children under ten, and was fortunate in his New Hampshire mother, who at once took charge. Eliza Law, so lately wed, was with Fanny during her illness and wrote to Washington to break the news to Martha, for whom it was a heavy blow, as Fanny was the daughter of her dearest sister Nancy, who had died young in the winter of '77-8.

Washington's letter to Lear was in his accustomed fatalistic style of condolence, but ended with a practical evidence of affection. "As you talked of coming to this place on business, let us press you to do so. The same Room that serves Mr. Dandridge & Washington is large enough to receive a Bed also for you; and it is needless to add, we shall be glad of your Company. The change may be serviceable to you; and if our wishes were of any avail, they would induce you to make your stay here as long as your convenience would permit......" Lear did return to the Washington household, but not until two more years had elapsed.

In a letter to Fanny's brother, Burwell Bassett II, in April, Washington took up the problem of what to do about Fanny's children by George Augustine Washington; the eldest, Maria, was eight years old, and had suffered from her mother's habitually lax discipline, as Harriot had done in her day. Bassett's marriage to Elizabeth McCarthy of Longwood was childless, and he had offered to take them into his own household at Eltham. "Mr. Lear is now in this City, and before the receipt of your letter we had some conversation respecting the disposition of the children," Washington wrote to Bassett. "At first, he seemed unwilling to part with any of them, but upon more mature reflection yielded to the propriety of your having Maria..... It was always my intention, as you probably may have understood, to take Fayette under my immediate care, but as they are now bereft of father and mother it would be best, I conceive, and more grateful to *their* feelings to keep them together, in whatsoever situation they may be placed; for this reason as I have mentioned before, the ultimate decision relative to them may be postponed until I bid adieu to public life; when I will advise with you and Mr. Lear on their future destination and shall readily acquiesce in any plan which shall appear most conducive to their permanent interest and advantage. . . . . ." Meanwhile, the children were left in Lear's mother's charge at Walnut Tree Farm near Mount Vernon.

Betty's attempt to maintain Millbank at Fredericksburg by running a school there had failed, and she was finally compelled to sell the house and move to Spotsylvania County, where she bought a place she called Millbrook, near the home of her married daughter. The change apparently precipitated a crisis in the affairs of young Harriot, who was being courted by a Fredericksburg man and probably had no desire to be buried in the hinterlands with an elderly ailing aunt. However she seems to have quailed before the prospect of presenting the case to her uncle, and persuaded Betty to break the news to him for her. At the end of March, '96, Betty wrote: "I am going to address you on a Subject which I am request'd to do by Harriot; there is a young jentleman in Fredericksburg Paying his addresses to her by the Name Andrew Parks, Merchant in that Town. She desired me to inform you that he is her Choice if it meets with your Approbation. He is One that is Very much respectted by all his acquaintances. He is a sober, sedate young man, and attentive to Business. He says his fortune Does not exceed Three Thousand Pounds, but has Expectations of some thing very handsome. You will receive a Letter from him, I Expect, with this. I have not receiv'd a line from you since I left Town, which Place I was oblig'd to quit as I should most sertainly have been ruined had I Contineu'd there one year more. The Place is more agrable to me than the one I left. The Place is Pore, but with the advantage of the Mill it will be more advantage to me than the other. . . . ."

Making allowance for the fact that both the Custis girls had married men who were already known to Washington, and they or their children were not likely in any case to become a further charge upon him, Washington's response to Harriot's projected engagement seems grudging and overly cautious, as he replied to Betty instead of directly to the person most concerned: "Harriot having very little fortune herself, has no *right* to expect a great one in the man she marry's; but if he has not a competency to support her in the way she has lived, in the circle of her friends, she will not find the matrimonial state so comfortable as she may have expected when a family is looking up to her and but scanty means to support it. . . . . . I do not wish to thwart Harriots inclination if her affects. are placed on Mr. Park and if upon the inquiries I shall make or cause to be made into his family and connexions, there shall be found nothing exceptionable in them. . . . . . I should have preferred, if a *good* match had not offer'd in the meanwhile that she shd. have remained single until I was once more settled at Mount Vernon and she a resident there, which, if life is spared to us, will certainly happen to me in ten or eleven Months; because then she would have had a much fairer prospect of matching respectably than with one who is little known, and of whose circumstances few or none can know much about. . . . . . I am persuaded you will enjoy more ease and quiet, and meet with fewer vexations where you now are, than where you did live. It is my sincere wish that you should do so, and that your days may be happy. . . . . ."

Betty's letter had been enclosed in one from Parks himself, in which he stated his prospects and fortune, and his Baltimore mercantile connections through a brother-in-law. Washington replied to him politely but non-committally, and the same day wrote to his always useful nephew George Lewis, asking him to look into Mr. Parks' background and circumstances, and report at once. Lewis was then living in Fredericksburg and had known Parks for the past year—"As to his family I am told his Father is an industrious Farmer in Maryland with a small property, from whom he can have no expectations," came George's reply. "In short his marrying Harriot at this time would be madness in the extreme, at all events. I think it would be well to put it off until your return to Virginia, by which time you can have an opportunity of being better acquainted with Mr. Parks prospects in life, and give them time to reflect seriously on what they are about, at present I conceive it has been an inconsiderate step on both sides. . . . . ."

But to Harriot, nineteen and in love, the year which must still elapse before the end of Washington's second term may have held the terror of losing a chance to establish a life of her own with some one to whom she was something more than a tiresome responsibility. By July she had fretted herself into an illness, and the subject was far from closed when Washington arrived at Mount Vernon for his summer visit. "I expected your coming through Baltimore that you would ascertain Mr. Parks fortune," Betty wrote to him there on the 5th, "though I believe he would not tell anything false on the occasion. Harriot's brother wrote her a letter from Baltimore and likewise one to Mr. Parks congratulating them on their intended union, which he says he makes no doubt will be a very happy one. Lawrence was here at the time that Mr. Parks first spoke to Harriot on the subject, and I begged of him to make all the inquire he could, but never heard from him until the letter I have mentioned here, and concluded from that that he had inquired and was well pleased." (This would be Harriot's next oldest brother, who was only a year her senior, and not her cousin Lawrence Lewis, who was old enough to judge.) "When Mr. Parks asked my consent I told him I had nothing to say to it," Betty continued, in the singularly ungracious tone which Harriot often engendered in the family, "and that you were the person to be applied to. I have never concerned myself with it, but I think Harriot is old enough now to make the choice for herself, and if they are not happy I believe it will be her own fault. He b[e]ars the best character of any young person that I know...... P.S. I fear you will hardly make out this, as I have a violent headache and a horrid cough. I believe Harriot is distressed to know how she is to be provided with things for her wedding dress."

The next development was Washington's Cash Memorandum: "By Cash sent Harriot Washington to buy her wedding clothes, $100."

The date is within a week of Betty's letter, and from a typically breathless, affectionate letter of thanks from Harriot to Washington on the 17th of July, one wonders what sort of wedding the poor girl had after all. "Aunt Lewis received a letter from my dear and honor'd Uncle a few days ago, wherein he was pleased to send me £30—also a great deal of good advice, which I am extremely obliged to you for, and intend adhering most strictly to. Believe me, my dear Uncle, my heart will ever with the liveliest gratitude most gratefully acknowledge and remember yours and Aunt Washington's great goodness and attention to me. And if my Uncle will only answer my letter and say he is not offended at my union (which took place yesterday, Aunt Lewis going immediately to Berkeley [County] to stay until the fall, and finding it not convenient to carry me with her, wished us married before she went) I shall be happy, for after my dear Uncle's protection and kindness towards me I should be a most miserable being to reflect that I had displeased my greatest friend......"

Martha sent her a pair of earrings as a wedding present. Harriot's marriage apparently turned out well—better, anyway, than Eliza's, which had recently received a much more indulgent blessing from Washington. The Parkses visited Mount Vernon after their marriage, and in April, '97, Washington gave Harriot 10 guineas—the last mention of her in the Diary being September 4, '98. In 1818 they moved to the Kanawha region in what is now West Virginia, where there came to be quite a Washington colony, and Harriot died there in her forties.

By mid-May Washington had begun to look forward to the end of the Congressional session, which would release him for another visit to Mount Vernon. His letters to Pearce reflected his inner excitement—a summer at home—a winter in Philadelphia—and then, in the spring of '97, he would be free. It is easy to see how jealously he measured out the time left to him—he was sixty-four—compared to all he still wanted to do.

"Let the house in the Upper Garden, called the School house, be cleaned and got in order against I return," he wrote Pearce. "Glass put in the windows if wanted; and a lock on the door. I cannot yet say with certainty when I shall be able to visit Mount Vernon, but *hope* it will be by, or before the middle of June. Have good meats ready for us by that time; and tell the Gardener I shall expect an abundance of everything in the Gardens; and to see everything in prime order there, and in the Lawns......"

"I have several times spoke concerning a necessary for the Quarter People, at Mansion House; and once or twice shewed Thomas

Green the precise spot to place it, viz., in the drain that leads from the old brick kiln back of the Well, towards the gully leading towards the gate; that having this advantage, the offensive matter might be washed off by the Rain water that collects in the gutter. I wish you would have this done before I come home that the yard of the Quarter may be always clean and Sweet. If the old necessary on the brow of the Hill can be moved with more ease than building one, let it be done, as it is not only useless where it is, but is an eyesore. Order the other two to be well cleaned and kept in good order. During my stay at Mount Vernon I expect much company there, and of the most respectable sort, it would be pleasing to us therefore to find everything in nice order......"

"In a few days after *we* get there, we shall be visited, I expect, by characters of distinction; I could therefore wish that the Gardens, Lawns, and everything else, in and about the Houses, may be got in clean and nice order. If the Gardener needs aid to accomplish as much of this as lyes within his line, let him have it; and let others rake, and scrape up all the trash, of every sort and kind about the houses, and in holes and corners, and throw it all (all I mean that will make dung) into the Stercorary and the rest into the gullied parts of the road, coming up to the House. And as the front gate of the Lawn (by the Ivies) is racked, and scarcely to be opened, I wish you would order a new one (like the old one) to be immediately made, and all the boarding of every kind that was white before, to be painted white again......."

"Let the Rooms in the Servants Hall, above and below, be well cleaned; and have the Beds and bedsteads therein put in order.... Let exactly the same things be done with the Rooms over the Kitchen, as there will be a white Cook with us that will require one of them, and the other may also be wanted for some other Servants, or use..... Tell the Gardener, I shall expect everything that a Garden ought to produce, in the most ample manner........"

"Take care to keep a sufficiency of Oats, and the best of your old Hay on hand. I shall have eight or ten horses of my own *with me*, and there will be *many others* with Visitors...... I perceive Mrs. Washington's Memm. herewith sent contains nearly the same requests that are made in this letter, but I send it notwithstanding........"

He relied on Alexander Hamilton now for consultation and advice, since Madison had been drawn away from him into the Jeffersonian circle. And before he left Philadelphia this time, he wrote and sent off to Hamilton for comment and criticism a draft copy of his Farewell Address.

XXXIV

THEY had been nearly a year away again, when they reached Mount Vernon late in June, '96. Eliza Custis, Harriot Washington, and Howell Lewis had all married in the interim. Bartholomew Dandridge, erratic at best, had apparently just walked out of his secretarial job in Philadelphia, leaving everything at a loose end, driven, it was said, by some private misdemeanor—only to turn up contrite at Mount Vernon in August and be reinstated, though meanwhile George Washington Craik, namesake and protégé of the President, had been lending a hand with the correspondence.

Fanny was dead, and her children were at nearby Walnut Tree Farm in Mrs. Lear's care, which was some consolation to Martha, as the two grandmothers were good friends. Betty Lewis had left Fredericksburg forever, for her house west of the Tidewater, and Washington's old friend William Fitzhugh of Chatham, across the river from Betty's Millbank, had sold his fine brick house because he complained that his many visitors had turned it into a tavern, that hospitality was impoverishing him, and that he could not even afford to feed the horses of his guests—a slight exaggeration, as he built a new house on his Ravensworth plantation west of Alexandria, and maintained another handsome residence on Orinoco Street in town.

This William was the son of the Eagle's Nest Fitzhugh and Lucy Carter, and was about ten years younger than Washington. He was educated at Eton and Oxford where he was a classmate of William Pitt, later Earl of Chatham, for whom he may have named the house he built on the Rappahannock, in the early '60's, probably at the time of his marriage to Ann Randolph of Chatsworth, when Washington was settling down at Mount Vernon. There is surprisingly little mention of Chatham in the Diary, but Washington regretted Fitzhugh's decision to leave the neighborhood of Fredericksburg, and wrote to him, about this time: "I have put my legs oftener under your mahogany at Chatham . . . . . and have enjoyed your good dinners, good wines, and good company more than any other. . . . ." It might have comforted him to know that Fitzhugh's little daughter Mary would grow up to marry Washington Custis, who was now attending Princeton Seminary in the President's hope of better discipline and instruction than the boy had been receiving in the Philadelphia school. The wedding would take place at Chatham, where a close connection was always maintained with the new occupants—and there Fitzhugh's granddaughter Mary Custis would be courted by Robert E. Lee.

They found old Bishop gone from Mount Vernon now, and Davenport, the miller who had been brought from Pennsylvania in '86 to replace the still lamented but too skylarky Robert, also had died inopportunely early this year. "It is an unlucky Circumstance," Pearce wrote Washington, "as it hapened at a time when we had a good head of water and was giting on with Grinding our wheat, but I have put my Son in the Mill with Ben and have kept her going as well as I Could. . . . . His wife and Child will be in a most distressed Situation and what will be done with them I know not. . . . . ." Washington as usual showed compassion to the widow and directed Pearce to aid her to return to her home.

Faithful Billy was aging and tippling; many of the older slaves were dropping away. The children of the 1786 inventory now had grown to usefulness, such as Cyrus, son of Sall the housemaid, a boy suspected of roguery the year before, now at seventeen in training as a waiter in the house. "I would have you stir up the pride of Cyrus," Washington had written Pearce in May, "that he may be the fitter for my purposes against I come home; some time before which . . . . . . I will direct him to be taken into the house and clothes to be made for him. In the meantime get him a strong horn comb and direct him to keep his head well combed, that the hair, or wool, may grow long." Cyrus was apparently a success, as three years later he was one of the several house servants dispatched at a gallop to summon the doctors when Washington's last illness began.

Despite the new gates, and the fresh white paint which had been bestowed as requested, the Mansion House and many of its dependencies were beginning to show the need of repair. Mount Vernon was getting seedy again, as it had done during the war, and time, labor, and money would be needed to bring it back to where he had left it for the first inauguration.

Lafayette, Jr., aged sixteen, and his tutor, M. Frestel, accompanied the Washingtons home for the summer, along with Nelly and Washington Custis, and except for the continued anxiety about his family in France, the President's French namesake seemed happy in his exile.

One of the most distinguished visitors to Mount Vernon that summer was young Benjamin Latrobe, who left in his journal and sketches one of the liveliest records of the household as he found it. He was the son of a Pennsylvania mother and a French Protestant refugee who had met at the Moravian school in Yorkshire, England, in the '50's. His parents were more lately members of the fascinating London circle which surrounded Dr. Johnson and Dr. Charles Burney, the most respected musician and teacher of music in his time. The latter's bluestocking daughter Fanny, whose novel *Evelina* caused a sensation in 1778, considered the musical talents of the Latrobe brothers better than amateur—Benjamin played the clarinet. He had lived a great deal on the Continent, and attended the University of Leipzig, emerging with a command of six languages, including Hebrew—and then chose architecture as a profession. He married an English girl and she died in childbirth in '93, just as the war with France discouraged building in England. Sensitive and highly strung, Latrobe went into a nervous breakdown, and when he recovered sailed for America, hoping to leave sorrow and the French Terror behind him.

He landed at Norfolk in March of '96, and travelled on through Williamsburg, Richmond and Petersburg, forming friendships with Bushrod Washington and his in-laws, the Blackburns of Rippon Lodge, and with Howell Lewis, who introduced him to the Petersburg races. Latrobe came inevitably to Mount Vernon, where he was of course cordially received. He was just past thirty, taller even than Washington, with dark wavy hair, an animated face, and great personal charm. He had travelled, and had stories to tell, and told them well. He knew London, and the most interesting people there. He was naturalist enough to appreciate the novel surroundings of Virginia, and to lead Washington on about his agricultural experiments and problems. He was an enchanting guest, and the family responded warmly to his enthusiasm for everything he saw.

His account of the visit began with a detailed rapture over the approach to the house and the view it commanded—"the good fences, clean grounds, and extensive cultivation, strike the eye as something uncommon in this part of the world, but the road is bad enough." To his European architect's eye the house itself "has no very striking appearance, though superior to every other house I have seen here."

"Having alighted at Mount Vernon," his Journal continued, "I sent in my letter of introduction and walked into the portico next to the River. In about ten minutes the President came to me. He was attired in a plain blue coat, his hair dressed and powdered. He shook me by the hand and desired me to sit down." It was a hot mid-July day. The conversation in the portico lasted about an hour and concerned the Bushrod Washingtons and their proposed journey to Berkeley Springs (now fashionably known as Bath) probably undertaken for the sake of Mrs. Washington's health, which since the death of her idolized sister was always frail. At the end of that time Latrobe rose to take his departure, but the President urged him "in a manner very like Dr. Johnson's" to remain, and the talk turned to affairs in England and Latrobe's object in coming to America, where he hoped to find employment as an architect. It developed that Washington was acquainted, perhaps from the war years, with Latrobe's mother's family in Pennsylvania.

When the President excused himself to finish some letters for the post, after inviting his guest to stay to dinner, Latrobe strolled about the grounds and made some sketches. Returning to the hall, he found Martha and Nelly there, and introduced himself as a friend of Bushrod's, whereupon Martha conversed about the members of her family "in a good-humored, free manner that was extremely pleasing and flattering. She retains strong remains of considerable beauty, seems to enjoy very good health, and to have a good humor. She has no affectation of superiority in the slightest degree, but acts completely in the character of the mistress of a respectable and opulent country gentleman."

George Washington Parke Custis is absent from Latrobe's narrative, doubtless on a visit to Hope Park or New Kent County. As to Nelly Custis, Latrobe was apparently very much smitten at sight. "Her granddaughter, Miss Eleanor Custis, the only one of four (sic) who is unmarried, has more perfection of form, of expression, of color, of softness, and of firmness of mind than I have ever seen before or conceived consistent with mortality," he wrote. "She is everything that the chisel of Phidias aimed at but could not reach, and the soul beaming through the countenance and glowing in her smile is as superior to her face as mind is to matter." Coming from so experienced and much-travelled a young man as Benjamin Latrobe, this is high praise. It is noticeable in the sketches he made of a family group on the portico that seventeen-year-old Nelly wore the new high-waisted classic gown in the latest Parisian style, with her dark hair in ringlets, while Martha dressed as she always had done, in full panniered skirts and an elaborate cap on a high, powdered coiffure.

"Young Lafayette with his tutor came down some time before dinner," Latrobe goes on. "He is a young man about seventeen, of a mild, pleasant countenance, favorably impressing one at first sight. His figure is rather awkward. His manners are easy, and he has very little of the usual French air about him. He talked much, especially with Miss Custis, and seemed to possess wit and fluency. .....Dinner was served about half after three. It had been postponed a half hour in hopes of Mr. Lear's arrival from Alexandria. .....There was very little conversation at dinner. A few jokes passed between the President and young Lafayette, whom he treated more as a child than as a guest. I felt a little embarrassed at the silent, reserved air that prevailed. As I drank no wine, and the President drank only three glasses, the party soon returned to the portico. Mr. Lear, Mr. Dandridge, and Mr. Lear's three boys soon after arrived and helped out the conversation. The President retired in about three quarters of an hour."

Latrobe's second move toward departure was again overruled with an invitation to stay the night. Coffee was served about six o'clock, when the President returned and discussed the crops in the country through which Latrobe had passed, gave an account of the Hessian fly, which was working down through Maryland from Long Island, explained the advantages of Indian corn as a diet for laborers, and went into the merits of several kinds of plow. Everyone retired early, and the visitor recorded with some surprise that no supper was served.

He rose with the sun and walked about the grounds, making his sketches, noting the boxwood planting in front of the greenhouse, still unusual in America, though Gunston had a remarkable display, and Latrobe considered it already outmoded: "On one side of this lawn is a plain kitchen garden," he wrote, "on the other a neat flower garden laid out in squares, and boxed with great precision. Along the north wall of this garden is a plain greenhouse. The plants were arranged in front and contained nothing very rare, nor were they numerous. For the first time since I left Germany I saw here a parterre clipped and trimmed with infinite care into the form of a richly flourished fleur-de-lis, the expiring groans, I hope, of our grandfathers' pedantry." Nowadays the parterre and hedges are kept equally well pruned and the rooted cuttings are preserved, so that it is possible for the visitor to bring away a living link with Washington and Lighthorse Harry Lee, who first sent the cuttings to Washington from Stratford ten years before.

Latrobe continued his account when Washington appeared about half past seven and breakfast was served "in the usual Virginia style —tea, coffee, and cold broiled meats"—and after the meal his host stood talking for a while on the steps of the west front. About ten o'clock Latrobe took his leave. "Washington had something uncommonly majestic and commanding in his walk, his address, his figure, and his countenance," he wrote in his Journal, reviewing his visit. "His face was characterized, however, more by intensive thought than by quick and fiery conception. There is a mildness about its expression, an air of reserve in his manner lowers its tone still more. He is sixty-four, and has sufficient apparent vigor to last many years yet. He was frequently entirely silent for many minutes, during which time an awkwardness seemed to prevail in everyone present. His answers were often short and sometimes approached to moroseness. He did not at any time speak with remarkable fluency. Perhaps the extreme correctness of his language, which almost seemed studied, prevented that effect. He appeared to enjoy a humorous observation, and made several himself. He laughed heartily several times, in a very good humored manner. On the morning of my departure he treated me as if I had lived many years in his house, with ease and attention, but I thought there was a slight air of moroseness about him, as though something had vexed him."

Washington's preoccupation may have had to do with the situation in France, where the American ambassador James Monroe was not giving satisfaction, and which soon necessitated another hurried journey to Philadelphia in the middle of his holiday, as had occurred the summer before. Latrobe was not the only guest to comment on Washington's silences, which may have been simply abstraction due to the many problems which weighed upon him, and here again is an indication of what may have been the same hesitation in his speech mentioned by Olney Winsor in '88.

Returning to Richmond, Latrobe completed his sketches of Mount Vernon and sent to the Bushrod Washingtons a delightful watercolor of the family group on the piazza. He settled in America and became one of several architects employed in the creation of the new Federal City which was named for the first president; caught Jefferson's fancy, was painted by Peale, and made a happy second marriage with a Philadelphia girl, who encouraged him to bring out from England the children by his first wife—whose daughter married a Roosevelt.

The summer was saddened by the death of Lund Washington at Hayfield, leaving his widow childless and in poor health. At Mount Vernon, manager Pearce was increasingly crippled by rheumatism, found himself unable to continue his duties according to his conscientious ideas of how they should be done, and talked of retirement to his Maryland farm. During his flying trip to Philadelphia in August Washington dined with his old friend and aide, Colonel Fitzgerald, at Alexandria, and from him heard of a man named Anderson who might be suitable in Pearce's place. Washington wrote to him at once, and after he returned to Mount Vernon Anderson came there for an interview, which resulted in a contract signed in October for him to take charge beginning with the new year.

When the Washingtons arrived back in Philadelphia for the winter of '96-7 the first contested Presidential campaign had begun—the chief candidates were John Adams and Thomas Jefferson—and the months which lay between then and the inauguration of his successor could now be counted on the fingers of one hand.

His letters to Pearce during that last winter away—the coldest in many years—were often concerned with information required to aid him in selecting the things he wished to bring home with him to Mount Vernon; the dimensions of the window frames on the west front, for new shutters; the pitch of the bedroom, from floor to ceiling; the length and breadth of the blue parlor, for a new carpet; as well as the usual admonitions about filling the ice-house, killing and salting the pork, getting up shelters for the cattle, and completing the new road. He also enclosed a certificate of highest praise for the services rendered by Pearce at Mount Vernon, and gave him the best of characters.

Now that the Harewood boys and Harriot were off his hands, the still younger set at Mount Vernon continued to harass him with their educational problems. "Washington Custis has got settled at Princeton College," he wrote Lear in November, "and I think under favorable auspices, but the change from his former habits is so great and sudden; and his hours for study so much increased beyond what he has been accustomed to, that though he promises to be attentive, it is easy to be perceived he is not at all reconciled to it yet. That of getting up an hour before day, to commence them, is, I will venture to pronounce, not the least irksome to him, at present."

It must have carried him back nearly a quarter of a century to find himself writing to Jacky's son the same admonitions which had so seldom adhered to Jacky during his Annapolis schooldays and his brief career at King's College. "You are now extending into that stage of life when good or bad habits are formed," he wrote in November from Philadelphia. "When the mind will be turned to things useful and praiseworthy or to dissipation and vice. Fix on whichever it may, it will stick by you; for you know it has been said, and truly, 'that as the twig is bent so it will grow'..... 'Tis well to be on good terms with all your fellow students, and I am pleased to hear you are so, but while a courteous behavior is due to all, select the most deserving only for your friendships, and before this becomes intimate, weigh their dispositions and character *well.* True friendship is a plant of slow growth; to be sincere, there must be congeniality of temper and pursuits..... Keep in mind that scarcely any change would be agreeable to you at *first* from the sudden transition, and from never having been accustomed to shift or rough it. And moreover, that if you meet with collegiate fare, it will be unmanly to complain..... P.S. I presume you received my letter covering a ten-dollar bill to pay for your gown, although it is not mentioned. To acknowledge the receipt of letters is always proper, to remove doubts of their miscarriage....."

He was at the same time concerned about Maria Washington, orphan daughter of Fanny and George Augustine, who after reaching the age of eight years under Fanny's lax and disorganized upbringing was proving too much of a handful for the elder Mrs. Lear, to whom Martha wrote in November, from Philadelphia:

"....As soon as we came to town the President sent Mr. Dandridge to enquire of the minister of the Moravian Church–if he could get Maria into the school at Bethlehem–I am sorry to tell you that his answer was that the school was full–so that it would be some time before she could be taken in–The President says he will write to Bethlehem and endeavour if its possible to get her in–if not–Mr. Lear, I think, would do well to send her to her uncle [Burwell Bassett II] till something better could be done for her–we cannot take the child in hear, our Family is large–and I could not pay the attention to Maria as I think would be necessary to such a child as she is–I have been told there is a very good bording school in Georgetown–if Maria was put to bord with Mrs. Smith, she might mannage her if she was put under her particular care and stayed with her altogether, which the President and myself think would be very much for the childs advantage.

"I was extremely sorry to be told after Maria went from Mr. Laws–how ill she had behaved to you; had I known it before I should have reprimanded her very seriously–she has always been a spoiled child–as indeed they were all–the Boys are more in Mr. Lear's way to mannage than a girl–I wish something may be done with her for her advantage. I loved the childs mother and I love her–it gives me pain to think that a child as circumstanced as she is should not have a disposition to make herself friends—her youth will plead for her.

"I have the pleasure to tell you that we had a very agreable journey hear, the weather was fine all the way, we arrived on Monday—take our compliments to Mr. Lear—and love to the Children—Nelly joins me in love and good wishes for you. . . . ."

As a result of Washington's intercession, the Dutch clergyman who ran the school consented to receive Maria in the spring, along with her cousin Milly Ball, daughter of George Augustine's sister Frances, who was to accompany her. In a letter to Lear which expressed a fervent hope that both the girls had had small-pox and measles and were therefore immune, the Reverend Mr. Van Vleck enclosed a list of the sundries his pupils were expected to bring with them.

"1 Double blanket (the rest of the bedding being found here)
1 Morning Gown
4-6 frocks
6 Pocket Handkerchiefs
6 Neck cloaths or handkecfs or Van Dykes [fichus?]
4 Night Caps
1 yd of Cambric for day-Caps
2 check aprons
2 Short Gowns
6 Shifts
3 Pockets
4 Towels
4 Napkins
1 Piece of Silk {pink / rose} Ribbon
2 Shawls
Table spoon, knife & fork, Cups & Saucers, Tea Spoon, Sugar box, &c.
Combs, tooth brushes
1 Slate
a Bible"

Music and needlework were extra. A school which considered pink ribbon a basic requirement would surely exert a beneficent influence over the most unruly girl child, but Maria never attended it. She was living with her aunt Mildred Hammond, another of her father's sisters, when she developed symptoms of what was feared to be the fatal consumption which was the family dread, and before the time came for her to be admitted to the school Washington wrote to thank the Reverend Mr. Van Vleck, and express his regrets for both girls. Maria grew up, however, to marry a Thornton, by whom she had several children.

John Adams, that prickly, outspoken, ambitious, but honorable man, won the Presidency by the narrow margin of three votes, and Thomas Jefferson, with the next highest number of votes, returned to public life from Monticello to act as vice-president—a combination which many thought might prove explosive in itself. The closing weeks of Washington's administration became emotional with farewells, and he was lionized almost to the danger of his habitual self-possession. Lear and young Dandridge were in charge of the final packing up and the distribution of remembrances to Philadelphia friends. In anticipation of more leisure to come, Washington resumed his daily Diary in January of '97, though at first it was little more than a record of his unflagging interest in the weather, and it even passed over the momentous day of John Adams's inauguration on March 4th with an exasperating entry of only twelve words: "Much such a day as yesterday in all respects. Mercury at 41." Yet this was the day he had walked alone, as a private citizen, wearing black velvet and with his hair powdered, to the Congress Hall to see his successor sworn in. The crowds through which he passed were strangely quiet, and some people wept.

On the 9th he wrote: "Wind changed to No. Wt. blew very hard and turned very cold. Mer: at 28; left Phila. on my return to Mt. Vernon, dined at Chester and lodged at Wilmington." One can only guess at the inner exultation behind the few sparse words. He was going home.

Young Lafayette and his tutor were still members of his household, and were to remain at Mount Vernon as his guests until the situation in France was clarified and the fate of the Marquis was known. Washington Custis was at Princeton, Dandridge and Lear were left behind in Philadelphia to see to the odds and ends. Nelly and Martha rode in the coach, and there was a cavalcade of baggage carts with maids and cooks, and the valet Christopher who had succeeded to Billy's duties. They travelled through a snowstorm to Baltimore, where they were met by a troop of horse and thundering huzzas from the crowd, and had to listen to an address by the Mayor and City Council. At Georgetown they dined with Eliza and Thomas Law, who were living luxuriously, and spent the night at Patty and Thomas Peter's more modest establishment.

On the 15th: "Recd. the Compliments of the Citizens of George Town as I had done the day before of those of the City of Washington, stopped in Alexandria, and got to Mt. V. to dinner."

On the 16th: "At home all day alone. Wind at East and very Cloudy all day."

But for him the sky was bright.

XXXV

HE had written to his nephew Robert Lewis during the previous summer that once he had completed his second term in March of '97 and returned to Mount Vernon "no consideration under heaven, that I can foresee, shall again with draw me from the walks of private life." Now at least he could settle in with a feeling of permanence. There was much to be done, and a new manager to make acquaintance with.

His correspondence with Pearce's successor, James Anderson, had begun in January, during the final weeks in Philadelphia. "There is nothing that fills my mind with more apprehension when I am from home than fire," he wrote during that month. "I request therefore that every charge and every precaution against the bad effects of it may be given and used during my absence, to guard against the danger of it. With this you will receive a box containing eggs of the silkworm, and a paper of grape seeds, which give to the gardener. The latter he will plant. The other I suppose he will know how to manage..... P.S. Mrs. Washington requests that you or Mrs. Anderson will pay particular attention to the bacon."

It may have been due to his Scottish ancestry that Anderson's first recommendation had been to establish a distillery in the cooper's shop at the Dogue Run mill. Washington replied that he had no objection, except that it should not be in the vicinity of the mill, where idlers and thieves could find a pretext to congregate by bringing in their grist; and he provided detailed instructions for the erection of such a building near what used to be the ferry landing. "The Potatoes and Turnips necessary for your own Table," he added, "you are very welcome to, without charging yourself for them."

His immediate concern in the spring of '97 was repairs. When Lear forwarded the bill of lading for the goods coming round by water from Philadelphia in the sloop—97 boxes, 14 trunks, 43 casks, 13 packages, 3 hampers, and a large number of "other things"—Washington wrote: "I have got Painters at work in order to prepare my rooms for the furniture which is expected; but I find I have begun at the wrong end, for some joiners work..... ought to have preceded theirs, as the fixing of the chimney pieces ought also to do..... The work *immediately* foreseen, and which must be done without delay, is, to refix the marble chimney piece in the Parlour, which is almost falling out; to fix the New one (expected from Philadelphia) in the small dining-room; to remove the one *now* there into what is called the School room; to fix the Grate which is coming round in the large dining-room; and to give some repairs to the steps; which (like most things else I have looked into since I have been at home) are sadly out of repair....."

To Washington Custis at Princeton, who was looking forward to a summer's escape from schooling, he wrote in April: "We are all in a litter and dirt, occasioned by joiners, masons, and painters, working in the house, all parts of which, as well as the outbuildings, I find upon examination to be exceedingly out of repairs...."

And to the Secretary of War, who was his old aide, James McHenry of Baltimore: "We got home without accident, and found the Roads drier, and better than I ever travelled them at that Season of the year......Mrs. Washington took a violent cold in Philadelphia, which hangs upon her still but not as bad as it did. I find myself in the situation, nearly, of a young beginner; for although I have not houses to build (except one, which I must erect for the accommodation and security of my Military, Civil, and private Papers which are voluminous, and may be interesting) yet I have not one or scarcely anything else about me that does not require considerable repairs. In a word I am already surrounded by Joiners, Masons, Painters, &ca. &ca. and such is my anxiety to get out of their hands, that I have scarcely a room to put a friend into or to set in myself, without the Music of hammers, or the odoriferous smell of Paint."

His orders to Biddle were resumed, for such things as picture frames—nineteen of them, with glass—Morse's *Gazeteer of America*, and something called Unguent Dalamere—4 dollars worth.

His homecoming had been blighted by the death of his sister Betty at her western home—but even now, in what may have been his keenest loss, his classic resignation to mortality is obvious in his letter to her son George on receipt of the news. Only Charles at Happy Retreat, the dimmest figure of all the Washingtons, was now left of George's generation.

He felt the gaps in his old circle, and perhaps his own childlessness, and the lack of an heir to Mount Vernon who had grown up to love and cherish it as he did. George Augustine had come the closest, but both he and Fanny were gone now, and their children were too small. Bushrod, son of John Augustine, was a successful, respected lawyer—and childless too. He would be appointed judge of the Supreme Court within a year, at the age of thirty-six. Washington was able to be proud of Bushrod, whose private life was spent in the twilight of his wife's increasing ill health, reading novels aloud to her in the patient evenings, fond of music, temperate, and mild of manner. It was to Bushrod he would finally entrust Mount Vernon.

Washington had returned to his own vine and fig-tree—the phrase recurred in his correspondence now as it had done at the end of the war—but the shadows were growing longer. He missed the youth and devotion of his aides and secretaries again, and turned back in his mind to old friendships. David Humphreys, the jolliest of them all, the most congenial, and the cheekiest, was now Minister Plenipotentiary to Madrid—seven years, since they had parted from Humphreys at Philadelphia. In a spasm of nostalgia, Washington wrote to him, suggesting that when he returned to America he would be most welcome at Mount Vernon, adding a wistful reference to his "desire of a companion for my latter days, in whom I could confide." The answer might have been expected—Humphreys was on the eve of matrimony with the daughter of an English banker at Lisbon, and had no immediate intention of leaving Europe. There remained but to wish him happiness.

Of the other aides, Robert Hanson Harrison, who used to come to dinner in the '80's with his maiden daughters, and Tilghman, a willing correspondent and agent at Baltimore, were both dead.

McHenry was in full career as Secretary at War to President John Adams, and Edmund Randolph, estranged and bitter, was trying to make a living for an invalid wife and family with a law practice at Williamsburg. Hamilton—Hamilton was only for Hamilton, pursuing his political career with a covetous eye on the Presidency. Fitzgerald, always like a rock, was still in business at Alexandria, and Lear would be in and out from Georgetown to Walnut Tree Farm, where his children were, but it was not quite like the old days when he lived under Mount Vernon's roof. Young Dandridge had accepted with Washington's blessing a job with a diplomatic mission to the Hague. "The career of life on which you are now entering will present new Scenes and frequent opportunities for the improvement of a mind desirous of obtaining useful knowledge," Washington wrote to him. "But I am sure you will never forget that, without Virtue and without integrity the finest talents or the most brilliant accomplishments can never gain the respect or conciliate the esteem of the truly valuable part of mankind."

It is not to be suggested that Washington gave himself time to repine. Writing to McHenry again in May, for their war-time friendship had been renewed with McHenry's entry into national politics during the Presidency, and he was always a favorite correspondent, Washington gave an account of himself which could hardly be better:

"I am indebted to you for several unacknowledged letters; but ne'er mind that; go on as if you had them. You are at the source of information, and can find many things to relate; while I have nothing to say, that could either inform or amuse a Secretary of War in Philadelphia.

"I might tell him that I begin my diurnal course with the Sun; that if my hirelings are not in their places at that time I send them messages expressive of my sorrow for their indisposition; then having put these wheels in motion, I examine the state of things further; and the more they are probed, the deeper I find the wounds are which my buildings have sustained by an absence and neglect of eight years; by the time I have accomplished these matters, breakfast (a little after seven O'clock, about the time I presume you are taking leave of Mrs. McHenry) is ready. This over, I mount my horse and ride round my farms, which employs me until it is time to dress for dinner; at which I rarely miss seeing strange faces; come, as they say, out of respect to me. Pray, would not the word curiosity answer as well? and how different this, from having a few social friends at a cheerful board? The usual time of sitting at Table; a walk, and Tea, brings me within the dawn of Candlelight; previous to which, if not prevented by company, I resolve that, as soon as the glimmering taper supplies the place of the great luminary, I will retire to my writing Table and acknowledge the letters I have received; but when the lights are brought, I feel tired, and disinclined to engage in this work, conceiving that the next night will do as well: the next comes, and with it the same causes for postponement, and effect, and so on.

"This will account for *your* letter remaining so long unacknowledged; and having given you the history of a day, it will serve for a year; and I am persuaded you will not require a second edition of it; but it may strike you that in this detail no mention is made of any portion of time allotted for reading; the remark would be just, for I have not looked into a book since I came home, nor shall I be able to do it until I have discharged my Workmen; probably not before the nights grow longer; when possibly I may be looking in doomsday book. On the score of the plated ware in your possession I will say more in a future letter. At present I shall only add, that I am always and affectionately yours....."

The Diary for the first half of 1797 is even briefer than was customary with him. It notes trips to Alexandria and Georgetown, and visitors from the same places—Dr. Stuart, Lawrence Washington of King George County, the Blackburns, assorted Lees and Fitzhughs—so that at the end of July he wrote to Lear: "I am alone at *present*, and shall be glad to see you this evening. Unless some one pops in, unexpectedly—Mrs. Washington and myself will do what I believe has not been done within the last twenty years by us —that is to set down to dinner by ourselves." (He had made almost the same entry in June, '85, when the war had been over for two years.) Lear was there briefly a fortnight later, and doubtless made many unrecorded calls from his nearby house at Walnut Tree Farm that summer.

One of the more exotic visitors this year was that French royal émigré Louis Philippe, whose spotty career included also the titles of Duc de Valois, Duc de Chartres, and Duc d'Orleans, and who in 1830 was to become—by proclamation—the "Citizen King" of France for eighteen years. Driven into exile again by the revolution of 1848, he would find refuge at Claremont in England, the house placed at his disposal by Queen Victoria—who wrote that he "in great as well as in small things took a pleasure in being cleverer and more cunning than others, often when there was no advantage to be gained by it." He died at Claremont at the age of seventy-seven under yet another alias, as the Comte de Neuilly.

At Mount Vernon in 1797 however he was a romantic-seeming wanderer of twenty-four, his father Philippe Egalité recently dead on the guillotine, himself ostentatiously republican in his views. He wrote home prophetically to his sister: "I love this nation; it will perhaps one day be a powerful ally of ours." He had been introduced to Washington in Philadelphia at the time of President Adams's inauguration, heard the Farewell Address delivered, and was invited to visit Mount Vernon.

He was particularly interested, as were most European travellers, in the institution of slavery, and recorded that Washington had forbidden the use of the whip on his lands. He was also impressed by the President's early rising and the long hours he spent in the saddle on his rounds of the plantation. When Louis Philippe's party left Mount Vernon—travelling on horseback—to continue their tour, they carried a map on which Washington had traced in red a route leading by way of Harper's Ferry to George Steptoe Washington's Harewood, and on to Winchester.

Betty's son Lawrence Lewis had not married again when it was rumored in '93 that he would. Now a highly presentable childless widower turning thirty, he lived in Fauquier County, almost the only unencumbered relative or friend remaining, and Washington wrote to him offering a position in the Mount Vernon household similar to that which he had had in mind for Humphreys—a companion and deputy host, some one to confide in, some one to count on, and in this case, some one of the blood. Lawrence accepted, and Washington wrote: "Whenever it is convenient to you to make this place your home I shall be glad to see you at it for that purpose, and that there may be no misunderstanding in the matter, I shall inform you beforehand that you, servant, (if you have one) and horses, will fare in all respects as we and mine do, but that I shall expect no Services from .you for which pecuniary compensation will be made. I have already as many on wages as are sufficient to carry on my business, and more indeed than I can find means to pay, conveniently....."

Lawrence arrived at Mount Vernon in the late summer of '97, a tall, commanding figure who was thought to resemble his uncle more than any of the other nephews, which might account for the attraction which soon existed between him and Nelly Custis, who was always the General's darling.

Another nephew, Samuel Washington, younger son of Charles and brother to the late George Augustine, about the same age as Lawrence Lewis, received one of Washington's thundering lectures to the younger generation, when he asked for a loan. Washington's reply reveals with a touching frankness the low state of his own finances. "I perceive by your letter of the 7th instant that you are under the same mistake that many others are, in supposing that I have money always at Command," he wrote. "The case is so much the reverse of it, that I found it expedient before I retired from public life to sell all my Lands (near 5000 acres) in Pennsylvania in the Counties of Washington and Fayette, and my lands in the Great Dismal Swamp in Virginia, in order to enable me to defray the expenses of my station and to raise money for other purposes. That these lands might not go at too low a rate (for they sold much below their value) I was induced after receiving prompt payment for part, to allow credit for the remainder, of the purchase money, in obtaining payment of which from two of the purchasers, I find much difficulty; but a third having within these few days paid me an installment of three thousand Dollars, I will rather than you should be compelled to sell your land, lend you a third of them, altho' it will be inconvenient for me to do so; and may be the means of retarding my purchase of wheat for my mill: which for want of it, has been very unproductive to me for several years; I might indeed say an expense to me. It is because you have assured me that misfortunes have brought on your present difficulties...... and because I have heard that you are industrious and sober, that I put myself to the inconvenience of parting with the above sum; . . . . . for you may be assured that there is no practice more dangerous than of borrowing money (instance as proof the case of your father and uncles) for when money can be had in this way, repayment is seldom thought of in time; the interest becomes a moth; exertions to raise it by dint of industry ceases, it comes easy and is spent freely; and many things indulged in that would never be thought of, if to be purchased by the sweat of the brow; in the mean time the debt is accumulating like a Snow ball in rolling. . . . . ."

Only a short time later, Lear, whose bank balance had sunk to $98, asked for a loan of $3000, which Washington had to refuse as being "more than I have in the Bank of Alexandria, and (for running calls) in my Desk." But Lear got another thousand from his dwindling fund, and in neither case would Washington accept interest, as the money was not lent, he wrote, "on usury." Lear was at this time establishing a permanent home at Walnut Tree Farm for his children.

Washington Custis continued to go from one schoolboy scrape to another, and in May of '97 Washington was writing to Princeton's Reverend Samuel Stanhope Smith much as he had written years before to Boucher at Annapolis: "From his infancy I have discovered an almost unconquerable disposition to indolence in everything that did not tend to his amusements; and have exhorted him in the most parental and friendly manner often, to devote his time to more useful pursuits. . . . . . In short I could say nothing to him now by way of admonition, encouragement, or advice, that has not been repeated over and over again. . . . . ." Young Custis wrote abject repentance, and Washington replied that his misdeeds should be kept a secret from all but his grandmother and his sister. Again in October Washington wrote darkly to Smith expressing regret at "the conduct and behaviour of young Custis. And as you have seen in a degree what my solicitude, advice and admonition have been, he will have himself only to upbraid for any consequence which may follow, and this perhaps may come too late." The rest is veiled in discretion and mystery.

Both Eliza Custis Law and Patty Custis Peter visited Mount Vernon that summer with their husbands and babies. Eliza had a daughter named for herself, and Patty by the end of the year had two. The constant entertaining and supervision of extra meals and service had begun to tire Martha, especially as the housekeeping routine had been deranged by the loss of Hercules—"Uncle Harklas" was a character, who became so inflated by his association with the President's household in Philadelphia that he would rig himself out in dandified clothes and parade through the streets to be admired by the lesser breeds. Life at Mount Vernon after Washington's retirement there had proved too dull for Hercules and he decamped, presumably back to Philadelphia. "The running off of my Cook has been a most inconvenient thing to this family," Washington wrote to George Lewis, "and what renders it more disagreeable is, that I had resolved never to become the Master of another Slave by *purchase;* but this resolution I fear I must break. I have endeavoured to hire black or white, but am not yet supplied. . . . ."

At the same time he turned again to the competent Bushrod at Richmond, requesting him to negotiate for a Mrs. Forbes who had recently been housekeeper to Governor Brooke. "Your aunt's distresses for want of a good housekeeper are such as to render the wages demanded by Mrs. Forbes (though unusually high) of no consideration," he wrote, "and we must, though very reluctantly, yield to the time she requires to prepare for her fixture here. We wish, however, that it might be shortened."

There followed a very comprehensive list of queries about a candidate they had already accepted, which reveals once more Washington's unflagging attention to detail in the organization of his estate: "Among other things it would be satisfactory to know—What country woman she is? Whether Widow or Wife? if the latter, Where her husband is? What family she has? What her age is? Of what temper? Whether active and spirited in the execution of her business? Whether sober and honest? Whether much knowledge in Cookery, and understands ordering and setting out a Table? What her appearance is? With other matters which may occur to you to ask, and necessary for me to know. Mrs. Forbes will have a warm, decent, and comfortable room to herself, to lodge in; and will eat of the Victuals from our Table, but not set at it, at any time *with us*, be her appearance what it may; for if this was *once admitted*, no line satisfactory to either party, perhaps, could be drawn thereafter. . . . . . Is it practicable do you think to get a good and well disposed Negro Cook, on hire, or purchase? Mention this want of ours to Mrs. Forbes. She, from the interest she would have therein might make inquiry......"

Bushrod's reply describes something no less than a jewel, and once Mrs. Forbes arrived at Mount Vernon in December she remained there for the rest of Washington's lifetime. "She is a widow," wrote Bushrod, "a native of England & without a family–about 50 yrs of age......her appearance is decent and respectable & such is her general deportment.–She does not expect to set at table with the family at any time never having been accustom'd to it–she regards not the trouble of cooking herself when necessary....."

There was also a new gardener, lately from Scotland, apparently to replace the Dutchman Ehler–"my old Gardener having left me, as I wished it might happen, about a fortnight before," Washington wrote to the new man's sponsor, Dr. Anderson, who like Arthur Young before him was prominent in English agricultural circles. Spence appeared to him younger than he would have chosen, but "goes to work handily, as one who knew what is to be done. He has deceived you or me, however, with his tale of Matrimony; for he has brought no wife with him, and says it was a *promise only*, of marriage from the Girl you saw; which, ultimately, she would not comply with. I am well satisfied as matters are, and perfectly approve, and thank you for every step you have taken in this business. ......" Washington's preference for unmarried workmen is always noticeable–perhaps because he was always being landed with their dependents.

George Washington Lafayette and his tutor, Felix Frestel, left Mount Vernon in October to return to France via New York, where they were again committed to Hamilton's care until sailing. Washington felt that the rumors of the Marquis's safe arrival at Hamburg after his imprisonment in Austria might be premature, but he gave the young men $300 for travelling expenses and sent by them affectionate letters to the family in France. After unqualified praise for the tutor Frestel, and his young charge, both of whom had endeared themselves to all by a modest and sensible behavior in a somewhat difficult position, Washington added his favorite kind of paragraph, to Lafayette Senior. "With what concerns myself, I shall not take up your time; further than to add, that I have once more retreated to the shades of my own Vine and Fig tree, where I shall remain with best vows for the prosperity of that country for whose happiness I have toiled many years, to establish its Independence—Constitution—& Laws—and for the good of mankind in general, until the days of my sojourment, wch cannot be many, are accomplished . . . . . ."

At the end of this first year of Washington's final retirement Nelly Custis, now eighteen, wrote a long letter to her friend Mrs. Wolcott in Philadelphia, wife of the Connecticut lawyer who was now Secretary of the Treasury. And in Nelly's letter lies preserved, like the fly in amber, the snug world of Mount Vernon as it was that winter—an island of family harmony in the fractious, bickering, unsettled new republic which was finding the pudgy hand of John Adams less firm on the reins than Washington's. "We have spent our summer and autumn very happily here, have in general been blessed with health," Nelly wrote in her fine, running hand, "have had many very agreeable visitors, and are now contentedly seated round our winter fireside, often speaking of and wishing to see again our good friends in Philadelphia, but never regretting its amusements, or a life of ceremony. I stay very much at home, have not been to the city for two or three months. My grandparents, brother, a nephew of the General, and *your humble servant* compose the family at present. I never have a dull or lonesome hour, never find a day too long, indeed the time seems to fly, and I sometimes think the years are much shorter for some time past than they ever were before. . . . ."

Nelly was falling in love with the General's nephew.

XXXVI

THE Diary for '98 showed a very busy social life at Mount Vernon that winter, and neglected the daily work going on outside. Lund's widow came over from Hayfield for the New Year, doubtless ailing and dismal, and "a Mr. Marshall, Music Master" tuned Nelly's harpsichord on January 8th. Lear was often mentioned as dining or lodging over night, as were George Washington Craik, Howell Lewis, and Dr. Stuart. Both Patty Peter and Eliza Law, accompanied by their husbands, brought their new babies for Martha's inspection. Washington dined with the faithful Colonel Fitzgerald at Alexandria, and attended a ball there in honor of his sixty-sixth birthday.

Washington Custis, seventeen, home for the holidays, had obviously not profited by his sojourn at Princeton, and the General in desperation sent him to his mother and step-father at Hope Park, with a letter to Dr. Stuart:

"Washington leaves this today, on a visit to Hope Park, which will afford you an opportunity to examine the progress he has made in the studies he was directed to pursue.

"I can, and I believe do, keep him in his room a certain portion of the 24 hours, but it will be impossible for me to make him attend to his Books, if inclination, on his part, is wanting; nor while I am out, if he chuses to be so too, is it in my power to prevent it. . . . .

"What is to be done with him, I know not. My opinion has always been that the University in Massachusetts [Harvard] would have been the most eligable Seminary to have sent him to, 1st, because it is on a larger Scale than any other; and 2d, because I believe that the habits of the youth there, whether from the discipline of the School, or from the greater attention of the People in general, to morals and a more regular course of life, are less prone to dissipation and debauchery than they are at the Colleges South of it. It may be asked, if this was my opinion, why did I not send him there? the answer is as short, as to me it was weighty, being the only male of his family, and knowing (although it would have been submitted to) that it would have proved a heartrending stroke to have him at that distance...... I have little doubt of his meaning well, but he has not resolution, or exertion enough to act well...."

Still following the unsatisfactory pattern set by Jacky a quarter of a century earlier, the boy was next sent to the College at Annapolis, as the Academy at Alexandria afforded too much opportunity for forming low associations—"With respect to his (Washington's) remaining at this place, I am perfectly satisfied from the experience of the last few months that he has been here, that even under the constant care of a more illumined Preceptor than I am sure there is the least chance of obtaining, he would progress very little; and as the case now is, he will forget what little he does know, so inert is his mind," Washington added in another letter to Stuart, who in March accompanied young Custis to Annapolis and saw him established there.

It was from Annapolis that Custis wrote in April, '98, to report:

"I was somewhat unwell for some time after coming here, owing to the water, but it is entirely removed now. I am going on with the class in college and attending the French master, who is, I believe, very competent. Every week we write dissertations on various subjects, which are both amusing and instructive, and create laudable emulation.

"I am very happily situated, perhaps better than many others; and could a repetition of those sentiments I have always vowed express my gratitude and obligations to you, they should be here expressed; but it is sufficient that they are indelibly engraven on my mind, and can never be erased while the principles on which they are grounded exist. These principles are innate. What could be a greater misfortune to me than your displeasure! What a greater happiness than your confidence!

"I find that young Mr. C. has been at Mount Vernon, and report says, to address my sister. It may be well to subjoin an opinion which I believe is general in this place, viz., that he is a young man of the strictest probity and morals, discreet without closeness, temperate without excess, and modest without vanity; possessed of those amiable qualities and friendship which are so commendable, and with few of the vices of the age. In short, I think it a most desirable match, and wish that it may take place with all my heart."

Young Mr. C. was Charles Carroll, IV, son of the Signer, Charles III, who had vast estates in Maryland where there was a legend that his slaves never quite numbered 1000 because something (like death) always intervened to hold the count to 999. Because of their Catholic faith the Carrolls were educated abroad, and Charles III in his day had been sixteen years absent in Europe and England, during which time he was bitterly disappointed in love by a Miss Baker, who conceivably did not want to come to America. Returning home at twenty-seven, Carroll fell in love with his cousin, Rachel Cooke, who died a month before their marriage was to take place in 1766. Her magnificent imported wedding dress, which was never worn, was carefully preserved in the family. Stricken again, Carroll finally married another cousin, Mary Darnell, who with her widowed mother had been living in the Carroll household for some years. She was nineteen, he was then thirty-one, and he wrote of her at the time: "She really is a sweet-tempered, charming, neat girl—a little too young for me, I confess, but especially as I am of a weak and puny constitution—of a good family, without any money, cheerful, sweet-tempered, virtuous, and sensible." This was young Charles IV's mother.

Washington's friendship with Carroll Senior went back to the easy '70's before the war, when during Jacky Custis's schooldays he had frequently attended the races at Annapolis, where the Carrolls had a town house overlooking Spa Creek. "Dined at Mr. Carroll's and went to the ball," Washington wrote in his Diary in September, '71. Carroll was a delegate to the Continental Congress, and signed the Declaration of Independence as Charles Carroll of Carrollton, a reference to his western lands around Frederick, to ensure his sole responsibility for the act, as there were five Charles Carrolls living at that time, in a genealogical puzzle as complicated as the Lees or the Randolphs.

The association and correspondence between Washington and Carroll continued through the war, when Carroll as a member of the Congressional Committee visited Valley Forge. During the Presidency Carroll was a senator from Maryland, and often dined at Washington's table. Only five years younger than Washington, Carroll outlived him by thirty-three years, and at ninety-five was the last surviving signer of the Declaration.

Like his father, Charles IV was educated abroad, having been sent over in '85 at the age of ten, and returning in '94 with his sister Kitty who had been at school at Liége since the age of eleven. There could have been no objection to his courtship of Nelly, apart from his religion, which would hardly have troubled Washington, but the General's reply to Nelly's officious brother was a thunderbolt directed at any form of gossip concerning the peerless Nelly: "Young Mr. C— came here about a fortnight ago to dinner, and left us next morning after breakfast. If his object was such as you say has been reported, it was not declared here; and therefore, the less said upon the subject, particularly by your sister's friends, the more prudent it will be until the subject develops itself more."

The glamor of young Mr. Carroll's European polish and famous name and fortune apparently had no weight with Nelly, and in 1800, when she was already a mother, he married Harriet Chew, whose home outside Philadelphia had been shot over, around, and into, during the battle of Germantown in '77. She had been one of Washington's favorite young ladies during the Presidency, and had been accustomed to accompany him to the boring sittings for his portrait by Gilbert Stuart in order, they pretended, to keep him awake while the painter worked. The bridegroom's father built for them the brick mansion called Homewood as a wedding gift.

It is unfortunate that the most widely known portrait of Washington was painted late in his life and by a man for whom he felt no friendship, as he had done for Peale, and very little respect, such as he had entertained for Houdon, Pine, and others. Stuart was a showy, dissipated, undisciplined, too-clever man, who was by his own admission incapable of venerating any man, not even his gentle London benefactor, Benjamin West—who said of his pupil in Stuart's early days, "he nails the face to the canvas"—at 30 gns. a head.

As to the figure, Stuart "could not get below the fifth button," having never learned to do line drawing, nor attended the Royal Academy school. But he had a certain trick of likeness. Having caught on in London and Dublin, where he fled to escape his debts, he next appeared in New York and Philadelphia, and became the fashion there. The Jays took him up, and the Binghams, and he set up a studio in Germantown. When General Knox somehow offended him, Stuart with his usual endearing ways used Knox's portrait as a door to his pig-sty, and took care that it was known.

He wanted to paint Washington simply because he knew that he could make money by selling Washington portraits, and later turned out copies of his own originals so fast and carelessly that they came to bear very little resemblance to his first canvas. By the time Washington sat to him in the Germantown studio, Stuart had drunk too much too long, and looked it, and despite his boast that he could talk shop to any subject who came to him, he complained that the minute Washington sat down in the painter's chair "an apathy seemed to seize him, and a vacuity spread over his countenance most appalling to paint." Boredom, to the nth degree. Stuart left a word-picture too: "There were features in his face totally different from what I had observed in any other human being. The sockets of the eyes, for instance, were larger than what I had ever met with before, and the upper part of the nose broader. All his features were indicative of the strongest passions; yet like Socrates his judgment and self-command made him appear a man of different cast in the eyes of the world."

Washington was somehow prevailed upon to sit to Stuart three times, the last at Martha's own request—she never received delivery of the canvas, because on one excuse or another the painter retained it to make his copies from. It was the third, or Athenaeum portrait, at which Harriet Chew assisted, and it was the dull, unperspicacious full-length which Dolley Madison rescued and preserved when the British burned Washington in 1812.

In June, '98, Washington Custis at Annapolis received another well-deserved dressing-down from his step-grandfather:

". . . . . It is now near five weeks since any person of this family has heard from you, though you were requested to write once a fortnight. Knowing how apt your grandmamma is to suspect that you are sick, or that some accident has happened to you, how could you omit this?

"I have said that none of us has heard from you, but it behooves me to add that from persons in Alexandria, lately from Annapolis, I have, with much surprise, been informed of your devoting much time, and paying much attention to a certain young lady of that place. Knowing that conjectures are often substituted for facts, and idle reports are circulated without foundation, we are not disposed to give greater credence to *these* than what arises from a fear that your application to books is not such as it ought to be, and that the hours that might be more profitably employed at your studies are misspent in this manner.

"Recollect again the saying of the wise man, 'There is a time for all things,' and sure I am that this is not the time for *a boy of your age* to enter into engagements which might end in sorrow and repentance. . . . . ."

Custis's reply was swift and rather ungallant, written from Marlborough where he had gone for a penitential meeting with his mother.

"The report, as mamma tells me, of my being *engaged* to the young lady in question, is strictly erroneous. That I gave her reason to believe in my attachment to her, I candidly allow, but that I would *enter into engagements* inconsistent with my duty or situation, I hope your good opinion of me will make you disbelieve. That I stated to her my prospects, duty, and dependence upon the absolute will of my friends, I solemnly affirm. That I solicited her affection, and hoped with the approbation of my family to bring about a union at some future day, I likewise allow. The conditions were not accepted, and my youth being alleged by me as an obstacle to the consummation of my wishes at the present time (which was farthest from my thought) I withdrew, and that on fair and honorable terms, to the satisfaction of my friends.

"Thus the matter ended, and should never have proceeded so far had I not been betrayed by my own feelings. However rash and imprudent I may be, I have always remembered my duty and obligation to you, which is the guide of my actions. . . . . To my mother I disclosed the whole affair. who is now perfectly satisfied. . . . . ."

He was seventeen. Jacky at eighteen had married the girl, and however mistaken his action may have seemed at the time, he looks a little better than his cautious son.

Nothing more is heard about the certain young lady in Annapolis. Washington Custis did not marry till 1804, when he was twenty-three, and his bride Mary Lee Fitzhugh of Chatham and Ravensworth was sixteen. For her he built at ruinous expense the white-columned house he called Arlington on land which was part of his Custis inheritance, near the new Federal City of Washington. It was the only one of their four daughters to survive who became the wife of Robert E. Lee.

Washington's need of a secretary to handle his accounts and correspondence continued, and Lawrence Lewis apparently did not fill the gap. Early in '98 there arrived at Mount Vernon a young man from Hanover County named Albin Rawlins, recommended by the Alexander Spotswood who had married a daughter of Jane and William Augustine Washington. His employer was as always specific about his duties: "That which I have to do would be easy in the execution, but the person must be always at hand and in readiness to perform it; and for so doing I had never contemplated giving more than $100; and for this sum characters have offered knowing that they would have an easy birth, and exposed to little or no expense, Bed, board, and washing being found them, but as they do not write so good a hand as you (presuming the letters I have received from you are of your own penning) I would allow you $150, provided you can bring sufficient testimony (as you are an entire stranger to me) of your Sobriety, integrity, and good dispositions, and provided also that you understand accounts, or could soon acquire a knowledge of them. In my last, I informed you where, and in what manner you would live if you came to me, that is, you would have rooms to yourself, and would eat and drink with my House keeper, who is a very respectable Character......" The duties included copying and recording papers and records, farm accounts, and journeys (expenses paid) on Washington's business to his more distant lands. Rawlins gave satisfaction from the first, and was a trusted member of the household at the time of Washington's death, while a brother of his seems to have acted as one of the overseers, at Union Farm.

A minor crisis in the nursery department emerges from the cryptic Diary early in April, during the visit of the Peter family to Mount Vernon.

"*22.* Doctr. Craik came on a visit to Eleanor Peter. [aged less than two years.]
"*23.* Mr. Peter returned. Sent for.
"*24.* Doctr. Craik came in the afternoon to visit Mr. Peter's children.
"*25.* Doctr. went away after breakfast.
"*26.* The Revd. Mr. Fairfax [Bryan] and Doctr. Craik (to visit Mr. Peter's children) came to dinner. The first returned afterwards.
"*27.* Dr. Craik went away after breakfast, and Mr. and Mrs. Law and a Mr. Ghan, a Swedish Gentleman, came to dinner.
"*29.* Mr. Ghan went away after breakfast.
"*30.* Mr. Law and Mr. Peter went away after breakfast, and Doctr. and Mrs. Craik and Son, Mr. and Mrs. Harrison, and Mrs. Jennifer and a Miss Barnes came to dinner and returned afterwards."

On the 8th of May the Peters and their children left Mount Vernon for their home in Georgetown, with everyone happily recovered.

There is no entry for the 16th of May, but on that day he wrote a long letter to Sally Fairfax in England, to be carried to her by Bryan, who had recently come into the title of Lord Fairfax, Baron Cameron, though he declined to use it. Washington also supplied letters of introduction for Bryan to several of his friends and correspondents in England, among them the American Ambassador, Rufus King, and Sir John Sinclair, the President of the British Board of Agriculture, who had sent Washington a complete set of the works and surveys of the Board, "neatly bound," along with inquiries about American crops and methods—which resulted in another transatlantic correspondence which was later published by Sinclair. "The manner in which the early Wheat (respecting which you inquire) came into this Country is not ascertained," Washington wrote at one time. "The history of it, so far as it has come to my knowledge, I will relate. A Farmer, walking in a field of Wheat when it was in bloom, discovered a plant or two that was perfectly ripe, and carefully separating it from the rest, sowed it at the usual time the following Autumn. From this *small* beginning (abt. seven years ago) this State, and those adjoining, are well in Seed. The grain is white, full, and heavy; weighing, generally, two or three pounds more in the bushel of Winchester measure. It makes excellent flour; and in tight, loamy land inclining to Sand it is said to be more productive of grain and less of Straw than Wheat in common. It is a tender plant, and apt to receive damage, both in the field and Garners. It will not, from report, bear transportation. Of a vessel sent to Philadelphia for Seed, hardly any of it vegitated; and some farmers go so far as to declare, that they are obliged to spread what is intended for Seed, thin on their Barn floors and turn it frequently to prevent the injury above mentioned. From my own experience I can add but little, for as my land is heavy, stiff, and slow, not much of it has been sown; but from the growth of the present year, I send you a sack; that by experimenting you may ascertain the utility of cultivating it in England." And to ensure the safety during the voyage of the precious grain, he had requested the captain of the ship to keep the sack in his cabin.

Such was the substance of these delightful contacts with men he was never to encounter in person, but whose thoughts and interests matched his own. Of Bryan Fairfax, now become so solid a citizen after an irresponsible youth, he wrote: "The integrity of his heart and benevolence of his mind, need only be known to procure him esteem, and as I can vouch for these I shall introduce him to you as a Gentleman worthy of your attention."

The letter to Sally Fairfax which Bryan was to carry with him was full of nostalgia for the lost sunny days of their youth before the war, when the Potomac neighborhood had sparkled with gaiety and well-being. "Five and twenty years, nearly, have passed away since I have considered myself as a permanent resident of this place," he wrote, "or have been in a situation to endulge myself in a familiar intercourse with my friends, by letter or otherwise." It was indeed twenty-three years since he had set out for the Second Congress at Philadelphia, and from there had ridden to Cambridge to begin the long exile of the war. And as he wrote on to Sally, there recurred the old favourite phrase from the Book of Micah about his vine and fig-tree, and the inevitable pessimism, like a crossing of his fingers, with regard to his future life span, and the desire to spend what time remained to him in rural retirement—"I have not been as far as Occoquan these seven years," he added.

He found it hard, in the compass of this long delayed letter, to give her any idea of the changes which had taken place in the scene she once knew so well; but his pen travelled on rather doggedly, in the verbal involutions and curlicues which often decorated his more personal correspondence: "Before the War, and even while it existed, altho' I was eight years from home at one stretch (except the *en passant visits* made to it on my march to and from the Siege of Yorktown) I made considerable additions to my dwelling house, and alterations in my Offices, and Gardens; but the dilapidations occasioned by time and those neglects which are co-extensive with the absence of Proprietors, have occupied as much of my time within the last twelve months in repairing them, as at any former period in the same space, and it is a matter of sore regret, when I cast my eyes towards Belvoir, as I often do, to reflect that the former Inhabitants of it, with whom we lived in such harmony and friendship, no longer reside there; and that the ruins can only be viewed as the memento of former pleasures; and permit me to add, that I have wondered often (your nearest relations being in this Country) that you should not prefer spending the evening of your life among them, rather than close the Sublunary Scene in a foreign Country, numerous as your acquaintance may be, and sincere as the friendships you may have formed......"

He left it to Martha to assemble in a letter of her own the sad toll of time in Alexandria, on the Maryland shore, and the nearer neighborhood, along with the arrival of offspring, particularly among Jacky's children, the babies who if he had lived would have called him grandfather. She made no mention of Jacky's widow, and the growth of her second family by Dr. Stuart—"My Dear Mother has just recovered from her confinement with her twentieth child,"

Nelly Custis wrote to her friend Mrs. Pinckney in 1802; "it is a fine Girl, large and healthy. Mamma has suffered extremely and is still weak. I passed a fortnight with her, and my two eldest single [half-] sisters have been here [Mount Vernon] with us since Christmas."

It was perhaps not surprising that Sally Fairfax had elected to remain at Bath, her beauty gone, her health poor, and her finances low. To return to Virginia alone after George William's death in '87 would have meant living as a dependent in the household of some relative of his or hers with whom she had long since lost touch—for she could hardly have imposed herself as a permanent guest at Mount Vernon, however cordial her welcome, and she had not the funds to make Belvoir livable again. She outlived both George and Martha Washington, and died at Bath in 1811 at the age of eighty-one.

On May 18th, '98, the Diary notes only that "the Horns, or points of the Moon" were upwards. The next day he and Martha set out on a visit to the Stuarts at Hope Park, to the Laws and the Peters in Georgetown, and on to Mount Eagle where they took leave of Bryan and delivered their letters to him for transport to Sally. They were away from home a week, during which time James Anderson sent off to Washington a letter announcing his resignation as manager, written out of a smouldering resentment over Washington's year-end summing up of Anderson's first year's service.

It seems odd that he should have seized this brief opportunity to write his dissatisfaction to his employer but it had probably been apparent for some time and Washington would not have been taken entirely by surprise. Anderson had already proved over-sensitive to anything which might be construed as criticism. "If I cannot remark upon my own business, passing every day under my eyes, without hurting your feelings, I must discontinue my rides, or become a cypher on my own Estate," Washington replied in a letter written during his absence in the Federal City. "You will, I am persuaded, do me the justice to say that I have never undertaken any new thing, or made any material change, or indeed any change at all in the old, without consulting you thereupon; and you must further acknowledge that I have never been tenacious of any matters I have suggested, when you have offered Reasons against the adoption of them. If your feelings have been hurt by my remarks on the bad

Clover Seed that was purchased, I cannot help that; my views and plan have been much more hurt by it..... Two things have appeared very clear to me for sometime past; one, that your attention is too much divided, and called to so many different objects, that notwithstanding your zeal and Industry, with wch I always have been, and still am, perfectly satisfied, some of them must suffer; the other, that my Mill and Distillery, under the uncertainty of Cropping of late years, would, with good management and close attention to them, be found my best and most certain support." And he then proposed at some length that hereafter Anderson should concentrate upon this department, and the fishery work.

Anderson's reply was slow in coming, and Washington learned through Lear that the manager had offered his services, as it were behind his employer's back, to William Fitzhugh of Chatham, who was then establishing his new dwelling place at Ravensworth. Instead of a justifiable resentment of this behavior, Washington merely wrote to Fitzhugh an appraisal of the man he still wished to retain at Mount Vernon—"honest, zealous, and well intentioned..... want of foresight, want of oeconomy...... To these may be added that although he expresses a wish to be governed in *all things;* you can find fault with *nothing* without hurting his feelings; but these do not show themselves in the least kind of indecency or impertinence; on the contrary there is no man more obliging......"

The differences were adjusted again, and Anderson remained at Mount Vernon, with Albin Rawlins and the overseer at River Farm taking over some of the activities which scattered Anderson's attention from the business of the mill and distillery, which was after all his first responsibility. Washington had the last word, in another long summing-up in mid-June: "It is no gratification to me to hurt the feelings of any person living by my observations," he wrote, "but in matters which relate to my *own* concerns I shall most assuredly express at all times my opinion of them....."

During the visit to the Laws at Georgetown, the Washingtons had met at that house the captivating Polish count, Julien Ursyn Niemcewicz, and invited him to Mount Vernon. Niemcewicz was a friend and comrade of Thaddeus Kościuszko, another Pole who like Pulaski had distinguished himself under Washington during the Revolution as a volunteer soldier of fortune. Kościuszko had seen action from

Saratoga to West Point to the Carolinas, and at the end of the war returned to Poland to join the almost perpetual fighting there against the Russian armies of Catherine the Great. At Cracow in '94 he had led a force of peasants armed mainly with scythes, against a Russian army twice their number, and seen the Russians routed. A few months later he was defeated and captured, covered with wounds, in a battle with the combined Russian, Prussian and Austrian armies. Both Kościuszko and Niemcewicz had suffered together a two years' imprisonment at St. Petersburg, until the accession of Czar Paul released them. The legend ran that Paul had endeavored to make some amends to the Polish patriot by returning his sword, which Kościuszko refused with a gesture: "I have no need of a sword. I have no country to defend," he told Paul, and went into permanent exile.

In '97 he and Niemcewicz set out together for America, which Niemcewicz had never seen and about which he must have heard some very tall tales. Homeless, and in bad health from his many wounds, with his fortunes at low ebb, Kościuszko had some high-flown idea of claiming a reward for his services in America all of fifteen years before, and Washington replied cordially to his letter announcing their arrival at Philadelphia: "I pray you to believe that at all times, and under any circumstances, it would make me happy to see you at my last retreat; from which I never expect to be more than twenty miles again."

Kościuszko was apparently prevented by his health from visiting Mount Vernon when his friend Niemcewicz went there in June of '98. He eventually returned to Europe alone, and settled in Switzerland, where he was to die, it is recorded briefly, "in a fall on his horse over a precipice." Niemcewicz, more than ten years younger, handsome, with dashing Continental manners, became the darling of New York society, where the Jays and the Hamiltons made much of him, and he remained to marry a wealthy American widow with Livingston connections in 1880. Seven years later he returned to Poland until another political upheaval there exiled him to England and then to Paris, where he died at an advanced age.

In this summer of '98, just turning forty, he was prepared to hero-worship the one-time American Commander-in-chief, who was all that he expected to see and more. "I sat down beside him,"

Niemcewicz wrote in his journal, of the first meeting with Washington at Mr. Law's house, "I was moved, dumb, and could not look at him enough. It is a majestic face, in which dignity is united with gentleness." Martha, in her middle sixties now, had something very charming about her, he wrote gallantly, and mentioned her "bright eyes" and "gay manner," her white dress and bonnet, and her white braided hair.

A few days later, accompanied by Mr. Law, he rode down to Mount Vernon along the Alexandria road, through rich cornfields and an oak forest and out towards the west front and the green carpet of the bowling lawn. They were greeted by Martha, who served up punch, and at two o'clock the General rode in from making his daily rounds, on a gray horse, which when he had dismounted went on alone to its stable.

While Washington disappeared to change for dinner, Niemcewicz was shown the house, room by room, noting as he went the key of the Bastille in its crystal lantern in the hall, as it is today; the Peale portrait of Washington in his old Virginia militia uniform, and one of "the divine Miss Custis;" the banquet hall, with its beautiful fireplace; the small parlor, where Miss Custis's harpsichord stood; and across the hall he mentioned a downstairs bedroom, the dining-room, and Washington's library. The long open gallery, as he called the piazza, where the family always spent their summer afternoons with their guests as the sun sank behind the house and a lovely lavender reflected light lay over the river, reminded him of Pulawy in Poland. During the afternoon, as though for his benefit, Nelly Custis made an entrance, from a visit to her mother at Hope Park.

"About three o'clock a carriage drawn by two horses, accompanied by a young man on horseback, stopped before the door. A young lady of the most wonderful beauty, closely followed by an elderly attendant, descended. She was one of those celestial beings so rarely produced by nature, sometimes dreamt of by poets and painters, which one cannot see without a feeling of ecstasy. Her sweetness equals her beauty, and that is perfect. She has many accomplishments. She plays on the piano, she sings and designs better than the usual woman of America or even of Europe.

"After dinner we adjourned again to the gallery in order to read newspapers. In the evening General Washington showed us round his garden. It is well cultivated, perfectly kept, and is quite in English style. Different kinds of berries—currants, raspberries, strawberries, gooseberries—a great quantity of peaches and cherries, but much inferior to ours; they are destroyed by robins, blackbirds, and negroes before they are ripe. There are very many beautiful trees: the tulip tree with flowers like the tulips, white with an orange touch at the base; magnolias, with flowers whose scent is almost as strong as the smell of an orange-tree, but not so pleasant; the sweeter scent —the small violet flowers have the pleasantest smell I have ever noticed, a mixture of strawberries and pineapple; the splendid catalpa is not yet in flower; the new Scotland spruce of beautiful dark green, and many other trees and shrubs, covered with flowers of different hues, planted so as to produce the best of color effects. The weeping willows were deprived of their best decoration: the amount of snow was so great last winter that their boughs were broken under its weight.

"The whole plantation, the garden, and the rest prove that a man born with natural taste may guess a beauty without ever having seen its model. The General has never left America; but when one sees his house and his home and his garden it seems as if he had copied the best samples of the grand old homesteads of England.

"At the hour of sunset we saw the General's herd coming home. A superb bull was noticeable, and had cost him some two hundred dollars. We went then to see the donkeys. Lafayette had sent him two stallions, one from Malta, another from Spain, with their females. They are tall and beautiful in their way. The General has about fifty mules, these animals being very good for work."

One hopes that Niemcewicz used the same praise in talking to Washington, for it would have pleased the General to hear that his beloved estate compared favorably with those seen abroad. The next day was Sunday, and he remained in his room, that day being sacred to his correspondence, while Mr. Law went for a ride with Niemcewicz. Eliza Law arrived during the afternoon, with her baby girl. There was no music during the evening, nor even a game of chess—it was Sunday—and everyone retired at nine.

On Monday they rode again, and visited the mill and the distillery. They entered some of the Negroes' huts, which Niemcewicz thought very poor compared to the dwellings of the Polish peasants, but "be it use or natural temper towards gaiety, I never saw negroes sorrowful," he noted. The following morning, Washington rode with them to another of the farms, where they saw a plow of his own invention. "In the middle of the axle a hollow cylinder is fitted. It is filled with corn. When the plow moves, the cylinder turns, and the grain falls in the hollow made by the share. A flat piece placed behind covered the grain with earth. The General is often censured for his reserve and taciturnity," the visitor observed. "It is true that he does not talk much; but he does not avoid conversation when one advances a subject worthy of remark...... At table, after the ladies' departure, or when sitting under the portico, he often talked with me for hours. His favorite subject is agriculture; but he answered with great kindness all the questions put to him on the Revolutionary war, armies, and so on." (The French Revolution could also rouse him, sometimes to heated speech.) "Mrs. Washington," Niemcewicz continued, "is one of the most delightful persons one can meet. Good, sweet, and exceedingly pleasant, she likes to talk and talks well, of old times....... I was considered in this home not as a stranger, but rather as a member of the family. They cared about everything which concerned myself."

And there perhaps we have it, the essence of grace and good manners—to care about the guest's own affairs, to listen, to draw out. Latrobe mentioned that he was treated as though he had lived for many years in their house—Lear writing to Prescott said that he was treated as a child of it. In a state renowned for hospitality, the Washingtons excelled in the not always easy art of putting a stranger at his ease in the family. This was true kindness of heart, genuine good will.

The usual flow of guests continued during Niemcewicz's stay. Besides the Laws, the Stuarts came, with three of their daughters; and the Fitzhughs from Alexandria with a daughter who may have been that Mary who would marry Washington Custis, but was at this time beneath his notice as a child of ten—her sister Ann married Dr. Craik's son William; Mrs. Beverly Randolph and her family—and Mr. Tracy, who was Nelly's music master. Niemcewicz won them all, and Martha presented him with a china cup which bore her initials. Nelly composed his cypher in flowers, and on the evening of the 13th played to him on the harpsichord for the last time.

Next morning he was awakened before sunrise. "Once more I walked around the green woods of Mount Vernon and glanced my last upon the wide, open view, on the waters of the Potomac," he wrote. "At six o'clock, more with silence than with words expressing my gratefulness for the hospitality and my sorrow on leaving that home, I bade farewell to General Washington and his worthy wife and the beautiful Miss Custis. In the company of Mr. and Mrs. Law, as well as their pretty baby daughter, we went back through Alexandria to Georgetown." Another lasting attachment had been formed at Mount Vernon.

Washington's formal reply to the bread-and-butter letter sent back by Niemcewicz from the Federal City contained a few extra flourishes: "The pleasure this family derived from the favour of your company in our retired situation," he wrote, "could only be equalled by the regret we felt at parting with you; and by our wishes if you should again visit this part of the United States, that you would not pass the shades of Mount Vernon without participating in the refreshment of them. . . . . . ."

The gala 4th of July celebration at Alexandria—on the twenty-third anniversary of the Declaration of Independence—was somewhat overhung by the worsening crisis with France under the Directory, arising from what had come to be called the XYZ Mission of Marshall, Gerry, and Pinckney to Paris. Washington attended, to review the parade, wearing full uniform and escorted by a troop of dragoons—listened to the speeches, attended a dinner of five hundred at Spring Gardens—while war with France must have seemed to him wholly fantastic.

But on the 11th he sent his carriage to Alexandria to meet the mail stage and convey James McHenry from there to Mount Vernon. Besides being an old aide and a cherished friend, McHenry was Secretary at War, and he carried a letter to Washington from President Adams. There was little doubt in anyone's mind what it would contain—the unanimous nomination of George Washington to be Commander-in-chief of all the armies raised or to be raised for the service of the United States. The Commission, dated July 4th, was enclosed. Twenty-three years had passed since that hot day in Philadelphia when he had ducked into the library to spare the Congress the embarrassment of his presence in the chamber if anyone had wished to dissent.......

With what a sinking of the heart he must have accepted again, and then laid down his reluctant, jealous stipulations—the actual invasion of our territorial rights—the conviction that it was the country's wish that its military force should be again committed to his charge—and the formation of an army which would be a credit to him in the field *before* he took command.

On the 12th he gave a dinner for McHenry—Fitzgerald, Craik and a son, Ludwell Lee from Shooter's Hill, Colonel Ramsay from Alexandria, Lear, and—surprisingly—Tracy, the music master. When McHenry returned the next day to Philadelphia he was in possession of Washington's personal estimate of the available officers for staff and field duty, surviving from the Revolution—sometimes not altogether flattering to them. The list included the names of Alexander Hamilton, Henry Knox, Harry Lee, and, at the bottom, James Craik as Director of Hospitals.

The mail increased, and the hospitality at Mount Vernon, as the summer wore on.

At the end of the school term, in July, Washington Custis wrote that he had finished the six books of Euclid, thus concluding the course marked out for him at Annapolis, and desired to know if he should pack to leave the College entirely. Again there was a roll of thunder from Washington: "Did I not, before you went to that Seminary, and since by letter, endeavor to fix indelibly on your mind, that the object for which you were sent there was to finish a course of education which you yourself were to derive the benefit of hereafter......"

The Diary notes the boy's return to Mount Vernon on the 5th of August from what after all proved to be his last term at school. On the 13th Washington was writing again in despair to Dr. Stuart: "If you, or Mrs. Stuart, could, by indirect means, discover the State of Washington Custis's mind, it would be to be wished. He appears to me to be moped and Stupid, says nothing, and is always in some hole or corner excluded from Company. Before he left Annapolis, he wrote to me desiring to know whether he was to return there, or not, that he might pack up accordingly; I answered, that I was astonished at the question! and that it appeared to me that nothing that could be said to him had the least effect, or left an impression beyond the moment. Whether this, by thwarting his views, is the cause of his present behaviour I know not. Enclosed is his letter and my answer, to be returned when read. We are as usual; and unite in best regards for you, Mrs. Stuart, and the family......"

Beset by additional duties and worries arising out of the French threat, Washington wrote to McHenry to inquire if his reappointment entitled him to the expenses of a secretary, having in mind, of course, the reliable Lear, "of whose abilities, prudence, and integrity I have received proof near fourteen years *in my own family.....*" Receiving a reply that pay and forage would be allowed to a secretary from the time of his joining the household at Mount Vernon, he then wrote to Lear, whose reply was pretty well predictable. He would come.

Next to a secretary, his need would be for a good horse, and the choice was nearly as weighty and as deserving of minute attention. He wrote to William Fitzhugh, as a good judge of horseflesh, to buy one for him in Alexandria, cash to be paid on delivery. "In age, I should not be willing to exceed Seven years, eight at most, younger, but not under four last Spring would be better; for Colour I would not contend, but would prefer a *Perfect* white, a dapple grey, a deep bay, a chestnut, a black, in the order they are mentioned. The Size and strength must be equal to my weight, which without the saddle may be estimated at 210 lbs. Being long legged, or tall, would be no recommendation; as it adds nothing to strength but a good deal to the inconvenience in mounting. Under my circumstances, I cannot limit you in price; but shall add, that I never expected to be master of a *riding* horse that would cost more than four hundred dollars....."

On the 18th of August Washington was seized with a severe bout of fever, struggled on till the 21st, and then much against his will and custom, called for Dr. Craik, who administered doses of Jesuit's bark, which was quinine. Weakness and loss of weight persisted for nearly a month, before he was himself again, and the illness was without doubt aggravated by his own nervous tension and depression at the prospect of being again called out of his precious retirement.

Lear apparently returned to the household, at the sacrifice of his partnership in business at Georgetown, during the gap in the Diary caused by Washington's illness, as he is mentioned soon after in the capacity of secretary, as well as being in charge of Washington Custis's further education at home.

The old Custis pattern persisted. In September Washington wrote to the head of Annapolis College that although the boy professed readiness to do whatever was required of him, "his unwillingness to return was too apparent to afford any hope that good would result from it in the prosecution of his studies. And therefore, as I have now a gentleman living with me who has abilities adequate thereto, will have sufficient leisure to attend to it, and has promised to do so accordingly, I thought best, upon the whole, to keep him here. . . . ."

As hospitality overflowed, Harriot and Andrew Parks came up from Fredericksburg for a visit of several days, and one hopes that Harriot enjoyed her new status and prestige as a married woman after her old role as mendicant. Her brother, George Steptoe Washington, and his wife Lucy, from Harewood, came to dinner, as did Bryan Fairfax's son Ferdinando and his wife—the younger generation was not as young as it had been.

In spite of his long affection for McHenry, Washington was not oblivious to the inadequacies of his former aide in the responsibilities of his present position as Secretary at War, and the years of friendship with General Knox did not prevent that old soldier from resenting what he considered a subordinate position in the new establishment, in which he was ranked by Alexander Hamilton. Early in November Washington recognized that he could not escape a journey to Philadelphia which might keep him as much as a month from home. Once again he sat down to write out for his manager, this time James Anderson, a detailed plan of what must be accomplished and guarded against during his absence, laying out a separate work sheet for the carpenters, the joiner, and the bricklayers. There was the additional bother of a man named Parkinson's unexpected arrival from England to take tenancy of the River Farm.

Arriving again in Philadelphia, he rode in full uniform through an almost continuous parade of escorts and welcoming committees, with Lear at his side, to the lodgings taken for him in Eighth Street.

He was six weeks in daily conferences, and once more made a hurried winter journey at top speed to reach Mount Vernon in time for the Christmas season. Stopping overnight at Thomas Law's on the way, he encountered there as a guest the same Richard Parkinson who had in mind to rent the River Farm, and spent the evening in cordial conversation. Parkinson had already inspected the farm in Washington's absence and was not favorably impressed, nor was Lawrence Lewis altogether taken with Parkinson, who finally bought a place outside Baltimore.

Nelly was spending Christmas with her mother's second family at Hope Park, Custis and Lawrence Lewis had gone to the Valley, probably to visit George Steptoe Washington at Harewood. Old friends like Craik and his sons, William Fitzhugh, Bushrod Washington, and a Digges from Warburton made up the holiday list at Mount Vernon, with the addition of two bright new names from outside the neighborhood.

It is probable that during his recent sojourn in Philadelphia Washington had renewed his acquaintance with the Massachusetts justice of the Supreme Court, William Cushing—whose father had presided over the trial of the British soldiers after the Boston Massacre in 1770—and with Charles Cotesworth Pinckney of South Carolina, lately returned from his hair-raising experiences as one of the Commissioners in the XYZ affair in France, and had extended to them both his cordial invitation to visit Mount Vernon during the coming holidays. Pinckney had been there before—having served briefly on the Staff at the time of Brandywine and Germantown before returning to the Southern Campaign, he then became a delegate to the Constitutional Congress in '87, and had stopped at Mount Vernon on his way home after that. He was an imposing but genial figure of enormous popularity, and must have contributed substantially to an atmosphere of elegant, adult good cheer and free and easy conversation at Washington's dinner table.

The last entry for 1798 in the Diary reads simply: "*31.* [*December.*] Calm and pleasant, thawing, Mer. higher than yesterday."

XXXVII

By the first of the year, '99, all the young men had begun to think of uniforms and commissions. In his desperation to know what to do with young Custis, Washington recommended him for Cornet in the troop of Light Dragoons which already included Lawrence Lewis, Lawrence Washington, Jr., of Chotank, and George Washington Craik. Even Bartholomew Dandridge II, now in London as secretary to the American Ambassador there, Rufus King, wrote to Washington about embarking on a military career, and was given a choice between continuing in diplomacy or returning home as a captain in the infantry. "Lawrence Lewis is appointed a Captn. in the Corps of Light Dragoons," Washington wrote him on January 25th, "but before he enters the Camp of Mars he is to engage in that of Venus with Nelly Custis, on the 22d. of next month; they having, while I was at Philadelphia, without my having the smallest suspicion that such an affair was in agitation, formed their Contract for this purpose. Washington Craik is appointed a Lieutenant in the said Corps, and Washington Custis is made a Cornet in Lewis's troop; for it was found impracticable to keep him longer at College with any prospect of advantages; so great was his aversion to study; tho' addicted to no extravagant or vicious habits; but from mere indolence, and a dereliction to exercise the powers of his mind, and those talents with which Nature had blessed him. The Army, generally will be very respectably Officered....."

No doubt Martha had observed the signs of the attachment between Nelly and Lawrence, but Nelly for once had not confided in her devoted Grandpapa—though possibly it was only in the increasing stress of the times that she had been able to make up her mind among a rather large field of suitors, which probably included young Carroll of Carrollton, and George Washington Craik, who besides his secretarial duties was a frequent visitor to Mount Vernon. Her somewhat sudden decision must have come as a surprise to others besides Washington.

Very little soldiering was done by the younger generation, after all. Dandridge declined his commission, to remain in London, and after that continued in the diplomatic service until 1802, when he died unmarried while acting on appointment by President Jefferson as American consul in San Domingo at the time of the revolution there led by Toussaint L'Ouverture. Lear appears to have joined or succeeded him in the post, and after a series of almost incredible adventures, according to Decatur, was sent out of the country by General Leclerc of the French army of occupation. Lear later acted as American consul at Algiers and Tripoli. In 1816 he was found shot, an apparent suicide, in the garden of his home in Washington city.

Lawrence Lewis, who seems to have kept very quiet in all directions and was of so little use about the place that after his arrival Washington still required both Rawlins and Lear to supplement whatever it was that Lawrence found to do, soon after his marriage to Nelly resigned his commission in the Light Dragoons. Young Custis, fretting over the delayed arrival of the cavalry equipment ordered for him by Washington, was in the end no more drawn to the military life than to any other form of discipline.

The order to Biddle for Custis's outfit had been sent early in June, and included "A pair of Pistols and Horseman's Sword, silver-mounted; . . . . . Holsters and caps, to suit the Pistols; A proper Horseman's Cap or Helmet, A Horseman's Cloak, suitable to the uniform. . . . ." More than a month later they had not arrived and Washington wrote to the Secretary at War, no less, about the delay. "Daily fruitless inquiries are made of me to know when they may be expected. Perhaps if you were to jog Mr. Frances the *Purveyor*, the sooner they might be *purveyed*, and the young Gentleman gratified. I wish them to be handsome, and proper for an officer, but not expensive. In my last on this subject I requested that the sword be silver-mounted, but any other mount, such as the officers of cavalry use, would answer just as well. . . . ."

Washington had ordered from a Philadelphia tailor a new uniform to be sent to him not later than February 22d, which Nelly had chosen for her wedding day out of compliment to him. He was, as usual, specific: "Let your blue cloth be of the best and softest French or Spanish; and the finest you can procure, of a deep colour. And the Buff of the very best sort, fine, and not inclining to yellow or Orange, like what I have been accustomed to wear. The buttons are to be plain, flat, and of the best double gilt. . . . . The Waistcoat should be straight-breasted, that is, without lapels, and the Cuffs of the Coat neither large, nor tight; observing a just medium between the two. . . ."

But he is said to have worn the old one after all, at Nelly's wedding, because the new one did not arrive in time.

An English visitor named Joshua Brookes visited Mount Vernon accompanied by two friends from Philadelphia and a letter of introduction, a short time before the wedding, and recorded in his journal some immediate impressions. He seemed to feel that his reception was not enormously cordial, which may have been due to the fact that they were three total strangers, or to the source of his introduction, which was not from a close friend of the General's.

"We arrived on horseback about 12," Brookes recorded, "and learnt from the servants that the General was gone to take a ride. We amused ourselves with viewing negroes at work at the back of the house in levelling the ground. After a short time Mr. Lear, his secretary, came out and invited us in. We had before been met by a jolly white servant in a white cloth coat turned up with red and laced. Mr. L. called for wine of which we had a glass each, from globular decanters; he then invited us to visit the drawing-room. He then accompanied us into a front small parlor. In this I was much charmed with the portrait of Miss Custis and, upon inquiring whose it was, was informed that I should see her, that she lived with the General.

"A short time after our return to the sitting room Miss C. was introduced to us by Mr. Lear. . . . . She appeared about twenty, dressed in white sprig muslin tied around the waist with a sky blue silk cord with six round balls at the end, head dress fillet round her head and hair hanging down behind in ringlets between three turns of the fillet; no powder, about 5 ft. 4 high, midling stature and size. Silk stockings. Black shoes with large roses."

Mr. Brookes was about twenty-five, and missed very little, but although the visitors owed their invitation to stay to dinner to Miss Custis's hospitable good manners, more than to anyone else, and he found himself seated next to her at the table, he considered the portrait which had first caught his eye too flattering. "She appeared modest, well bred, intelligent and sensible, has a piercing eye, grecian nose, made judicious remarks and conversed with propriety," he added, it seems grudgingly. Martha, who wore a "Mazareen blue satin gown," pleased him most, he concluded, with "mildness and affability depicted in her countenance. She enquired for news, said she was no politician but liked to read the newspapers, wore a loose cap, hair combed straight, grey locks. . . . ."

The General came in from his ride, "dressed in a blue great coat, large buttons, blue overalls and bespattered boots, a blue coat, coquelico cassimere waistcoat, blue small clothes, cocked hat with a cockade. In conversation he informed us his clothes were all of American manufacture. . . . . . He is near six feet high, has a roman nose, projection under the chin, rough, weather beaten countenance, healthy look, large hands. He appears a reserved man but became pleasant, free and sociable at dinner, seems naturally austere and reflective. . . . ."

Dinner was enlivened, luckily, by the arrival of Dr. Craik, with whom Nelly seemed "intimate and free, but with us reserved." This is hardly remarkable, as she had known Dr. Craik all her life and the writer was a stranger. Mr. Brookes described the meal briefly: "Leg of boil[ed] pork, top [at head of table]; goose, bot [at foot of table]; roast beef, round cold boil[ed] beef, mutton chops, hommony, cabbage, potatoes, pickles, fried tripe, onions, etc. Table cloth wiped [crumbs brushed off], mince pies, tarts, cheese; cloth of[f]; port, madeira, two kinds of nuts, apples, raisins. Three servants." After dinner Washington had their horses brought to the door, stood punctiliously with Lear until they had mounted, and saw them off with his habitual courtesy, which seemed to Mr. Brookes a trifle stiff. One wonders what further hospitality he imagined he was entitled to.

On the evening of February 22d, echoing the entry for Fanny

Bassett and George Augustine in '83, Washington wrote in the Diary: "The Revd. Mr. Davis and Mr. George Calvert came to dinner, and Miss Custis was married about candlelight to Mr. Lawrence Lewis." The young couple paid visits in the Federal City and at Hope Park—and in May set off for a summer honeymoon in the Valley.

In June, no doubt with a rueful smile, Washington undertook once more to solve his difficulties at the mill with a letter to the incorrigible miller William Roberts, whose loss nearly fifteen years before he had never ceased to regret. Roberts may have smiled also, on its receipt:

"I have caused some inquiries to be made, lately, respecting your present situation and conduct," Washington wrote, "and am sorry to learn that the first is not eligable; and that the latter is far from being such as one would have hoped that experience, reflection, and I might add misfortunes, would have produced.

"Had these enabled you to overcome a practice which has involved you in the most heartfelt distress, and in a manner brought you to the brink of Ruin, or, if I could entertain any well grounded hope that you would, by shifting the scene, and entering into your old walks at my Mill, refrain from Drink, and the evils which it has produced, I would employ you again.

"Whether you are able to accomplish the latter, or not, none but yourself can tell, and to you only I apply. If then you would seriously resolve, and religiously adhere to a determination to be sober, and orderly in your deportment; and would be content with such wages and allowances as I give, and beyond which I cannot go, I would receive you as a Miller after the term of the person who looks after it at present, expires, which will be the 12th of August. . . . . . .

"The Work at my Mill is by no means hard; and a Man and a boy when there is water sufficient assists; It follows of course that a Miller cannot be more at his ease any where; and you know from experience, that no man discharges the demand of wages, or fulfills his agreements with more punctuality than I do. Such a place, then, to a man in the decline of life, might be more desirable than one with higher wages accompanied with infinite more trouble and uncertainty: In a word, if you could keep yourself within bounds, it might be considered as a settlement, as it were, for life. . . . . ."

Roberts agreed, but at the end of August he was still missing, and Washington wrote again with some impatience, as his present miller's time was up. A week later he had apparently sent Anderson to see what was the trouble. Roberts proved to be ill, or incapacitated, and the services of Dr. Craik were indicated. "If it be found that he is not *now* nor soon *will* be, in a condition to discharge the duties of a miller, some other *must*, undoubtedly, be got; as I cannot loose the Fall work of the mill. He may have medicine, or anything else from here. . . . . ."

But Roberts never made it back to Mount Vernon.

At this time Martha had a frightening illness, and Dr. Craik was sent for. Lawrence and Nelly were at the Springs, in the hope of improving his health—an old familiar anxiety for Washington. Anderson himself was in poor health and found the work too much for him. Even Lear was away to consult a doctor about a persistent lameness. And at the end of September word came of the death of Charles Washington at Happy Retreat. "I was the *first*, and am now the *last*, of my father's children by the second marriage who remain," he wrote to Charles's son-in-law, Burgess Ball. "When I shall be called upon to follow them, is known only to the giver of life. When the summons comes, I shall endeavour to obey it with a good grace." And to Charles's always impecunious son, Samuel, he wrote: "By this event, you have become the Guardian of your mother; and as it were, the father, of your father's family; and by care, industry, and sobriety will merit the appellation of one. . . . . . ."

With the precedent of George Augustine again before him, while Nelly and Lawrence were still away in the west Washington wrote to Lawrence outlining a plan for the future: "The expense at which I live, and the unproductiveness of my Estate together, will admit of no diminution of income, while I remain in my present situation," he confessed, burdened as always with his own financial difficulties. "On the contrary, were it not for occasional supplies of money in payment for Lands sold within the last four or five years, to the amount of upwards of Fifty thousand dollars; I should not be able to support the former without involving myself in debt and difficulties." He offered to release to Lawrence at once the tract of land which was left to them jointly in his will, including Gray's Hill, which he considered the best site roundabout to build on, and to rent to them the adjoining Dogue Run farm, its mill and distillery, which would provide Lawrence with suitable employment in its management. "Idleness is disreputable under any circumstances," he wrote, "productive of no good, even when unaccompanied with vicious habits; and you might commence building as soon as you please; during the progress of which Mount Vernon might be made your home." Nothing was said this time about the nuisance of children, or of two women under his roof at the same time. And when the young Lewises returned, it was plain that a child would be born in the autumn.

Before Washington could receive an answer to this letter, however, Anderson and his son applied to rent the mill and distillery to run themselves, and Washington was inclined to consent, as it would suit his project of reducing his staff and responsibilities for the future, without the necessity of dismissing Anderson entirely. "As the old man is extremely obliging and zealous in my service," he wrote in a second letter to Lawrence, "I am unwilling by any act of mine to hurt his feelings or (by discarding of him) to lessen his respectability in the eyes of the world. But if it should appear to be his own act (by engaging in this business) both our ends will be answered. I should be lessened, by so much, of my general concerns; and if you take Dogue Run farm (by odds the best and most productive I possess) I can, if I remain quiet at home, with great ease attend to the other three, and the Mansion House, and thereby ease myself of the expense of a manager......"

The offer of a home at Mount Vernon and a building site was accepted by the young couple, and Lawrence appears finally to have taken over the Mill and Distillery as well. Washington did not live to see the spacious brick mansion which the Lewises built on the site he chose for it, which they called Woodlawn.

During the autumn of '99, however, things brightened in all directions. Lear came back, restored in health, and Martha was much improved after a series of colds and fevers. September was full of visitors, including Colonel William Washington of Sandy Hill near Charleston, who smelled gunpowder again in the worsening relations with France, and was on his way to Philadelphia and a brigadier general's commission. The Laws and the Peters and the Bushrod Washingtons, with the widow of John Augustine from Bushfield, and of course the Stuarts from Hope Park, were all in and out of Mount Vernon as Nelly's time drew near.

In late November, when the midwife was already in the house, the Carringtons of Richmond arrived for a visit. Edward and Betsy Carrington were old friends from the war days, and since then Colonel Carrington had attended the Congress in '87, and joined in the fight for the Constitution which resulted in Virginia's ratification in spite of the oratory of Patrick Henry and Richard Henry Lee. He had been several times an overnight guest at Mount Vernon during the '80's, and in a letter to her sister written from Mount Vernon during this present visit, Mrs. Carrington recorded with pride that on their arrival Washington's reception of her husband "was that of a Brother; he took us each by the hand & with a warmth of expression not to be described pressed mine & told me that I had conferred a favour never to be forgotten in bringing his old friend to see him: then bidding a servant to call the ladies entertained us most facetiously till they appeared. . . . ."

Mrs. Carrington's letter is the last intimate account penned by a guest during Washington's lifetime, and like everyone else who wrote about Nelly she fell into extravagance: ". . . . Mrs. W—, venerable, kind and plain, & resembling very much our Aunt A—[mbler].—Mrs. Stewart her daughter-in-law, once Mrs. Custis, with her two young daughters, Misses S—, all pleasant and agreeable—Mrs. H—[owell] Lewis, formerly Miss P—[ollard] of Richmond, and last tho' not least Mrs. L. Lewis—but how describe her —once I heard my neighbour, Mrs. Tucker, give a romantic account of her, when Miss Custis—her lovely figure made doubly interesting by a light fanciful summer dress with a garland of flowers she had just entwined, and an apronfull she had selected—came in to throw them at her grandmamma's feet;—all which I considered as the fanciful effusions of my friends romantic turn of mind, but now when I see her the Matron, for such her situation makes her appear, though she has been only ten months a wife, lovely as nature could form her, improved in every female accomplishment & what is still more interesting, amiable & obliging in every department that makes a woman most charming, particularly in her conduct to her aged Grandmother & the General, whom she always calls Grampa, I seem actually transported in beholding her. . . . ."

Good manners, or real friendliness, prompted Nelly to show Mrs. Carrington the bedchamber which had been prepared for the birth, and to urge her to remain in the house until "this dreaded event" had passed, which she readily promised to do, but Colonel Carrington was either embarrassed by the imminence of the crisis or had other ideas of propriety in the circumstances. "In this promise I thought this morning I should be indulged," his wife's letter continued, "for on entering the breakfast room, I understood she had been complaining all night, but unfortunately my husband spied the arm-chair carried upstairs, & a moment after ordered our carriage;— In vain does the General insist upon our stay, promising to take him over the grounds and farm, & and showing him the mill &c &c which will occupy him till 3—but no—the world would not tempt him to stay at a time when he said, everyone should leave the family entirely undisturbed; but that after a few days, when we had finished our visit to our friends in Maryland, we would again see them and prolong our visit;—is it not vexatious to have so scrupulous a husband; nothing would distress me more than to leave that charming family at such a moment, but I am bound to obey, & at 12 we are to leave this place for Washington; when I return you may expect to hear from me. . . . ."

So the Carringtons tactfully withdrew, and Nelly's child was born with Dr. Craik in attendance on the 27th of November, a daughter to be named Frances and become another Fanny. The continuation of Mrs. Carrington's letter on their return to Mount Vernon is of the same date, so they must have barely missed the peak of excitement, after all, though she gives no indication of having been present when the child was actually born. "It is really an enjoyment to be here, to witness the tranquil happiness that reigns throughout the house," she wrote, having missed the post and so scribbling on. Washington Custis had at last been permitted to kill a stag among the deer which were now half wild—provided that he undertook "to kill with ball, to use no hounds, and on no account to kill any but an old buck," Washington noted in the Diary. These stipulations having been duly observed, he gave the carcase a brief nod of approval on his way to dress for dinner, and Eliza Carrington had the honor of seasoning the venison stew. Her letter continued:

"My mornings are spent charmingly alternately in the different chambers; first an hour after breakfast with the lady in the straw —dressing the pretty little stranger, who is the delight of the Grand-ma; then we repair to the old lady's room, which is precisely in the style of our good old aunt's, that is to say nicely fixed for all sorts of work—on one side sits the chamber-maid with her knitting, on the other a little coloured pet learning to sew, an old, decent woman with her table and shears cutting out the negroes winter clothes, while the good old lady directs them all, incessantly knitting herself, & pointing out to me several pair of nice coloured stockings and gloves she had just finished & presenting me with a pair half done, begs me to finish & wear for her sake........

"It is wonderful after a life spent as these good people have necessarily spent theirs to see them in retirement assume domestic manners that prevail in our country, when but a year since they were forced to forego all the innocent delights which are so congenial to their years and tastes, to sacrifice to the parade of the drawing-room & the Levee.

"The recollection of these lost days, as Mrs. W— calls them, seem to fill her with regret, but the extensive knowledge she has gained in this general intercourse with persons from all parts of the world has made her a most interesting companion, & having a retentive memory, she presents an entire history of half a century....."

The weather was too wintry to enjoy being outdoors, but the Carringtons visited the greenhouse, "which at this season is a vast, a great source of pleasure. Plants from every part of the world seem to flourish in the neatly furnished apartment, & from the arrangement of the whole, I conclude that it is managed by a skilful hand, but whose I cannot tell—neither the General nor Mrs. W— seem more interested in it than the visitors—We have met with no company here, but are told that scarcely a week passes without some, and often more than is comfortable or agreeable. When transient persons who call from curiosity, they are treated with civility, but never interfere with the General's disposition of time, which is as regular as when at the head of the Army or in the President's chair. Even friends who make a point of visiting him are left much to themselves, indeed scarcely see him from breakfast to dinner, unless he engages them in a ride, which is very agreeable to him. . . . . ."

The days were short, and the fireside cheerful, and doubtless the punch bowl steamed. Nelly was safe, the baby was well, and Washington relaxed into reminiscence and anecdote with one of the few men who succeeded in disrupting his lifelong habit of early to bed and early to rise. "Indeed," wrote Mrs. Carrington with some pride, "one evening the General was so fascinating and drew my husband out into so many old stories, relating to several campaigns where they had been much together, & had so many inquiries to make respecting mutual friends, particularly Kościuszko & Pulaski, who have always corresponded with Col. C–, whose characters afford great interest, that it was long after twelve when we separated... At breakfast, I feel quite at home, everything is so plain–"

Here the letter breaks off, at a tantalizing point, because the rest of the text has been lost.

Before the Carringtons departed, Howell Lewis arrived to collect his wife, who was already staying in the house, and to inspect his new niece. Everything was so serene that Lawrence Lewis and Washington Custis decided on a visit to the Burwell Bassetts at Eltham, setting out at the same time as the Howell Lewises, and Washington stood on the steps at the west door to see them all off. "It was a bright, frosty morning," Howell remembered. "He had taken his usual ride, and the clear, healthy flush on his cheek and his sprightly manner brought the remark from both of us that we had never seen the General look so well. I have sometimes thought him decidedly the handsomest man I ever saw; and when in that lively mood, so full of pleasantry, so agreeable to all with whom he associated, that I could hardly realize he was the same Washington whose dignity awed all who approached him."

From there Washington turned indoors to begin the long, detailed layout of the coming year's work on the estate, farm by farm, field by field. It ran to thirty pages before he had finished, in his level, unhurried script. On the 11th of December there was a spate of dinner guests, including Bryan Fairfax, safely returned from England, and Warner Washington's widow, who had been Hannah Fairfax.

On the 12th Washington rode out on his usual rounds and encountered bad weather, but would not cut short his accustomed tour, returning to a belated dinner which had been kept waiting for him past the regular hour of three o'clock. There were no guests that day, and he sat down at the dinner-table without making his habitual change of clothes, though Lear protested that there was snow even in his hair. That evening he wrote in the Diary: "Morning cloudy, Wind at No. Et. and Mer. 33. A large circle round the Moon last Night. About ten o'clock it began to snow, soon after to Hail, and then to a settled cold Rain. Mer. 28 at Night."

Lear himself later set down an account of the slowly mounting tragedy of the next two days, aware of his own unique position in history as the hours ran out—it is a simple, moving account of Washington's last battle:

"A heavy fall of snow took place on Friday, (which prevented the General from riding out as usual)," Lear wrote. "He had taken cold (undoubtedly from being so much exposed the day before) and complained of a sore throat: he however went out in the afternoon into the ground between the House and the River to mark some trees which were to be cut down in the improvement of that spot. He had a Hoarseness which increased in the evening; but he made light of it. In the evening the Papers were brought from the Post Office, and he sat in the Parlour, with Mrs. Washington and myself, reading them till about nine o'clock—when Mrs. Washington went up into Mrs. Lewis's room, who was confined in Child Bed, and left the General & myself reading the papers. He was very cheerful, and when he met with anything interesting or entertaining he wd. read it aloud as well as his hoarseness would permit him. He requested me to read to him the debates of the Virginia Assembly on the election of a Senator and a Governor—and on hearing Mr. Madison's observations respecting Mr. Monroe, he appeared much affected and spoke with some degree of asperity on the subject, which I endeavoured to moderate, as I always did on such occasions. On his retiring, I observed to him that he had better take something to remove his cold. He answered no: 'you know I never take anything for a cold. Let it go as it came.' "

During the morning of that day, while the snow kept him indoors, Washington had had time to write a letter to Anderson, with whom he had missed connections the day before in the storm. "Such a Pen as I saw yesterday at Union Farm would, if the Cattle were kept in it one Week, destroy the Whole of them," he pointed out, and no compromise this time with the manager's sensitive feelings. "They would be infinitely more comfortable in this, or any weather, in the open fields. . . . ."

That evening he again made up his Diary: "13. [December] Morning Snowing and abt. 3 inches deep. Wind at No. Et., and Mer. at 30. contg. Snowing till 1 o'clock, and abt. 4 it became perfectly clear. Wind in the same place, but not hard. Mer. at 28 at Night." It was the last entry in the little almanac book, and his reprimand to Anderson about the welfare of his cattle was the last letter he wrote. Returning to Lear's account:

"Between two & three o'clock on Saturday morning he awoke Mrs. Washington, and told her he was very unwell, and had had an ague. She observed that he could scarcely speak and breathed with difficulty; and would have got up to call a Servant; but he would not permit her lest she should take cold. As soon as the day appeared, the Woman (Caroline) went into the Room to make a fire, and Mrs. Washington sent her immediately to call me. I got up, put on my clothes as quickly as possible, and went to his Chamber. Mrs. Washington was then up, and related to me his being taken ill as before stated. I found the General breathing with difficulty, and hardly able to utter a word intelligibly. He desired that Mr. Rawlins (one of his overseers) might be sent for to bleed him before the Dr. could arrive. I dispatched a servant instantly for Rawlins, and another for Dr. Craik, and returned again to the General's Chamber, where I found him in the same situation as I had left him. A Mixture of Molasses, Vinegar & butter was prepared to try its effects in the throat; but he could not swallow a drop. Whenever he attempted it he appeared to be distressed, convulsed, and almost suffocated. Rawlins came in soon after sunrise, and prepared to bleed him. When the arm was ready the General observing that Rawlins appeared to be agitated, said, as well as he could speak, '*Don't be afraid.*' And after the incision was made, he observed, '*The orifice is not large enough.*' However, the blood ran pretty freely. Mrs. Washington not knowing whether bleeding was proper or not in the General's situation, begged that much might not be taken from him, lest it should be injurious, and desired me to stop it; but when I was about to untie the string the General put up his hand to prevent it, and as soon as he could speak, said,—'*More, more.*' Mrs. Washington being still very uneasy lest too much blood should be taken, it was stopped after taking about half a pint. Finding that no relief was obtained from bleeding, and that nothing would go down the throat, I proposed bathing it externally with salvolatila, which was done; and in the operation, which was with the hand, and in the gentlest manner, he observed, '*'tis very sore.*' A piece of flannel dip'd in salvolita was put around his neck, and his feet bathed in warm water; but without affording any relief.

"In the meantime, before Dr. Craik arrived, Mrs. Washington desired me to send for Dr. Brown of Port Tobacco, whom Dr. Craik had recommended to be called if any case should ever occur that was seriously alarming. I dispatched a messenger (Cyrus) immediately for Dr. Brown (between 8 & 9 o'clock.) Dr. Craik came in soon after, and upon examining the General, he put a blister of Cantharides on the throat, took some more blood from him, and had a gargle of Vinegar and sage tea, and ordered some Vinegar and hot water for him to inhale the steam, which he did;—but in attempting to use the gargle he was almost suffocated. . . . ."

Craik, who was a year or so older than Washington and had tended and advised him since the frontier days of their youth, had at once recognized crisis when he reached his friend's bedside, and diagnosed inflammatory quinsy. He wanted a consultant, and around eleven o'clock another messenger was dispatched to Alexandria for young Dr. Dick, who might still manage to arrive before Dr. Brown. Craik then resorted again to bleeding, and Washington by now could not swallow, cough, or speak, and had such difficulty in breathing that Lear leaned or lay on the bed beside him trying to raise or turn the big body in his arms, to bring what comfort he could by a change of position.

Dr. Dick rode in about three o'clock, and Dr. Brown soon after. Dr. Dick wanted to open the trachea as a last resort but was overruled by his two seniors, as he was also in the matter of bleeding, which was done twice more during the afternoon. It was the old school against the new. Craik and Brown were graduates of Edinburgh, for whom Dr. William Cullen's textbooks were a Bible of medicine. Brown had "walked" the London hospitals to gain the practical experience which Craik had found in the wilderness camps and battlefields of western Virginia in the '50's. His Maryland home called Rose Hill was one of the handsomest in the neighborhood, and famous for its gardens. The junior Dr. Dick was Pennsylvania born and schooled under the crusty Dr. Rush who had so distinguished himself during the yellow fever years in Philadelphia, and Dr. Shippen, the high and mighty Director-General of Hospitals during the war. Dick was an immediate social success when he set up his practice in Alexandria—having a handsome presence, a bedside manner, and some talent as a musician, while his conviction that doctors should "spare the lancet" for elderly patients was somewhat in advance of his time.

During the afternoon the two consultants withdrew and Craik, compelled by his anxiety to do *something*, even if it was not the right thing, prescribed a dose of calomel and tartar emetic, naturally with no good result, and Washington roused enough to motion the faithful Christopher to a chair from his weary post near the door in readiness to run any conceivable errand. Always a fatalist about his own illnesses, he then requested Martha to bring him the two Wills she would find in his desk, and when they came he chose the later one, and directed her to burn the other. For the second time in the day he was helped to a chair by the fire, but after half an hour returned to the bed, and said to the three helpless physicians, "I feel myself going...... you had better not take any more trouble about me....."

Lear hung above him, cradling his hand, trying to support him against the pillows; Martha sat by the foot of the bed; the two consultants tactfully withdrew, and Craik sat by the fire to grieve. About eight o'clock they tried again, despairingly, with blisters and cataplasms of wheat and bran to his feet and legs, without, said Lear, a ray of hope. Washington submitted to these administrations, Dick recorded later, rather as his duty to his physicians, than in any expectation of any benefit therefrom—his courtesy and self-discipline unimpaired, and his mind perfectly clear.

The clock struck ten, and Lear leaned closer to catch what Washington wanted to say—"I am just going," he heard, and then the strange injunction: "Have me decently buried, and do not let my body be put into the vault in less than two days after I am dead." Lear was unable to speak above his own emotion, and Washington added, "Do you understand me?" "Yes, sir," Lear managed to reply, and Washington's last words were: " 'Tis well."

Lear's narrative plods on: "About ten minutes before he expired (which was between ten & eleven o'clock) his breathing became easier and he lay quietly;—he withdrew his hand from mine, and felt his own pulse. I saw his countenance change. I spoke to Dr. Craik who sat by the fire;—he came to the bedside. The General's hand fell from his wrist—I took it in mine and put it into my bosom. Dr. Craik put his hands over his eyes and he expired without a struggle or a sigh. . . . ."

Martha's composure was seldom less than his. No one saw her weep. But Lear sank into the fireside chair with his head in his hands, and Dr. Craik's worn, ruddy countenance was drawn with sorrow, while Christopher and the other servants, Caroline, Molly, and Charlotte, besides the housekeeper Mrs. Forbes, who were clustered near the door, gave way to tears. Poor Nelly, always his favorite, and still unable to leave her room since the birth of her daughter, must have found it very hard to bear.

"As soon as Dr. Craik could speak after the distressing scene was closed," Lear concluded his account, "he desired one of the servants to ask the Gentln. below to come upstairs. When they came to the bedside, I kissed the cold hand which I had held to my bosom, laid it down, and went to the other end of the room; where I was for some time in profound grief; until roused by Christopher desiring me to take care of the General's keys and other things which were taken out of his pockets and which Mrs. Washington directed him to give to me; I wrapped them in the General's handkerchief, & took them with me to my room. About 12 o'clock the

Corpse was brought down stairs and laid out in the large room. . . . ."

Lear's duty was far from done. It was he who wrote the sad news over and over again for dispatch to President Adams, the Cabinet, the relatives, and nearby friends. Washington Custis and Lawrence, on their holiday at Eltham, received it as a stunning blow, and hurried back too late for the funeral, which was made impressive by a large delegation from the Masonic Society at Alexandria and Washington City. The solemn procession from the piazza to the vault was led by a troop of militia, horse and foot, a band playing a dirge, and four clergymen. Washington's horse, wearing its saddle, holster and pistols, was led by his two grooms, and followed by the principal mourners—Martha remaining inside the house with Nelly. On Christmas Day Lear attended the closing of the coffin by plumbers from Alexandria who soldered down the lid—"and beheld for the last time that face wh. shall be seen no more here; but *wh. I hope to meet in Heaven.*"

Washington was sixty-seven when he died, and for those times and considering the critical illnesses he had already survived, to say nothing of the hazards of war, it was a fairly good age. If medical knowledge and skill had been greater in his day, he might have gained a few more years of inevitable decline. But for him, and for his devoted wife, the story had a happy ending—since he died at home, at peace, in his own bed, with his people and his beloved acres all around him.

Footnote, Acknowledgments, and Bibliography

The mansion of Mount Vernon stands today as the symbol of a man's life—a great but simple man. His chosen work is here, for he thought of himself as a planter or farmer, rather than as a soldier or statesman, and would take off his coat and employ his own strength and skill alongside his workmen—so that his handiwork literally survives. His ambition is here, for he desired above all things to see his land productive, to make Mount Vernon support itself and show a profit. His dreams are here, for he lived to see the house and its dependencies and gardens completed pretty much as he had planned them during four frustrating decades when absence, conflicting responsibilities, and always a financial pinch conspired to delay the realization. And his love is here, because the house sheltered his happy marriage and his devoted family and his many friends.

To understand George Washington, to *believe* him, one must come to Mount Vernon. No American child should reach voting age without standing here on the bank of the Potomac where at one time there dwelt the living symbol of the courage, the convictions, the dogged determination, and the flaming spirit of the infant nation which today, along with its mother country, still embodies those embattled beliefs which it defended at Valley Forge and Guildford Courthouse and Yorktown.

Not everyone can be privileged as I have been to see Mount Vernon alone and tranquil, when the gates are closed for the day and the pilgrims have all departed—to sit silent in one of the windsor chairs on the long piazza and watch the lavender twilight fall across the broad River as he must have done, and to feel in some degree the serenity of spirit which he must have found here, and which he left here as his legacy to the troubled generations to come. Because of my sincere wish to capture within the pages of a book something of what will always exist at Mount

Vernon I was permitted to come closer to it, and to him, than the daily visitor. But anyone who arrives with a receptive mind will become aware, even in a crowd, of the enduring magic which resides here.

Under its present management Mount Vernon maintains its tradition of hospitality and freedom—you can walk on the grass, you can sit on the benches, you can take your own pictures, you can spend all the time you want to, you can enter and re-enter the mansion and the dependencies and the greenhouse, stables and tomb—you can buy souvenirs, and even cuttings and plants and seeds from the gardens—the whole atmosphere is cordial and generous and without *verbotens.* How all this is possible, with more than a million visitors a year, is a mystery. But it works. Even from behind the scenes, where I have been, it works. Perhaps because it comes naturally to people, as Washington's guests, to behave well.

There is a handsome, easy to read Handbook to Mount Vernon, but without it one does not as a rule anticipate all that is in store. The house is not a restoration, like the beautiful Birthplace at Wakefield down the River. The kitchen, spinning-house, greenhouse, and others have been reconstructed on the original plans, but the house itself is the true fabric, miraculously preserved. This is the very staircase Washington trod when he carried his candle upstairs at bedtime, this smooth walnut rail has felt the warmth of his big hand. These are the rooms where the wilful Custis children romped away from their colored nurses. This is the dining-room fireplace which smoked, Lund wrote during alterations, like anything in the Negro quarters. In the banquet-room is the handsome Vaughan mantel-piece which Washington must have seen unpacked, piece by piece, recognizing with delight its agricultural motifs, and designing the ceiling of the room to reflect and complement the gift.

Not all the movable furnishings have had an uninterrupted residence, as the Houdon bust has had since its delivery in 1785, or the Bastille key which has always hung where Washington placed it in 1790. But by gift and purchase many of the authentic original inhabitants of the house have returned to it—from Martha's bits of jewelry (pathetically simple and inexpensive) and household china to the big secretary-desk in the library where Washington sat to do his accounts and write his letters till the end of his life—at which he probably made the last entry in his Diary the day before he died.

It is difficult now to separate the actual pieces from the carefully chosen contemporary things which surround them, but apart from the Museum itself many of the furnishings which were in daily use during his lifetime are here now, under your eyes, including the great bed he died in. Paintings he chose—over the mantel in the west parlor and in the banquet-room; portraits by Savage and Pine; Chippendale and Sheraton chairs; the mirrored plateau on the dining-room table; the small breakfast-table in the pantry and the blue and white china on the shelves; Nelly Custis's harpsichord and music-books; a trunk with the simple inscription: "G. Washington, Virginia"; many of his own books, including the copy of his friend de Chastellux's *Travels in America;* and in the garden, the box and the fig-trees are living links with the man who planted them. In the stable are the Fairfax riding-chair and the Powel coach—both of them familiar visitors there, though not Washington's own. But the main thing at Mount Vernon is invisible—intangible. When you are there, it exists.

My own indebtedness to the present staff, which leads its obscure, enchanted life in the quiet administration building behind the North Lane, is immense. The unpublished material which they allowed me to read, and from which I have been permitted to quote, is literally priceless, in reconstructing the part of Washington's life which has been submerged in his always reluctant public career. There was never a strong man who wailed so loudly in private while doing his duty so nobly wherever it led him. Washington grumbled. In letters to his brothers, to his sister, to nephews, fellow generals and beloved aides, and to Lafayette, he complained and fulminated and let off steam. And then, wearing the famous poker-face, he did with dignity and resolution all those things he did not want to do, usually with resounding success. To the numerous young, both of his family and Martha's, he was an alternate and sometimes an only father, regarded by them with both awe and devotion. His letters to them are full of sound advice, severe reprimand, genuine affection, and sometimes an avuncular playfulness. Without children of his own, he was nevertheless beset by nurseries. And apparently for the most part he enjoyed it, though the irresponsible Custis boys, father and son, were a perpetual exasperation.

Once again I express my thanks to the New York Society Library and its mailing service, without which I have never been able to assemble a book requiring research; also to patient correspondents in the various Historical Societies. Above all, I reiterate my gratitude to the Mount Vernon Ladies' Association, by whose permission the excerpts from the family letters in their possession are given here—from Lund Washington's wartime reports, and George Augustine Washington's during the Presidency, and letters from the other managers; from Martha to Fanny Bassett; and from Harriot Washington to her uncle. It is to be hoped that some day all this correspondence may be published in full. Washington's Ledgers were made available to me during my work at the library, as was material relating to the visits at Mount Vernon of Count Niemcewicz and the future Louis Philippe. Also of tremendous value was the set of illustrated Annual Reports of the Association, covering the last twenty-one years, which the librarian presented to me. Among this book's illustrations, the floor plans, the dining-room, the Parkyns print, and the Pine portraits are all reproduced through the courtesy of the Association.

The Powel Journal is owned by the Pennsylvania Genealogical Society; the letter from Tobias Lear to Prescott, by Roger Wolcott of Boston; the letter from Olney Winsor to his wife by the Rhode Island Historical Society; and the William Hunter Diary by the Huntington Library.

It would be redundant to give the full Bibliography for a book of this kind, and there is no estimating the number of books which have passed through my hands during nearly four years of work. Obviously indispensable are the thirty-nine volumes of the Collected Writings, edited by John C. Fitzpatrick, which the New York Society Library placed at my disposal by extended privilege; and the four-volume published Diary, also edited by Dr. Fitzpatrick, which I was able to buy. It is safe to say that nothing authoritative can be written about Washington henceforth without daily reference to Douglas Southall Freeman's seven-volume *Life of Washington,* which has superseded and outdone all former works of a similar nature. A short list of some less well-known sources follows.

BOUCHER, JONATHAN. *Recollections of an American Loyalist.* 1925.

CHASTELLUX, MARQUIS DE. *Travels in North America.* 1787.

CUSTIS, GEORGE WASHINGTON PARKE. *Recollections and Private Memoirs of Washington.* 1860.

DECATUR, STEPHEN. *Private Affairs of Washington.* 1933.

DODGE, HARRISON H. *Mount Vernon.* 1932.

DUKE, JANE TAYLOR. *Kenmore and the Lewises.* 1949.

EARLE, SWEPSON. *Chesapeake Bay Country.*

FITHIAN, PHILIP. *Journal and Letters.* Ed. by Hunter Dickinson Farish. 1957.

FITZPATRICK, JOHN C. *Washington Himself.* 1933.

FORD, PAUL LEICESTER. *The True George Washington.* 1896.

FUSSELL, G. E. *More Old English Farming Books.* 1950.

HAMILTON, STANISLAW MURRAY. [Ed.] *Letters to Washington.* 1898.

HAWORTH, PAUL. *George Washington, Country Gentleman.* 1925.

HENDRICK, B. J. *The Lees of Virginia.* 1935.

HUGHES, RUPERT. *George Washington.* 1926.

JOHNSON, GERALD, and C. C. WALL. *Mount Vernon: the Story of a Shrine.* 1953.

LEAR, TOBIAS. *Letters and Recollections of Washington.* 1906.

LONG ISLAND HISTORICAL SOCIETY. Vol. IV. 1889. *George Washington and Mount Vernon.*

Miller, Helen Day Hill. *George Mason, Constitutionalist.* 1938.
Moore, Charles. *The Family Life of George Washington.* 1926.
Mount Vernon Handbook.
Ritter, Halsted Lockwood. *Washington as a Businessman.* 1931.
Rousby. *Maryland Homes.*
Rowland, Kate Mason. *Life of George Mason.* 1892.
Rutland, Robert. *George Mason.* 1961.
Shippen, Nancy. *Journal.* Ed. by Ethel Armes. 1935.
Snowden, W. H. *Some Old Historic Landmarks of Virginia and Maryland.* 1894.
Stetson, Charles. *Washington and his Neighbors.* 1956.
Virginia Cavalcade Magazine.
Waterman, T. T. *The Mansions of Virginia.* 1946.
Watson, Elkanah. *Men and Times of the Revolution.* 1856.
Watson, John F. *Annals of Philadelphia.* 1830.
Wayland, John. *The Washingtons and Their Homes.*
Wilstach, Paul. *Mount Vernon.* 1916.

Index

Abingdon, 187, 188, 197, 200, 220, 234, 238, 261, 275, 280, 298
Accotink Creek, 115
Adam, William, 11
Adams, John, 227, 260, 288, 290, 343, 359, 362, 367, 369, 374, 391, 412
Adams, John Quincy, 240
Addison, Eleanor (Mrs. Jonathan Boucher), 120-123, 125, 156
Addison, Henry, 121, 122, 156
Addison, Mrs. John, 121, 122
Albany, 210
Albemarle County, 99, 199
Alexander family, 87, 188, 298
Allegheny Mountains, 163
Allegheny River, 38
Allison, 331
Alton, Ann (Mrs. Walker), 246, 330
Alton, John, 13-15, 17, 19, 26, 31, 37, 45, 47, 78, 239, 246, 330
Ambler, Edward, 12
Ambler, Mrs. Edward. *See* Mary Cary.
Ambler, Eliza. *See* Mrs. Edward Carrington.
Amson, Dr., 31
Anderson, Dr. James, 373
Anderson, James (overseer), 358, 364, 385, 386, 394, 401, 402, 408
Appenines, 52
Aquia, 173
Arlington, 381
Arnold, Benedict, 191-193, 213, 270, 284
Arnold, Mrs. Benedict. *See* Peggy Shippen.
Arris, John, 11, 44, 63, 71
Askew, John, 77, 78
Augusta County, 52
Austin, 253, 309, 330
Austria, 223, 341
Aylett, Anne. *See* Mrs. "Austin" Washington.
Aylett, John, 96, 292
Aylett, Mrs. John. *See* Betsy Dandridge.
Aylett, William, 96
Aylett family, 7

Bahamas, 5, 25, 237
Balch, Rev. Mr., 245, 246
Ball, Burgess, 318, 319, 401
Ball, Mrs. Burgess (Frances Washington), 318, 361
Ball, John, 106, 107
Ball, Milly, 361, 362
Ballendine, John, 145
Baltimore, 5th Lord, 127
Baltimore, 6th Lord, 112
Barbados, 9, 11, 61, 210, 224
Barnes, Mrs., 163-165
Barry, John, 168
Bassett, Betsy, 115, 127, 128
Bassett, Billy, 138
Bassett, Burwell, xi, 24, 57, 58, 87, 95, 98, 110, 115, 116, 127, 129, 135, 138, 155, 182, 198, 220, 224, 225, 238, 247, 263, 309, 310, 316, 317
Bassett, Mrs. Burwell (Nancy Dandridge), xi, 24, 57, 58, 83, 84, 98, 115, 128, 129, 134, 138, 191, 220, 224, 345
Bassett, Burwell II, 191, 220, 237, 238, 241, 322, 345, 360, 406
Bassett, Mrs. Burwell II (Elizabeth McCarthy), 322, 345, 406
Bassett, Elizabeth. *See* Mrs. Benjamin Harrison V.
Bassett, Fanny (Mrs. George Augustine Washington, Mrs. Tobias Lear), xi, 83, 115, 134, 138, 191, 220, 224, 225, 236, 237, 238, 241, 242, 247, 268, 274, 280, 293, 295, 298, 301, 303, 307, 309, 311, 314, 316, 317, 319, 320, 322, 323, 340, 345, 352, 360, 366, 399, 400; death, 345; marries George Augustine Washington, 241; death of George Augustine Washington, 316; marries Tobias Lear, 340
Bassett, John, 191, 220, 237, 238, 241
Bastille, 297, 388
Bateman, 206
Bater, Philip, 268, 269
Bath (England), 15, 191, 229, 237, 277, 385
Bath (W. Va.). *See* Berkeley Springs.
Bayliss, Richard, 58
Baylor, George, Jr., 156
Beck, 47, 60

Beggar's Opera, 111
Bel Air, 45, 59
Belle Grove, 336
Belleview, xii, 42, 148
Belvale, 155
Belvoir, xiii, 5, 8, 9, 12, 15, 20, 24, 25, 30, 31, 39, 46, 58, 87, 92, 97, 100, 117, 125, 129, 132, 133, 138, 141, 142, 205, 228, 229, 248, 277, 384, 385; auction, 141, 142
Bemis Heights, 249
Bensons, Miss, 212
Berkeley, xii, 135, 136
Berkeley County, 46, 145, 146, 148, 154, 177, 199, 200, 289, 349
Berkeley Springs (Frederick Springs, or Bath, W. Va.), 71, 100-102, 237, 241, 302, 355, 401
Berkshire, 256
Bermuda, 225, 237
Berwickshire, 256
Bet, 182
Bethlehem (Pa.), 360
Betty, 47, 253, 330
Biddle, Clement, 215, 216, 225, 256, 263, 284, 297, 366, 397
Biddle, Rebecca (Mrs. Clement), 215
Billy (Will, William), 93, 216, 228, 234, 253, 261, 264, 280, 292, 298, 324, 353, 363
Bishop, Sally (Mrs. Thomas Green), 189, 246, 293, 328-330
Bishop, Susannah (Mrs. Thomas), 189, 246
Bishop, Thomas, 17, 31, 39, 47, 71, 115, 167, 180, 189, 246, 329, 330, 353
Blackburn, Julia Anne. *See* Mrs. Bushrod Washington.
Blackburn, Thomas, xiii, 134, 219, 354, 368
Blair, President John, 31, 86
Bland, Richard, 43, 141
Bland, Theodorick, 156, 249, 296, 299
Bland, Mrs. Theodorick (Martha Dangerfield), 249
Blenheim, 199
Bloxham, James, 254, 256, 293, 329
Blue Ridge, 101
Boston Massacre, 105, 108, 149, 395
Boston Port Bill, 138
Boston Tea-party, 132, 137, 138
Bosun, 168, 254, 312
Boswell, James, 278
Botetourt, Governor, 95, 96, 99, 103, 104, 111, 138
Botetourt County, 182
Boucher, Miss Jinny, 91, 121, 123, 125, 156
Boucher, Jonathan, 90, 92, 99, 109-116, 120-127, 156, 213, 245, 371; letter, 91, 109, 114, 115, 156; marriage, 120, 124
Boucher, Mrs. Jonathan. *See* Eleanor Addison.
Braddock, General Edward, 13, 14, 17, 32, 34, 63, 141, 148, 174, 189
Bradley, xiii, 97
Brandon, xii, 94
Brandywine, 179, 395
Breechy, 47, 60
Bréhan, Marchioness de, 287, 288
Brent, Robert, 173
Brent, Sarah. *See* Mrs. George Mason.
Bridgetown, 9
Bristol, 253, 332
Broad, John, 168
Broadwater, Major Charles, 140
Bronaugh, Anne (Mrs. Martin Cockburn), 97
Bronaugh, Betsy (Mrs. Lee Massey), 97
Brooke, Governor Robert, 372
Brookes, Joshua, 398, 399
Brown, Dr. Gustavus, 409, 410
Brunswick, 254
Buckland, William, 41
Bullskin, 8, 15, 61, 67, 98, 102
Bunker Hill, 153
Burgoyne, General John, 171
Burnaby, Andrew, 50-52
Burney, Dr. Charles, 258, 279, 354
Burney, Fanny, 258, 278, 354
Burr, Aaron, 336
Burwell, Nathaniel, xii, 58
Burwell, Mrs. Nathaniel. *See* Elizabeth Carter of Corotoman.
Bushfield, x, xiv, 18, 28, 33, 42, 47, 88, 94, 107, 111, 129, 146, 152, 266, 403
Bushrod, Mrs., 99
Butler, James, 326
Butler, Jane. *See* Mrs. Augustine Washington.
Byrd, Anne. *See* Mrs. Charles Carter of Cleve.
Byrd, Evelyn, 134, 135
Byrd, William II, 134, 135
Byrd, William III, 51, 52, 59, 134, 135, 145, 191, 214
Byrd, Mrs. William III (Mary Willing), 134, 191, 214, 275

Cadwallader, John, 234
Calvert, Benedict, 112, 123, 124, 126-128, 142, 154
Calvert, Governor Charles, 127
Calvert, Eleanor ("Nelly"). *See* Mrs. John Parke Custis.
Calvert, Elizabeth ("Betsy"), 123, 124, 127, 131, 142, 145
Calvert, George, 400
Cambridge (Mass.), 151, 153, 155, 157, 159, 165, 166, 220, 341, 384
Camden (N.C.), 192
Cameron, 99
Campbell, Mrs., 104
Carlyle, George, 145
Carlyle, Colonel John, xiii, 9, 23, 24, 28, 33, 37, 62, 63, 87, 98

Carlyle, Mrs. John (Sarah Fairfax), xiii, 9, 20, 24, 28, 63, 138
Carlyle, Mrs. John (Sybil West), 87
Carlyle, Nancy, 63, 87, 137, 145
Carlyle, Sally, 63, 87, 145
Carolinas, 145, 148, 193, 210, 242, 245, 387
Caroline, 253, 301, 320, 408, 411
Caroline County, 90, 91, 109, 156
Carpenter James, 184
Carpenter Sam, 56
Carrington, Colonel Edward, 403-406
Carrington, Mrs. Edward (Eliza Ambler), viii, 403-406
Carroll, Charles III (of Carrollton), 377, 378
Carroll, Mrs. Charles III (Mary Darnell), 377, 378
Carroll, Charles IV (of Homewood), 377, 378, 397
Carroll, Mrs. Charles IV (Harriet Chew), 378
Carroll, Kitty, 378
Cartagena, 5, 9
Carter, Anne (of Cleve, Mrs. John Champe, Jr.), 59
Carter, Anne (of Corotoman, Mrs. Benjamin Harrison IV), xii
Carter, Anne Hill (of Shirley). *See* Mrs. Henry Lee II.
Carter, Charles (of Blenheim), 199
Carter, Mrs. Charles. *See* Elizabeth ("Betty") Lewis, Jr.
Carter, Charles (of Cleve), xii, 43, 58, 59, 148
Carter, Mrs. Charles (Anne Byrd), 59
Carter, Charles (of Shirley), 136
Carter, Mrs. Charles (Mary Carter of Cleve), 136
Carter, Elizabeth (Mrs. Nathaniel Burwell), xii, 58
Carter, John, xii, 136
Carter, Mrs. John (Elizabeth Hill), xii, 136
Carter, Judith (Mrs. Mann Page), xii
Carter, Landon, xii, 43
Carter, Lucy (Mrs. Henry Fitzhugh, Mrs. Nathaniel Harrison), xii, xiii, 94
Carter, Mary (of Cleve). *See* Mrs. Charles Carter of Shirley.
Carter, Robert ("King"), xii, 43, 58, 136
Carter, Robert, Jr. (of Nomini Hall), xii, 89, 107, 111, 191
Carters, xii, 43, 58, 111, 136, 215, 219
Carter's Grove, xii, 58
Cary, Ann (Mrs. Robert Carter Nicholas), 9, 12, 88, 191
Cary, Elizabeth ("Betsy," Mrs. Bryan Fairfax), 9, 12, 25, 46, 191
Cary, Mary (Mrs. Edward Ambler), 9, 12, 30, 125, 191
Cary, Sally. *See* Mrs. George William Fairfax.
Cary, Willson, 9
Catherine the Great, 387
Cawsons, 156
Cedar Grove, 145, 215
Ceeleys, 9
Champe, Jane. *See* Mrs. Samuel Washington.
Champe, John, 59
Champe, John, Jr., 59
Champe, Mrs. John, Jr. *See* Anne Carter of Cleve.
Chantilly, xii, 89, 103, 245, 250, 267
Charlotte, 301, 312, 331, 411
Chartres, Duc de. *See* Louis Philippe.
Chastellux, Marquis de, 260, 275, 276, 287
Chatham, xiii, 352, 353, 381, 386
Chatham, Earl of. *See* William Pitt.
Chatsworth, 352
Chesapeake, 112, 192
Chester, 309, 362
Chotank, xi, 78, 88, 107, 396
Christian, Mr., 107, 108
Christopher, 297, 324, 363, 410, 411
Claremont, 369
Cleve, xii, 43, 58, 136, 148
Clifton, William, 52, 65, 263, 314
Clifton's Farm. *See* Mount Vernon; River Farm.
Clinton, General Sir Henry, 171, 187, 192
Cockburn, Martin, xiii, 96, 97, 139, 145, 157, 231
Cockburn, Mrs. Martin. *See* Anne Bronaugh.
Colchester, 50, 57, 110, 245
Concord (Mass.), 149, 262
Cone River, 164
Constitution, 263, 268, 269, 272, 274, 275, 279, 283, 287, 299, 315, 337, 403
Conway, Richard, 169, 292
Conway, General Thomas, 181, 234
Conway Cabal, 181
Cook Jack, 66, 168, 253, 254
Cooke, Rachel, 377
Cooper, President, 128, 136, 137
Copley, John Singleton, 116
Corbins, xii, xiv
Cornwallis, General Charles, Earl of, 177, 192, 193, 196, 197, 198, 249
Corotoman, xii, 43, 58, 136
Cracow, 387
Craik, George Washington, 60, 239, 285, 352, 375, 395-397
Craik, Dr. James, xiii, 27, 28, 31, 43, 44, 59, 60, 130, 137, 142, 145, 147, 219, 223, 238, 239, 245, 248, 256, 285, 288, 294, 303, 312, 317, 331, 382, 390, 392, 395, 399, 401, 404, 408-411; letters, 27, 28, 43, 44; marriage, 59
Craik, Mrs. James (Marianne Ewell), 59
Craik, James, Jr., 137
Craik, Nancy, 288
Craik, William, 390, 395
Craik, Mrs. William. *See* Anne Fitzhugh.
Crawford, Val, 61, 67, 102

Crawford, William, 102
Crow, Hyland, 325, 326
Crump, Turner, 78
Cullen, Dr. William, 410
Culpeper County, 324, 333
Culpeper family, 8
Cumberland, Fort, 14, 16, 21, 34
Cupid, 60
Cushing, Judge William, 395
Custis, Daniel Parke, 24-26, 32
Custis, Eleanor Parke ("Nelly," Mrs. Lawrence Lewis), x, xi, 190, 197, 198, 200, 206, 208, 221, 238, 244, 259, 267, 268, 277, 281, 288, 293, 296, 298, 299, 306, 307, 308, 321, 322, 324, 335, 337, 344, 354, 356, 361, 362, 370, 371, 374, 375, 378, 385, 388, 390, 391, 395, 396, 400, 402, 404, 406, 407, 411, 412; Latrobe on, 356; letters, 374, 384, 385; marriage, 400; Mrs. Carrington on, 403, 404; Niemcewicz on, 388
Custis, Eliza Parke (Mrs. Thomas Law), xi, 183, 197, 198, 206, 220, 264, 298, 337-339, 343-346, 349, 352, 363, 371, 375, 384, 386, 389, 390, 391, 403; Adams on, 343, 344; marriage, 339, 343, 345
Custis, George Washington Parke, xi, 197, 198, 200, 206, 208, 220, 221, 238, 244, 259, 268, 269, 277, 281, 293, 296, 298, 299, 302, 306, 308, 321, 322, 324, 335, 338, 345, 353, 354, 356, 359, 362, 365, 371, 375, 380, 381, 384, 390, 395, 396, 397, 404, 406, 412; letter, 376, 377
Custis, Mrs. George Washington Parke. *See* Mary Lee Fitzhugh.
Custis, John Parke ("Jacky"), ix, xi, xii, 32, 47, 49, 72, 73, 82, 85, 87, 88, 90, 92, 95, 97, 99, 103, 104, 107, 109-117, 120, 123, 124, 126-129, 133-138, 141, 142, 145, 154, 159, 172, 173, 179, 181-183, 187, 188, 190, 197-199, 205, 208, 213, 220, 245, 247, 289, 298, 359, 376, 377, 381, 384; death, 198; marriage, 137
Custis, Mrs. John Parke (Eleanor Calvert, Mrs. David Stuart), xi, 112, 123, 124, 126-129, 131, 134, 136, 141, 145, 154, 159, 183, 193, 198, 205, 206, 208, 220, 221, 298, 301, 310, 380, 381, 384, 385, 390, 392, 403; marries John Parke Custis, 137; marries David Stuart, 208
Custis, Martha (Dandridge). *See* Mrs. George Washington.
Custis, Martha Parke ("Patsy"), ix, 32, 47, 49, 72, 73, 83, 85, 87, 88, 90, 92, 94, 95, 98, 100, 102-104, 107, 109, 110, 113, 115, 117, 118, 120, 123-125, 129, 130, 133, 137, 142, 145, 208, 224; death, 129
Custis, Martha Parke II ("Patty", Mrs. Thomas Peter), xi, 183, 197, 198, 206, 220, 264, 298, 337-339, 344, 346, 363, 371, 375, 384, 403; marriage, 338, 339
Custis, Mary Anne Randolph (Mrs. Robert E. Lee), 353, 381
Cyrus, 254, 333, 353, 409

Dandridge, Anne ("Nancy"). *See* Mrs. Burwell Bassett.
Dandridge, Bartholomew, xi, 61, 83, 110, 134, 198, 234
Dandridge, Bartholomew II, xi, 235, 299, 304, 308, 317, 321, 323, 345, 352, 356, 360, 362, 367, 396, 397
Dandridge, Dorothea (Mrs. Patrick Henry), 171
Dandridge, Elizabeth ("Betsy," Mrs. John Aylett, Mrs. Leonard Henley), 96, 98, 191, 234, 292
Dandridge, Mrs. John, 234
Daphne, 333
Darnell, Mary. *See* Mrs. Charles Carroll III.
Davenport, Joseph, 233, 234, 253
Davis, Reverend Mr., 400
Davis, Tom, 76, 137, 314
Davy, 86, 326
Dawson, Mrs., 87, 104
Declaration of Independence, 140, 170, 250, 270, 314, 378, 391
Declaration of Rights, 170, 314
Delia, 304
Delphy, 254
Dick, 332
Dick, Dr. Elisha, 409-411
Dickinson, Governor John, 235
Digges, Elizabeth, xiii, 87
Digges, George, xiii, 145, 238
Digges, Ignatius, xiii, 112, 124
Digges, Jenny, xiii, 145
Digges, Nancy, xiii, 145
Digges, Theresa ("Tracy"), xii, 87
Digges, William, xiii, 87, 100, 111, 112, 123, 124
Digges family, xiii, 100, 112, 125, 145, 219, 249, 395
Dinwiddie, Governor Robert, 10, 12, 15, 18, 21, 24, 26, 27, 86
Directory, The, 391
Dogue Run, 35, 55, 67, 106
Dogue Run Farm. *See* Mount Vernon; Farms.
Doll, 47, 60, 66, 168, 253, 304, 313, 331
Dolly, 253
Dolshy, 288
Donaldson, James, 329, 341
Douglass, David, 110
Dulany, Benjamin, 57, 246
Dulany, Daniel, 145
Dulany family, 125, 246
Dumfries, xii, 45, 50, 58, 59, 96, 103, 134, 147, 156, 193
Dunmore, Governor, Lord, 88, 113, 115, 138, 140, 149, 150, 153, 159, 164, 173
Dunmore, Lady, 139
Duquesne, Fort, 22, 32, 38, 52, 142

Eagle's Nest, xii, xiii, 94, 352
Eden, Governor Robert, 103, 109, 111, 112, 123, 124, 156
Edinburgh, 95, 410
Ehler, John Christian, 293, 313, 327, 332, 333, 335, 373
Ehler, Mrs. John Christian, 314
Eltham, xi, 24, 87, 103, 115, 134, 138, 158, 191, 198, 220, 247, 307, 309, 312, 316, 322, 323, 345, 406, 412
Epsom (Surrey), 123
Estaing, Admiral Comte d', 187
Evans, Joshua, 92
Ewell, Marianne. *See* Mrs. James Craik.
Ewell family, 45

Fairfax, Anne. *See* Mrs. Lawrence Washington.
Fairfax, Bryan, xiii, 24, 25, 46, 86, 92, 100, 140, 148, 191, 199, 248, 382, 383, 394, 407
Fairfax, Mrs. Bryan. *See* Elizabeth Cary.
Fairfax, Mrs. Bryan (Jane Donaldson), 248
Fairfax, Ferdinando, 100, 394
Fairfax, George William, xiii, 7-9, 20, 24, 25, 28, 31, 33, 35, 37, 45, 46, 51, 56, 63, 71, 77, 78, 81, 86, 87, 92, 96, 100-102, 125, 129, 131, 132, 141, 142, 191, 204, 205, 229, 230, 235, 247, 254, 277, 385; death, 277; letters, 35, 36; marriage, 9
Fairfax, Mrs. George William (Sally Cary), 3, 9, 12, 19, 20, 25, 30, 46, 57, 71, 82, 86, 92, 96, 100, 125, 129, 131, 132, 191, 205, 229, 277, 382-385; death, 385
Fairfax, Hannah (Mrs. Warner Washington), xiii, xiv, 9, 12, 20, 25, 71, 98, 99, 407
Fairfax, Lord, xiii, 8, 51, 66, 98, 101, 102, 117, 199
Fairfax, Robert, 8
Fairfax, Sarah. *See* Mrs. John Carlyle.
Fairfax, Colonel William, xiii, 5, 7, 8, 24, 27
Fairfax, Mrs. William, 5, 7, 9
Fairfax County, 44, 53, 59
Fairfax Resolves, 140, 314
Fairfield, xiv, 71, 101, 281
Falls Church, 163
Fauchet, Jean, 341
Fauntleroy, Betsy, 20, 30
Fauquier County, 369
Fauquier, Governor Francis, 32, 39, 50, 84, 85, 86
Fendall, Philip, 267
Fendall, Mrs. Philip (Elizabeth Steptoe, Mrs. Ludwell Lee), 267
Ferry Farm (Fredericksburg), xiii, 1, 5, 6, 10, 24, 82, 124
Ferry Farm (Mount Vernon). *See* Mount Vernon: farms.
Fielding, Henry, 222
Fithian, Philip, xii, 89, 107, 108, 111, 191
Fitzgerald, John, 156, 238, 241, 242, 245, 249, 288, 358, 367, 375, 392
Fitzgerald, Mrs. John (Miss Digges), 249
Fitzhugh, Anne (Mrs. William Craik), 390
Fitzhugh, Henry (of Eagle's Nest), xiii, 94, 352
Fitzhugh, Mrs. Henry. *See* Lucy Carter.
Fitzhugh, John (of Marmion), xiii, 125
Fitzhugh, Mary Lee (Mrs. George Washington Parke Custis), 353, 381, 390
Fitzhugh, Miss, 121
Fitzhugh, William (of Chatham and Ravensworth), xiii, 352, 353, 386, 390, 393, 395
Fitzhugh, Mrs. William (Anne Randolph of Chatsworth), 352
Fitzhugh, William (of Marmion and Rousby Hall), xiii, 125
Fitzhugh, Mrs. William (Anne Rousby), 125
Fitzhugh family, xii, xiii, 78, 94, 219, 368
Fitzpatrick, Dr. John C., 2-4, 20, 211
Foote, Elizabeth. *See* Mrs. Lund Washington.
Forbes, General, 32, 34, 38, 55, 142
Forbes, Mrs., 372, 373, 411
Ford, Paul Leicester, 19
Foster, 78
Frank (House), 93, 253, 313, 322
Franklin, Benjamin, 227, 237, 240, 243, 260, 269, 270, 274, 278
Fraunce's Tavern, 207
Frederick County, 8, 61, 67, 71, 100, 342, 378
Freeman, Douglas Southall, viii, 19, 20
French, Daniel, 53, 55, 56, 82
French, Mrs. Daniel, 56, 264
French, Elizabeth, 56, 57, 246
French Revolution, 285, 297, 341, 354
Frestel, Felix, 341, 354, 362, 373

Gage, General Thomas, 128
Galloway, Joseph, xiii
Galloway, Samuel, xiii, 111, 112
Galloway, Mrs. Samuel (Anne Chew), 112
Galloway, Miss, xiii, 112
Garrick, David, 235, 279
Gates, General Horatio, 148, 192, 235
Gates, Mrs. Horatio, 148
George, 66, 86
George I, 135
George III, xiv, 95, 99, 113, 126, 138, 140, 146, 153, 157, 189, 257
Gerry, Elbridge, 391
Gibbon, Edward, 279
Giles, 253, 300, 301
Gloucester County, 173, 251
Gloucestershire, 254, 255
Gordon, William, 220-222, 237
Graham, William, 237
Grasse, Admiral Comte de, 196
Grayson, Mr., 241

Grayson, Colonel William, 96, 145, 156, 173, 283, 299
Green, Dr. Charles, xiii, 28, 57, 69, 85, 129
Green, Thomas, 246, 272, 291, 293, 313, 318, 326, 329, 349, 350
Green, Mrs. Thomas. *See* Sally Bishop.
Greene, General Nathanael, 148, 245, 260
Greenway Court, xiii, 8, 51, 101
Greenwich (England), 50
Grymes, Lucy. *See* Mrs. Henry Lee.
Grymes family, 277
Gubner, Domenicus, 105
Gunner, 168
Gunston Hall, xiii, 4, 12, 41, 42, 46, 69, 70, 76, 83, 97, 98, 107, 110, 130, 131, 141, 143, 191, 214, 245, 299, 314, 357; John Mason's account, 69-71, 130, 131
Guy, 168
Gwynne's Island, 173

Hague, The, 227, 367
Hallams, 110
Hamburg, 373
Hamilton, Alexander, 3, 210, 269, 275, 287, 315, 317, 321, 337, 351, 367, 373, 387, 392, 394
Hamilton, Mrs. Alexander (Betsy Schuyler), 210, 321, 387
Hammond, Mrs. (Mildred Washington), 362
Hampton, 157
Hancock, John, 290
Hanover County, 91, 381
Hanson, Colonel, 285, 286
Happy Retreat, x, 147, 199, 211, 266, 366, 401
Hardwicke, Christopher, 61, 62, 67
Harewood, x, 46, 147, 198, 312, 321, 336, 359, 369, 394, 395
Harford (Md.), 309
Harlem, 173-175
Harper's Ferry, 369
Harrison, Benjamin IV (of Berkeley), xii
Harrison, Mrs. Benjamin. *See* Anne Carter of Corotoman.
Harrison, Benjamin V (of Berkeley), 135, 141, 202, 215, 250, 274
Harrison, Mrs. Benjamin (Elizabeth Bassett), 135
Harrison, Nathaniel (of Brandon and Eagle's Nest), xii, 94, 145
Harrison, Mrs. Nathaniel. *See* Lucy Carter.
Harrison, Robert Hanson, xiii, 81, 155, 156, 210, 238, 245, 366
Harvard, 3, 259, 281, 375
Hay, Anthony, 99, 104
Hayfield, xi, 163, 228, 261, 275, 358, 375
Head of Elk, 197, 216
Hell Hole, 98, 161, 230
Henderson, Mr., 57
Henley, Frances, 234
Henley, Leonard, 234, 292
Henley, Mrs. Leonard. *See* Betsy Dandridge.
Henry, Patrick, 138, 141, 143, 145, 146, 170, 171, 215, 263, 274, 403
Henry, Mrs. Patrick. *See* Dorothea Dandridge.
Hercules, 253, 300, 372
Hessians, 171, 176
Hill, Elizabeth. *See* Mrs. John Carter.
Hite, Mrs. Isaac, 336
Holland, 227
Hollin Hall, 215
Home, Henry (Lord Kames), 256
Home, Reverend John, 94
Homewood, 378
Homony Club, 113
Hope Park, xii, 298, 339, 375, 385, 388, 395, 400, 403
Hopkinson, Francis, 235
Houdon, Jean Antoine, 240, 241
Howe, General Sir William, 171, 187, 270
Hudson River, 83, 151, 174, 192, 196, 198
Humphreys, Colonel David, 196, 208, 210, 240, 258, 260, 263, 270, 277, 279, 281, 284, 290, 291, 292, 297, 304, 307, 316, 366, 369
Hunter, William, viii, 241-245
Hunting Creek, 5, 65

Indiana, 83
Ipswich (England), 222
Isaac, 300, 304

Jack, 330, 331
Jackson, Colonel William, 297, 299, 304
Jamaica, 97, 218
James, Captain, 173
James River, xii, xiv, 4, 9, 52, 58, 94, 134, 156, 164, 190, 192, 214, 316
Jamestown, 12, 191
Jay, John, 250, 280, 340, 387
Jay, Mrs. John (Sarah Livingston), 235, 387
Jefferson, Thomas, 3, 99, 126, 138, 140, 182, 191, 193, 215, 249, 260, 279, 284, 285, 287, 305, 315, 327, 342, 351, 358, 359, 397
Jenny, 47, 253
Joe, 253, 331
Johnson, Dr. Samuel, 3, 237, 258, 278, 279, 354, 355
Johnston, George, 155
Johnston, George, Jr., 156
Jones, Commodore John Paul, 273
Julius, 47
Jupiter, 86, 330

Kames, Lord. *See* Henry Home.
Kanawha, 349
Kenmore. *See* Millbank.
King, Rufus, 382, 396
King George County, 125, 368

King's College, 126, 127, 129, 133, 136, 137
Kip's Bay, 173
Kitty, 254, 313
Knight, Humphrey, 31, 33, 35, 37
Knowles, John, 167, 168, 172
Knox, General Henry, 209, 210, 268, 291, 341, 392, 394
Kosciuszko, General Thaddeus, 386, 387, 406

Lafayette, George Washington, 223, 341, 354, 356, 362, 373
Lafayette, Marquis de, 187, 193, 194, 196, 209, 215, 216, 222, 223, 237, 240, 245, 247, 282, 283, 287, 297, 317, 341, 362, 373, 389
Lafayette, Marquise de, 223, 341
Lafayette, Virginie, 223
Lame Alice, 183, 254
Lanphier, Going, 142, 144, 154, 165, 167, 172, 180, 183, 185, 188
Latrobe, Benjamin, viii, 354-358, 390
Laurie, Dr. James, xiii, 57, 60, 61, 63
Law, Thomas, 343, 345, 360, 363, 371, 375, 382, 385, 388, 391, 395, 403
Law, Mrs. Thomas. *See* Eliza Parke Custis.
Lear, Lincoln, 298, 308, 317, 321, 324, 335, 342, 356, 367
Lear, Mrs. (Senior), 321, 335, 345, 346, 352, 360
Lear, Tobias, xi, 3, 258-261, 264, 273, 277, 280, 281, 291, 292, 296, 298, 299, 302, 308, 309, 317, 321, 322, 324, 335, 340, 342, 345, 346, 356, 359, 360, 362, 365, 367, 368, 371, 375, 386, 390, 392, 394, 397, 398, 401, 402, 407-412; marries Mary Long, 296; her death, 321; marries Fanny Bassett, 340; her death, 345; returns to Mount Vernon, 394
Lear, Mrs. Tobias. *See* Fanny Bassett.
Lear, Mrs. Tobias (Mary Long), 296, 298, 308, 317, 321, 340
Lear, Mrs. Tobias (Frances Henley), 234
Lee, Alice (of Stratford, Mrs. William Shippen), xii
Lee, Arthur, xii
Lee, General Charles, 145, 148, 151
Lee, Flora (of Stratford, Mrs. Ludwell Lee), 267, 288, 303
Lee, Francis Lightfoot, xii, 43
Lee, George, 1, 9, 12, 18, 75
Lee, George II, 238
Lee, Hannah (of Stratford, Mrs. Gawen Corbin II), xii
Lee, Hannah (of Chantilly, Mrs. Corbin Washington), 89
Lee, Colonel Henry (of Leesylvania), 43, 103, 193
Lee, Mrs. Henry (Lucy Grymes), 30, 43, 103, 278
Lee, Colonel Henry II ("Lighthorse Harry"), xii, 43, 100, 103, 125, 126, 136, 148, 156, 193, 245, 250, 251, 262, 268, 275, 299, 316, 317, 357, 392
Lee, Mrs. Henry II (Anne Hill Carter of Shirley), xii, 136, 316
Lee, Mrs. Henry II (Matilda Lee of Stratford), 245, 267, 299
Lee, Ludwell (of Chantilly and Shooter's Hill), 267, 288, 303, 392
Lee, Mrs. Ludwell. *See* Flora Lee.
Lee, Mary (of Chantilly, Mrs. William Augustine Washington), 89
Lee, Philip Ludwell (of Stratford), xii, 43, 267
Lee, Mrs. Philip Ludwell (Elizabeth Steptoe). *See* Mrs. Philip Fendall.
Lee, Richard Henry (of Chantilly), xii, 43, 89, 139, 141, 148, 181, 238, 241, 243, 245, 250, 275, 403
Lee, Richard ("Squire," of Lee Hall), 100, 146
Lee, Mrs. Richard (Sally Poythress), 100
Lee, Richarda, 100
Lee, Robert E., xii, 136, 353, 381
Lee, Mrs. Robert E. *See* Mary Anne Randolph Custis.
Lee, Thomas (of Stratford), xii, 100
Lee, Thomas (of Chantilly), 89
Lee, Mrs. Thomas (of Chantilly). *See* Milly Washington.
Lee, Thomas Ludwell (of Belleview), xii, 42, 148
Lee, William, xii, 278
Lee, Mrs. William (Hannah Ludwell of Green Spring), 278
Lee family, xiv, 215, 219, 241, 250, 278, 368, 378
Lee Hall, 100
Leeds Castle, 8
Leesylvania, xii, 43, 103, 125, 148, 156, 193
Lewis, Charles, 16
Lewis, Elizabeth ("Betty," Jr., Mrs. Charles Carter), ix, 199, 310, 324, 333, 346
Lewis, Fielding, ix, xiii, 11, 16, 23, 26, 44, 59, 87, 88, 94, 95, 102, 103, 124-126, 130, 147, 166, 167, 176, 191, 199, 211; death, 199
Lewis, Mrs. Fielding ("Betty" Washington), ix, xiii, 4, 11, 24, 44, 59, 83, 101, 103, 124-126, 147, 191, 199, 211, 212, 266, 268, 269, 292, 294, 304, 310, 311, 323, 333, 336, 340, 346, 349, 352, 366; death, 366; letters, 211, 298, 310, 323, 333, 346, 347
Lewis, Mrs. Fielding (Catherine Washington), 11
Lewis, Fielding, Jr., ix, 310
Lewis, Frances, 404, 406, 411
Lewis, George Fielding, ix, 24, 156, 220, 347, 366, 372
Lewis, Howell, ix, 199, 212, 304, 307, 308, 310, 318, 321, 322, 324, 352, 354, 375, 406; letter, 318

Lewis, Mrs. Howell (Ellen Pollard), 403, 406
Lewis, John, 220
Lewis, Lawrence, ix, 199, 212, 298, 318, 319, 348, 369, 370, 374, 381, 395-402, 406, 412; first marriage, 298, 319; marries Nelly Custis, 400
Lewis, Mrs. Lawrence. *See* Eleanor Parke Custis.
Lewis, Robert, ix, 199, 212, 292, 297, 301, 302, 304, 307, 310, 342, 364
Lexington (Va.), 215
Lincoln, General Benjamin, 192, 249, 258, 259, 287, 297
Livingston, Henry Beekman, 213
Livingston, Mrs. Henry Beekman. *See* Nancy Shippen.
Livingston family, 387
Long Island, 171, 357
Longwood, 145, 322, 345
Loudoun, Fort, 22, 24, 26, 32, 44, 46, 48
Loudoun, Lord, 21, 22, 32
Loudoun County, 43, 154, 182, 264
Louis XVI, 317
Louis Philippe (Duc de Chartres, Duc d' Orléans, Duc de Valois, Comte de Neuilly), 369, 415
L'Ouverture, Toussaint, 397
Lucy, 60, 313, 322
Ludwell, Hannah. *See* Mrs. William Lee.
Ludwell, Lucy. *See* Mrs. John Paradise.
Ludwell, Philippa, 278
Lynch, Thomas, 151

Macauley-Graham, Catherine, 237, 238
Madison, James, 249, 250, 263, 268, 271, 275, 283, 284, 287, 290, 306, 336, 337, 351, 407; marries Dolley Todd, 336
Madison, Mrs. James (Dolley Payne Todd), 320, 336, 337
Magowan, Walter, 72, 85, 90, 99, 125, 245
Maine, 219
Malta, 247
Mansion House Farm. *See* Mount Vernon: farms
Markham, Gervase, 66
Marlborough (Md.), 52, 280, 380
Marmion, xiii, 125
Marshall, John, 391
Marshall, Thomas, 187
Marshall Hall, 55, 187
Mason, George, xiii, 4, 12, 41, 42, 54, 56, 65, 69, 70, 96-99, 107, 110, 130, 131, 139-141, 143-145, 157, 164, 175, 181, 191, 194, 199, 214, 215, 219, 231, 245, 263, 264, 270, 274, 275, 283, 299, 314, 315; death, 314, 315; letters, 98, 139, 140, 157
Mason, Mrs. George (Anne Eilbeck), 41, 97, 130, 131, 194, 214
Mason, Mrs. George (Sarah Brent), 191, 194, 199, 214, 264
Mason, George V, 215
Mason, John, 69, 70, 130, 131, 215, 270
Mason, Sally (Mrs. Daniel McCarthy III), 99, 140, 194, 215
Mason, Thomson, 65
Mason, Thomson II, 215
Massey, Lee, xiii, 97, 129, 139
Massey, Mrs. Lee. *See* Betsy Bronaugh.
Mattapony River, 31, 87, 96
McCarthy, Captain Daniel II, 98
McCarthy, Daniel III, 215
McCarthy, Mrs. Daniel III. *See* Sally Mason.
McCarthy, Elizabeth. *See* Mrs. Burwell Bassett II.
McCarthy family, 145, 322
McHenry, James, 365, 367, 368, 391-394, 397
McKoy (overseer), 318, 325, 326, 332
Meade, Colonel Richard Kidder, 156
Menokin, xii
Mercer, George, 17, 100
Mercer, Hugh, xii, 147
Mercer, John Francis, 252
Middlebrook (N.J.), 186-189
Millbank (Kenmore), ix, 11, 12, 44, 45, 63, 71, 101, 103, 104, 124, 147, 166, 212, 310, 346, 352
Millbrook, 346, 352, 366
Minitree, David, 58
Molly, 47, 411
Monmouth, 145, 187
Monongahela, 17, 32, 79, 174, 330
Monroe, James, 249, 290, 358, 407
Monroe, Mrs. James (Eliza Kortwright), 249
Monticello, 327, 342, 362
Moore, Charles, 173
More, Miss, 57
Morgan Library, 20, 338
Morris (overseer), 159, 165
Morris, Gouverneur, 260, 284, 285, 294, 301
Morris, Robert, 218, 235, 236, 269, 270, 275, 284, 295, 298
Morris, Roger, 174
Morris, Mrs. Roger. *See* Mary Philipse.
Morristown (N.J.), 178, 190-192, 249
Morton, Reverend Mr., 141
Mount Airy (Md.), xi, 112, 127, 137, 145, 173
Mount Airy (Va.), 127
Mount Eagle, 248, 385
Mount Pleasant, 9
Mount Vernon:
agreements, 94, 105, 106, 182, 188, 254, 268, 269, 322, 323, 329, 381, 382, 400
banquet room (New Room), 142, 165, 166, 172, 173, 175, 218, 219, 252, 268, 271, 273, 274, 388, 414
barns, 78, 90, 284, 288, 290, 293, 300, 301
bedroom, 142, 166, 171
botanical garden, 238, 239, 251, 271, 280

Mount Vernon (*Continued*)
bowling green, 226, 240, 243, 252
bricklayers, 76, 167, 216, 244
building, 33, 39, 142, 144, 149, 154, 165-167, 171, 173, 183, 186, 326, 365
bull, 167, 168
ceilings, 165, 166
chariot, 92, 93, 103, 111, 112, 192, 244
chimney-pieces, 23, 154, 166, 175, 218, 219, 252, 274, 365, 414
covered ways (colonnades, palisades), 167, 186, 188, 193, 217, 232, 272
crops, 66, 76, 93, 95, 100, 105, 169, 179, 184, 188, 189, 203, 239, 244, 251, 257, 258, 269, 271, 272, 273, 280, 285, 293, 304, 309, 312, 318, 341, 342, 357
cupola, 217, 272, 273
deer, 229, 230, 240, 244, 252, 271, 288, 333, 404, 405
dining-room, 38, 154, 161, 165, 365, 388, 414
distillery, 364, 390, 402
dogs, 21, 90, 95, 100, 208, 240, 244, 246, 264, 404
farms, *Dogue Run,* 47, 60, 65, 71, 78, 95, 169, 184, 185, 226, 238, 251, 264, 269, 300, 301, 318, 325, 332, 342, 364, 402; *Ferry Farm,* 82, 94, 114, 188, 226, 264, 269, 313, 331; see also *Union Farm; Mansion House* (*Home House*), 65, 87, 90, 95, 252, 312, 313, 322-325, 331, 332, 350, 354, 402; *Muddy Hole,* 65, 86, 94, 226, 238, 239, 251, 254, 269, 293, 300, 326; *River Farm* (*Clifton's or Neck*), 60, 65, 71, 76, 239, 254, 263, 264, 293, 314, 316, 325, 333, 340, 386, 395; *Union Farm,* 65, 82, 288, 325, 342, 408
fences, 66, 77, 78, 280, 285, 293, 300, 251, 343, 350, 355
fishing, 55, 88, 94, 105, 107, 116, 120, 232, 269, 280, 313
flower garden, 227, 232, 349, 357, 389
French officers at, 197
fruits, 4, 69-71, 169, 208, 231, 240, 251, 335, 389
garden houses, 251, 252, 349
garden walks, 300, 312
gardeners, 206, 300, 332, 333, 349, 350, *see also* Bateman, Ehler and Christian
gates, 77, 230, 239, 300, 343, 350, 354
greenhouse, 240, 272, 308, 314, 329, 357, 405, 414
ha-ha's, 226, 232
hay, 71, 169, 293
hedges, 171, 172, 182, 183, 193, 251, 312, 328, 343
Hell Hole, 98, 161, 230
horses, 15, 38, 66-68, 77, 80, 100, 101, 111, 112, 114, 123, 128, 134, 167, 172, 176, 177, 184, 185, 193, 198, 208, 241, 244, 248, 296, 300, 301, 308, 309, 312, 325, 350, 352, 388, 393
hot beds, 300
hunting, 55, 78, 85-88, 97, 98, 103, 106, 107, 137, 180, 244, 245, 246, 248, 277, 281, 404
ice, 218, 226, 251, 280, 304
ice-house, 218, 300, 304, 312, 359
inventories, 60, 183, 241, 252-254
invoices, 22-24, 29, 30, 48-50, 72-75, 92, 93, 118-120, 129, 133, 134, 215, 216, 256, 258, 263, 284, 294, 295, 297, 366
jackasses, 247, 252, 280, 290, 389
kitchen garden, 206, 227, 357
library, 142, 144, 149, 166, 171, 216-218, 222, 252, 256, 257, 258, 388
machinery, 74, 75, 257, 258, 290, 318, 390
mill, 35, 37, 67, 68, 69, 76, 90, 105-107, 114-116, 144, 184, 185, 206, 226, 277, 285, 364, 390, 400, 402, 404
miller, *see* William Poole, William Roberts.
mules, 290, 389
necessaries, 230, 232, 300, 349, 350
overseers, 31, 34-37, 61, 62, 67, 78, 86, 161, 312, 318, 319, 325, 326, 341, 342
palisades, *see* covered ways
piazza, 46, 193, 217, 240, 252, 358, 388
plateaux, 294, 295, 301
ploughing, 66, 67, 184, 232, 269
ploughs, 4, 66, 67, 255, 258, 357, 390
racing, 99, 111, 113, 133, 241, 264
roads, 98, 226, 232, 243, 269, 309, 343, 359
roof, 205, 240
salt shortage, 169, 182
school house, 349
scythes, 133, 134
seed drill, 257
serpentine walks, 226, 230, 232, 239, 272, 273, 300, 312
shooting, 86, 87, 107
sieves, 118, 216
slavery, 184, 188, 189, 252
slaves, 13, 47, 55, 56, 60, 62, 76, 77, 83, 93, 105, 114, 168, 176, 182-184, 188, 189, 194, 195, 252-254, 300, 301, 303, 304, 312, 313, 318, 323, 324, 325, 326, 329-333, 390
stables, 198, 244, 251, 318, 388, 415
tobacco, 76, 93, 105
trees, 169, 171, 172, 176, 182, 183, 193, 200, 201, 208, 225-228, 230, 232, 233, 251, 272, 285, 312, 389, 407, 415
vineyard, 312
wall-paper, 23, 216, 252
weather, 54, 57-59, 61, 67, 68, 71, 83, 84, 86, 98, 114, 115, 122, 125, 182, 184, 186, 188, 210, 230, 232, 251, 254, 285, 304, 309, 361, 363, 395, 407, 408
weather-vane, 217, 272, 273
weaving, 76, 105, 137, 168, 182, 414

Mount Vernon (*Continued*)
well, 154, 167, 193, 226, 273, 284, 300, 308, 314, 350
wildernesses, 226, 232, 239, 300, 312
windsor chairs, 216
wine-coolers, 295
Moustier, Comte de, 287, 288
Moylan, Colonel Stephen, 234
Muddy Hole Farm. *See* Mount Vernon: farms.
Muhlenberg, General Peter, 156
Mulatto Jack, 47, 57, 66, 67
Myrtilla, 168, 254

Nathan, 253, 301, 331
Neabsco Bay, 134
Neale, John, 341
Neck, The. *See* Mount Vernon; River Farm.
Ned, 37, 86
Nelson, General Thomas, 215, 298
Nelson, Thomas, Jr., 298
Neuilly, Comte de. *See* Louis Philippe.
Newburgh (N.Y.), 198, 200, 204, 205, 213, 214, 220
New England, 139, 157, 295
New Hampshire, 259, 262, 284, 296, 308, 321, 342, 345
New Jersey, 89, 107, 178, 186
New Kent County, xi, 24, 57, 58, 154, 158, 241
Newport (R.I.), 187, 192, 193
Newton (Pa.), 177
New Town, 97
New Windsor (N.Y.), 83, 151, 192, 194, 197
Nicholas, Robert Carter, 12, 88, 104, 115, 138, 149, 191
Nicholas, Mrs. Robert Carter. *See* Anne Cary.
Niemcewicz, Count Julien, viii, 386-391, 415
Nomini Creek, xiv, 18
Nomini Hall, xii, 89, 107, 111
Norfolk (Va.), 157, 164, 225, 285, 354
North Carolina, 192, 225

Occoquan, 52, 58, 97, 145, 215, 384
Ohio River, 12, 13, 25, 38, 53
Orléans, Duc d'. *See* Louis Philippe.
Overdoncks, 264
Oxford (England), 278
Oxon Hill, 120, 121, 123

Page, Mann, xii, xiv
Palmer, Jonathan, 93, 94
Pamunkey River, xi, 26, 32, 39, 44, 47, 48, 82
Paradise, John, 277-279
Paradise, Mrs. John (Lucy Ludwell), 277-279
Paradise, Peter, 277, 278
Paris (France), 227, 237, 240, 243, 260, 279, 285, 287, 294, 301, 387
Paris (slave), 253, 300, 330
Parkinson, Richard, 394, 395
Parks, Andrew, 346-349, 394
Parks, Mrs. Andrew. *See* Harriot Washington.
Patterson (overseer), 31, 33, 34, 38
Patuxent River, 125
Paul, Czar, 387
Payne, Anna, 336
Payne, Lucy (Mrs. George Steptoe Washington), 321, 336
Payne, Mrs., 320, 336
Peacey, William, 255
Peake, Nancy, 145
Peale, Charles Willson, 116-117, 358, 388
Pearce, William, 322-326, 328-333, 340, 341, 343, 349, 350, 353, 359, 364
Peccatone, xii, xiv
Pendleton, Edmund, 43, 141, 143, 152
Pensacola (Fla.), 82
Peter, 67, 254, 313
Peter, Judge Robert, 338
Peter, Thomas, 338, 344, 346, 371, 375, 382, 384
Peter, Mrs. Thomas. *See* Martha Parke Custis.
Petersburg (Va.), 354
Philippe Egalité, 369
Philipse, Mary (Mrs. Roger Morris), 17, 174
Pinckney, Charles Coatsworth, 391, 395
Pinckney, Mrs. Charles Coatsworth, 385
Pine, William, 235, 236, 241, 415, 416
Piscataway Creek, 112, 276
Pitt, William (Earl of Chatham), 257, 260, 352
Pleasant Hill, 31, 87
Plymouth (Mass.), 227
Pohick Bay, 97
Pohick Church, 56, 57, 129, 144, 261
Pohick Creek, 215
Poland, 387
Poole, William, 35, 68
Pope's Creek, ix, 6, 42
Port Royal, 58, 91
Port Tobacco, 59, 210, 409
Portsmouth (N.H.), 259
Portugal, 297, 316
Posey, Hanson, 80
Posey, Captain John, 53, 55, 56, 78-83, 87, 94, 137, 187, 199
Posey, Milly, 55, 83, 100, 107, 152, 173, 180, 193, 195
Posey, Price, 79, 82, 83, 199
Posey, Thomas, 83
Potomac River, xiii, xiv, 5, 6, 12, 18, 23, 26, 30, 33, 34, 38, 41, 42, 46, 52, 57, 63, 82, 86, 96, 99, 102, 103, 125, 153, 155, 159, 173, 191, 193, 209, 242, 244, 261, 276, 309, 324
Powel, Samuel, 275-277, 321, 415, 416

Powel, Mrs. Samuel (Elizabeth Willing), 275-277, 321
Poythress, Sally. *See* Mrs. Richard Lee.
Prescott, William, 281, 282, 416
Princeton, 125, 126, 147, 206, 211, 249, 353, 359, 362, 365, 371, 375
Pulaski, Count Casimir, 234, 386, 406
Putnam, General Isaac, 260

Quebec, 242

Raleigh Tavern, 24, 41, 99, 104, 124, 138
Ramsay, Betty, 145
Ramsay, Colonel, 392
Ramsay, William, xiii, 98
Randolph, Anne (of Chatsworth). *See* Mrs. William Fitzhugh of Chatham.
Randolph, Mrs. Beverley, 390
Randolph, Edmund, 155, 249, 263, 268, 274, 275, 284, 320, 323, 327, 341, 367
Randolph, Mrs. Edmund (Betsy Nicholas), 367
Randolph, John, 43, 88, 96, 104, 110, 155, 173
Randolph, Peyton, 43, 88, 96, 99, 104, 110, 113, 115, 135, 141, 144, 149, 155
Randolph, Mrs. Peyton (Elizabeth Harrison of Berkeley), 135
Randolph family, 378
Rapahannock River, xii, xiii, 1, 5, 8, 10, 11, 14, 23, 24, 44, 50, 58, 59, 78, 82, 111, 173, 212, 245, 352
Ravensworth, xiii, 55, 78, 352, 381, 386
Rawlins, Albin, 381, 382, 386, 397
Rawlins, John, 252, 268
Rawlins (overseer), 382, 408
Recruiting Officer, The, 110
Reed, Joseph, 151
Reynolds, Joshua, 279
Rhode Island, 187, 262
Richardson, Samuel, 3
Richmond (slave), 254
Richmond Convention, 146, 157
Richmond County, 146
Rippon Lodge, x, xiii, 134, 219, 241
River Farm. *See* Mount Vernon: farms.
Roberts, William, 184, 185, 206, 233, 234, 353, 400, 401
Robinson, Beverly, 17, 174
Robinson, John, 22, 24, 31, 43, 87, 88, 174
Rochambeau, General the Comte de, 193, 197, 287
Roosevelt, 358
Rose, 47
Rosegill, xiv, 111
Rose Hill (Md.), 410
Rose Hill (Va.), 55
Rosewell, xii, xiv
Round Hill, xiii, 179
Rousby, Anne. *See* Mrs. William Fitzhugh.
Rousby Hall, 125
Rover's Delight, 55, 78, 82, 94. *See also* Mount Vernon, Union Farm.
Roxbury (Mass.), 220
Rumney, Dr. William, xiii, 63, 64, 85, 87, 92, 96, 106, 121, 125
Rush, Dr. Benjamin, 410
Ruth, 37, 332

Sabine Hall, xii, 43
St. Clair, General Sir John, 32, 34
Salem (Mass.), 5
Sall, 253, 353
Sall Brass, 253
Sam, 331, 332
San Domingo, 397
Sandy Hill, 211, 225, 402
Sarah, 313, 332
Saratoga, 387
Savage, Edward, 415
Savannah, 198
Schomberg, 168, 254
Schuyler, Betsy. *See* Mrs. Alexander Hamilton.
Schuyler, General Philip, 210
Sears, 154, 166
Shakespeare, William, 95, 142, 236
Shaw, William, 245, 258, 261
Shays' Rebellion, 262
Shenandoah River, 71, 101
Shenandoah Valley, xiii, xiv, 8, 51, 90, 147, 156, 237, 266, 281, 289, 395
Shippen, Nancy (Mrs. Henry Beekman Livingston), 213
Shippen, Peggy (Mrs. Benedict Arnold), 213, 270
Shippen, Dr. William, xii, 410
Shippen, Mrs. William. *See* Alice Lee.
Shippen family, xii, 213, 214
Shirley, xii, 136, 316
Shirley, Governor, 17, 21
Shooter's Hill, 267, 303, 307, 334, 392
Siddons, Mrs. Sarah, 95, 260
Simcoe, Colonel John, 111
Sinah, 254, 313
Sinclair, Sir John, 382, 383
Smith, Reverend Samuel Stanhope, 371
South Carolina, 151, 192, 225, 395
Spain, 247, 297
Sparks, Jared, 291
Spence, William, 373
Spotswood, Alexander, 381
Spotsylvania County, 26, 346
Springfield, xiii, 97, 139, 157
Springfield (Mass.), 262
Springs. *See* Berkeley Springs.
Stamp Act, 83, 86
Staten Island, 171, 173
Stephens family, 60, 62
Steuben, General Frederick, 187, 235
Stewart, Captain Robert, 17, 26, 27, 44
Strasburg (Va.), 336
Stratford, xii, 42, 100, 103, 245, 250, 267, 278, 299, 357
Stuart, Dr. David, xii, 205, 206, 208, 220, 221, 234, 238, 280, 284, 289, 296, 298, 368, 375, 376, 384, 385, 390, 392, 403

Stuart, Mrs. David. *See* Mrs. John Parke Custis.
Stuart, Gilbert, 378, 379
Stuart, William, 325
Summer Seat, 176
Supreme Court, 366
Switzerland, 387

Tarleton, Colonel Banastre, 193
Tayloe family, 127
Thomson, Charles, 291
Thomson, James, 217
Thornton, Mildred. *See* Mrs. Charles Washington.
Thornton, Mildred. *See* Mrs. Samuel Washington.
Thornton, William, 276
Tilghman, Tench, 252, 366
Todd, Dolley. *See* Mrs. James Madison.
Tom, 77
Towelston, 25, 46, 86, 100
Townshend Acts, 86, 98, 103
Trenton (N.J.), 4, 147, 176, 249
Triplett, Captain Thomas, xiii, 179, 183
Triplett, William, xiii, 35
Truro Parish, 57
Tulip Hill, xiii, 112
Tull, Jethro, 256, 257
Turberville, Miss, 24, 25
Turberville family, xiv

Union Farm. *See* Mount Vernon: farms.

Valentine, Joseph, 47, 48
Valley Forge, 4, 83, 85, 147, 179, 182, 183, 187, 191, 203, 210, 215, 224, 234, 378, 413
Valois, Duc de. *See* Louis Philippe.
Van Vleck, Reverend Jacob, 361, 362
Vaughan, Samuel, 218, 219, 252, 274, 414
Victoria, Queen, 369

Wakefield, ix, x, xiv, 1, 6, 88, 111, 414
Wakefield (England), 43
Walnut Tree Farm (Wellington), 340, 346, 352, 367, 368, 371
Walpole, Horace, 279
Wanstead (England), 219
Warburton Hall, xiii, 87, 112, 238
Ward, Colonel, 221
Warville, Brissot de, 289
Washington, Augustine, ix, xiv, 5, 7, 8, 11, 68
Washington, Mrs. Augustine (Mary Ball), ix, xii, 5, 10, 11, 14, 24, 26, 44, 59, 82, 103, 104, 125, 144, 147, 201, 202, 210, 212, 266, 267, 269, 283, 292, 294
Washington, Mrs. Augustine (Jane Butler), ix
Washington, Augustine II ("Austin"), ix, xiv, 1, 5, 7, 24, 42, 47, 49, 50, 83, 88, 111, 191
Washington, Mrs. "Austin" (Anne Aylett), ix, 1, 83, 88, 111
Washington, Betty. *See* Mrs. Fielding Lewis.
Washington, Bushrod, x, 83, 89, 134, 191, 201, 206, 212-214, 219, 220, 241, 248, 266, 289, 298, 354, 355, 358, 366, 372, 373, 395
Washington, Mrs. Bushrod (Julia Anne Blackburn), x, 134, 220, 241, 248, 307, 358, 366
Washington, Catherine. *See* Mrs. Fielding Lewis.
Washington, Charles, ix, x, xiv, 26, 46, 59, 83, 86, 88, 90, 94, 96, 100, 133, 147, 199, 211, 212, 224, 238, 266, 267, 281, 289, 366, 370, 401; death, 401
Washington, Mrs. Charles (Mildred Thornton), x, 26, 46, 90
Washington, Charles Augustine, xi, 303, 316, 317, 342, 345, 346, 352, 356, 366, 367
Washington, Corbin, x, 89, 218
Washington, Mrs. Corbin. *See* Hannah Lee of Chantilly.
Washington, Fayette, I and II, xi, 269, 295, 298, 316, 317, 342, 345, 346, 352, 356, 366, 367
Washington, Ferdinand, x, 90, 191, 280
Washington, Frances. *See* Mrs. Burgess Ball.
Washington, George:
- Diary, 53, 62, 65-69, 71, 82-84, 86, 87, 90, 92, 94, 95, 97-99, 102-104, 106, 107, 111, 114, 116, 123, 124, 129, 138, 140, 147, 148, 151, 195, 197, 198, 208, 219, 224, 226, 228, 230-235, 238-241, 245, 246, 248, 251, 252, 254, 259, 264, 268, 269, 271, 274, 277, 280-285, 288, 291, 293, 295, 296, 298, 362, 363, 368, 375, 382, 385, 392, 394, 395, 400, 407, 408, 414
- finances, 4, 24, 53, 76, 105, 125, 133, 137, 147, 161, 180, 181, 183, 184, 189, 203, 204, 211, 212, 214, 224, 256, 289, 292, 320, 342, 348, 370, 371, 401, 402
- frontier service, 1, 10, 12-18, 21, 27, 32, 34, 38, 39
- health, 9, 12, 14, 15, 25, 28, 31, 33, 38, 39, 61, 71, 72, 87, 115, 256, 294, 296, 297, 321, 393, 407-412
- letters:
  - to London agent, 22, 23, 29, 30, 48-50, 72-75, 133-134
  - to John Alton, 45
  - to Dr. Anderson, 373
  - to James Anderson, 364, 385, 386, 401, 408
  - to Burgess Ball, 318, 401
  - to Burwell Bassett, 57, 128, 129, 236, 237
  - to Burwell Bassett II, 345, 346
  - to Fanny Bassett, 316
  - to Clement Biddle, 216, 263, 297

Washington, George, letters (*Continued*)
to Thomas Bishop, 189
to Jonathan Boucher, 90, 91, 115, 116
to President Cooper, 136
to Dr. Craik, 285, 294, 401
to Eliza Parke Custis, 338, 339, 344
to George Washington Parke Custis, 359, 360, 365, 378, 380, 392
to Bartholomew Dandridge, 83
to Bartholomew Dandridge II, 367, 396
to Governor Dinwiddie, 18, 25
to Christian Ehler, 327, 335
to Bryan Fairfax, 140
to George William Fairfax, 77, 78, 204, 205, 229, 230, 254
to Sally Fairfax, 19, 383, 384
to Governor Fauquier, 39
to William Fitzhugh, 353, 386, 393
to William Gordon, 221
to Thomas Green, 327
to Alexander Hamilton, 315
to Colonel Hanson, 286
to Benjamin Harrison, 250
to Robert Hanson Harrison, 81, 82
to Francis Hopkinson, 235
to David Humphreys, 258, 260-263, 277, 316, 317, 366
to John Jay, 250, 251
to Thomas Jefferson, 342, 343
to Henry Knox, 209, 210, 291, 341
to Lafayette, 209, 215, 223, 237, 247, 282, 283, 373, 374
to Virginie Lafayette, 223
to Tobias Lear, 299, 300, 302, 308-310, 322, 324, 335, 345, 359, 365, 368, 371
to Richard Henry Lee, 238
to Charles Lewis, 16
to Mrs. Fielding Lewis, 294, 304, 310, 311, 347
to George Lewis, 372
to Howell Lewis, 318
to Lawrence Lewis, 369, 370, 401, 402
to Benjamin Lincoln, 259, 287
to James Madison, 284, 306
to James McHenry, 365, 367, 368, 393
to McKoy, 326
to John Francis Mercer, 252
to Mitchell, 192
to Gouverneur Morris, 260, 294, 295
to Robert Morris, 218, 269
to Count Niemcewicz, 391
to the overseers, 318, 326, 327
to William Peacey, 255
to William Pearce, 322, 323, 325, 326, 328-333, 340-343, 349-351, 353, 359
to Captain Posey, 79-81
to Price Posey, 199
to Albin Rawlins, 381, 382
to William Roberts, 400, 401
to John Robinson, 21, 22
to a sea captain, 77
to Sir John Sinclair, 383
to Reverend Samuel Smith, 371
to David Stuart, 289, 296-297, 375, 376, 392, 393
to a tailor, 398
to Samuel Vaughan, 219
to Bushrod Washington, 201, 213, 214, 289, 372, 373
to George Augustine Washington, 225, 263, 264, 271-273
to George Steptoe Washington, 286, 293
to Harriot Washington, 303
to John Augustine Washington, 14, 15, 146, 152, 153, 157, 158, 201, 202
to Lund Washington, 154, 161, 162, 171-177, 180, 182, 188-190, 193-195, 200-205
to Martha Washington, 102, 103, 151, 152
to Mary Ball Washington, 26, 266, 267
to Samuel Washington II, 370, 371, 401
to Anthony Whiting, 308, 312-314
to Arthur Young, 290, 324
marriage, 32, 33, 39, 41
portraits, 116, 117, 235, 240, 241, 378, 379, 415
True Happiness, 40
uniform, 10, 116, 139, 144, 398
Washington, Mrs. George (Martha Dandridge Custis):
arrives Mount Vernon, 45, 46
fortune, 47
health, 53, 57, 63
letters, 84, 118, 301, 302, 307, 319, 320, 338, 360, 361, 415
marriage, 39, 41
Washington, George Augustine, x, xi, 83, 90, 100, 199, 200, 210, 211, 224, 226, 236, 237, 241, 242, 244, 245, 247, 252, 256, 261, 269, 272, 274, 277, 281, 284, 292, 293, 298, 302-304, 307, 309, 310, 312, 314, 316, 317, 333, 342, 360, 366, 370, 400, 401, 415; death, 316; letters, 293; marriage, 241
Washington, Mrs. George Augustine. *See* Fanny Bassett.
Washington, George Steptoe, x, 90, 191, 199, 212, 220, 245, 246, 267, 285, 286, 289, 293, 294, 298, 299, 311, 312, 320, 321, 336, 359, 369, 394, 395; marriage, 321
Washington, Mrs. George Steptoe. *See* Lucy Payne.
Washington, Harriot (Mrs. Andrew Parks), x, 90, 191, 199, 212, 246, 267, 268, 280, 293, 295, 296, 298, 299, 302, 303, 307, 310, 311, 316, 323, 333-337, 340, 346-349, 352, 359, 394; death, 349; letters, 295, 296, 302, 307, 333, 337, 348, 349, 415; marriage, 348, 349

Washington, Jane (Mrs. William Augustine Washington), x, 47, 88, 89, 191, 381
Washington, John, xiv, 11
Washington, John Augustine, ix, x, xiv. 14, 15, 18, 22, 28, 30, 31, 33, 42, 47, 83, 88, 94, 96, 99, 107, 111, 128, 129, 134, 146, 152, 154, 157, 158, 174, 175, 191, 201, 202, 212, 218, 231, 266, 366, 371, 403; death, 266; marriage, 18
Washington, Mrs. John Augustine (Hannah Bushrod), x, 18, 47, 94, 128, 129, 158, 266, 403
Washington, Lawrence, ix, 1, 5, 7-10, 12, 28, 31, 43, 68, 75, 130, 210, 224; death, 9
Washington, Mrs. Lawrence (Anne Fairfax), ix, xiii, 1, 5, 7-10, 12, 20, 75
Washington, Lawrence (of Chotank), 88, 90, 94, 107, 111, 231, 368
Washington, Lawrence, Jr. (of Chotank), 396
Washington, Lawrence Augustine (of Harewood), x, 90, 191, 199, 212, 220, 245, 246, 267, 285, 286, 289, 293, 294, 298, 299, 311, 312, 320, 348, 359
Washington, Lucinda, 280
Washington, Lund, xi, 2, 54, 56, 78, 83, 84, 87, 88, 137, 142, 149, 152-155, 157-169, 171-173, 175-177, 179-190, 192-195, 197-206, 217, 228, 229, 234, 239, 245, 246, 248, 252, 264, 271, 273, 277, 280, 292, 294, 302, 358; death, 358; letters, 84, 154, 155, 157-169, 171-173, 175-177, 179-190, 192-195, 197-206, 294, 415; marriage, 190
Washington, Mrs. Lund (Elizabeth Foote), xi, 83, 190, 200, 221, 229, 248, 358, 375
Washington, Anna Maria, xi, 280, 298, 316, 317, 342, 345, 346, 352, 360, 361, 362, 366
Washington, Mildred. *See* Mrs. Hammond.
Washington, Milly (Mrs. Thomas Lee of Chantilly), x, 89
Washington, Samuel, ix, x, xiv, 46, 59, 88-90, 94, 96, 107, 133, 183, 191, 198, 199, 201, 211, 212, 220, 267, 280, 285, 289, 310, 320; death, 198, 199, 211, 371
Washington, Mrs. Samuel (Jane Champe), 59
Washington, Mrs. Samuel (Anne Steptoe), 90, 133, 191
Washington, Mrs. Samuel (Mrs. Perrin), 199
Washington, Mrs. Samuel (Mildred Thornton), 46, 90
Washington, Samuel II, 370, 371, 401
Washington, Thornton, x, 90, 199, 212, 267
Washington, Tristram, x, 90
Washington, Warner, xiv, 71, 98, 101, 102, 281, 407
Washington, Mrs. Warner. *See* Hannah Fairfax.
Washington, William Augustine, ix, x, 24, 83, 89, 191, 381
Washington, Mrs. William Augustine. *See* Jane Washington.
Washington, Mrs. William Augustine. *See* Mary Lee.
Washington, William Augustine II, 191
Washington, Colonel William, 210, 211, 225, 226, 402, 403
Washington, D.C. (the Federal City), 343, 358, 363, 381, 412
Watertown (Mass.), 220
Watson, Elkanah, x, 226-228
Watson, John, 302
Webster, Noah, 236
Weedon, George, xiii, 46, 147, 156
Wellington. *See* Walnut Tree Farm.
West, Benjamin, 116
West, Colonel, 84, 97
West Indies, 9, 77, 97, 120, 218, 237, 261, 321
West, Nancy, 19
West Point, 174, 192, 387
Westmoreland County, xii, xiv, 6, 9, 18, 31, 75, 107, 249
Westover, 52, 134, 135, 191, 214
West Virginia, 349
Whiskey Rebellion, 335
White Plains, 175
Whiting, Anthony, 300, 302, 303, 306, 308, 311-314, 316, 317, 322, 325; letters, 314
Will, William. *See* Billy.
William and Mary College, 126, 191
Willing, Elizabeth. *See* Mrs. Samuel Powel.
Willing, Mary. *See* Mrs. William Byrd III.
Wilmington (Del.), 362
Winchester, xiv, 8, 10, 18, 21, 33, 39, 43, 51, 61, 336, 369
Winsor, Olney, viii, 282, 358, 416
Woffington, Peg, 95
Wolcott, Mrs., 374
Woodford, General William, 156
Woodlawn, 402
Woodstock, 173, 191
Woodstock (Shenandoah), 156
Wormeley, John, 111
Wormeley, Ralph, 111
Wormeley family, xiv, 111

XYZ Mission, 391, 395

Yale, 260
Yellow fever, 320, 321
York County, 99
York River, xii, xiv, 47, 110, 124, 134, 153
Yorkshire (England), 25, 43, 71, 354
Yorktown, 4, 50, 151, 157, 176, 191, 196, 197, 212, 215, 249, 260, 270, 287, 384, 413
Young, Arthur, 216, 256-258, 280, 289, 290, 324, 325, 373